ENDC

This is exactly the book I have been waiting for. The more I have discovered the Jewish roots of the scriptures, the more my eyes have been opened, the clearer my understanding of the heart of God, and the greater my passion for going even deeper into the Bible. This book could not have come at a better time. I only hope this is just a beginning for Rabbi Barney.

Pastor Ray Bentley
Maranatha Chapel
San Diego, Calif.

------ :: ------

Barney Kasdan has done a wonderful job presenting a Messianic Jewish commentary that has unique insights for interpretation from Jewish sources. His commentary has agreement with moderate dispensationalism, but is not dogmatic and is truly of benefit to believers from many streams of teaching. I heartily recommend it.

Dr. Daniel Juster, first president of the Union of Messianic Jewish Congregations, Director, Tikkun International, Gaithersburg, Md.

------ :: ------

Best-selling author Rabbi Barney Kasdan has once again illuminated the Jewish worldview of Scripture in ways that deepen understanding and strengthen faith. If you want to look at Scripture through Matthew's eyes, Barney Kasdan's commentary opens that world to you.

Jeffrey Feinberg, Ph.D.
Rabbi, Etz Chaim Congregation
Lake Forest, Ill.

------ :: ------

With this commentary Rabbi Barney Kasdan has provided a definite service for all eager and serious students of the Gospels. Writing in his usual plain and straightforward style, he provides the vital, missing dimension of a Messianic Jewish vantage point on Matthew's presentation of the very Jewish Jesus the Messiah. Integrating the often-ignored rabbinic sources with significant exegetical insights from the gospel text, as well as important religious, cultural, and historical information, Kasdan has made a valuable contribution to the study of the gospels.

Rabbi Dr. John Fischer
Vice President of Academics, St. Petersburg Seminary and Yeshiva
Rabbi, Ohr Chadash Messianic Synagogue, Clearwater, Fla.
President, International Messianic Jewish Alliance

MATTHEW

PRESENTS

YESHUA, KING MESSIAH

A MESSIANIC COMMENTARY

MATTHEW

PRESENTS

YESHUA, KING MESSIAH
A MESSIANIC COMMENTARY

RABBI BARNEY KASDAN

Lederer Books
A division of
Messianic Jewish Publishers
Clarksville, Maryland

ISBN #9781936716265
Library of Congress Control Number: 2011930968

Cover by Josh Huhn of DesignPoint Graphics
Page Design and Layout by Yvonne Vermillion

15 14 13 12 11   5 4 3 2 1

Published by:
Lederer Books
A Division of Messianic Jewish Publishers
6120 Day Long Lane
Clarksville, MD 21029

Distributed by:
Messianic Jewish Resources Int'l.
Order line: (800) 410-7367
Lederer@messianicjewish.net
www.messianicjewish.net

Use above contact information to obtain
quantity discounts for resale, bible study groups or other purposes.

Printed in the United States of America

CONTENTS

Foreword ix
Preface xi
Acknowledgments.. xv
Introduction 1

The Preparation for King Messiah 1:1-4:16......................... 7
  Messiah Prepared Through His Lineage   1:1-17 8
  Messiah Prepared by His Unusual Birth   1:18-25 13
  Messiah Prepared by Regal Acclaim   2:1-23 18
  Messiah Prepared by Mikveh   3:1-17 26
  Messiah Prepared by Testing   4:1-16...33

The Program of King Messiah 4:17-16:12 39
  The Initiation of the Kingdom   4:17-25 40
  The Precepts of King Messiah   5:1-7:29 43
  Proofs of King Messiah   8:1-9:38...79
  The Disciples of the Kingdom   10:1-42 102
  Responses to King Messiah   11:1-30...111
  The Opposition to Yeshua as King Messiah   12:1-50..................................118
  The Mysteries of the Kingdom   13:1-52 132
  The Might of the King   14:1-16:12...147

The Final Presentation of King Messiah 16:13-28:20 169
  The New Revelations of King Messiah 16:13-17:27...................................170
  Instructions for the Messianic Life   18:1-20:34 194
  The Aliyah of King Messiah   21:1-23:39..229
  Predictions of King Messiah   24:1-25:46..283
  The Redemption of King Messiah   26:1-27:66 328
  The Victory of King Messiah   28:1-20 383

Glossary 401
Bibliography... 408
About the Author 432

FOREWORD

I n this very readable explanation of the account of Matthew, Rabbi Kasdan opens with an emphasis on explaining the whys behind Matthew's focus on the Davidic lineage of Rabbenu Yeshua. In particular, this contains a valuable perspective for the Christian student of the Newer Testament writings. His unfolding of this book is done methodically, looking equally at all parts of it. This helps the reader discover a 1st century Jewish perspective from which to evaluate the Messiah's teachings.

As I read through the commentary, I became appreciative of Rabbi Kasdan's style, which reminds me of that of the renowned scholar Alfred Edersheim. Kasdan always digs deep into the Jewish backgrounds and concepts that underlie everything that Yeshua taught in the book of Matthew. His look at Matthew 5-7 in light of the rabbinic literature that is quoted invites the student deeper into the world in which Yeshua grew up, while building some deserved appreciation for rabbinic literature. I am reminded of the late Rabbi Dr. Shmuel Safrai's comment: "Unless you understand some simple things about the *Talmud*, you will never understand Yeshua's teachings." Rabbi Kasdan includes some of the *Talmud*'s foundations as he explains the meaning of Yeshua's words, which is consistent with Rabbi Safrai's contention.

In particular, I appreciate the strong connection that he builds between the teachings of Yeshua and the teachings of the *Torah*. His handling of Matthew 27-28 and the trial and death of Messiah was done with particular attention given to relevant sources, in particular the *Talmud* and Josephus' histories. I believe that this is exactly what is needed in order to place Yeshua in his proper context. And this is exactly what the entire commentary does—it places the book of Matthew back where it belongs...into its historic Jewish context.

Just as one example, Kasdan's short summary on the seven different types of Pharisees, as found in rabbinic literature, is crucial to understanding which Pharisees were the recipients of Yeshua's criticism.

I certainly recommend Rabbi Kasdan's commentary as part of everyone's reference library. In particular, I believe it is a valuable resource for Christian students who know how necessary it is to understand the historic context of Rabbenu Yeshua. This commentary will help students understand the book of Matthew more accurately.

Rabbi Dr. D. Friedman
Former academic dean
King of Kings College
Jerusalem, Israel

PREFACE

As the year 2008 began, *Time* magazine came out with its customary 10 upcoming trends for that year. Among the "Future Revolutions" predicted by the venerable publication were ideas ranging from "The End of Customer Service" to "The New Austerity." What may have surprised some people was the listing of the tenth phenomena; namely, "Re-Judaizing Jesus." It probably seems like a radical thought but many scholars and people of faith already realize that the revival of the Jewish Jesus has been in the works for the last several decades. Certainly the historical Jesus has become a point of interest to many at the start of the 21st century. Both Jewish and Christian scholars debate his original context, with many affirming that he was certainly a traditional Jew of his day. Many see Jesus as an amazing rabbi and enlightened teacher. On the Jewish side, most can be comfortable with that conclusion while stopping short of debating his claims as the Messiah. On the other side of the spectrum, Christians by definition receive him as the Messiah but many times do not understand the historical and cultural context from which Jesus originated.

There is a third group that in essence can serve as a bridge of understanding between these diverse views. That group consists of Jews who appreciate the Jewishness of Jesus and likewise embrace his full message as being the Messiah for both Jews and non-Jews. We like to call ourselves "Messianic Jews" which describes both sides of our philosophy. We are Jewish in background and greatly appreciate our heritage. We also, in the midst of our heritage, have come to the conviction that Jesus is the true Messiah. We even prefer to call him by his original Hebrew name "Yeshua" which means "salvation." Unlike the common historical understanding, we do not see ourselves as converts to a new religion—rather, in the spirit of the *Time* magazine observation—we relate to the "Re-Judaized Jesus," as this is in fact his original context.

Many people today affirm that the earliest followers of Yeshua were all Jews, as were all the writers of the New Testament. What is not so commonly understood is that these early Messianic Jews did not start a new religion but simply believed they were following the one who is the promised Mashiach/Messiah for Israel. Their lifestyle continued to testify of this belief as the New Testament notes that in the early decades there were "many tens of thousands of believers among the Jews and they are all zealots for the *Torah*" (Acts 21:20). A careful study of the New Testament confirms time and again that the early Yeshua movement was birthed among Jews and matured through the leadership of the Jewish disciples.

Of course, the messianic concept in Judaism also realized that the promise of Messiah would be welcomed by many of the nations outside of the Jewish people. In the course of those early decades of the first century, the message of Yeshua would spread from Jews to Gentiles throughout the known world (Acts 1:8). In essence there developed two distinct yet unified people movements around personal faith in Yeshua—the Jewish branch and the Gentile branch (Romans 11:17-18). Since faith in Yeshua could be adapted to any culture, each of these groups had their own faith expression based on their own identity. This had many benefits, as the Yeshua faith could fulfill its destiny of being a truly international community. It also had a potential danger when the Gentile majority ultimately forgot or de-emphasized (or worse, despised) the Jewish roots of their faith. This ironically created the impression that faith in Yeshua is somehow a totally non-Jewish religion. As a result, there has existed, for much of the last 1800 years, a great gap of misunderstanding about the Jewish background of the faith of Yeshua.

This brings me to the vision of this new commentary on the life of Yeshua from a Messianic Jewish perspective. It is my hope that this book will serve as a bridge of understanding and respect between my Jewish brethren and the Christian community. For my Jewish *landsmen* it is my hope that we can take a fresh look at Yeshua, even his more controversial claims, and evaluate for ourselves with an open mind. Needless to say, I have used various sections of the New Testament as well as the *Tanakh* to explore what the Bible says about the Messiah doctrine. To better understand the Jewish religious and cultural connection, I have made significant use of quotes from the *Talmud* and other rabbinic sources. This in itself is a challenge as it includes a massive amount of often complex material. As one studies this amazing resource, one is often reminded that there is no single "Jewish view." The *Talmud* is essentially a record of a multitude of rabbinic opinions, whether they are considered correct, incorrect, or just intriguing discussions!

By quoting Talmudic and other rabbinic sources, I do not mean to imply that they agree with our philosophy in Messianic Judaism but I am simply illustrating that similar concepts have been discussed by other Jewish sources as well. It is my belief that it is imperative for the rabbinic background to be included in the search for the first-century Jesus. Professor Shmuel Safrai is among many Jewish scholars who have likewise argued that the rabbinic literature (even that dated well beyond the Second Temple period) must be consulted to understand the context of first-century Judaism (Safrai, "The Value of Rabbinic Literature as an Historical Source," *Jerusalem Perspective Online*, September 2009).

On the other side of the spectrum, I would hope that non-Jewish Christian readers will better understand the one they call Messiah within his original Jewish context. The "Yeshua" of the New Testament might be somewhat different from the "Christ" of the Church or later history, but I believe true Christians will greatly appreciate knowing their savior in a more intimate way. To assist in this pursuit, I have included an extensive bibliography of good sources on this topic. For more details on the background of the biblical Holy Days and customs from a messianic perspective, I recommend my earlier works (*God's Appointed Times* and *God's Appointed Customs* by Messianic Jewish Publishers).

This Messianic Jewish commentary is not meant to be strictly exegetic (though there is a fair amount), nor is it meant to be merely devotional (although that is present as well). I am writing as a Jewish believer since 1971 and a Messianic Rabbi since 1979. As such, I take a popularized approach with this commentary with the hope that all readers (including my own faith community of Messianic Judaism) will benefit. Wherever you are in your religious journey (Jew, Gentile, believer, seeker, or skeptic), I trust you will be enlightened and inspired as you explore the "Re-Judaized Jesus."

Rabbi Barney Kasdan (M.Div.)
April 5, 2011 / 1 Nisan 5771

ACKNOWLEDGMENTS

I would like to thank many people for their assistance with this commentary. Rabbi Barry Rubin (President of Messianic Jewish Resources Int'l.) and his crew of editors have been essential in putting together this extensive work. Their comments and insights (along with those from my rabbinic colleagues) have made this a better manuscript. I am so blessed by my supportive family: my *eshet chayil*/Proverbs 31 wife, Liz (also a Messianic Jew), our four grown kids (David, Aaron, Zhava, and Dvora), my father Shelley, and my mother Norma (of blessed memory). Thank you for the encouragement (and extra time!) for this project. It is a blessing to have a united walk together with our Messiah. Many thanks go to the Messianic synagogue where I serve, Kehilat Ariel of San Diego, California. It is a joy to explore Yeshua and to continue in our Jewish heritage together. Finally, I wish to dedicate this commentary to the growing Messianic Jewish movement worldwide. *Chazak/Be strong!* The best is yet to come!

INTRODUCTION

Writer

The Gospel of Matthew is distinctive in a number of ways. For starters, maybe it is God's sense of humor that one of the most beloved scrolls of the New Testament was written by an internal revenue agent! It is well documented even by Matthew's own writings that he was a tax collector for the Romans during the first century (Matthew 9:9; Luke 5:27). As such, he would have often been at odds with the larger Jewish community, especially because he himself was a Jew. Although his Hebrew name "Mattityahu" means "Gift of God," no doubt many of his acquaintances would have questioned its validity in his case. As a *talmid*/disciple, Matthew walked with Yeshua and his circle of *talmidim* for about three and a half years. During that time he was an eyewitness to most of the events he records, and he personally lived with Yeshua during the amazing time of his earthly ministry to Israel. He is listed among the *talmidim* who saw the resurrected Yeshua and who awaited the pouring out of the *Ruach HaKodesh*/Holy Spirit on the day of *Shavuot*/Pentecost (Acts 1:13).

From there, Matthew's name is not specifically mentioned again, although he was no doubt included in the subsequent references to the ministry of the *sh'lichim*/apostles in the expansion of the early Yeshua movement. Historians speculate that, after his years in Israel,

Matthew was sent as a *shaliach*/apostle to Ethiopia and Persia. Some have questioned the authorship of this scroll since Matthew is not specifically named as the writer. The consensus of early historians (Irenaeus, Origen, and others) is that Matthew was indeed the writer. This seems to be a logical conclusion, as it would be strange for some other writer to attribute the scroll to a despised tax collector if it were not so. Other internal evidences also point to Matthew's authorship.

Jewish Context

It is for good reason that the Gospel of Matthew was placed first in the canonical order of the New Testament. His account of the life of Yeshua has long been appreciated for its Jewish context and, as such, is a natural bridge between the *Tanakh* (Hebrew Scriptures) and the entire *Brit Chadashah* (New Testament). For example, the writer begins his account with the genealogical link to the forefather of the Jewish people (Avraham) and in the same verse connects Yeshua to the messianic house of King David (1:1).

It is noteworthy that Matthew also does not find it necessary to explain certain religious observances (15:1-9). He likewise addresses issues of importance to observant first-century Jews, such as *Shabbat* (12:1-14) and the Temple tax (17:24-27). In the course of his record, Matthew invokes many of the great messianic prophecies of the *Tanakh* in order to make his case for Yeshua as the King Messiah. It is documented that Matthew uses nearly twice as many references to the *Tanakh* than do the other Gospel writers (61 quotes for Matthew, 31 in Mark, 26 in Luke, 16 in John).

It is evident that Matthew is writing with a strong focus on his own people. Matthew also includes several conflicts between Yeshua and some of the religious leaders of the day. Some have tried to portray this as anti-Semitism but, in the proper context, it actually confirms the Jewishness of the gospel. Matthew honestly records the realistic "inner-family" debate between various Jews—some believers and some skeptics. Add to all this a significant historical point concerning the strong Jewish context of Matthew: There is reference to Hebrew being the original language of the scroll. As the early church historian Eusebius notes, "Matthew composed the oracles in the Hebrew language, and each one interpreted them as he was able" (*Ecclesiastical History*, III, xxxix, 16).

While we have not found this Hebrew gospel account (yet), it is not surprising to Messianic Jews that Matthew as a Jew wrote to Jews in Hebrew! Eusebius' account that the gospel was translated into Greek for universal appeal makes sense, and is one that even Matthew himself affirms (28:19). Based on the internal evidences of all the gospels, I believe that all four gospel accounts were actually written by Jews for Jews (Romans 3:2). It is fitting that the glorious message of this Good News should go to all peoples, but we must not forget the original context of the entire New Testament. No doubt the Gospel of Matthew stands out as a message for all peoples—to the Jew first and also to the non-Jew (Romans 1:16). With this in mind, we should say that Matthew's account describes faith in Yeshua not as a conversion to a new religion for Jews but as the fulfillment of the messianic hope for Israel (5:17-18).

Time and Place

There is considerable debate as to the exact dating of the Gospel of Matthew. There is no clear statement internally or from external sources that can date the scroll with certainty. Some scholars have dated the book as being written after the destruction of the Temple and as late as 80 CE/AD. This is based on the assumption that Matthew 24 and other passages are descriptive of history and not predictive of a future event. Some early fathers dated Matthew as early as even the late 30s CE/AD, speculating that it was probably the earliest Gospel. It is quite possible, however, that Matthew made use of an earlier source found in Mark's scroll, although this has never been proven beyond any doubt. Many today feel best about a date of 50-70 CE/AD, as this would satisfy most of the questions. The year 50 CE approximates the dispersion of the early Messianic Jews from Jerusalem,which would include Matthew himself.

It seems that Yeshua's words in Matthew 24 are therefore not descriptive of the 70 AD destruction, but predictive. If the Roman catastrophe had already taken place, we would expect Matthew to make that very clear in his record. His record of Yeshua's words even seems to predate the start of the First Jewish Revolt against Rome in 66 CE. By contrast, the writer addresses such issues as the Temple tax that would be irrelevant on any date after 70 CE (17:24-27). It is more logical that Matthew is recording his gospel for the benefit of the Jewish community in Israel to prepare for the challenges of the near future.

Purposes

The purpose of Matthew seems abundantly clear from the very first verse of the Gospel: "This is the genealogy of Yeshua the Messiah, son of David, son of Avraham" (1:1). As a son of Avraham, the Jewishness of Yeshua is accentuated, which is a prerequisite to qualify as the Messiah (Genesis 12:1-3). As a descendant of King David, Yeshua is shown to be from the very family that the Messiah must come from (II Samuel 7:11-16). From this compelling opening verse all the way through his closing chapter, Matthew's purpose is to confirm that Yeshua of Nazareth is King Messiah, the promised one for Israel. He is the Messiah in all that the concept implies. Yeshua is certainly the King who will offer and ultimately bring the promised Kingdom of God through the Messianic Kingdom. Israel will be the center of the world and Jerusalem will be the center of international worship in this promised kingdom.

As this King Messiah, Yeshua heals the hurting, feeds the hungry, and teaches the depths of the *Torah*. Yeshua is born in the city of David (Beit-Lechem), and the messianic title *Mashiach ben David* (Messiah Son of David) is found nine times in Matthew's account. What is surprising at first glance is that Matthew also highlights a secondary mission of the Messiah as the suffering one, *Mashiach ben Yosef* (Messiah Son of Joseph). It is debated in the rabbinic literature just how the Messiah can fulfill the two apparently conflicting pictures of his work. He is undoubtedly to be the King of Israel, but many scriptures describe the Messiah as also suffering and even being killed (Isaiah 53; Zechariah 12). Matthew addresses this issue, as do the Talmudic rabbis. Some rabbis had the view that there might be two messiahs to fulfill the two different missions (Tractate Sukkah 52a), whereas Matthew reconciles this issue by describing one messiah coming at two different times (24:30-31). While the debate continues even to this day, Matthew's purpose is nonetheless clear. Based on the evidence he sees and presents, Yeshua is King Messiah for Israel and ultimately for all the nations.

THE PREPARATION
FOR KING MESSIAH
1:1-4:16

"Seven things were created before the world was created:
Torah, repentance, the Garden of Eden, Gehinnom, the
Throne of Glory, the Temple, and the name of the Messiah."

(Tractate Pesachim 54a)

Messiah Prepared Through His Lineage 1:1-17

Matthew begins his account of the life of Yeshua in a way that would no doubt grab the attention of any first-century Jew. All of the names attributed to Yeshua speak to his messianic qualifications. Indeed, the name Yeshua, from the Hebrew root for "salvation," reminds us of his purpose for coming into the world (cf. Matthew 1:21). Yeshua is the original form of the name that the Greeks translated into *Yesous*, which, in turn, was later translated into various dialects around the world (e.g., *Hesous, Jesus*, etc.). Although it is understandable and proper that the name of Yeshua be translated into the various languages, it is also ironic that many have forgotten (or are unaware of) the very name by which he was called when he lived in Israel in the first century. The name Yeshua would truly have a beautiful ring to it, as it still does for his followers today.

In many English Bibles, this proper name is followed by what may appear to be a second name, Christ. In the western world, we hear this combination (Jesus Christ) so often that we frequently forget that the second part is not a name but, in fact, a title. The Greek word *Christos* is a direct translation of the Hebrew *Mashiach* or the anglicized *Messiah*. The term in all these cases means "anointed one" or "poured-upon one," as when a priest or king was ordained for service with the symbolic pouring out of oil. In this sense of the word, there are many "messiahs" in the *Tanakh*.

However, it became clear in the Scriptures and Jewish tradition that there was a promised Messiah who would be a unique king of Israel (cf. Daniel 9:24-26; Isaiah 11:1-10, as quoted in Tractate Sanhedrin 93b and Targum Yonaton; Isaiah 53, as quoted in Tractate Sanhedrin 98a). It is in this more technical manner that Matthew states the background of Yeshua of Nazareth. He is the *Mashiach* and all that title implies to the Jewish mind.

The other names in this opening verse likewise accentuate vital aspects of this Messiah's lineage. It is important for the writer to confirm that this Yeshua is a *son of Avraham*, emphasizing that he is a Jew by birth. Since the early chapters of the *Torah*, it has been established that through Avraham the Jewish nation would arise. Not only would this patriarch be blessed by his covenant with the Lord God, but also through Avraham there would be blessings for the larger Gentile world. Consequently, the phrase *son of Avraham* implies that Yeshua is qualified to be the redeemer promised not only to the Jewish people but also to all nations (cf. Genesis 12:3).

The other phrase *son of David* provides an important link in the qualifications of the Messiah. It was to King David that God promised an eternal throne from which one of his descendants would rule (cf. II Samuel 7:8-13). Since the days of David, it has been a tradition that the *Mashiach* must therefore not only be a Jew, but be from the specific family of the house of David. This Davidic emphasis provides Matthew and Jewish readers with the recurring theme of this gospel account. Yeshua is the promised King Messiah and has the proper qualifications to prove it. This opening verse likewise confirms that Matthew is presenting a beautiful completion of the covenants as seen through the cornerstone of the Jewish faith in the coming of Messiah.

The writer now segues into a rather lengthy genealogical list that gives further details of the qualifications of Yeshua as the Messiah-King. While many readers may be tempted to skip these details, this list answers some important questions. Various names in the genealogy are familiar, such as Ya'akov, Boaz, and Shlomo (Jacob, Boaz and Solomon). Many others are lesser-known, yet vital, connections in the ancestry of Yeshua. From a Jewish perspective, these details are not only incumbent upon, but also quite enlightening to, the messianic qualifications. Several points should be highlighted.

First, the Davidic emphasis of Matthew's account is affirmed once again. This is seen in the division of the list into three distinct groups, as the writer himself confirms (see verse 17). A closer study of the list reveals that there are gaps between names, sometimes of several generations. This is allowed in the Jewish way of recording genealogies, as the word for *son* can many times mean a descendant who is not an immediate progeny (cf. Ezra 2 and Nehemiah 7). This practice is justified many times if the writer has a particular point to make. In Matthew's case, he is clearly focusing on the three sets of 14 names.

While some commentators seem bewildered by this fact, there is good Jewish reasoning implemented here by the writer. Anyone familiar with Hebrew knows that from ancient times the language had a numeric value associated with each of its letters. It is not coincidental that one of the numeric values of the number 14 may be expressed in the three Hebrew letters (D/dalet=4, V/vav=6, D/dalet=4), the Hebrew letters for David. By intentionally skipping over particular names that could have been included in the list, the writer is emphasizing the Davidic connection to Yeshua as King Messiah, the Son of David.

A second notable detail is the inclusion of Y'khanyahu (Jeconiah, also known as Coniah or Jehoiachin) in verse 11. As Matthew recounts the ancestors of Yosef, the adoptive father of Yeshua (v. 16), this former king of Judah would seem to present a looming problem. As one traces the history of this troubled leader, a major potential obstacle arises when it comes to the throne of David. Though Coniah was indeed from the family line of David, he was inflicted with a curse because of his rebelliousness against the Lord in his day. Jeremiah 22:24-30 records the incident in which the prophet is told to remove the signet ring from the king's hand as a symbol of God's displeasure. Such a problem was Coniah that his reign lasted only three months in the year 597 BCE. Not only was a judgment placed on this evil king, but the prophet was also told to extend the curse to all of Coniah's descendants. Specifically, the *Tanakh* says:

> Thus says the Lord, "Write this man down childless, a man who will not prosper in his days; for no man of his descendants will prosper sitting on the throne of David or ruling in Judah." (Jeremiah 22:30).

Here we discover a potentially enormous problem in Matthew's list. In recounting the genealogy of Yosef, the writer cannot escape the historical fact that this same Yosef, though in the messianic line of David, is also in the direct line of the cursed king of Judah! Consequently, if Yeshua were the biological son of Yosef, ironically he would be disqualified to inherit the messianic throne of King David. Amazingly, what seems to be an insurmountable problem in Matthew's account actually affirms another vital New Covenant truth, that Yeshua was not the born son of Yosef but was conceived by the miraculous intervention of the Holy Spirit.

This apparent problem in Matthew's genealogy also answers for us the question of why there are two different lists of individuals in Yeshua's line in the New Testament. When one compares Matthew's account with that of Luke (3:23-38), it becomes apparent that these are two different branches entirely. While Matthew affirms that Ya'akov is the father of Yosef (v. 16), Luke unabashedly states that Eli was the father of Yosef (Luke 3:23). How could Matthew and Luke have differed on this vital issue? Skeptics have even pointed to this apparent contradiction as proof of the so-called mistakes in the New Testament. Yet, a closer look at Luke reveals an amazing truth. Since Yosef's line is under the curse of Coniah, Luke is, in fact, giving the genealogy of Yeshua's mother's line, namely Miryam. This is confirmed by a number of details. In Luke's list, all of the names have the article "the" attached to them in the original language—all of them, that is, except Yosef in verse 23.

In the Greek language, this would be a red flag to the reader that something unusual is happening in the case of Yosef. Virtually all ancient genealogies in the Bible exclusively focused on the male side. However, if a first-century Jewish writer included a woman's line, the reason for this would be worth pursuing. It seems that the men whom Luke cites in his listing are actually related to Yeshua's mother and not his apparent father, Yosef. Therefore, the odd Greek construction would be a tip-off to the observant reader. An extra-biblical source that confirms these details is found in the *Talmud*, where the father of the New Testament Miryam is said to be a man by the name of Eli, just as Luke attests (cf. Tractate Hagigah 2:4).

To state this another way, Luke gives the practical answer to the problem presented in Matthew 1. In reality, both Yosef and Miryam are of Davidic descent and in the messianic line. It could be said that whereas Matthew presents Yeshua's line through the cursed line of Solomon and Coniah, Luke presents the Davidic connection of Yeshua through the acceptable line of Nathan (Luke 3:31). For those who would contend that the normal procedure is to pass the inheritance through the father's line, there is a precedent for such an unusual adaptation. Most notably, the daughters of Tz'lof'chad (Numbers 27:1-11) were told that they could receive the family's inheritance because they had no brother to fulfill this obligation. Legally speaking, Miryam could pass on the Davidic right to her son Yeshua, thus bypassing Yosef's line entirely if there was an important justification for this.

This is more than just biblical trivia. The human connection of Yeshua through his mother has vast theological implications for the essence of the messianic mission, as we shall see.

A final interesting detail of Matthew's genealogy is the fact that his list includes four women, which, in itself, is unusual. Moreover, all of these women are non-Jews, and each had her own share of spiritual problems. Tamar, Rahav, and Batsheva were all involved in sexual immorality. Ruth, although she joined the Jewish people, was a part of the cursed Moabites, who were not allowed to fully participate in the riches of Israel because of their historical opposition to God's people (cf. Deuteronomy 23:3). Matthew's point seems to be that the Messiah would come into this fallen world to redeem all categories of humanity: Jew, Gentile, man, woman, slave, and free (cf. Galatians 3:28). These intricate details confirm to us the amazing plan of God as he sets forth his messianic redemption.

Messiah Prepared by His Unusual Birth   1:18-25

Having verified that Yeshua's lineage met the criteria for him to be the *Mashiach,* Matthew now turns to the actual events of his birth in Israel some 2000 years ago. As with the previous genealogies, we find that Matthew's emphasis is on Yeshua's birth from the vantage point of Yosef, whereas Luke focuses on Miryam's experience. Of chief importance here is the technical relationship between Yosef and Miryam as a young couple. It is noted that they were *engaged*; that is, they had entered into the second step of the first-century Jewish wedding ceremony.

Essentially, the ceremony was broken into three distinct parts, two of which can still be observed in the modern Jewish wedding. The first step was called *shiddukhin*, meaning "the arrangement." At this stage, the respective fathers of two children would *arrange* for the future marriage. This would naturally be initiated at a very young age, with hopes of joining two families for the common good. If they had some trouble making a proper match, families might enlist the services of a *shadkhan* (matchmaker), in the hope of finding a future mate.

As time passed, there would come a point when the couple was old enough to confirm their desire to be wed. This would lead to the second stage of the ceremony, known as *erusin,* or "engagement."

Our modern, westernized understanding of engagement does not fully capture its meaning for the people of New Testament times.

Today, an engaged couple may break off their commitment with no legal repercussions, but a couple in first-century Judea were bound by a much stronger agreement. To enter into this *erusin* period, the couple would have a public ceremony, under a *huppah*/canopy, and sign a written contract called a *ketubah*. In this document, both parties would stipulate what they were agreeing to bring into this new household. The groom would promise his protection and provision for his espoused, while the bride would indicate her family dowry that she could bring into the marriage.

As the *Ketubah* was signed, the first cup of the ceremony was blessed, thus declaring publicly their sincere intention. The *erusin* was now official, which would bring the couple into their engagement period. However, unlike the modern understanding, this engagement was as binding as a legal marriage with one notable exception. They were not to live together nor were they to enter into sexual relations. The ancient understanding of *erusin* was that it was a time of preparation for the final marriage step.

During what was usually a one-year period, the espoused couple had their own distinct obligations. The groom undoubtedly needed to get their new household in order. The bride, for her part, needed to attend to her dowry and garments for the upcoming *simcha* (joyous occasion). If, for some serious reason, the *erusin* needed to be voided, the covenant was much more binding than the modern concept of engagement. Based upon the requirements for divorce (cf. Deuteronomy 24:1-4), the couple would be obligated to obtain a *Get* or *Sefer Keritut* (Hebrew for "bill of divorce"), a procedure that is still followed in Orthodox Jewish law to this day. In other words, a couple who had entered the *erusin* stage were, in fact, considered completely married, although they were not living together yet as husband and wife.

The final stage of the ceremony, *nisuin* (marriage), would take place after the one-year engagement. At a time the groom's father would dictate, usually by sounding a *shofar* (ram's horn), the groom would go with his procession to the house of his betrothed. He would take the bride, and she would literally be carried (the meaning of the Hebrew root *nasa*, from where the word, *nisuin,* comes) to the place of the ceremony. Once again, under the *huppah*/canopy, the couple would affirm their intention to enter the marriage. This was done as the second cup of wine was blessed with the beautiful *sheva b'rakhot* (seven blessings). After this part of the *nisuin* ceremony, the couple would celebrate their marriage with a seven-day feast, after which the newlyweds would live together at the place prepared by the groom.

Any reader familiar with these details of the Jewish wedding ceremony will readily recognize the spiritual application in the Scriptures. Several times, in both the *Tanakh* and the New Covenant, parallels are drawn between marriage and the relationship between the believer and God. Two entire books of the Prophets highlight this fact, as is evident in the love stories of Hosea and the Song of Solomon. Not coincidentally, Yeshua and Sha'ul/Paul refer to marital terms such as the *shiddukhin* (cf. II Cor. 11:2; Eph. 1:3-6), *erusin* (cf. Yochanan 14:1-4), and *nisuin* (cf. I Thess. 4:13-18). Indeed, the details of the wedding ceremony illustrate many exciting truths about how God views followers of Yeshua, the Bridegroom sent from the Father.

This background provides an enlightening context for the particular situation Matthew is relating. We are told that Miryam was engaged to Yosef, meaning that the couple had entered into the second stage of the ceremony. They had exchanged public vows, taken the first cup of wine under the *huppah,* and were in the one-year *erusin* period. One can understand Yosef's shock and dismay as his betrothed announces that she is pregnant. He knew that they had not had sexual relations, yet her story of a miraculous conception must have been puzzling to say the least! Additionally, Yosef realized that a violation of sexual chastity during any part of the marriage covenant was punishable by stoning to death (cf. Deuteronomy 22:13-21) or at least by putting away the adulterous wife by obtaining a *Get* (cf. Deuteronomy 24:1). Because of his deep love for Miryam, we find Yosef contemplating the latter action when the angel reveals the truth to him. Of course, the unusual circumstances surrounding the pregnancy confirm the uniqueness of this child. In fulfillment of Isaiah's ancient prophecy (7:14), this is the son born of a *virgin.*

While there is considerable debate in both Jewish and Christian circles about the meaning of this prophecy, Matthew quotes it because it perfectly captures an important truth about the birth of the Messiah. If the *Mashiach* is to have the uniquely divine task of removing the sins of mankind, we should expect him to have a uniquely divine nature.

Most Jewish commentators would argue that the controversial term used in Isaiah 7:14, the Hebrew word *almah,* can have a number of meanings. No doubt it is used many times to refer to a woman of marriageable age who is not yet married and, in that culture, presumably a virgin. However, it is true that the term is broad enough to include a woman who is married. Some would argue that Isaiah's prophecy would have been quite clear if he had used the common Hebrew term for virgin (*betulah*). Yet, the Scriptures use both of these Hebrew terms interchangeably at times, as seen in Genesis 24 where Rebecca is called both an *almah* and a *betulah* (cf. Genesis 24:13 and 24:43)!

Similarly, the great rabbinic commentator Rashi translates *almah* as "young woman" in Isaiah 7:14, but as "virgin" elsewhere in the *Tanakh* (Song of Solomon 1:3 and 6:8). When the etymology of a word seems so inconclusive, one must rely on the context of the verses to help define its meaning. Ironically, the intricate details of Isaiah's prophecy would not have been clearly fulfilled if the term *betulah* were employed. A close reading of Isaiah 7 reveals that the prophet is speaking of a dual fulfillment, of a child born in his day, as well as of a future son born by miraculous means. To put it another way, what term would best communicate the natural birth of a son in 8th century BCE, as well as a supernatural conception some 700 years later? Amazingly, the term *betulah* would not cover the former situation, but the term *almah* would be adequately flexible to describe both events.

An important piece of corroborative evidence emerges when we consider how this passage was interpreted pre-Yeshua. Most notably, the Septuagint (LXX) gives a most interesting interpretation some 200 years before the events Matthew is recounting. Without having any axe to grind regarding the New Testament, these 70 rabbis translated the Hebrew *almah* into a term that was equivalent from their perspective, the Greek *parthenos*, which normally means "virgin." Evidently, in the minds of many scholars, the simple yet profound way to understand Isaiah 7:14 is to conclude that the birth of this later son would somehow be usual. This is strongly implied by the overall context, as Isaiah says that this conception would be a "sign," the Hebrew term *ot* often used of a miraculous event. The symbolic name given to this son testifies to this uniqueness as well: *Immanuel* (God with us).

Finally, the Hebrew actually reads *Ha-almah* (the virgin) with the definite article. Isaiah thus seems to be referring to a particular woman whom his readers would know. This seems to fit with the earlier details given in the *Torah* that in some unusual way the "seed of the woman" will come and crush the seed of the serpent (cf. Genesis 3:15). Indeed, the statements of Isaiah fill in some necessary detail given to Moses. According to the New Testament, Miryam is revealed as the woman who fulfills both Genesis 3:15 and Isaiah 7:14

by bringing forth that promised Redeemer. She is to be honored as a woman who showed incredible faith in God, yet is not to be exalted beyond her humanity. Consequently, Matthew recounts how, after the birth of Yeshua, the couple lived together in a normative marriage relationship. As would be expected, their newborn son is given his prophetic name, Yeshua, after his *brit milah* (circumcision) on the eighth day (cf. Luke 2:21).

Messiah Prepared by Regal Acclaim   2:1-23

In another vital proof of Yeshua's messianic qualifications, Matthew informs his readers that this son of David was also born in the city of David. Since the birth of King David, Beit-Lechem (Bethlehem) was designated as the city of this beloved leader of Israel. Although not much more than a village just five miles outside of Jerusalem, the town took on even greater importance as the revelation came through Micah the prophet that it would be at Beit-Lechem that the Messiah, David's greater son, would be born. This is later affirmed by rabbinic tradition, as one translation of this verse actually uses the Aramaic word for Messiah in Micah's prophecy (cf. Tractate Berakhot II.4; Targum Jonathan on Micah 5:1).

Specifically, it would be Beit-Lechem in the land of Y'hudah as opposed to another village by the same name, Beit-Lechem in the land of Zevulun, which was some seven miles north of Nazareth. Of course, the tribal cities of *Y'hudah*/Judah would need to be the place of *Mashiach's* birth, as this would fit another piece of the puzzle, that King Messiah must come from the kingly tribe of Judah (cf. Genesis 49:10).

Interestingly, there is another piece of evidence from the *Talmud*, in conjunction with Luke's biography of Yeshua, which indirectly points to Beit-Lechem as the birthplace of the Messiah. In one discussion, some of the rabbinic scholars conclude that the *Mashiach* must be revealed at a place called *Migdal Eder* (Tower of the Flock). This is known to be the place where the shepherds who specialized in the animals for Temple sacrifice would watch their flocks, especially during the time of any holy day (cf. Targum Pseudo-Yonaton 35.21). This, of course, perfectly fits Luke's description of the place of the Messiah's first revelation, as well as that of the original witnesses, the shepherds in the fields of Beit-Lechem (cf. Luke 2:8).

The place of Yeshua's birth is not important only to Matthew but also to those who were seeking this newborn king. The term *magi* can be understood to mean magicians, wise men, or astrologers. Because some of these practices are condemned in the *Torah*, it is assumed that this group consists of non-Jews (cf. Deuteronomy 18:9-13). However, if this were so, we are faced with a challenging question: How would pagan astrologers know about a coming Messiah, and why would they even care?

An important clue to the answer lies in the phrase identifying where they came from, that is, *from the east*. As an Israeli Jew, Matthew had little doubt as to the location of the eastern land. Despite the famous Christmas carol identifying them with the "orient," these wise men would have most assuredly originated from the huge province known as Babylon. This being so, we can more easily understand how these magi would have knowledge of such details of Jewish theology.

Long a home for Diaspora Jews, Babylon was still the place of residence for the majority of the Jewish community even as Matthew was writing in the first century. At one point in history, there was even a famous Jew who arose to political prominence in the kingdom of Nebuchadnezzar around the year 500 BCE. This was Daniel, who lived among the dispersed in the land while awaiting the time when the remnant would be able to return to Israel. In a most interesting note, it is stated that several Jewish youth were recruited by the pagan king to be trained in "every matter of wisdom [*chochmah*] and understanding [*bina*]" (Daniel 1:17-20). This would provide a natural connection between these wise men (Heb. *chachamim*) and their understanding of Jewish tradition. At the very least, it would seem these magi would be Gentile converts who were familiar with the writings of Daniel or, in fact, born Jews from Babylon in search of the *Mashiach*.

Of particular interest to these magi is the star that appears to be directing them to the Jerusalem area (v. 2, 9). There are those who would explain this unusual manifestation in the naturalistic terms of a certain alignment of planets or meteorites. While this is possible, it would fail to explain the unnatural behavior of this star. It moves over Jerusalem, disappears, and then reappears directly over the nearby village of Beit-Lechem. This was no regular star but would better be explained as a manifestation of the *Sh'chinah* (glory) of God that appears at many dramatic events in history. This would catch the attention all the more of these biblically literate magi, as they undoubtedly were familiar with the messianic prophecy declaring that "a star shall come forth from Ya'akov" to deliver Israel in the day of redemption (Numbers 24:17). A later *midrash* (Rabbinic commentary) confirms how some even speculated about the details of the star:

> It was taught in the name of the rabbis: In the septenary in which the Son of David comes, in the first year there will be insufficient food; in the second, arrows of famine are sent out; in the third, great famine; in the fourth, neither famine nor abundance; in the fifth, great abundance, and a star will sprout up from the east. This is the star of the Messiah, and it will abide in the east fifteen days, and if it tarries longer, it will be to the good of Israel (Aggadat Mashiach, BhM 3:141-143).

Traditional Jewish sources have long regarded this verse as referring to the coming of the Messiah (Tractate Taanit IV. 8; Targum Onkelos). During the Second Jewish Revolt against Rome (132-135

CE), Rabbi Akiva used this verse to identify the Jewish military general as the Messiah, even calling him by the Aramaic name "*Bar-Kochba*/Son of the Star" (Tractate Taanit 68d)! How appropriate that God would use the *Sh'chinah* in the manifestation of a star to direct these seekers to the true King Messiah, Yeshua.

Undoubtedly, the wise men would have paid special attention to Daniel's prophecies in regard to the exact time of the Messiah's birth as well. In the amazing revelation of Daniel 9:24-27, the prophet is given a vision of 70 "sevens" as they relate to the history of his people Israel. Additionally, the details of this scripture seem to point to the exact time when the Messiah would be revealed. Exactly 483 years (69 "sevens") after the decree to rebuild Jerusalem, Messiah the Prince will be "cut off." Many scholars agree that, from Daniel's vantage point, this decree would have to be the one issued by Artexerxes in the year 444 BCE (Nehemiah 2:1-8). After doing all the math, as well as factoring in the biblical calendar year, one comes up with the cutting off of the Messiah around the year 30 CE. Thus, not only did the wise men see the star of the Messiah, but it also appeared at the very time they might have been expecting his appearance in Israel.

As for the chronology of when the magi came to Jerusalem, we should consider several important details. It should be noted that the writer takes a jump forward in time, probably about two years after the birth of Yeshua. We can deduce this from the fact that Herod, upon hearing of his potential competition for the throne, gives the command to murder all Hebrew boys up to two years of age (cf. 2:16). According to the historian Josephus, there was a lunar eclipse just before Herod's death in 6 BCE on the Roman calendar (Josephus Antiquities xvii. 6.4, 167). Considering all these events, the birth of Yeshua likely occurred between the years 4-6 BCE. That this visit of the magi was later than Yeshua's time of birth is also confirmed by the phrase *upon entering the house* (v. 11). This is a quite different term than that given to his original place of birth in the hillside stable or manger (cf. Luke 2:7). Once in the house, they proceed to offer gifts to the new king—*gold, frankincense and myrrh.*

Each of these gifts is highly symbolic of spiritual truth. Gold was considered an expensive gift fit for royalty. Frankincense was often used as a perfume even for a bridegroom, as illustrated in Solomon's love story (cf. *Shir HaShirim*/Song of Songs 3:6). Myrrh (Hebrew *mor*) was often an anointing oil used in preparation for death (cf. *Yochanan*/John 19:39-40). A *midrash* on the verse from *Shir HaShirim* makes a connection to Avraham offering Isaac on Mount Moriah, *the Mor of God* (Shir HaShirim Raba 3:6). All three ingredients are prophetic symbols of the purpose of the Messiah's arrival—to be King, Groom, and Redeemer. Although the popular Christmas carol speaks of "we three kings," it should be pointed out that the text describes only three kinds of gifts. There may have been three *chachamim* or a much larger entourage. Whatever the number, they bent the knee in *worship,* an act that would be offered only to God himself (v. 11).

It would seem that the original description in Luke's account would fit with the view that the Messiah was born in a temporary shelter. While there is considerable debate about the exact time of Yeshua's birth, the details suggest that it could have occurred during the feast of *Sukkot* (Tabernacles), when Jews would be dwelling in such temporary structures. Appropriately, this fall holy day focuses on the fact that God dwelt with Israel in the wilderness for 40 years (cf. Leviticus 23:33-44). Additional evidence of this view includes the chronology of the gospels, which record the public ministry of Yeshua as lasting three and a half years. If one backtracks from the known point of the terminus of his ministry (his death on Passover), the three and a half years places his birth, not in December, but in the late fall around the time of *Sukkot.* Perhaps this is why *Yochanan*/John 1:14 speaks of the birth of Yeshua in the context of God "dwelling" or "tabernacling" in the midst of Israel.

After the magi return to their homeland, *an angel* appears to Yosef once again, this time to warn him to flee the dangerous situation in Judea. *Herod* was infamous for his paranoia and erratic behavior. It didn't help matters that he was a puppet king appointed by the Romans. Although his family was officially Jewish as a result of the mass conversion of the Idumeans around the year 200 BCE, Herod was clearly identified more as a pagan king than a leader of Israel. So ruthless was he that, at one point, Herod actually killed his own sons because he feared that his throne was in jeopardy. Consequently, a saying arose that it was better to be Herod's pig than his son. Herod lived a superficial Jewish lifestyle.

It is easy to understand the danger at this point of Yeshua's young life, as Herod would find it a great threat that another "king" was residing within his jurisdiction. The family, therefore, heeds the warning of the angel and flees by cover of night to the historic land of *Egypt*. Matthew notes that this action is part of a dual fulfillment of Hosea 11:1. Most certainly, the original text refers to the Exodus from Egypt of the whole nation in the days of Moses. There are, however, references in the rabbinic literature in which some equated the son of Exodus 4:22 with the Messiah himself (cf. Midrash on Psalm 2:7).

Matthew likewise sees a secondary fulfillment of this prediction in the specific son of Israel, Yeshua, coming out of Egypt as well. In a strange way, the Talmudic rabbis also confirm the fact of Yeshua's Egyptian connection by attributing his miracles to sorceries that he learned in that land (Tractate Sotah 12a). Matthew's point is that the Messiah is the collective representative of all of Israel.

True to his reputation, Herod goes into a fit of paranoid rage. To quell any perceived threat to his throne, he gives orders to murder every Jewish boy under the age of two who happens to be residing around Beit-Lechem. Matthew once again sees a dual fulfillment of prophecy in which history, in a sense, is repeating itself. The famous quote is from Jeremiah 31:15 (v. 14 in Hebrew), where the prophet hears a voice of grief over the destruction of the Jewish people by Babylon's army in 586 BCE. It is the resurrected *Rachel*, one of the mothers of Israel, who is in anguish over the plight of her people. In Jeremiah 40:1, we are told that it was in *Ramah* that Nebuchadnezzer gathered the exiles before their deportation to Babylon. This prophetic word is doubly appropriate, as Rachel is the mother of the very tribe where the village of Ramah is located in the territory of Benjamin, about 10 miles from Beit-Lechem. As the first event was fulfilled by the Babylonian deportation, so too is there anguish in Ramah in the first century over the tragic murder of Jewish children. How much greater the grief would be if the Messiah, the hope of Israel, had been slain prematurely.

The family sojourned in Egypt until the *death of Herod* was confirmed. Upon his death in 4 BCE, the kingdom was divided among the three sons of Herod the Great, with Archelaus receiving the territories of Judea, Samaria, and Idumaea. We know that the Jewish people dreaded Archelaus as much as they did his father. It is quite understandable that Yosef, in obedience to the angelic vision, avoided the land of Judea and, Herod's son, in the process. So the family returned directly to the *Galil* and settled in their original hometown of Natzeret.

Matthew again brings out a messianic prophecy, which relates to this part of the life of Yeshua. As spoken by the prophets, the Messiah would be called a *Natzrati* (Nazarene) which, in the mind of the writer, directly relates to the town in the Galilee. The only problem is that the town of Nazareth is not mentioned in the *Tanakh*, nor does any specific prophecy make this statement.

While some accuse Matthew of a gross error or biblical ignorance, verse 23 actually confirms the accuracy of the writer. Too often people read the Bible while presuming western (i.e., Aristotelian) logic, which mandates that every statement must have a linear format. Even most modern Jews have been trained in this westernized approach. Yet we must remember that the Bible (both *Tanakh* and *Brit Chadashah/*

New Testament) was written within the Jewish culture of the Middle East more than 2000 years ago. With these things in mind, we can understand that Matthew, as a good first-century Jew, is using one of the several methods of biblical interpretation common in rabbinic literature. These methods of interpretation can be summarized as follows:

1. *Peshat* (simple) is the plain, literal meaning of the passage.

2. *Remez* (hint) is where the passage somehow alludes to a truth beyond the plain meaning.

3. *Derash/Midrash* (search) is a sermonic application or illustration drawn from the text.

4. *Sod* (secret) is a mystical or esoteric meaning derived from the verse.

These four hermeneutical principles are remembered by the acronym based on the first letters of each method: PRDS, or "PARDES" meaning "garden," also anglicized by the word "paradise." While the modern bible interpreter may not necessarily endorse all of these principles outright, there is no doubt that Matthew must be read with an understanding of their use in first-century Jewish literature.

In the context of Matthew 2:23 and other similar verses, this would be more of a *midrashic* approach, a broad application derived from specific biblical statements. It is not that Matthew is ignorant of the fact that there is no such verse that specifically mentions Natzeret. But in good Semitic fashion, he sees a sermonic application to many of the events recorded in the life of Yeshua. In this case, any educated Jew would understand the connection between the town of Natzeret and the *Mashiach*. The town's name is, in fact, derived from the Hebrew word for "branch," which would call to mind a common term for the Messiah himself (cf. Isaiah 11:1; Zechariah 6:12, as well as the synonym "tzemach" found in Jeremiah 23:5 and Tractate Berachot 2.5).

What Matthew is pointing out is a good play on words that the *Netzer* (Branch) is now residing in the city called *Natzeret* (Branch). In his mind, this is a perfect midrashic fulfillment of this concept that is indeed mentioned by several writers of the *Tanakh* (note the plural "prophets" in verse 23). Instead of being a contradiction or mistake, this verse actually underscores the messianic qualifications of Yeshua in a manner that many first-century (and modern) Jews would appreciate. In Matthew's mind, Yeshua is perfectly qualified to be Israel's King Messiah, and he no doubt hopes that his readers will continue to explore that possibility.

Messiah Prepared by Mikveh   3:1-17

Matthew now jumps ahead in his chronology of the life of Messiah to the start of his public ministry. The details of Yeshua's early life seem to be of little consequence to the writer, as he skips from the young boy of about two years old to the mature man of about 30 (cf. Luke 3:23). Luke, however, feels compelled to record the family's visit to Jerusalem when Yeshua was 12 years old. This has been noted as the age of accountability in Judaism, when a young person takes on the responsibilities of the religious community. While the official *bar mitzvah* ceremony did not fully develop in the synagogue until the Middle Ages, there is little doubt that Luke's account records this event because it served as an important transition in the life of Yeshua as a traditional Jew (Pirke Avot 5.24). Matthew picks up the story at the next vital transition in the preparation of the Messiah. If Yeshua is indeed the promised King and redeemer of Israel, then he must go through a final preparation for his holy task. Since *mikveh* (ritual immersion) must play an essential role, Matthew shares the historical details leading up to this highly symbolic event.

First, the writer draws our attention to the person administering the *mikveh* in the wilderness, the itinerant preacher by the name of

Yochanan. He turns out to be one of the more colorful characters described in the New Testament. Yochanan was in fact a cousin of Yeshua, born just six months before him (cf. Luke 1:56-57). His name means, "God is gracious," which is an apt description of the one who will prepare the way of *Mashiach*.

The secondary title given to him is the The Immerser (*ha-matbil*), not because he was a member of a particular modern denomination, but because he was one who performed ritual immersions within the context of Judaism. The Hebrew noun form of "immersion" is *t'vilah*, which the Greeks called *baptidzo*, meaning "to totally immerse or dip." In secular usage, the term is often used to describe the process of dipping a piece of cloth in a dye in order to change its appearance. Perhaps the best word is "identification," as the cloth is now identified with the color of the dye. This gives us the meaning of immersion. *T'vilah* is a complete immersion to identify with a particular event or message. This act of immersion would take place in a proper pool, called *mikveh* (from *Kaveh*, a collection of water). Numerous *mikva'ot* were found on the Temple Mount in Jerusalem, as well as in any sizable community throughout the Land. Certainly, the *Yarden* (Jordan) would serve as a "kosher" *mikveh*, as it would have more than the minimal requirements of fresh water.

While the term "baptism" sounds so non-Jewish to most people, it should be noted that the act of *t'vilah* has ancient roots in Judaism. For example, there were prescribed ritual cleansings for the priests as they served the community (cf. Leviticus 8; 16) and for the common Israelite who had been healed of a disease like leprosy (cf. Leviticus 15). While these practices are no longer followed in modern Judaism, ritual immersion still takes place to acknowledge the cleansing of a woman after her monthly period (*nidah*) and to welcome new Gentile converts who are said to be spiritually cleansed at their immersion. The great rabbi of the middle ages, *Maimonides*, even attributes the verse in the prophet Ezekiel to convert immersion:

I will sprinkle clean water on you, and you will be clean; I will cleanse you from all your impurities and from all your idols (cf. Ezekiel 36:25 as quoted in the Mishneh *Torah*, Mikva'ot, 11:12).

T'vilah/mikveh within Judaism expresses cleansing, repentance, and identification. Yochanan, therefore, was not teaching something new but calling on Israel to identify with the message God had given to him.

The fact that he centered his ministry in the *desert of Y'hudah* has led some to speculate that perhaps Yochanan was associated with the *Qumran* community. Because of the common themes of their messages and the general location in the Dead Sea area, this could very well be the case. His message was a powerful one that attracted no small following: *Turn from your sins to God.* It is noteworthy that Yochanan was not calling Israel to convert to a new religion but to return (*t'shuvah*) to the source of any religious Jew's faith, the God of Abraham. The problem in the first century was not a faulty *Torah* or Temple service, but that so many in Israel had turned away from that spiritual relationship with the Lord.

Some modern commentators have questioned Matthew's use of the term "Kingdom of Heaven." Some even wonder if Matthew is speaking of a different, spiritual kingdom versus the earthly kingdom (Kingdom of God) alluded to by the other gospel writers. From Matthew's perspective, the answer is rather simple. As a traditional Jew writing to a Jewish audience, it would be common to refrain from pronouncing or writing the holy name of God (*YHVH*). As the *Talmud* clarifies, "In the Sanctuary the Name was pronounced as written, but beyond its confines a substituted Name was employed" (Tractate Sotah VII.6). A solution still common today in the Jewish community is to use substitute terms for *YHVH* such as *ADONAI* (LORD) or *HaShem* (the Name). In the Talmudic writings, we often find the word "*Shamayim*/heavens" as a substitute for the name of God since it refers to the entire universe that he has created. When Matthew uses the term "Kingdom of Heaven," then, he is not speaking of a different kingdom but is simply using a very Jewish way of referring to the Creator. For such traditional Jews of the first century, the Kingdom of Heaven is, in fact, the Kingdom of God.

As if to prove the point that Yochanan was not speaking of a different kingdom or new religion, Matthew quotes a famous prophecy that there will be a voice in the wilderness to *prepare the way of* ADONAI (cf. Isaiah 40:3). From the writer's perspective, Yochanan is fulfilling this vital ministry of preparing the way for Messiah. This is why the New Testament elsewhere affirms that Yochanan is fulfilling the prophetic work of the latter-day Elijah, who will usher in the days of *Mashiach* (cf. Luke 1:17). Even the appearance of this *magid*/ preacher in the wilderness would have brought back memories of the beloved Eliyahu with his *clothes of camel's hair with a leather belt* (cf. II Kings 1:8).

The surprising note that his food consisted of locusts and wild honey has certainly raised some questions. It is true that locusts may be eaten according to the laws of *kashrut* (dietary laws), as seen in Leviticus 11:22, and there is a discussion in the *Talmud* defining the characteristics of kosher versus unkosher locusts (Tractate Chullin 65a). Yet, a more viable translation has been offered as the Greek word for "locust" (*akis*) has a very similar sound to the word for "carob" (*karis*). Indeed, to this day in Israel, the carob tree is called the "St. John's tree," which probably sounds more appetizing than the insect! Whatever the case, the people who were heeding the message of Yochanan were coming in droves to make the symbolic gesture of their repentance and were fully immersed in the Yarden. By this *mikveh* of repentance, they were identifying with what Yochanan preached and preparing themselves for the imminent appearance of the Messiah.

Matthew shares some intriguing details of the *mikveh* ministry of Yochanan. It is not surprising that many traditional Jews came to hear the message of Yochanan and received his exhortation. Even many of the *P'rushim* and *Tz'dukim* (Pharisees and Sadducees) responded favorably by seeking this *mikveh* of repentance. Notice again that they did not perceive this immersion as some new religious expression or conversion, but they understood that this particular *mikveh* was one of repentance and preparation for the *Mashiach*. This all looked good on the surface, yet Yochanan perceives that the respondents' hearts are not right. Yochanan is clearly not seeking popular approval when he cries out, *"You snakes! Who warned you to escape the coming punishment?"* While it is a shockingly straightforward rebuke, it is no different from what the prophets of previous generations have spoken (cf. Psalm 58). The Immerser even calls into question their motives for seeking this *mikveh* of repentance since they have *no fruit that will prove it.*

Yochanan also reproves this particular crowd for their anticipated response, which relies on their relationship with Father Abraham. The belief is that all Jews, by virtue of our relational connection to righteous Abraham, enjoy the benefits of his standing before God. This common doctrine is found often in the prayer service and rabbinic writings (e.g., *Avot* section of the *Amidah* prayer). The *Talmud* even assures us that *all Israel has a place in the world to come* (cf. Tractate Sanhedrin 10.1).

To this, Yochanan issues a rebuke that *God can raise up for Avraham sons from these stones!* Besides the veracity of this statement, there is clearly a classic play on words in the Hebrew text as well. The Hebrew for "sons/*banim*" would closely relate to the word for "stones/*avanim*," thus reinforcing the problem of trusting only in the merits of the fathers. Indeed, *the axe is at the root of the trees* in anticipation of God's judgment on all that is false.

At this point, Yochanan clarifies some of the distinctions between his *mikveh* of repentance and the *mikveh* of the coming

Messiah. The current immersion is said to be only *in water* to symbolize the act of *t'shuvah*/repentance. But the *Mashiach* will immerse the people in *the Ruach HaKodesh* (Holy Spirit) *and with fire*. While the immersion of Yochanan was important, the immersion of Messiah would go even deeper into the spiritual call of Israel. The first was an outward call to prepare for the Kingdom. The second would be the reality of the Kingdom as experienced by the indwelling of the Holy Spirit.

The promise of the *Ruach HaKodesh* goes back to prophecies of Joel and Ezekiel. Joel predicts a time to come when the *Ruach* will be poured out on all humanity, especially upon Israel (2:28 English/3:1 Hebrew). Similarly, Ezekiel foresees a time in the Messianic Age when Israel will receive a new heart and a new Spirit (36:24-27). In other words, Yochanan's *mikveh* was similar to other types of immersions found in first-century Judaism, whereas Yeshua's *mikveh* would be of a different, spiritual dynamic.

The promise here is of Yeshua bringing the predicted times of spiritual filling to those who desired it. This seems to be why Yochanan humbly asserts that he is *not worthy to carry his sandals*, the sandals of his master. It could also be an allusion to an ancient practice of *Torah* called *chalitzah*/untying. In Deuteronomy 25:5-9, we are told of a case in which a man is obligated to marry the wife of his deceased brother. A central theme in the scroll of Ruth, this custom of exchanging a sandal is described as a symbol of a transfer of property or a renunciation of the same (Ruth 4:7). If the custom of *chalitzah* were in the mind of Yochanan, then he would be saying he did not feel worthy even to be connected to this coming Messiah.

A secondary part of Yeshua's immersion would include *fire* as well. Usually, the symbolism of fire in the Scriptures represents judgment or purification. The context of Yochanan's statement here emphasizes that when this Messiah appears, there will be not only the blessing of the Spirit, but also judgment by fire for those who refuse to follow.

In ancient days, the winnowing fork was a farm instrument used to throw the harvested grain into the air. The wind would then separate the heavier wheat grain from the lighter straw of the kernel. The valued wheat would then be stored for future use, while the scrap would be burnt or destroyed as useless.

In this case of spiritual harvest, that which is useless would be burnt with unquenchable fire, a graphic depiction of the judgment known as *Gei-Hinnom* in Jewish literature (later called *Gehenna* or Hell in Greek literature). This is a valley outside Jerusalem used in ancient times as a trash dump and was even a place of pagan, human sacrifice at times. *Gei-Hinnom* (valley of Hinnom) was, therefore, an apt symbol for the real place of judgment to come in the Messianic Age. In short, this passage teaches that every person, believer or non-believer, will experience an immersion of the Messiah when he appears. It will either be a *mikveh* of blessing with the indwelling Holy Spirit, or it will be a *mikveh* of fire and judgment. This message caused quite a stir in Israel at this time. It is still a vital message for all of us to consider for our own spiritual lives today.

What transpires next is truly amazing, as Yeshua himself makes that trip from the Galilee to the place of Yochanan's immersion ministry. Yochanan clearly realizes his submission to Yeshua, as reflected in his question as to why Yeshua is coming for the *mikveh*. We may ask the same question: If Yeshua is the true Messiah, why would he need to be immersed by Yochanan? Yeshua gives the answer in stating that *we should do everything righteousness requires.* It is important to remember that the key symbolism of *mikveh* in Judaism is that of identification. Yeshua clearly did not need to repent of any sins, since he is described as the sinless son of God. However, it does make sense that he would identify with the message of Yochanan and put his stamp of approval upon it. Likewise, it makes sense that part of everything righteous would include the symbolic cleansing of a priest before the start of a time of ministry. It is fitting for Yeshua

THE PREPARATION FOR KING MESSIAH / 33

to take a *mikveh* as a public testimony that this is the start of his ministry to Israel. As Yeshua comes out of the water, there is a public manifestation of the Holy Spirit, which appeared *like a dove.*

Interestingly, this is the same symbolism for the Holy Spirit seen in rabbinic literature. One passage of the *Talmud*, in dealing with the Creation account of Genesis 1:2, states that "The Spirit of God hovered over the face of the waters—like a dove which hovers over her young without touching them" (Tractate Hagigah 15a). In another Talmudic expression, the text says that *a voice from heaven* testified, "This is my son, whom I love; I am well pleased with him."

The classical rabbis called this mysterious manifestation the *bat-kol* (daughter of the voice). After the last of the prophets, it was considered that God provided the *bat-kol* to still give guidance to the people (Tractate Yoma 9b). How interesting it is that the *bat-kol* testified, after the last of the prophets and before the New Covenant was established, that Yeshua is indeed God's son. To Matthew's audience, this was a voice to be taken seriously. God is said to have a son according to Psalm 2, Proverbs 30, Isaiah 9:5 (in Hebrew Scriptures, 9:6 in English), and elsewhere. Now this person has come to Israel and started his priestly ministry in the traditional way of *mikveh*.

Messiah Prepared by Testing   4:1-16

Matthew now moves us to a new phase of Messiah's preparation for ministry. As Yeshua received the confirmation of the Spirit and the *bat-kol* in Chapter 3, now that same Spirit leads him up to the wilderness for a confrontation with the Adversary. This is an apt translation of the Hebrew word *satan*, as it describes the fallen angel who opposes all that God is trying to establish. Satan is not a "Christian" invention but appears numerous times in the Hebrew Scriptures and Jewish tradition. The most famous case is where Job is tested, as God allows Satan to afflict him in numerous ways

(Job 1). Likewise, it is Satan who is accusing Joshua, the priestly representative of Israel (Zechariah 3). Isaiah 14, as well as Ezekiel 28, graphically describe the fall of this anointed cherub who once was at the very throne of God. In rabbinic literature, Satan is said to be involved in three specific actions—he seduces people, he accuses them before God, and he brings the punishment of death (Tractate Bava Batra 16a). Satan is also said to have instigated the Golden Calf incident in the wilderness by, after forty days, stirring up turmoil in Israel and casting doubt on the return of Moses from the mountain (Tractate Shabbat 89a). Since his rebellion before the Creation, Satan/Lucifer has opposed God's plan, which now would certainly focus on the Messiah.

Not surprisingly, Satan comes to oppose Yeshua, yet the Father will use it as a test to prepare his son for the messianic mission. From the Jordan River valley (site of the *mikveh*), the site of the test was most likely the wilderness of Judea, which consists of the desert foothills. The fast of *forty days and nights* would sound familiar to Matthew's readers, as this parallels the experience of both Moses (Exodus 34:28) and of Elijah (I Kings 19:8).

These two personalities are central to historic Judaism, as *Moshe* represents the *Torah* and *Eliyahu* is the first of the prophets. Their connection to Yeshua is a central focus for Matthew both in this context and later at the Transfiguration (cf. Matthew 17:1-9). After the forty days, the writer makes what seems to be an obvious understatement—*he was hungry.* It is known that after the initial hunger pangs of a fast, a person may have an extended period of time during which the body is strong and there are no ill effects from lack of food. However, around forty days into a fast, there will be some new pangs. These are not due merely to hunger but actually indicate that the body is beginning to starve itself. Yeshua was at this critical junction when the Adversary came to him with some incredible tests.

The first test centers on the claim that Yeshua is the Son of God. What was clearly testified to by the *bat-kol* in the previous chapter is now called into question. *If you are the Son of God* is an informative question in itself. The Greek conditional clause would be better translated *since you are the Son of God.* The Adversary is evidently not questioning the earlier testimony, but, in a deceitful move, seeks to cause this Anointed One sent from the Father to stumble. The temptation of bread after a 40-day fast must have been almost overwhelming, especially in light of the fact that Yeshua could have created the bread himself as suggested.

We sometimes forget that the *Mashiach,* by definition, is the God-man. Thus, in his humanity Yeshua could feel the intensity of any physical test. However, because of his divine nature, he could not succumb to such testing, as that would disqualify him from being the sinless redeemer (cf. Heb. 4:15) Accordingly, Yeshua answers with the spiritual insight that *man does not live on bread alone,* a direct quote from the *Torah* (Deuteronomy 8:3). The Messiah must be totally dependent on his Heavenly Father and not succumb to using his powers for causes that may be contrary to the revealed will of God.

Satan, having failed at his first test of the Messiah, now turns to another angle of temptation. *The highest point of the Temple* refers to the corner of the Second Temple where the priests would sound the trumpet to call the crowd to worship.

An amazing archaeological discovery amid the broken stones of the Temple Mount confirms the location of this spot. In 1969, archaeologists uncovered a stone that had been at the top of the Temple with the Hebrew inscription reading, "To the place of the trumpeting for…." Presumably the end of the phrase would have read "for the Priest" or contained equivalent wording. Such a place, with its commanding view for the multitude of worshippers, would have been the ideal location for a dramatic, messianic miracle.

A *midrash* puts particular emphasis on this exact place, as it states:

> Our teachers taught, at the time when the King Messiah will
> appear, he will come and stand upon the roof of the Temple.
> He will proclaim to Israel and will say to the humble, "The
> time of your redemption has arrived" (Peshikta Rabbati 36).

To add to the weight of this temptation, the Adversary even quotes part of Psalm 91:11, stating that *he will order his angels to be responsible for you.* It is a sobering thought to realize that Satan knows the Scripture and will even quote it out of context for his own evil purposes. The whole context of the Psalm is trusting God (v. 1-2). To test the Father would imply that Yeshua had a lack of trust in him. Yeshua's response is to quote Scripture in proper context, *Do not put ADONAI your God to the test* (Deut. 6:16). The one who truly trusts the Father is perfectly comfortable not testing the veracity of his promises. Perhaps some people test God because they do not know him well enough to rest in him.

The Adversary takes one last shot at discrediting this designated Messiah by pulling out perhaps the strongest temptation of all. By showing Yeshua *all the kingdoms of the world in all their glory,* Satan was appealing once again to something that rightly belongs to the Messiah. At the moment, the kingdoms of the world are controlled by (or given over by God to) Satan, the ruler of this age (cf. Eph. 2:2). In this temporal sense, Satan could make a legitimate offer of these kingdoms. Yet, the preconditions are what subtly undercut the sincerity of this offer. If Yeshua were to *bow down and worship* Satan, he would be placing himself in submission to and acknowledging the superiority of the Adversary. Again, it must have been an incredible temptation to the humanity of Messiah, as he in fact had a legal right to all those kingdoms. But the timing was premature, and ADONAI is the only One worthy of worship and service (Deuteronomy 6:16). With that scriptural response, *the Adversary let him alone.*

Not only did Yeshua pass these critical tests of his messiahship, but he also provided vital lessons for his followers today. No doubt, Satan is still seeking to harass and devour the Messianic remnant of believers (cf. I Pet. 5:8-9). Yet we are called to resist the Evil One. And we should not do so by arguing, binding, or debating in some spiritual manner. The rabbis understood that Israel possessed a secret weapon to overcome Satan:

> The Holy One, blessed be He, said to Israel, My children, I have created the evil impulse, and I have created the *Torah* as an antidote to it; if you occupy yourselves with *Torah* you will not be delivered into its power (Tractate Kiddushin 30b).

We also can have great victory by following Yeshua's example of resisting with the Word of God. It is also informative which section of the Word that he used. For some believers, the New Covenant is the only source of power, yet Messiah consistently quotes the *Torah* in his spiritual confrontation with Satan. Of course, the book of Ephesians had not yet been written! Likewise, we see that Yeshua did not try to "bind" the enemy but powerfully resisted the Adversary through the proper use of the promises of God. We can still find spiritual power today as we stand on the entire Word of ADONAI—including the *Torah*, the foundation of it all.

After this intense time of testing in the wilderness, Yeshua is said to have gone to the Galilee after *Yochanan had been put in prison.* Herod had evidently become tired of Yochanan's prophetic denunciations of his family and administration, so he had him imprisoned in hopes of stopping his light from shining (cf. Matthew 14:1-11). Yeshua makes a stop at his hometown of Nazareth and even has a dramatic *aliyah* (calling up to the *bima*/platform at synagogue) where he proclaims his messiahship (cf. Luke 4:14ff). After he is driven out of the town, Yeshua sets up his ministry base *in* K'far-Nachum/Capernaum, just down the hill from Nazareth and on the shoreline of the Sea of Galilee. It is important to Matthew to note that this area of the Kinneret has a major prophetic role in the Hebrew Scriptures. It is this *Galil-of-the-Goyim* (Galilee of the Nations) where great light will permeate the darkness of history, according to Isaiah 9.

The name reflects the historical experience of the region, which was the territory of some of the ten tribes of the Northern Kingdom of Israel. It was an area of sordid idolatry and paganism, especially in the tribe of Dan to the north. In 722 BCE, the Assyrians came in and captured the area, sending the people into dispersion or intermarrying within the land. Thus, the region became a mixture of Jews, non-Jews, and intermarried Jews who later started their own culture and religion as the Samaritans.

Truly, the Galilee was a land of darkness for many centuries. Yet, in a rather strange promise, it is in this Galilee (not religious Jerusalem) that *the people living in darkness have seen a great light.* What Isaiah predicted in his generation was affirmed in rabbinic tradition multiple times with the expressed hope of the coming Messiah. In the mystical literature of the *Zohar*, some of the rabbis even saw a logical reason for this promise of Isaiah: "The Messiah will arise and reveal himself in the Land of Galilee because that was the first place to be destroyed in the Holy Land" (Zohar 2:7b). Matthew's point is that Yeshua fulfills even the minute details concerning the promised Messiah as spoken in the *Tanakh*.

THE PROGRAM
OF KING MESSIAH
4:17-16:12

"The Holy One, blessed be He, will sit and expound the new Torah which He will give through the Messiah. 'New Torah' means the secrets and the mysteries of the Torah which have remained hidden until now."

(Midrash Talpiyot 58a)

The writer now turns his attention to some important details concerning the life of Yeshua. When will he start his ministry to Israel? What will be his message to the people? How will this message compare to the Jewish teaching and understanding of the day? The answers to these questions will be compelling to the first-century audience as well as to us today.

The Initiation of the Kingdom   4:17-25

Having completed the required preparation, Yeshua now commences his actual messianic program for Israel. Matthew records the simple yet powerful message that was the theme of Yeshua's ministry in a two-fold division. *Turn from your sins to God* reflects a key element in traditional Judaism. Repentance (*t'shuvah*) encompasses more than just a change of heart but actually turning one's life in a different direction. In this case, the challenge is to turn from that which misses the mark that God has placed before us, and come back to the Father's call on our life. It is noteworthy that Israel is not called to convert to a new religion or new God but simply to turn around and come back to the God of our Fathers. That *the Kingdom of Heaven is near* likewise would sound familiar to the audience.

If one had to pick a summary theme of the entire message of the Scriptures, it might be God's desire to establish his kingdom on Earth. This has been the foundational hope given to Israel in the *Torah* (Exodus 19:6), the Prophets (Isa. 11:1-9), and the Writings (I Chron. 29:11). It is only natural for Jewish tradition to conclude that the Messiah would be the King over this earthly kingdom (cf. Isa. 9:6, 9:5 in Hebrew). How perfectly consistent it is that since Yeshua is the promised King Messiah, he would start his public ministry with the proclamation that the Kingdom is near.

Some have tried to draw a distinction between the "Kingdom of God" and the "Kingdom of Heaven" that is mentioned here.

Sometimes commentators establish the former as the earthly kingdom, whereas the latter would be the spiritual kingdom. However, the biblical understanding is that there is no such dichotomy. The various terms that are used describe the same kingdom spoken of in the *Tanakh*. The clear reason for multiple terms, from the perspective of Matthew's audience, is that Jews do not normally attempt to pronounce the holy name of God (*YHVH*), as mentioned previously. Out of respect for the third commandment, Jews to this day often use substitute terms when referring to God. A common Talmudic term is the word *shamayim*/heaven, as this designated the One who is omnipresent. Consequently, Matthew's use of the term "Kingdom of Heaven" is not a reference to a secondary kingdom.

Also noteworthy is that the content of Yeshua's message apparently correlates with the timing of the start of his public ministry to Israel. It is commonly shown that the chronological aspects of the gospels suggest that Yeshua's entire public ministry was about three and a half years in length. This is based on internal evidence, including the fact that he is said to have celebrated four Passovers over that period. This being so, we can trace the beginning of his ministry back from the point where it came to a finish at Passover. Tracing back the three and a half years from Passover, we arrive at the fall season. It is quite interesting to note that the high holy days in the fall commence with the strong message of *t'shuvah*/repentance at Rosh Hashanah.

Not only is the message of Yeshua significant, but the timing would add that much more power as he seemed to start his ministry during this holy season of turning back to God during Rosh Hashanah. Likewise, these chronological clues seem to lead us to the time of year in which the Messiah was actually born in Bethlehem. According to Luke 3:23, Yeshua was "about 30 years old when he began his public ministry." Although not an exact date, the reference implies that Yeshua was close to 30 in the fall of the year, contrary to the tradition of celebrating his birth in late December. This evidence shows that Messiah was born during one of the fall holy days. I have suggested that these details lend credence to the possibility that Yeshua was born during the festival of *Sukkot*/Tabernacles, a time when Israel celebrates God dwelling with his people.

It was in conjunction with the message during the High Holy Day season that Yeshua officially called his first disciples. The concept of discipleship was not new. Any significant rabbi would have faithful followers who would be called to a commitment of both following and learning (thus the word *talmid*/learner). This entailed more than just passing on information, as it also involved a close personal relationship with one's rabbi.

This is beautifully stated in the *Talmud* where a disciple is called to, "Let your house be a meeting place for the rabbis, and cover yourself in the dust of their feet, and drink in their words thirstily" (Pirke Avot 1:4). The best disciples were the ones who stayed so close to their rabbi that they could take in every detail of their mentorship. That should be a fresh challenge today as we consider the call of Yeshua upon our lives!

It is noteworthy that Yeshua did not start calling disciples from among the rabbis in the *yeshivot*/seminaries of Jerusalem. Instead, Yeshua sought simple fishermen toiling around the Kinneret (so named for its shape like a harp or violin).

Not that these men would have been ignorant. They surely received the mandatory training of any Jewish boy growing up in ancient Israel. Yet it was a bit surprising to some that many of the followers of this self-proclaimed Messiah were more from the common people (*am ha-aretz*). *Shim'on* was the Hebrew name for the one also known in Greek as *Petros*/Peter. The former name means "hearing," as in the conviction that God has heard the prayers of the parents. *Petros* means "rock" and is equivalent to a third name in Aramaic, *Kefa*. Although shaky at times, Shim'on will turn out to be one of the foundational rocks of the Yeshua movement. *Andrew* (Greek for "manly") is simply noted as the brother of Shim'on. However, both respond with incredible faith to the call of this rabbi/messiah to become *fishers of men*. Similarly, the call goes forth to two brothers working at the seashore. *Ya'akov Ben-Zavdai* and *Yochanan* are working with their father when they prioritize the invitation of Yeshua and immediately leave their profession. Although their family name was Zavdai (Hebrew for "gift of God"), Yeshua would later give these zealous brothers the nickname *"Boanerges*/thunder," which would be an apt description of their personality (cf. Mark 3:17).

The chapter closes with the note that Yeshua was *proclaiming the Good News of the Kingdom in the synagogues of the Galil*. To testify to the validity of his message, many were being healed of diseases and illnesses. Likewise, as Messiah, he was bringing demonic activity under the submission of his rule. Little wonder that word of these deeds was spreading swiftly and huge crowds were following him throughout the region. How about us? Is our life covered with the dust of our Rabbi Yeshua?

The Precepts of King Messiah   5:1-7:29

With the initiation of his ministry to Israel, Yeshua now presents his specific teaching and interpretations concerning the coming Messianic Kingdom. There are numerous perspectives on the intent of the Sermon on the Mount. Some see the teaching merely as a moral code to be followed to the best of our human ability. Others see it as a description of the utopia of the Messianic Kingdom that is unattainable in this present age. Within the context of Matthew, it seems best to regard the following three chapters as Messiah's interpretation of the *Torah*. That this would be one of the primary ministries of the *Mashiach* is made clear in the rabbinic commentaries. In one text, it is written:

> Rabbi Hizqiya in the name of Rabbi Shimon bar Zivdi said: "The whole *Torah* which you learn in this world is vanity as against the *Torah* of the world to come. For in this world a man learns *Torah* and forgets, but in the world to come he will not forget, as it is written, I will put My *Torah* in their inward parts and in their heart will I write it" (Eccles. Rabba 11:1).

Just how the *Torah* would be written on the heart of God's children is debated. Yet, the person who would be instrumental in bringing us the true meaning of *Torah* would undoubtedly be the Messiah himself. "When he, about whom it is written, 'Lowly and riding upon an ass will come…' (Zech. 9:9) he will elucidate for them the words of the *Torah*…and elucidate for them their errors" (Gen. Rabba 98:9). It is a humble yet accurate admission that we need help to fully understand God's teaching to us. With this backdrop, the Sermon on the Mount can be understood to be a logical presentation of the Messiah, clarifying the true intent of *Torah* for all of Israel and those in the Nations who will seek him.

The Subjects of the King   5:1-16

The mention of *the crowds* reminds us that Yeshua's popularity was growing at this point of his ministry. There was a simple yet powerful truth to his message of repentance and preparing for the Kingdom of God. This was especially appealing to the common people who were in desperate need of hope and purpose during this tumultuous time in Israel. Many had become true *talmidim*/disciples as they chose to learn at the feet of their rabbi/Messiah from Galilee. Since the Messiah would be the ultimate *Torah* teacher, it is quite appropriate that the context here is reminiscent of the first giving of the *Torah* on another mountain. In accurate cultural detail, Matthew notes that Yeshua *sat down* to teach, which was the traditional mode of teaching for rabbis in the first century (Tractate Berachot 27b).

What follows in verses 3-12 are the characteristics of those who will dwell in the Messianic Kingdom. The opening segment, often called the Beatitudes (Latin for *blessed*), of course can be traced back to an earlier Jewish concept. The phrase "How blessed" would sound familiar to any educated Jew. The Hebrew word *ashrey* is common throughout the Psalms and the *siddur*/prayer book. The root word (*asher*) would more accurately mean "happy," not in some superficial sense in the temporal world, but in the most fulfilling reality of doing the will of God. Some of the specific beatitudes do not seem good in themselves; yet if a person fulfills God's will in these ways, there is a blessing and even a sense of happiness that the world cannot offer.

The first characteristic of those who will dwell in the kingdom is revealed in the statement *How blessed are the poor in spirit.* The Hebrew term *oni* is often used to refer to material poverty; yet the Messiah challenges his disciples, who are so destitute in their own spirits. This is a foundational place to start as we seek to know the true interpretation of *Torah*. Our own spirit must be devoid of any pride or self-merit. Interestingly, a similar phrase (*oniye ha-ruach*) was used in the Dead Sea Scrolls to describe the character of this first-century sect living in the Judean desert. If we are to even begin our search for Messiah's kingdom, we must humbly realize our need for God. Those who look at themselves as so impoverished will participate in the *Kingdom of Heaven*.

The second beatitude invokes a blessing on *those who mourn*. Unfortunately, Israel has a long history of mourning, as it has endured many times of trials and attacks from enemies. The crowds on this mountain would easily relate to the concept expressed in the Hebrew term *aval*, which is a common response to the tragedies of life. The promise of Yeshua here is similar to that of the prophet Isaiah, who promised Israel the oil of gladness instead of mourning (Isa. 61:3).

In speaking of the spiritual reality of the kingdom, Yeshua could also be alluding to our need to mourn over our sins before we can *be comforted*. It is interesting that one of the Talmudic titles given to the Messiah is the name "Menachem" (Hebrew *nacham*), which means "Comforter," as this would be an important ministry of King Messiah (Tractate Sanhedrin 98b). In Yeshua's later teaching, we are told that another comforter will come to us as well—the Holy Spirit, who will dwell with all Messianic believers (cf. Yochanan 14:15-17).

The third *ashrey* spoken by Yeshua will be encountered by *the meek*. Some have misinterpreted this concept to mean that a disciple of Yeshua must be a weakling or a doormat. However, the Hebrew word *anav* implies power under control. Such a person is not pushy or self-centered, but purposely limits his own power and rights.

A good illustration would be a high-powered sports car cruising at 60 miles per hour down a freeway. Surely such a car could double that speed, yet, out of meekness, its power is brought under control. The Messianic Kingdom calls for people who are willing to walk in such a humble manner so they may *inherit the Land*. The latter phrase implies both a physical inheritance in *Eretz-Yisra'el* (Land of Israel), as promised to the Jewish people, and a spiritual inheritance of eternal life in the future Kingdom of God for all believers in Yeshua.

How blessed are those who hunger and thirst is clearly applied to the moral/spiritual life of any seeker. As those seekers hunger (*ra-eyv*) not just for physical food but also for righteousness, *they will be filled*. The body naturally hungers for provision, yet the spirit has an even stronger need. It is those who hunger for the things of God who will be filled. The Talmudic tradition mentions with delight the prospect of the coming kingdom of Messiah.

One much-anticipated highlight will be the banquet of Messiah that is said to take place in the restored Garden of Eden. As the

Mashiach gathers his redeemed people together, a cup of wine is blessed that has been aged from the days of Creation. King David himself is said to have the honor of singing the *brachah*/blessing (cf. Patai, pp. 238-239). As great as the physical banquet may be, Yeshua emphasizes the greater blessing of having our spiritual hunger completely satisfied in the kingdom.

The fifth blessing is pronounced over *those who show mercy*. The Hebrew word *racham* speaks of withholding something that is truly deserved. Someone may be guilty of a crime in a judicial sense and therefore deserving of the appropriate sentence, yet mercy spares the defendant of the rightly earned penalty. Yeshua teaches that those who will enter into the kingdom of Messiah must have this attribute that beautifully reflects the character of God himself. We *will be shown mercy* from God as we show that same kind of mercy to those around us. Certainly those who understand the mercy of Yeshua, who removes the judgments against us, will be slow to judge others.

The requirements get even stricter with the sixth beatitude, *How blessed are the pure in heart* (Hebrew *barey lavav*). Being pure in heart seems to be an impossible condition for mankind to attain and maintain. We all fall short of the standard of God as reflected in the *Torah*. Even with our best intentions, our actions and thoughts do not come close to fulfilling the requirements of a righteous God.

Although we should continue to strive for more of the character of God to be active within our hearts, this beatitude clearly convicts us of our need for the help of God. If we will *see God* only when we have a pure heart, all of humanity is in trouble. The more we dig into the words of Yeshua, the more we find that his interpretations of *Torah* are even more difficult to fulfill than the original covenant. The principles are so lofty that they should convict us of our desperate need for what the Messiah offers. It is only in his purity and righteousness that we can dare hope of enjoying the kingdom to come. In other words, Yeshua the Messiah came not just to teach us about

God but also to actually pay the proper price of redemption to bring us into the Kingdom of God.

Shalom/peace is the theme of the seventh *ashrey*. It is a concept that is perhaps the most treasured among Jewish people, as it is one of our favorite words. The Hebrew term (*shalom*) is significantly different from the commonly known Greek concept (*eirene*). In the Greek culture, the term was used to describe a situation in which there was an absence of conflict. When a war stopped, that was *eirene*. In the Jewish culture, the term is much broader and deeper. Not only does it describe the absence of war but also a state of completeness, fulfillment, and positive blessing. It's no wonder that those who seek true *shalom will be called sons of God.*

Blessing number eight again illustrates the values of Messiah's kingdom, which are often so different from the present age. In our worldly society, we usually seek acceptance from others. However, Yeshua exhorts these disciples to prepare to be *persecuted* as they *pursue righteousness.* The fact is that the world's system ultimately is not seeking the righteousness of God. It may seek a certain standard of righteousness that is usually based on the relative values of society. Those who pursue the holy righteousness of God can expect to get some negative reactions from those around them. The darkness does not enjoy the light and must react. Perhaps this concept explains much of the anti-Semitism throughout history. Many times the community was identified with the righteousness of God, even when we ourselves did not walk entirely in it. True believers in Yeshua can expect a negative reaction from a world that does not seek the presence of God.

While this is not always easy, Messiah gives the assurance that *the Kingdom of Heaven is theirs.* Perhaps it is significant that Yeshua elaborates on this truth, noting that people will even *insult you* and *tell all kinds of vicious lies about you.* It is bad enough that some people would do such things, but it becomes all the more stunning when we realize it is, as Yeshua says, *because you follow me.* Sometimes, people just have problems with those who follow Yeshua. This seems totally unfair and is quite disheartening, yet it is for this very reason we are told to *rejoice* and *be glad.* Our reward in heaven is great, and we can also take some comfort in the reality that even *the prophets* of Israel were *persecuted in the same way.* Indeed, Yeshua himself was fiercely persecuted by those who were threatened by his message. Can those who identify with him expect anything less?

Yeshua now moves from the characteristics of his followers to their specific calling. He illustrates the responsibilities of his disciples with a series of practical pictures. Messianic believers are *salt for the Land,* which may reflect a number of truths. Salt in the ancient world was vitally important, so much so that the *Talmud* states that "the world cannot exist without salt" (Tractate Soferim 15.8).

Salt was an important commodity for trade, as seen in the covenant of salt in the *Torah* (Numbers 18:19). Even our modern saying of someone "being worth his salt" recounts the days when salt was traded with great value. Salt was required for many of the sacrifices in the Temple (cf. Leviticus 2:13). Since salt was a preservative and would draw out the blood in the meat, it was vital for kosher sacrifices. Kosher salt is still used today to help prepare meat for cooking. A common tradition today is to sprinkle salt on the *hallah* (*Shabbat* bread) to remind us of the sprinkled sacrifices.

All of these ideas can come into play with Yeshua's teaching. We are to be like koshering salt that preserves society as well as draws out impurities. Yet potential problems can occur. What if the *salt becomes tasteless?* Messiah warns us that we can lose our effectiveness in the world around us if we lose close contact with him. This teaching seems especially applicable to Jewish followers of Yeshua today. It is one thing to choose to follow Yeshua as Messiah, but we miss an important part of our calling if we assimilate instead of choosing to remain true to our Jewish heritage (cf. I Cor. 7:17-20). The modern

Messianic synagogue movement provides a practical way for Jews to embrace Yeshua and to continue to live as Jews in a practical sense, not losing our saltiness. Tasteless salt may be used only *for people to trample on.* On the other hand, sometimes we may be salty enough, but hidden in the saltshaker. Don't be surprised if God has to shake us a bit to get us out to the world.

A second picture given is that Messianic believers are *light for the world.* This calling is actually nothing new in the understanding of Israel. Isaiah the prophet long ago reminded his generation that they were to be a light to the Nations, spreading the salvation of the one true God (cf. Isaiah 49:6). The lampstand/*menorah* in the Temple was to be a constant reminder that God's light was manifested to Israel. Yet, as Yeshua clarifies here, what good is the light if you *cover it with a bowl?*

Messiah calls his followers to let their light shine even beyond the Temple, to the nations of the world. The *town built on a hill* is most likely a reference to a common practice of the Second Temple period. It was customary to announce the start of the New Moon festival (*Rosh Chodesh*) by igniting a fire on strategic mountaintops around Israel. Since the new moon must be verified by a *Beit-Din* (rabbinic court) in Jerusalem, the fires were set to quickly announce to the countryside that the festival had officially begun.

As Yeshua spoke these words in the Galilee, it is likely he was pointing to the mountain city of *Tsfat,* designated as one of the places where such fires were built (Tractate Rosh Hashanah 2.4). Such a visible city was a graphic reminder of the spiritual calling of his Messianic community. How can this light shine in practical terms? It can shine in *the good things you do* that can be outwardly observed by others. This has always been a strong value—that our beliefs are reflected by our actions. In fact, how can the non-believing world understand our spiritual walk unless they see some practical, outward manifestation? In the words of Ya'akov, "Faith by itself, unaccompanied by actions, is dead" (*Ya'akov*/James 2:17). Are we letting the light of Messiah shine in the world around us?

Yeshua and the *Torah*   5:17-20

These verses give us a vital clarification of Yeshua's interpretations of *Torah*. Undoubtedly, the strong message of Yeshua's early ministry would cause some to question his ultimate objective. He already perceived that some, especially in the rabbinic community, were seeing his message as a theological threat to Judaism or even to the Scriptures themselves. As the Messiah reveals his interpretation of the *Torah*, he feels the need to clarify his position in regard to the earlier revelations given to Israel.

By his own words, Yeshua is not bringing a new teaching or new *Torah* to his people; he is coming to complete the covenants that were previously given. The word "complete" (Greek *plerao*) is not used here in the sense of destroying something or making an end. It is better understood as completing or reaching a goal. Rabbi Sha'ul uses the same word to exhort the believers to be filled with the Holy Spirit (cf. Ephesians 5:18). The idea is to fill up like a sail on a boat.

It has been an unfortunate tendency in some Christian theologies to deprecate or devalue the *Torah*. Although the *Torah* must be used in a proper way, the Messianic Jewish view is that *Torah* becomes all the more beautiful when we find the completion of the picture in Yeshua. For this reason, many Messianic Jews appreciate our God-given heritage even more than we did before we understood the place of Yeshua in our Jewish faith.

As if to emphasize the importance of this teaching, Yeshua elaborates even further. *Yes indeed!* (Hebrew *ameyn*) *not even a yud or a stroke will pass from the Torah* until all is accomplished. The *yud* is the smallest letter of the Hebrew alphabet. The stroke (Hebrew *tag*) is the smallest extension of a letter. In Hebrew, the difference of a *tag* can change the whole meaning of a word, as in the case of a *dalet* or a *resh* (cf. *Echad*/one or *Acher*/another) in Deuteronomy 6:4. Not only does Yeshua respect the message of *Torah*, but he is not advocating altering one of the smallest letters or even the part of a letter. He could not have emphasized his regard for *Torah* in stronger terms. Although there is considerable debate today about the inspiration of Scripture, the teaching of Yeshua makes it abundantly clear where he stood on the issue. All Scripture (indeed every letter!) is directly from God. Messiah's followers today (both Jew and non-Jew) would do well to hold such a high regard for the entire Word today.

He goes on to uphold the relevance of *Torah* by warning that *whoever disobeys* its message will be *called the least in the Kingdom.* The concept of heavier and lighter commandments is a common theme in the rabbinic understanding of *Torah.* For example, a lighter commandment would be freeing a mother bird in nature, whereas a heavier commandment would be to honor one's parents (cf. Tractate Kiddushin 61b).

Yeshua teaches here that just as there are heavier and lighter commandments, there are also heavier and lighter people in the Kingdom of God. This parallels the situation with the pagan king Belshazzar, who was weighed by God and found to be light (cf. Daniel 7:25). Lest Yeshua's disciples begin to think they can enter the kingdom through their own power of obedience to *Torah*, he states a rather shocking truth. Unless their *righteousness is far greater* than that of the top rabbis and observant Pharisees, they themselves have no hope of entering Messiah's kingdom. This seems to be the general principle *(klal)* of Yeshua's perspective on *Torah.* If we must have more righteousness than even the most religious and observant Jews, we indeed are in great trouble.

Here we are reminded of one of the clear purposes of the Sermon on the Mount. While we can glean much about life from Yeshua's teaching, the bottom-line truth is that we all will fall short of fulfilling these exalted values. Perhaps it is ironic that the Sermon on the Mount is given not so that we can earn our place in Messiah's kingdom, but that we will realize our desperate need for all that the *Mashiach* offers. As Rabbi Sha'ul would say, "He delivered us...not on the ground of any righteous deeds we had done, but on the ground of his own mercy" (cf. Titus 3:5). Messianic Judaism can appreciate the special place of *Torah* as a guide, while leaning on the work of Yeshua for our spiritual salvation. Ultimately, he is the only hope for Jew and Gentile alike.

Yeshua and *Halakhah*   5:21-48

Precepts on Murder   5:21-26

As the perfect interpreter of the *Torah*, Yeshua now addresses several moral issues facing humanity. Of course, the written *Torah* is set forever as the Word of God. But the process of deriving practical application from the *Torah* is called *halakhah*/the walk. Yeshua now gives his interpretation on various *halakhic* perspectives of his day.

He starts with his teaching on the commandment, *"Do not murder."* Yet a closer look at Yeshua's words shows that he is not just commenting on the written *Torah* (*Torah she-biktav*) but also on something much broader. In the phrase *you have heard that our fathers were told,* we find Messiah alluding to what is often called the Oral *Torah* (*Torah she'baal pey*).

Since the days of Mount Sinai, traditional Jews have largely been in agreement that the *Torah* Moses wrote down is the inspired Word of God. However, over the course of the centuries, another body of tradition developed that was the rabbinic commentary on this written *Torah*. Of course, it is not necessarily wrong and it may even be a good thing to have scholars offering their understanding of the holy text. From the Jewish point of view, the written *Torah* is so holy that we should protect it to the best of our ability. Subsequently, the classical rabbis developed a concept called the "fence around the *Torah*" (*seyag la-Torah*) that was to protect the perimeter of the commandments. "Moses received *Torah* from Sinai and handed it on to Joshua, and Joshua to the Elders, and the Elders to the Prophets, and the Prophets handed it on to the men of the Great Assembly. They said three things: Be deliberate in judgment, raise many disciples, and make a hedge around the *Torah*" (Pirke Avot 1:1).

The idea is that if we set up a fence and don't break through its boundaries, then we will certainly not break the actual commandments of God. The subtle danger, however, both in Judaism and Christianity, is that over time these commentaries may take on almost equal weight with the original Scripture. In this passage, Yeshua refers to both of these bodies of tradition. He quotes directly from the Ten Commandments regarding the prohibition of murder. Yet, the secondary phrase shows us that he is addressing specifically how the rabbis applied this command. Matthew specifies that he does not say "it is written" but "you have heard it said," clearly alluding not to the written *Torah* but to the interpretations of oral *Torah*, as later incorporated in the *Talmud* (*Mishnah* and *Gemara*).

For generations, these commentaries were literally passed down by word-of-mouth teaching. The word *Mishnah*/repetition describes how the interpretations were passed down by oral repetition until the students mastered them. Some sectors of rabbinic Judaism in Yeshua's day were overly concerned with the fence, ironically even to the point of breaking the original intention of the *Torah*. Once again we see a primary focus of Yeshua's ministry, which was to bring our people back to a purer understanding of the *Torah* given through Moses.

Yeshua, in addressing the various rabbinic views of this *Torah* commandment, strikes at the heart of the issue. His messianic interpretation is different than many of the existing views as is evident by his statement *but I tell you*. It is not enough merely to fulfill the *mitzvah*/commandment of not murdering, but we are called to a higher standard of even refraining from holding *anger against* our *brother.* The precepts of the kingdom go beyond external obedience to the motivations and thoughts of the heart. Of course, the horrific act of murder has its seeds in ungodly attitudes. One's language will often reflect such anger, as in the case of calling a brother *You good-for-nothing* or *fool*. The former term (Hebrew *reyk*) is used in Talmudic literature as an insult meaning "vacant" or "empty-headed." The latter (Hebrew *eyvil*) has the stronger connotation of evil. Those who express their anger with such language might be *brought before the Sanhedrin* (rabbinic court) or even be in danger of *burning in the fire of Gei-Hinnom* (literally "valley of Hinnom," symbolic of Hell).

Certainly, Yeshua's statements underscore the seriousness of harboring and expressing inappropriate anger. The Messiah does not leave his hearers without concrete direction in dealing with this kind of anger. So important is this issue that if people are offering a *gift at the Temple*, they must make it a top priority first to resolve any conflicts in their relationships. Although the worship sacrifice is important, the true spirit behind such a sacrifice requires the person to *make peace* with an offended brother. Only after the interpersonal relationship is restored can the sacrifice then be offered. The same principle applies if you happen to be the object of a lawsuit. Messiah's directive is to *come to terms with him quickly* so that you may avert a worse situation. Since the price of ungodly anger is so high, it is to everyone's advantage to seek a peaceful resolution with any offended parties.

Precepts on Adultery   5:27-32

Yeshua continues his *halakhic* commentary on the *Torah* with the technical phrase *you have heard*. Again, he is clearly referring to the oral *Torah* tradition as opposed to the written Word found in the Law. *Do not commit adultery* is the written command, yet there were various rabbinic interpretations of this important statute. Since the *mitzvah* (good deed) of marriage is one of the earliest in the Bible, it is obviously of great importance. Likewise, marriage is called a covenant (Hebrew *brit*) between a man and a woman (cf. Malachi

2:14). Adultery is most certainly an attack on this holy covenant; therefore, Yeshua addresses this problem early in his teaching. Adultery is not merely an outward action of immorality but has its beginning in the inward part of a person. The rabbis understood this concept, as they pointed out that the Hebrew verb for "to commit adultery" consists of four letters. These letters are to remind us that this sin may be committed with the hand, or with the foot, or with the eye, or with the heart (Midrash Hagadol Ex. 20:14).

In classic fashion, the Messiah brings out the deep, inward intention of the *Torah* when he says that even the one who lusts *has already committed adultery with her in his heart*. The solution seems extreme: If your eye causes you to sin, you are told to *gouge it out*. Similarly, if *your right hand makes you sin*, you are told to cut it off. Better to lose a body part than to *have your whole body cast into Gei-Hinnom*. This must be seen as classic hyperbole, often used in rabbinic teaching. Cutting off one's hand or plucking out one's eye will not guarantee the removal of this terrible sin since it is ultimately a matter of the heart. However, by these strong statements Yeshua clearly emphasizes the seriousness of breaking the covenant and the vows that one has promised.

Since marriage has always been a cherished covenant in Judaism, the rabbis had much to say about maintaining a blessed relationship. God's perfect plan is for a man and woman to enjoy a fulfilling marriage until death separates them. Yet, because the marriage agreement is between two people who have fallen natures, marriage does not always work out so smoothly. For this reason, the *Torah* also made some provision for limited cases of divorce. It was possible and obligatory in such cases for the husband to give his wife a *get* (certificate of divorce).

So important was this document that an entire tractate of the *Talmud* deals with various interpretations and details of issuing a *get*. Among some of the particulars, the document must be written and signed before witnesses. Likewise, the *get* will be approved by the *Beit-Din* only after a delay of some time. This is due to the hope that there still may be some possibility of restoring the marriage (Tractate Gittin 9:3). In Deuteronomy 24:1, the document is called a *"sefer kritut"* (certificate of divorce), which literally means a "scroll of cutting off." Divorce is likened to cutting off a limb. It is so tragic that it was stated that even the altar of the Temple sheds tears at the news of a divorce (Tractate Sanhedrin 22a).

The one exception in the *Torah* is expressed by the term *ervat devar* ("unclean thing" or "nakedness") found in Deuteronomy 24:1. The rabbis debate various meanings of this phrase. *Hillel* makes the statement that if a wife deliberately burns her husband's food, a *get* is permitted. *Akiva* said if a husband found someone better-looking, divorce was acceptable. *Shammai* took the position that the phrase was limited strictly to sexual immorality on the part of the wife. Yeshua affirms the position of Shammai that divorce is allowed under very narrow terms. He defines the Hebrew term *ervat devar* as adultery, the literal implication of the term. Yeshua affirms the tragedy of divorce, yet addresses some of the problematic situations. To cut off a marriage covenant *except on the ground of fornication* (Greek *pornea*) is to actually open the door to future adultery.

The summary of Messiah's interpretation concerning marriage is that it is a holy covenant, worthy of a lifelong commitment. The only biblical ground for divorce is that of adultery. In later New Covenant teaching, Rabbi Sha'ul would also add to this the case of desertion on the part of a non-believing spouse (I Cor. 7). This teaching has even greater relevance in our day of widespread divorce. For Messianic believers, divorce in response to anything short of biblical grounds is sin and can lead to future adultery in the event of an unbiblical remarriage. However, if a divorce is in response to one of these biblical grounds, there should not be a sense of false guilt, and biblical remarriage should even be allowed. Followers of Yeshua would do well to evaluate their own family situations in light of his teaching and with the guidance of mature spiritual leadership.

Precepts on Oaths 5:33-37

Again, Yeshua addresses a common theme in first-century Judaism. The use of one's word in vows and oaths was to be guarded carefully. Two tractates of the *Talmud* address the multitude of details and interpretations regarding oaths (cf. Tractates Shevuot and Nedarim). It is some of these rabbinic interpretations that Yeshua is addressing when he says, *"you have heard that our fathers were told."* Most interpreters would be satisfied with the outward fulfillment of any vow. However, Yeshua draws our attention to a more fundamental issue, which is the integrity of our promises at all times.

People may believe that their vow will carry more weight if they appeal to the authority of *heaven, the earth,* or even *by Yerushalayim... the city of the Great King.* The *Talmud* gives an example in which a vow is firmly upheld if it is made under the auspices of "Jerusalem, for Jerusalem, by Jerusalem...the Temple, for the Temple, by the Temple" (Tractate Nedarim 1).

While the practice of making vows and taking oaths was accepted in first-century Judaism, this kind of extra reinforcement implies that our original word may not be good enough. Yeshua himself came under an oath (Matt. 26), as did Sha'ul with the nazarite vow (Acts 21). But Messiah is clarifying that there should be no need for such reinforcements of our word when spoken with integrity. An extra oath cannot *make a single hair white or black.* Let our word stand on its own merit without the undergirding of an extra vow.

Precepts on Revenge 5:38-42

You have heard various interpretations of the precept of vengeance. It is true that the *Torah* teaches *"Eye for eye and tooth for tooth"* (Exodus 21:24). At first glance, many people think this precept is incredibly harsh by modern standards. Yet, in the ancient world, *"ayin tachat ayin"* (Hebrew) would have been extremely merciful. Pagan peoples of antiquity, and even many today, believe that vengeance is the appropriate response to some forms of injustice. In some cultures, if a man steals from you, you may cut off his hand. Judaism and the Bible speak of giving just compensation without excessive revenge. In fact, it limits retribution. So in that sense, if a man loses an eye, let him be repaid with appropriate "eye compensation."

As we analyze the details of this commandment, it becomes apparent that it is problematic to try to achieve an equal compensation in the literal sense. The *Talmud* debates some of these challenges by noting the differences between two people and even their two eyes. A common interpretation, therefore, was that monetary compensation was a universal solution. "Eye for eye—that means a payment of money. The *Torah* declares, 'You shall have one manner of law (Lev. 24:22)—that means, a law which shall be the same for all of you'" (Tractate Bava Kama 83b). Through his teaching, Yeshua affirms the *Torah*'s emphasis on withholding personal revenge.

Some may have misunderstood Yeshua's teaching about letting an aggressor *hit you on the left cheek too*. This is not intended to turn his disciples into doormats for mistreatment by the bullies of the world. Even when we may be wronged, the way of Messiah means we do not necessarily have to demand personal revenge. Yet it would be sinful if we let some gross injustice go unchallenged. As the *Torah* says, "Do not stand by the blood of your neighbor" (cf. Lev. 19:16). Yeshua himself did not always turn the other cheek. As the High Priest questioned him, he questioned some of the injustice that was taking place (Yochanan 18:23).

God's character demands righteousness and justice; however, too often people push for their own personal rights at the expense of what is best overall. A good question would be, "Is this important enough to oppose, or would it be even more redemptive to not press for my rights?" Similarly, if someone sues for *your shirt*, you are called to let him have *your coat as well*. The coat would be the outer garment adorned with the fringes as dictated by the *Torah* (cf. Num. 15:37). Since this outer garment was also an important means of protection from the elements, it was important not to take it from a brother overnight (Deut. 24:13).

So this scenario was actually testing a person, as he was given an opportunity to prove love to his neighbor, as defined by this command. Even if a pagan Roman obliged you to *carry his pack for one mile* (as he could legally do under the Roman occupation), you could prove your relationship to God by carrying it for the extra mile. It is the heart of God for his people to be sharing and generous individuals.

Precepts on Love   5:43-48

In a final commentary on the common Oral Law of the day, Yeshua now focuses on the main point of all the *Torah*. *Love your neighbor* is clearly an important summary of all the Law, even if the Hebrew word *reah* was usually applied only to fellow Jews (Lev. 19:18). Yet some have debated to what degree that would apply and even if there is a time to *hate your enemy*. For Yeshua to emphasize the need to *love your enemy* was taking the *mitzvah* to another level. This would apply not only to Jews, but also to Gentiles and even those who hate you. Here we are reminded once again that these lofty teachings of Messiah are not meant to be accomplished by our own strength. Such love requires a new heart and spirit within us in order to let the love of God shine to others. The Sermon on the Mount is not meant to be an idealized goal, but it reminds us that we need the living power of Messiah within us to fulfill his *mitzvot*. To *pray for those who persecute* us will go a long way toward giving us a tender heart and new perspective on our enemies.

When it comes down to it, we are all equal before our Heavenly Father. We are not any better than anyone else, if it were not for the mercy of God. If we *love only those who love* us, how are we any different from the pagans? We have a higher calling in Yeshua. In fact, it is so high that it is ultimately beyond our ability. Messianic Judaism is not just a religious philosophy or a system of morals to try to follow. Ultimately, it is about allowing the living Messiah and his Holy Spirit to give us new life. We can never *be perfect* as our Heavenly Father is, but we can receive the gift of Yeshua, who makes us perfect as we stand before the Father. The more we study Yeshua's interpretation of the *Torah* in this sermon, the more we should realize our desperate need for God's help. Blessed be God who has provided the way of redemption through his son, *Yeshua HaMashiach!*

The Practice of the Kingdom   6:1-7:12

Chapter 5 of Yeshua's great Sermon on the Mount dealt with the values and precepts of his kingdom. He now turns the attention of his disciples to more practical applications of these values. Although many of these topics were of vital importance in first-century Judaism, they continue to be important to the modern-day believer in Messiah.

Tzedakah   6:1-4

Since much of Yeshua's interpretation of the *Torah* deals with the need for righteousness, it is fitting that he now addresses specific acts of charity. The Hebrew concept of *tzedakah* carries with it a varied meaning—righteousness, charity, or alms for the needy. So important is the action of *tzedakah* that it is said, "alms obtain the world to come" (Tractate Rosh Hashanah 4.1). During the High Holy Days, Jews seek "*t'shuvah*/repentance, *t'fillah*/prayer and *tzedakah*/charity" to avert any judgment. *Tzedakah* has long been a central value within Judaism, with the rabbis often discussing options for fulfilling this *mitzvah. Rambam*/Maimonides (1200 AD) compiled a list of ten levels of *tzedakah,* ranging from helping one's own family to making an anonymous contribution to a community fund. Every Jew is to fulfill the *mitzvah* of *tzedakah,* with even the poor donating to a cause (Mishneh *Torah,* Gifts to the Poor).

Charity is obviously a positive act of expressing good to others, yet Messiah exhorts his listeners to also look deeply into their motive for giving. In fact, Yeshua assumes that his followers will live in this spirit as he says, *"When you do tzedakah. . . ."* The problem is not the lack of righteous actions but the attitude behind the actions. *To parade your acts in front of people in order to be seen* reveals a less than honorable motive.

Especially troubling to Messiah are those who, in a hypocritical fashion, seek to make a big public show of their deed *in the synagogues and on the streets.* They may even make use of *trumpets to win people's praise.* This could be an exaggerated statement about those who would sound the *shofar* to draw attention to themselves. It could, however, refer to the shape of the offering/*tzedakah* boxes placed in the Temple. The *Mishnah* describes these 13 boxes as narrow at the top and wide at the bottom, thus resembling a shofar ram's horn (Tractate Shekalim 6.1). In either case, Yeshua warns against making a big public display of our acts of *tzedakah.* If we are concerned merely about the reaction of people at that moment, then that is all the reward we will receive. Much better is the right heart attitude to perform your *tzedakah* in secret so that your *Father will reward you.*

T'fillah   6:5-15

In logical fashion, Yeshua now turns to the second pillar of this rabbinic triad, *t'fillah*/prayer. In Jewish tradition, one is obligated to pray three times daily—*shakharit*/morning, *minchah*/afternoon, and *ma'ariv*/evening. These specific times were based upon some of the statements of the *Torah* in which the patriarchs prayed at these times, as well as the illustration in the life of Daniel (Dan. 6:10). As a traditional Jew himself, Messiah assumes his disciples will follow the spiritual discipline of prayer. A beautiful definition of the attitude toward *t'fillah* is that it is a way of serving God. It is called "the service of the heart" (Tractate Taanit 2b). Yeshua's warning, however, is against those who would pray in a hypocritical fashion. There is nothing wrong with praying in the synagogue or even on the street (Yeshua himself did both), yet the reward is lost if this is done only so *that people can see them.*

Instead of making a public spectacle of one's prayers, it is much better to *go into your room, close the door and pray to your Father in secret.* Not only is the place for *t'fillah* discussed, but also the content of prayer. God's people are not to *babble on and on like the pagans.* Once again we must note that repetition, in itself, is not necessarily a problem. Many of the Psalms, which are the foundation of the Jewish prayer book, have repetitious themes. Yeshua himself prayed in the Garden three times that the cup of death be removed from him (Matt. 26:39-44). The problem is not repetitive prayers but meaningless babbling, thinking that the pagan mantra will elicit a response from God. There is no need for that kind of prayer, as *your Father knows what you need before you ask.*

What follows is the beautiful example of prayer known as "The Lord's Prayer," or, more accurately, "The Disciples' Prayer." That Yeshua is merely giving a model of prayer is clear from the statement *pray like this.* How ironic it is that some groups have used this model prayer in the very way that Yeshua warns against! It is not meant to be a magical mantra but, rather, a paradigm for how to pray effectively. Messiah's model prayer beautifully shows us the vital themes and principles desired for effective worship in the Messianic Kingdom. Yeshua starts with the commonly known address *Our Father in heaven.*

This is not some new concept, as Jews have always understood that God is comparable to a loving Father. Israel was called his son (cf. Ex. 4:22). In regard to the redemption from Egypt, Israel is reminded that it was our Heavenly Father who purchased us out of slavery (cf. Deut. 32:6). Isaiah proclaims to his generation, "You are our Father" (cf. Isa. 63:16). Of course, innumerable prayers in the *siddur*/prayer book also address God as *avinu*/our Father. The crowds would have related well to Yeshua's exhortation to pray directly to God the Father. Some might want to evaluate their own prayers in light of this. The New Covenant consistently, with rare exceptions, admonishes us to direct our prayers to the Father, through the work of the Son, by the power of the Holy Spirit (cf. Eph. 2:18). Our Father, the God of Israel, is still to be the focus of our prayers.

In typical Jewish fashion, Messiah adds the phrase *"may your Name be kept holy."* Names in the Bible are more than just identification tags. They reflect the character of a person. How much more with the Name of God. It is to be uniquely set apart as holy. Many traditional prayers rightly focus on the holiness of the Name of God. The well-known *Kaddish*, chanted several times in each synagogue service, starts with the Aramaic phrase *Yitgadal v'yitkadash shemey raba* (Magnified and sanctified be His Great Name). An entire tractate of the *Talmud* deals with the details of how to offer up proper prayer and blessings (cf. Tractate Berakhot). The common formula continues today: *"Barukh Atah Adonai"* (Blessed are You, Lord), reminding us of our holy responsibility to bless God before any other prayers are offered.

Moving to the area of petition, Yeshua now teaches his followers to focus on the coming Kingdom. By praying *May your Kingdom come,* they were reminded that prayer is not merely a list of personal requests. We are to be involved in helping to establish the Kingdom of Messiah *on Earth, as in heaven* through our prayers and our tangible work. As mentioned earlier, this reality of the Kingdom of God (Hebrew *malchut hashamayim*) could be said to be the main theme of the entire Scripture. Whatever else is happening in our personal life and world events should align with the coming kingdom of *Mashiach*. It is significant to note that this kingdom is already established in the heavens. Consequently, our prayers are to be for that same kingdom to be established on Earth in our days. Yeshua's model prayer once again would sound familiar to those aware of the synagogue liturgy. The *Kaddish* elaborates on this vital theme (*May his Kingdom come*), as does the liturgy of the *Torah* service, which quotes I Chronicles 29:11-12 (*The Kingdom is Yours, ADONAI*). Believers in Yeshua today should be reminded that their prayers are to be centered around God's will and Kingdom, rather than just around their personal desires and own kingdom.

While it is essential to focus our prayers on the bigger picture of God and his Kingdom, Messiah does remind us that the Father is also concerned about our personal needs. Such basic essentials as *the food we need daily* are appropriate prayer requests to bring to God. The language here is reminiscent of the experience of our people in the wilderness. For forty years, the Father took care of the practical needs of his children down to the very provisions of water, shade, and manna. The latter is an especially graphic reminder for us, as it was edible only on the very day it was given. The people in the wilderness learned to thank God for their daily bread without worrying much about the future. In Jewish tradition to this day, we give thanks to the Father for providing our food with blessings before and after meals. Some people have the erroneous belief that we are "blessing the food." But the blessings remind us that we are not blessing food, but blessing God for providing our food. The distinction is important.

The next phrase deals with a vital element of human relationships— forgiveness. In the state of our humanity, we are sure to sin and offend others. Our first thought should be to ask others to *forgive us*. No excuses or justifications will do. We simply need to own up to the fact that we have wronged others. When we admit our sin and seek the forgiveness of others (including from God himself), we open up a positive door for sincere relationships. Messiah's prayer gives us a logical yet powerful motivation to seek such forgiveness. Since *we too have forgiven those who have wronged us,* we can ask for the same kind of forgiveness. The themes of granting and receiving forgiveness are common in Judaism. The sixth blessing of the *Amidah* prayer beseeches us to deal kindly in forgiveness.

The High Holy Days of Rosh Hashanah and Yom Kippur are filled with this as a central theme. The *Avinu Malkeynu* prayer calls on us to both forgive others and to receive forgiveness for our many sins. Forgiveness, it should be noted, is not necessarily forgetting the past sins and trespasses. The perfect model is God's actions toward us. He does not forget our sins, but chooses not to make them an issue once we are in Yeshua. Likewise, as God's children, our forgiveness of others cannot be conditional. This is illustrated in a special ceremony that takes place on the first day of the Jewish New Year (Rosh Hashanah). Traditional Jews go down to a body of water and cast breadcrumbs or stones into the lake or ocean. This ceremony is called *Tashlikh* (You will send/throw), based on the verse in Micah the Prophet that says, "You will throw all their sins into the depths of the sea" (cf. Micah 7:19). If God has buried our sins in the sea, we would do well to let them stay there and not go fishing! Messiah's teaching on forgiveness certainly underscores this important dynamic.

The next part of Yeshua's prayer is a reminder that we need God's help for our spiritual walk. Life is difficult, with many strange twists and turns. We will all be tested, yet it is appropriate for us to pray that the Father will *not lead us into hard testing.* According to James 1:13, God is not the one who tempts anyone to do evil. That is entirely contrary to the nature of God and his hopes for his people. Sin is more often our surrender to the evil inclination within us. Yet we are told to pray that we might endure hard testing, no matter the source. Yeshua mentions the other source of temptation, besides our own flesh, which is *the Evil One*. Satan (Hebrew for "Adversary") is alive and well and seeking to devour any unsuspecting soul (cf. Job 1:6-7; Zech. 3:1; I Peter 5:8). Although there is a great spiritual battle for our souls, this part of the prayer reminds us to call out to God to *keep us safe*. The Father has not left us to fend for ourselves, but has provided powerful spiritual armor for our deliverance. As we walk through this life, the battle rages around us. We must keep on the helmet of salvation, wear the breastplate of righteousness, and use the sword of the Spirit, which is the Word of God (cf. Eph. 6:10-18). Assuredly, the battle will be intense many times, yet we are promised victory as we abide in Messiah (cf. I John 4:4).

Yeshua's teaching on prayer culminates with a reminder of the sovereignty of God. Despite the difficulties, sins, and blindness of this present time, the Father is in control of all. The liturgy is replete with this theme of God's kingdom. The second line of the most central prayer, called the *Sh'ma*, is actually an affirmation of this truth. *Barukh shem kevod malchuto le'olam vaed!* "Blessed be his Name, whose glorious Kingdom is forever and ever!" Whatever we do and say as followers of Yeshua, it should in some way assist in building the wonderful Kingdom of HaShem. Our prayer life should focus on the Kingdom, and our very actions must be for the *glory* of God. This would seem to be the ultimate test of a true, spiritual prayer. It is not about our needs or our desires, but seeks God's will on the matter. When we can submit to this truth, our own prayers will be in line with the heart of our loving Heavenly Father.

A fitting close is captured in the word *Amen*. This Hebrew word is not just a tag on the end of a prayer, but means "So be it" or "He is faithful." It is a great way to end any prayer by affirming that the answer is not found with our limited power, but that our trust is in the omnipotent One of the Universe. The last phrase, though not part of the actual prayer, is connected thematically. The prayer for forgiveness is given additional emphasis in that it is directly related to our relationship with our Heavenly Father. As we have experienced the forgiveness available through Messiah, we are to *forgive others their offenses*. If we refuse and hold grudges, our *heavenly Father will not forgive us*. That truth should give us all pause to think about our attitudes toward those around us.

Fasting   6:16-18

Another important practice in Judaism is fasting. There are fasts observed throughout the spiritual year as a means of remembrance, sacrifice, and focus. The prophet Zechariah mentions four such fasts that were observed in his generation and that continue to this day in the traditional community. The fast of the fourth month (9th of *Tammuz*/July) marks the breach of the walls of Jerusalem in 586 BCE. The fifth month's fast (9th of *Av*/August) recalls the many tragedies that have befallen Israel, especially the destruction of both the first and second Temples on this very day. The fast of the seventh month (Fast of *Gedaliah*/September) marks the assassination of the last king of the first Temple period. The tenth month (10th of *Tevet*/January) commemorates the tragic time when the Babylonians set the siege against Jerusalem.

While there is no biblical command to observe these fasts, many Messianic believers find that they keep connected to our people and history by observing them. Zechariah beautifully notes that these fast days will someday be turned to *joyful and glad occasions* in the Messianic Age (cf. Zech. 8:19). In addition to these traditional fasts in Judaism, there is the one supreme fast on *Yom Kippur*/ Day of Atonement. Some may argue that even this is not a directly commanded fast, yet the similarity of language in Leviticus and Isaiah leads to this natural connection. The same word, *oni* ("humble your soul" in Lev. 23:27) is used specifically of fasting in Isaiah 58:5, making Yom Kippur the preeminent fast of the spiritual year.

It should be noted that Yeshua does not denounce the act of fasting itself. In fact, he assumes his disciples will continue in this spiritual discipline, as he says, *"When you fast...."* Yet again, he challenges his hearers to check their motives during their religious duties. We are not to *go around looking miserable, like the hypocrites* because that would make it more of an outward show. The purpose of fasting is to simplify our physical life so that we may focus more clearly on our spiritual walk. It is self-contradictory to allow such an outward distraction during a fast. In fact, it is best *to wash your face and groom yourself so that no one will know you are fasting.* On Yom Kippur, one is allowed such minimum washing as well, yet it may be tempting for some to maximize their outward religious appearance. In the *Talmud*, it is noted that some zealous worshippers even put ashes on their faces to illustrate their spiritual poverty on this holy day (Tractate Yoma 8). If fasting is to be a true spiritual discipline, we must remember that the focus is seeking our Heavenly Father. It is he who *sees what is done in secret* and will reward accordingly.

Material Wealth   6:19-34

Yeshua now turns his attention to an important part of the human existence—attitudes toward material possessions. He again issues a challenge to evaluate our inner priorities and values in light of the world around us. There is nothing inherently wrong with wealth and property. The Bible is filled with the stories of godly men and women who were people of great means (Abraham, Solomon, etc.). Yet, assuredly, there is danger in having skewed and worldly attitudes toward our wealth. It is good to have a financial plan, but Messiah reminds us not to put our entire faith in the material world. It is too susceptible to problems like *moths, rust and burglars.* It is much better to store our treasures and *wealth in heaven* where they will reap eternal dividends. It is often said that you can't take your wealth with you to the next life. This is graphically illustrated in the traditional burial clothes, which purposely have no pockets! The reality is that our checkbook actually reflects our priorities. We will invest our money according to the values of our heart.

At first glance, the next phrase may seem out of context. What does a *good eye* have to do with wealth? Here is a classic case in which a Hebrew idiom has often been mistranslated and, consequently, misunderstood. It has nothing to do with sight but relates to one's attitudes toward material wealth. A good eye (*tov ayin* or *ayin tovah*) is descriptive in the Scriptures of a person who is generous, whereas an *evil eye* (*ra ayin* or *ayin raah*) refers to someone who is stingy (cf. Proverbs 22:9; 23:6). Consequently, it is the one with a good eye who gives a generous sacrifice according to the rabbinic literature (Tractate Trumot IV. 3).

Perhaps there is a parallel between the physical and spiritual in this idea, after all. As the eye brings physical light into the body, so does a generous spirit make a person *full of light*. When it comes to our attitudes toward our material possessions, we must be very careful. You cannot have two owners or *two masters*. Multiple loyalties will naturally be divided. You cannot serve wholeheartedly both *God and money* or, as the Aramaic term implies, *mammon*/material things.

A *midrash* of Rabbi Shimeon illustrates this in a creative manner. He notes that the word "*va-yitzer*/and He created" in Genesis 2:7 is spelled in an unusual way—with a double Hebrew letter *yod*. The rabbi applied this phrase to the fact that we serve two masters— the evil and good inclinations known in Hebrew as the *yetzer ha-ra* and *yetzer ha-tov* (Tractate Berachot 61a). Yeshua speaks in similar fashion as he applies the dual choice between material things and our relationship with God. The discipleship of Messiah is a call to make him both savior and Lord of all that we are, including our material possessions. Wealth is not inherently evil. On the contrary, it can be an essential part of accomplishing God's will on the material earth. It is simply an issue of loyalties. This is one reason why the biblical principle of tithing is quite healthy for the soul of the believer. Every time we give financially to the work of our local congregation, we not only help to further the kingdom of Yeshua on Earth, but are also reminded that we are merely stewards of what God has given us. Our Messiah taught many lessons on the importance of financial faithfulness. We would do well in our day to be generous with all that God has blessed us to have through his riches.

Yeshua continues this train of thought as he expands the principle from wealth to worry. We may give and sacrifice for the Kingdom of God, but it is never a lost investment. We are told *not to worry about what we will eat or drink or about the body.* The original present tense is better translated as "stop being anxious." Life is much more than our daily material needs. We can learn a good lesson from even the birds of the Galilee (the place of this *Torah* teaching), who don't seem to worry much about such things, yet the *heavenly Father feeds them.* Surely mankind is *worth more than they,* as the Genesis account of Creation testifies. Our worry cannot add a single hour to our life. Even the *wild irises* (*shoshanim*) of the Galil can teach us deep lessons of faith. They don't work or spin thread, yet even King Solomon was not *clothed as beautifully* as one of them. If God takes such good care of his wild creation, how *much more* will he take special care of his spiritual children?

The language at this point is especially relevant to the crowd, as Yeshua uses a rabbinic principle of interpretation first elaborated in seven principles by Rabbi Hillel (10 CE/AD). Because these principles were used in the days of Yeshua, it is relevant to understand his words. Here, Yeshua uses one of the Middot principles to challenge the faith of his hearers: If God provides for his natural creation, how much more can we be assured that he will provide for those who call him their Heavenly Father?

The culmination of this part of the sermon comes with a strong exhortation to trust our caring Father. Stop being anxious about what we will eat, drink, or wear. It is *the pagans* of the world who put such great emphasis on these things. Israel is not to be like the Nations. Certainly, believers in Yeshua, both Jews and non-Jews, in this present age have a different calling and perspective than those who have no heavenly Father.

Our calling is a rather simple, yet profound, one. As we *seek first his Kingdom and his righteousness*, all our material needs will be provided. It doesn't even pay to *worry about tomorrow*. Today will bring us *enough tsuris*/troubles about which to worry. Being a follower of Yeshua may not be easy, but he promises the presence of the Father along the journey. We could always find something to worry about, but with Messiah in control of our life, why expend the energy?

Rendering Judgment   7:1-6

Perhaps no other verse in the Sermon on the Mount has been so misapplied as this opening verse of Chapter 7. Yeshua has previously taught his disciples about the vital importance of forgiveness in Chapter 6. Now we come to the flip side of that teaching with his call to withhold certain kinds of judgments. That the Messiah is not forbidding any kind of judgment is clear from other passages. We are to discern and judge between right and wrong or light and darkness. Even in this particular passage, we are exhorted to make a certain judgment when we are called to *remove the splinter from your brother's eye*. However, this passage deals with the human propensity to render unfair judgment upon others. The present, imperfect tense of the verb suggests that this is a continual habit or attitude of judging others. The first-century Rabbi Hillel noted that we should not judge a man until we have been in his situation.

We are forbidden to judge in this manner for several logical reasons. We may have impure motives or an imbalanced understanding of what's fair. We often are too hasty in our conclusions, not to mention

THE PROGRAM OF KING MESSIAH / 73

that we may not have adequate knowledge of a given situation. Of course, it is assumed that only God can be the ultimate judge of a person's eternal destiny. The plain truth is that we too often make terrible judges in our own fallen condition. Yeshua has a simple way of helping his *talmidim* resist this ungodly behavior. He reminds them that they will be judged by *the way you judge others.*

We should proceed carefully before attempting to remove *the splinter in* our *brother's eye* when we have *a log in our own eye.* It is interesting to note that both the splinter and the log consist of the same material. How true it is that many times we are quick to pick on our brother's fault when the same kind of sin actually exists in our own lives. In a rather humorous hyperbole, Yeshua says that the other person often has only a splinter whereas we ourselves have a roofing beam, as the original language implies. It is indeed hypocritical to be so focused on the faults of others when we have plenty to judge in our own lives. We are, however, to exercise discernment in our walk with Messiah. If we are not to *give dogs what is holy,* then the implication is that we should, in fact, judge between the holy and profane.

In another strikingly humorous statement, Yeshua notes that we are not to throw our *pearls to the pigs.* The vision of this unkosher animal sporting a valuable necklace would surely stir up some laughs in that crowd (cf. Prov. 11:22). However, in the spiritual realm, the metaphor becomes quite serious. The same pigs will not only trample the jewelry under their *feet* but will also *then turn and attack you.* The lesson is clear. Those who have no discernment about the distinction between the holy and the profane will have no appreciation for the spiritual riches of Yeshua. In fact, some will become downright antagonistic! If a person is so turned off by the treasures of the New Covenant, then it is better not to confront them further. There are many people even in our day who are seeking and hungry for what Yeshua offers. Our time is better spent with those who want to dialogue in a respectful manner.

Finding God's Will   7:7-14

Having addressed some earlier questions concerning prayer, Messiah now highlights some important principles on seeking the plan of God. The language here reminds us that prayer is also a key element in finding the will of God. *Keep asking, keep seeking, keep knocking* all are in the present tense to emphasize the need for persistent effort. Answered prayer does not often come easily or quickly. More often, it is the result of a longer process of seeking the Father. This is probably why prayer is one of the most difficult disciplines of the messianic life. It takes diligent work over the long haul. However, as believers continue in these efforts, the answers will be provided and doors *will be opened.* The Father promises to answer our prayers, but his answer may not be what we had hoped for. The answer is sometimes "yes," other times "no," and even sometimes "wait." But be assured, the answer will come in God's perfect time.

For those who may doubt Yeshua's promise here, he gives a short parable to affirm this truth. A son who *asks for a loaf of bread* will not be given *a stone,* will he? Similarly, if the son *asks for a fish,* he will not be given *a snake.* A fish is a legitimate kosher meal, whereas a snake (or possibly an eel from the Sea of Galilee) is obviously not. If an earthly father would faithfully answer his son with such good things, *how much more will your Father in heaven* do the same. Again Yeshua uses the rabbinic *"kal v'chomer"* argument to reinforce his teaching (see comment on Matt. 6:30). Most certainly, the heavenly Father will provide for his spiritual children.

What follows next, in essence, can be considered one of the summary statements of the entire Sermon on the Mount. In a famous Talmudic story, Rabbi Hillel was one day asked by a non-Jew to summarize all of the *Torah* while standing on one foot. He obviously wanted the quick answer! Hillel is said to have answered, "What is hateful to you, do not do to your neighbor. This is the whole *Torah*" (Tractate Sanhedrin 31a). What Hillel describes in a negative fashion, Yeshua frames in a positive manner when he says, *"always treat others as you would like them to treat you."* This, in essence, summarizes the principle of *Torah*: "You shall love your neighbor as yourself," which Yeshua elsewhere identifies as the second greatest commandment (cf. Mark 12:28-31). The technique of giving a general summary of a teaching closely parallels what the rabbis call a *klal*/general principle. Indeed, all 613 *mitzvot*/commandments can be summarized by the principle of love. For Messianic Jews and all followers of Yeshua, this is our simple but vital priority.

Finally, the Messiah gives us a dramatic picture of attaining God's will. It will never be easy, as portrayed by *the narrow gate.* The term *bava* is a common rabbinic designation for gate and is used of legal contracts and laws (Tractate Bava Metzia). In Yeshua's kingdom, the gate to life is not easy, but narrow. But the way of the world is the wide *gate that leads to destruction.* Consequently, there are many people on the broad road yet *only a few* on the more difficult path of *Mashiach.* Truth is never dictated by a majority vote or popular opinion. Yet, the more difficult path of Messiah *leads to life*, both now and in the world to come. These are encouraging words to those who have chosen to stand with Yeshua in this current generation.

The Wise Disciple   7:15-29

Yeshua now turns his attention to the finer points of his discipleship. It is an incredibly high standard to which we should aspire. It is so high, in fact, that the sermon should ultimately convince all people of their need for Messiah's help. With all of the challenges before a follower of Yeshua, what is it that we are to keep in the forefront of our vision? With all of the blessings brought to us by our faith, we must also be on guard for potential dangers. *False prophets* unfortunately have always harassed our people, Israel. Where the truth of God has been revealed, the enemies of that truth will certainly try to stir up confusion or deception. So cunning are some of these false teachers that they even wear *sheep's clothing* to try to disguise the fact that they are actually ravenous *wolves*. With such outward trickery, how can one truly discern between the true sheep and the false? When all is said and done, the most accurate indicator of spiritual reality is *their fruit*. Any farmer in the Galilee can tell you *that every healthy tree produces good fruit*.

The most telling indicators of one's spiritual condition are the actions that come forth from the heart. We should be able to discern between the good and bad teachers by checking the corresponding fruit in their lives. Is there peace, love, and joy? Or is there negativity, oppression, and spiritual death? We should be easily able to *recognize them by their fruit*.

Messiah also has a strong warning for such teachers who would try to mislead his sheep. *Any tree that does not produce good fruit is cut down and thrown in the fire*. In graphic terms, Yeshua alludes to the judgment that awaits those who produce such bad fruit. The fire certainly would remind the crowd of the common belief in the afterlife and the place of judgment known as *Gei-Hinnom*. Whereas this passage specifically warns false teachers, the concept also applies throughout the Bible to those who bear unacceptable fruit in their spiritual lives. It is always timely to ask ourselves, "What kind of fruit am I bearing today in my own life?"

Spiritual deception is not only about false outward appearances, but it also has much to do with false words. Anyone can say *Lord, Lord* with his or her mouth. Not everyone who professes the Lord will enter the *Kingdom of Heaven,* according to Yeshua. What is the accurate measurement in this case? It is only those *who do what my Father in heaven wants* who will pass the test of authenticity. Some people who profess that they have eternal life may not, in fact, possess it at all. The ultimate test of Yeshua's discipleship is whether we are doing the will of the Father. Many say they are children of God. Are they obeying the Father? They may even argue that they did many fantastic works in the name of Yeshua. It is an impressive list indeed that includes expelling demons and performing *many miracles*. Yet the response of Messiah is that he never knew them and that these *workers of lawlessness* should be cast away.

This verse, while troubling to many people, actually provides hope and light to those seeking the truth of God. So many terrible, lawless deeds have been done throughout history in the name of Jesus. Especially in regard to our people, there has been much injustice perpetrated in the form of crusades, inquisitions, and holocausts. It would shock some people to realize how often these things were carried out by nominal, outward followers of Yeshua. This passage provides us with some important insight into the reality of these things. Just because people say that they are believers does not make it so. According to Yeshua's own words, they must do the will of the Father to prove that they are for real. Messiah never taught people to murder or to persecute others. In fact, he taught his true followers just the opposite, as they are to exemplify love and peace. If people live in a manner that is contrary to such teaching, we can assume they are not true followers of the One who came from the Father or, at best, are not obeying the clear teachings of the Messiah.

The importance of applying the truth of Messiah is illustrated in the next passage. It is the disciple who not only *hears these words of mine* who finds life. It is the one who *acts on them* who finds the blessing. He will be *like a sensible man who built his house on bedrock*. Even though natural catastrophes came, the house didn't collapse because it was built on a solid foundation of obedience. In contrast to this is the person who *hears these words of mine and does not act on them*. He stupidly tried to build his spiritual *house on sand*, which caused the house to collapse under pressure. We should note here that both individuals have one thing in common: They heard the words of Yeshua. However, they have differing responses. The one who acts on these words finds that his house stands amidst the trouble of the world and the future judgment. The other who does not act will see his entire house fall in a horrendous disaster.

It is not enough to simply hear or understand the words of Messiah. They will benefit us today only if we too act and apply them to our own lives. Today, as in the first century, there are many who are in danger of this future judgment. They have heard Messiah's words. They may have them memorized. Maybe they even teach them. The simple yet profound question for us today is, "Are we acting on these words?" Our spiritual blessing, both now and for eternity, rests on the answer. Let us be wise people who hear and act upon these powerful words of our *Mashiach*!

The crowd was truly *amazed* at the end of Yeshua's *halakhic* teaching on the mountain. Much of this, undoubtedly, was because of the spiritual focus and content of the message. There were certainly some new truths and applications revealed by the Rabbi from Galilee. Yet, part of the crowd's amazement was in response to *the way he taught*. The common practice among the rabbis of the *mishnaic* period was to appeal to the authority of previous teachers. If one expected to present a weighty argument, he would need to support it with other authorities.

In the *Talmud*, the phrase *tannu rabbanan* (our rabbis taught) is often used in such cases. Frequently, there would be a direct reference to rabbinic scholars (e.g., "Rabbi Joshua said in the name of Rabbi Akiva"). Any rabbi worth his salt would have a significant number of sources behind his teaching in order to establish strong authority.

However, here the crowd is amazed despite the technique of Yeshua's teaching. In his entire sermon, he does not feel the need to quote one other rabbinic source. It was apparent that Yeshua did not need an extra authority, as he claimed to be the holy Messiah sent directly from the Father. Indeed, he could teach as one who had authority himself.

In this sense, Yeshua actually is fulfilling one of the anticipated ministries of the *Mashiach*:

> The Holy One, blessed be He, will sit and expound the new *Torah* which He will give through the Messiah. "New *Torah*" means the secrets and the mysteries of the *Torah* that have remained hidden until now. It does not refer to another *Torah*, heaven forbid, for surely the *Torah* which He gave us through Moses our Master, peace be upon him, is the eternal *Torah*; but the revelation of her hidden secrets is called "new *Torah*" (Midrash Talpiyot 58a).

What a fitting end to Yeshua's dynamic teaching! The Messiah has come to reveal the deep meaning of the *Torah*. May we be wise people who build on that rock even today!

Proofs of King Messiah   8:1-9:38

Matthew's chronology followed a logical order as he presented the evidence for the messiahship of Yeshua of Nazareth. The early chapters of his gospel deal with the preparations for the King, whereas the Sermon on the Mount reveals the precepts of Messiah. We now come to a section that is vitally important to the Jewish mind, i.e., proofs to substantiate the words of Yeshua. It is one thing to claim to be a messiah. It is quite another to offer tangible, physical evidence to validate those claims. This certainly would have been a central focus of the rabbinic leadership of the first century, as they were the ones called to discern truth from error. Many false messiahs had tried to capture Israel's attention over the years. The rabbis therefore developed certain criteria based on the Scriptures for how to recognize the true *Mashiach* when he appears. Matthew, as a traditional Jew, makes note of some of the actions of Yeshua and how they strongly support his claims of being the King of Israel.

Power Over Disease   8:1-17

During his descent *down the hill* after his Galilee sermon, Yeshua encounters *large crowds* that include some of the most needy individuals. The *man afflicted with tzara'at* certainly would stand out in the multitude. There is some debate as to the exact nature of this disease that is usually translated "leprosy." In our modern medical understanding, this term applies to Hansen's Disease. However, in ancient times the Hebrew term was used to designate a rather wide variety of ailments. Some of these were curable, and thus we find the *Torah* requirements for such a healing (cf. Lev. 13-14). There was a severe form that was incurable and thus rendered the person without any hope. As with our modern form of leprosy, there was not much to do medically except to quarantine the afflicted so as to spare the community both physical and spiritual defilement. Because of the unique challenges this disease presented, the classical rabbis had an understanding that such cases were beyond the normal prayers of the sages.

A by-product of this quarantine would be a certain amount of humiliation for being separated and thus feared by the community. Not only were lepers required to live in their own compounds, but they also had to warn others of their presence, even to the point of calling out "*tamey*/unclean" (cf. Lev. 13:45-46). This man must have been an extreme case, as Luke, a medical doctor, describes the disease as "completely covering" his body (cf. Lk. 5:12). As the disease would literally consume the flesh, this man must have been actually near death according to this description.

It is this desperate person who *kneeled down* in front of Yeshua in an act of complete humility as he sought help. Sometimes this is actually an act of worship, which would make sense if this man understood the divine nature of Messiah. Many times it is simply a gesture of respect and humility, fitting the context of this encounter. Similarly, the term *Sir* (Hebrew *adon/adonai*) also has a double meaning. It can be used in the simple manner of addressing someone, or it can ascribe sovereignty that belongs only to God himself.

The leper's petition is to the point—*you can make me clean.* Evidently, this man had heard some of the amazing words of this rabbi from Galilee. He expresses faith that just a touch from Yeshua could be the remedy for his illness. It is not insignificant that Yeshua *reached out his hand* and *touched* the leper. Of course, any healthy person or even a fellow rabbi would shrink back from being exposed to this dreaded disease and consequent defilement (cf. Lev. 5:3). No doubt this man had gone a long time without the touch of another person, yet it is Yeshua who literally reaches out to him. Not only is Messiah *willing* to make him clean, but he commands it to be so. Immediately, this extreme case of *tzara'at* is healed and cleansed.

It was important for the man not to broadcast his healing publicly without first fulfilling the requirements of *Torah*. In Leviticus 14, the community was given the prescribed details for the priests to confirm a healing of leprosy. Evidently, this was exceedingly rare even in the religious community of Israel. So rare was it, in fact, that it is easy to understand why many would view the healing of leprosy as a sign of the end days and the Messianic Age. An informative passage in the *Talmud* illustrates this:

> Rabbi Joshua ben Levi met Elijah [the prophet]...and asked him, "When will the Messiah come?" "Go and ask him for yourself," was his reply. "Where is he sitting?" "At the entrance." "And by what sign may I recognize him?" "He is sitting among the poor lepers: all of them untie their bandages all at once, and rebandage them together, whereas he unties and rebandages each separately, before treating the next...The rabbis said: His name is "the leper scholar," as it is written, Surely he hath borne our griefs, and carried our sorrows: yet we did esteem him a leper, smitten of God and afflicted (Tractate Sanhedrin 98a + b).

It is significant that the Talmudic rabbis attribute the classic chapter, Isaiah 53, to the person of *Mashiach*. Unfortunately, modern Judaism often interprets this passage differently from the earliest commentators, by applying it to the sufferings of Israel and not to a suffering Messiah. Nonetheless, the prevalent first-century view was that when the Messiah comes, he would have a healing ministry that would include some unique miracles. No wonder that this healing of a leper is the first testifying miracle in Matthew's record.

Yeshua directs the man to *let the cohen examine you* in order to be a testimony to them. This is consistent with the *Talmud* regarding the response to this dreaded disease. At the time of this event, there was a courtyard in the Temple called the Chamber of the Lepers, where those who had experienced a healing were to take a *mikveh*/immersion and allow the priests to verify their healing (Tractate Nega'im 14:8). The priests were the ones who had an especially vested interest in determining whether the true Messiah had appeared. They were the designated judges to determine whether a claim of messiahship was true or false. The healed leper would stir up an excited response, both among the priesthood and the common people, as they realized a messianic sign had been performed in their midst.

Yeshua continues on his itinerant ministry as he travels back to the town that served as his home base, K'far-Nachum. It is here that *a Roman army officer came up and pleaded for help*. As K'far-Nachum was a Jewish town under the occupation of the Romans, this situation offered the first opportunity for Yeshua to publicly minister to a non-Jew. There is a good possibility that the officer belonged to a special category of non-Jews known as the *Yirey HaShamayim*/ God Fearers. These were Gentiles who had a great respect for the faith of Israel and even attended the local synagogue. However, they stopped short of becoming full converts *(gerim)* who not only attended synagogue but also kept the required commandments for a convert, such as circumcision, immersion, and Temple sacrifice. Luke notes that this Roman military officer even loved the Jewish people to such an extent that he assisted in building the local synagogue in K'far-Nachum (cf. Luke 7:5). The man had a servant at home who was *suffering terribly* with some debilitating disease.

As Yeshua agrees to go to the home, the officer makes a rather astounding statement. He confesses that he is *unfit* to have the Messiah come to his home. Most observant Jews would have been repelled at the suggestion of socializing with a non-Jew. The religious barriers such as *kashrut* (kosher) and *Shabbat* would have kept traditional Jews at a distance from their Gentile neighbors. While there was no direct biblical prohibition keeping a Jew from entering the house of a non-Jew, it is understandable that most would refrain from such an action so as not to become ritually defiled (cf. Acts 10:28; Tractate Oholot 18:7). This Roman officer already understood such convictions and expected that Yeshua, a rabbi, would not come to his own home.

The record in Luke's Gospel account tells us that the man even recruited some of the Jewish elders to present this request to Yeshua, another indication of his understanding of these cultural issues (Luke 7:3). However, the man asks Yeshua to merely *give the command* and his servant can still be touched with the healing power of the God of Israel. The officer uses his own military structure to illustrate why Yeshua need not come to his home. Since he is *a man under authority* in the Roman army, he trusted that the spoken word of Messiah is all that is needed for the healing of his servant.

This is one of the few times in the New Covenant that Yeshua is said to be *amazed*. Not even among the crowds of Israelis had Yeshua seen an example of such strong faith. One would think that many in the covenant community of Israel would have a greater faith in the testimony of this Messiah. After all, it was to Israel that the covenants and promises were given, which were all to be realized in the Messianic Kingdom to come. Yeshua was amazed that a non-Jew, a Roman soldier from a pagan background, could exceed the faith of his own people, Israel. In fact, it is people with such faith as this non-Jew who will *feast in the kingdom of Heaven with Avraham, Yitz'chak and Ya'akov.* What a sad irony that *many of those born for the Kingdom will be thrown outside in the dark!* God is not a respecter of persons. Even those who have the promises and covenants (Israel) must have personal faith and trust in the God who gave those beautiful promises.

The Talmudic statement that "all Israel has a place in the world to come" (Tractate Sanhedrin 10.1) does not totally match up with the biblical revelation both in *Tanakh* and here in the New Covenant. For this reason, the *Mashiach* was to come to us, to provide physical blessing as well as spiritual connection to the Father. Because of the sincere faith of this Roman officer, it is not surprising that his servant *was healed at that very moment.* This man stands as a great example of a Gentile believer who has personal faith in the God of Israel and, consequently, a love for the people of Israel. We would do well to ask ourselves today if we have this kind of personal faith in Messiah. If you have been touched by the blessings of God through Israel, what are you doing to return the blessing to the Jewish people today?

After the encounter with the Roman God-fearer, Matthew now records an important episode with Peter's mother-in-law. The other gospel accounts note the event as occurring when the disciples were returning from the synagogue previously mentioned in K'far-Nachum. As they return home, they find that Shi'mon's *mother-in-law was sick in bed with a fever.*

Dr. Luke, in his characteristic fashion, notes with some medical detail that it was a "great fever" (Luke 4:38). It is not insignificant that the Rabbi from Galilee *touched her hand.* The teaching of the *Talmud* is that a man (and how much more a rabbi) should not make contact with a woman's hand, even when counting money from his hand to hers (Tractate Berachot 61a). After the instantaneous healing of the fever, the woman shows her appreciation by serving the band of disciples.

That same evening, *many people held in the power of demons were brought to him.* If the synagogue service was on *Shabbat*, this would be when such healings should not take place. Yet, as the promised Messiah, Yeshua once again substantiates his word by exerting his power over all forms of disease, even on the Sabbath. Matthew distinguishes between problems that had a spiritual source and those caused by natural illnesses. In either case, Yeshua *healed all who were ill.* These healings were for a particular purpose, as Matthew quotes from the prophet Isaiah: *He himself took our weaknesses and bore our diseases* (Isaiah 53:4). As mentioned above, this passage was applied in many rabbinic commentaries to the coming of *Mashiach* (cf. Sanhedrin 98a).

The Hebrew of Isaiah 53 (*choli*/disease) allows for both the physical and spiritual aspects of healing. No doubt, a most important work of Messiah would be to take our sins away as a guilt offering (Isaiah 53:11). It should be noted that physical healing is not necessarily guaranteed in the atonement of Messiah at this present time. There are too many examples of unrealized healings both in the Bible and in the modern-day lives of godly believers (cf. II Corinthians 12). There is some mystery why God does not always heal in every case, yet clearly he uses these cases many times to teach his children different lessons. Nonetheless, a day will come when the physical aspect of Yeshua's work will be fully realized by all who call on his name (Revelation 21:4).

Power Over Nature   8:18-27

After a time of ministering to the gathered crowd, Yeshua *gave orders to cross to the other side of the lake.* It is here that a rabbi approaches him with the zealous comment: *I will follow you wherever you go.* The fact that a fellow rabbi and *Torah* scholar would seek the mentoring of Yeshua shows the great respect he was receiving. However, even given such high regard, Yeshua was calling his followers to some costly sacrifices that many people were not prepared to make. By using the term "Son of Man," Yeshua was again alluding to his clear claim of being the promised Messiah of Israel. The Prophet Daniel used the term prophetically to describe the *Mashiach* coming from the clouds of heaven (Daniel 7:13-14). That this is a messianic title is confirmed by the Talmudic sages, who designated the Messiah with the secondary name *"Bar Nafel*/Son of the Falling One," based on this passage (Tractate Sanhedrin 96b).

Another potential disciple gave a different response. At first glance, it seems like he had a valid excuse to delay his discipleship. To first *go and bury* his father could have several meanings. First, it is possible that his father was not yet dead and that this man was offering an excuse because of family pressure. If so, this would clearly be an unacceptable response to the high calling of Yeshua's discipleship. First-century cultural practices also provide a possible second explanation—that the would-be disciple wanted to provide a proper burial for his father. But this cannot be the case.

Yeshua would never instruct someone to break a clear biblical command (cf. Matthew 5:17). Add to this the rabbinic exemptions when one is faced with a burial, such as the normal requirements of daily prayers, *Torah* study, and attendance at the Temple service (Tractate Berachot 3:1) However, it makes more sense that the burial custom of that day, not a biblical commandment, is at issue here. It is known that in the Second Temple period there were two burials for a traditional Jew. The first burial was immediately after death, at which time the body was properly prepared and then placed in a burial niche in a cave or tomb. The second burial would take place after the one-year mourning period, in which the bones of the deceased were then placed in a special burial box known as an ossuary.

This custom was followed only during the Second Temple period, which included the time of the New Testament. We still see an interesting parallel to this custom in modern Judaism in that the immediate family of a departed loved one is called to a period of mourning for one year. At the end of this time, the headstone of the grave is unveiled to symbolize the end of the mourning period. If this is the allusion, then this potential disciple was saying that he would wholeheartedly follow Yeshua only after the one-year period of mourning for his recently deceased father.

Since this custom is not a *Torah* requirement, he in essence would be placing his personal preference over his personal call to follow the Messiah immediately. This, too, is unacceptable to Yeshua, as he exhorts the dead to *bury their own dead.* Matthew does not tell us what the final decision was of these two individuals. Clearly, it cannot be a halfhearted commitment to become a follower of Yeshua even today, whether one is Jewish or non-Jewish. We should count the cost of discipleship before taking up the calling of *Mashiach.*

Finally boarding *the boat,* Yeshua and his small band of close disciples set out for the other side of the Kinneret/Sea of Galilee. An unforeseen storm rose up, surprising even the experienced fishermen who were on the boat. So strong was the squall that Matthew uses an unusual word normally associated with an earthquake (Greek *seismos,* also in Matthew 28:2) to describe it.

While *the waves were sweeping over* the small vessel, Yeshua is said to have been *sleeping* after his exhausting day. With a sense of urgency, the disciples *roused him* and cried out, "Sir! Help! We're about to die!" There is a sense of irony here if the title "Sir" is translated "Lord," which would indicate that the disciples understood the deity of the Messiah. Yet, their urgent cry reveals a lack of faith on some level. We cannot be too hard on these followers, however. At least they got in the boat with Yeshua and followed his calling, which is more than most people are willing to do. Nevertheless, it is a teachable moment for these growing disciples, as they are reprimanded for their *little trust* in this miracle-working Messiah. As *he rebuked the wind and the waves*, the sea became astonishingly silent. Even with the wind stopping immediately, such a large lake as the Kinneret would not become completely calm in an instant unless it was a miracle of God.

Although they had experienced the healing and teaching ministry of Yeshua, the disciples were shocked and wondered aloud, "What kind of man is this?" Of course the real answer is that this could not be the work of any mere man or even a gifted rabbi. Once again, Yeshua unveiled his eternal power to confirm he is the promised Messiah sent from the Father. The disciples, meanwhile, learned yet another important lesson. Their faith undoubtedly grew in new ways from having gone through a storm with Yeshua. The same holds true for Messianic believers today. The storms of life can be intense. But the question is not how bad the storms are, but, rather, do we have Yeshua in our boat? He is the one who calms the storms of those who cling to him by faith.

Power Over Spiritual Forces   8:28-34

After the calmed storm on the Kinneret, Yeshua and his disciples *arrived at the other side of the lake, in the Gadarenes' territory.* Presumably it was predominantly a non-Jewish area, as witnessed by the fact that the people raised pigs. It was here that Messiah was confronted by two men coming out of some of the *burial caves* in that vicinity. To add to the strange sight, the writer notes that they were *controlled by demons* and the men were therefore known for their violent behavior. In the larger context of Scripture, demons are part of the fallen angels who rebelled against God before the foundations of the world (cf. Isaiah 14; Ezekiel 28). The chief *cherub* became known as *Satan* and he, in turn, leads a multitude of lesser spirits known as demons.

While the reality and power of Satan are never doubted in Scripture, demonic activity seems to wax and wane at various times in biblical history. It should not be surprising that, with the earthly ministry of the Messiah, the manifestations of evil spiritual forces would intensify as Satan opposes all that God is trying to accomplish through Yeshua. What these two men screamed, under the influence of the demonic spirits, is quite informative.

First, they actually affirm the divine power of Yeshua as the *Son of God.* Second, they seem to plead for mercy because it is *before the appointed time.* It is known, evidently by the demons as well, that there is a coming day of judgment when Satan and all his accomplices will be cast into *Gei-Hinnom* (cf. Revelation 20:1-3). Since this Messiah has shown his power over evil, these demons seem to fear the possibility that the time had come. They themselves came up with an alternative solution as they noted *a large herd of pig*s feeding nearby. Yeshua allowed the demons to enter the swine, which in turn *rushed down the hillside into the lake and drowned.* Having witnessed such an amazing event, the herdsmen *went off to the town and told the whole story* to those who would listen. With such an astounding testimony, it is not surprising that the whole town went out to meet Yeshua.

Yet, not all the people responded positively to this act of spiritual power. In fact, many *begged him to leave their district.* This could be for several reasons. In a practical sense, a significant part of the wealth of the Gadarenes had been destroyed, which must have been very troubling. Also, it should be noted that Mark's and Luke's accounts of this event reveal that the people were unsettled as they witnessed the healing of the two men. So it is even today. To encounter the living *Mashiach* can be unsettling. Yet with any uneasiness that may come, there is healing and restoration in his Name. Some today still would rather ask Yeshua to leave their presence because they are not willing to let him deal with some problems in their midst.

Power to Pardon   9:1-17

Matthew now records further evidence of the messiahship of Yeshua. These situations occur in a very open and public setting so that no one can doubt Yeshua's messiahship. Having previously dealt with physical elements in Chapter 8, Matthew's account now shows some of the deeper, spiritual implications of Messiah's supernatural power.

A Paralyzed Man   9:1-8

After some of the dramatic signs of Chapter 8, Yeshua now crosses back over the Kinneret and comes to his own city. The context dictates that this is his new home base of K'far-Nachum, which is situated on the Kinneret. For the first time in Matthew's account, Yeshua will experience strong opposition to his actions and subsequent teachings from some of the leaders. As he is abiding in a local house, some people bring him a paralyzed man. Luke's account gives an important detail by noting that among the crowd were specifically Pharisees and *Torah*-teachers, some even from as far away as Jerusalem (cf. 5:17). Evidently they were there to examine this self-proclaimed Messiah and the reports of his miraculous works.

As previously noted, such rabbinic authorities would be especially interested in the rumors of such "messianic" miracles as the healing of the leper in the previous chapter. It must have been a full house. The other gospel writers note that there was not sufficient room to enter the house by the door. The afflicted man was therefore lowered to Yeshua through the roof, which could be easily opened by removing some tiles or other materials. Messiah saw their trust, although we have no record of the friends speaking a single word. Obviously, their actions spoke loudly of their faith. They believed this rabbi from their own town had the power to help their paralyzed friend.

It is here that Yeshua proclaims to the paralyzed man, "Courage, son! Your sins are forgiven." This, no doubt, would be a shocking statement in any Jewish crowd and especially to some of the rabbinic leaders who were present. They come to the quick conclusion that this so-called messiah is blaspheming. This is not an illogical response. Indeed, only God himself is able to forgive someone's sins and transgressions.

In the Talmudic literature, there is ample debate about the definition of blasphemy and its consequences. One opinion states that "the blasphemer is not culpable unless he pronounces the Name [of God] itself" (Tractate Sanhedrin 7:5). Of course, this was one of the most serious religious crimes for a Jew, enforceable by death through stoning. While it is unclear if Yeshua pronounced the Name of God in this situation, clearly the impression given was that he was acting with the authority that belongs only to God himself.

It is noteworthy that the leaders are quoted as calling Yeshua "this man," which is a reflection of the growing desire of some not to even pronounce the name of this controversial teacher. In another act of spiritual discernment, Yeshua challenges the evil thoughts of some of the leaders by posing a question to them: *Which is easier, to pronounce the forgiveness of sins or to raise a paralytic up to walk?* Words can come easy, but it is action that validates the words. To exhibit the power of healing over something as devastating as paralysis is, in fact, a much more potent proof.

It is with this in mind that Yeshua turns his attention back to the afflicted man and commands him to pick up his mattress and go home. He specifically proclaims that his intention is to prove *that the Son of Man has authority* for both the physical and spiritual aspects of his ministry. When the man rose *up and went home*, the crowd was *awestruck* (literally "filled with fear") by witnessing such a manifestation of God's power. They gave glory to God by making a *b'rakhah*, a blessing, to attribute praise to the source of all healing.

It is likely that some of the rabbinic witnesses returned to Jerusalem to report their disturbing findings to the proper authorities. Irrespective of how these things were interpreted, one thing was for sure: Yeshua had given a strong exhibition of word and power that could not be taken lightly. It was becoming increasingly clear that this was no ordinary rabbi in their midst.

A Publican   9:9-17

In a most intriguing account, we have here Matthew's own personal testimony of how he became a follower of Yeshua. As he was continuing his ministry throughout the Galil, Yeshua spotted a tax collector named *Mattityahu* collecting his fees. The name means "gift of God," which was ironic considering this particular individual. As a tax collector, Mattityahu would have been doubly despised by his own people. First, he was a collaborator with, and employee of, the occupying forces of Rome. If this wasn't bad enough, it was commonly known that such agents would make their living by overcharging and often extorting higher fees. Not exactly the "gift of God" that most first-century Jews would appreciate!

It was not uncommon for Jews to have two names, as is the practice today. Jews in the Diaspora have both a Hebrew name as well as a name common for the country in which they live. We know from the other gospel writers that this man's secondary name was "Levi." If this means that he was also from priestly descent, then the enigma of this person is even greater. Because of the problems associated with such "publicans," the rabbis issued a series of judgments against them, such as their disqualification as legal witnesses and even the unlikelihood of their real repentance (Tractate Sanhedrin 25b).

The abrupt change in Mattityahu indicates that he was not a stranger to Yeshua or his message. He had probably encountered this Messiah several times as he passed along the shores of the Kinneret. Upon hearing the call to "Follow me!" Mattityahu abandons his previous occupation and joins the other disciples. As a sign of heartfelt appreciation for his new calling, a meal is provided at a house (probably Mattityahu's) where there are all sorts of controversial guests. The Pharisees were appalled at the sight of many other tax collectors and sinners dining in the presence of the Galilean rabbi. From their perspective, such apostate Jews were not only beyond personal fellowship, but this kind of crowd would certainly render any observant Jew ritually unclean.

By its very name (*P'rushim*/Separate ones), the Pharisaic sect of Judaism denoted that its members would keep far from anyone considered wicked. The *Talmud* states it this way: "If tax collectors entered a house, all within it become unclean. People may not be believed if they say, 'We entered but we touched nothing'" (Tractate Toharot 7:6). Yet, Yeshua breaks down some commonly accepted norms once again, as he not only goes to such a meeting but also shares intimate fellowship with the crowd by partaking in a meal! From Messiah's perspective, these are the very ones who need his help.

Although such actions may have raised some objections from the traditional community, Yeshua reminds all those present that this principle of acceptance is an important value of the Prophets of old: "I want compassion rather than animal sacrifice" (Hosea 6:6). This summary statement clearly conveys one of the primary purposes of Messiah's mission to Israel—not to call the righteous, but the sinners. Of course, the irony of this statement is that all people, including those who considered themselves *frum* (*Torah* observant), were in need of the righteousness that only the *Mashiach* could provide. The need of all people, Jews or non-Jews, religious or pagan, for this unique work of Yeshua continues. Though this idea may sound strange in today's postmodern, relativistic world, it should not deter us from acting on the urgency to share the Good News of Yeshua with all those around us. Apparently this is one reason why Mattityahu sponsored this celebration dinner in the first place.

An opportunity to elaborate on these points presented itself as some of Yochanan's *talmidim* (John the Immerser's disciples) came to Yeshua with some questions. Why, they wondered, do the Pharisees fast often, while Yeshua's followers don't fast at all? The informative response comes using the description of a Jewish wedding. Clearly, the guests do not mourn while the bridegroom is still with them. Yet, if the bridegroom is taken away, that is a time when fasting is appropriate. These statements correlate with the first-century wedding ceremony (see comments on Matthew 1:18ff). In this passage, Yeshua focuses on one of the finer details that illustrates an important spiritual lesson from the wedding ceremony. It is true that at any good Jewish wedding there is tremendous joy and feasting. Yet, a detail of the wedding day is that it is considered a *mitzvah* (good deed) for the bride and groom to fast on the day of their wedding, before the ceremony. This is a special act of preparation as they focus on the holy occasion and seek God, even as Jews do during the fast of Yom Kippur.

It is this that Yeshua alludes to when he notes that his disciples need not currently fast because the groom is in their midst. Yet the time will come when the separated bride and groom will fast to prepare for the final stage of their wedding ceremony. How informative this is in regard to our present status! We Messianic Jews and Gentile believers are engaged to our groom Yeshua. But we are currently in the state of separation as we prepare for the final stage of our spiritual wedding at his Second Coming, when he will share the second cup with us. Therefore, fasting is appropriate at this time, but the day will soon come when the feast will begin. Are you keeping your wedding garments ready? May that day come soon!

The next illustration also holds some deep truth. No one patches an old coat with a new piece of cloth. This is an allusion to the outer garment worn by the average Jew of that day. It was vital for protection from the elements, which is why it is forbidden in the *Torah* to confiscate an outer garment overnight (cf. Exodus 22:26-27). Moreover, this garment would also be adorned with fringes (*tzitziot*), as mandated in Numbers 15:37-39, in order for Israel to remember the calling to the *Torah*. Orthodox and other Jews continue to observe this command by wearing a garment called a *tallit katan* (small prayer shawl) to display the fringes. Most Jewish men (and some women in contemporary branches of Judaism) wear a modern tallit today in synagogue or at other religious occasions to fulfill this commandment. It is this important garment that Yeshua uses as an illustration. If a worn tallit is patched with new material, it will surely tear. It is not a proper fit and can even be damaging to the original purpose of the garment.

The next word-picture also illuminates a similar truth. People do not put new wine in old wineskins, as the newer skin will expand and burst. New wine that is still fermenting, if it is to be properly stored, requires freshly prepared wineskins. If not, then the fermentation process will expand the skins to the point of destruction.

The point of these last two illustrations has been greatly debated. Many Christian expositors will try to make the point that Yeshua is proposing a whole new religion which cannot be contained in the existing forms of Judaism or even the Old Testament. This cannot be the case in light of Yeshua's own words about the consistency between his teachings and the older covenants (cf. Matthew 5:17). Yet, in the context of his disputes with some of the Pharisees, it seems more logical that Yeshua's references to old wine and old garments are an allusion to the *Mishnah* and certain rabbinic interpretations of the *Torah*.

True to his mission, Yeshua is not calling Israel to abandon the previous covenants nor their biblical foundations. Instead, these verses are a challenge to Israel, and specifically the rabbis, to return to a more correct view of *Torah* and the Prophets without getting sidetracked by some of the traditions of men. I should say that most Jewish tradition is based upon the Scriptures, but this fact is easily forgotten.

For those of us within modern Messianic Judaism, it is important to note that we appreciate and express our faith in Yeshua, often through the cultural expression of our Jewish heritage. We follow the model of the earliest followers of Yeshua, who walked according to the *Torah* and traditions of Judaism, the cultural expression of their faith (cf. Acts 21:20). It is also clear from the New Testament that the early Jewish believers (and the Gentiles as well) followed much of the rabbinic Jewish tradition.

One example of this is the fact that the third cup of the Passover *seder* meal is used by Yeshua to illustrate his redemptive work. This cup is not mentioned in the *Torah* details pertaining to Passover, but is actually a rabbinic idea added during Talmudic times. It would be surprising for some to realize that not only are the Jewish believers exhorted to remember the lessons of this cup (cf. Matthew 26:26-29), but the non-Jewish believers of Corinth are also (cf. I Corinthians 11:23-26).

So, according to Yeshua's own words and the example of his first followers, we find a balance between the Bible and some extra-biblical cultural practices. With a proper biblical balance, many Messianic Jews would affirm the great blessing it is to don a *tallit* in prayer with the knowledge of Messiah's work for us! Similarly, what a joy it is to celebrate the feast days and many of the customs with the full picture of Messiah in view!

Yeshua's warning in this current passage must therefore be balanced with the other passages that speak to this issue. Certainly, care must be taken not to simply look at Yeshua's teaching as just another "addition" to the rabbinic commentaries. The fact is that the teaching of Messiah cannot be applied in the old skins of rabbinic Judaism. If we were to do so, then we would be faced with some inherent contradictions, such as the fact that the Mishnaic teaching of the rabbis clearly rejects Yeshua as the promised Messiah.

On the other hand, we should not jump to the erroneous conclusions of some that Yeshua is making a blanket condemnation of anything rabbinic or traditional. As usual, the balance lies somewhere in the middle. The fact that the *Mashiach* has come clearly has implications for our perspective of *Torah* and tradition.

Some of the classical rabbis actually anticipated this, as reflected in the statement

> When he, about whom it is written, *Lowly and riding upon an ass* (Zech. 9:9) will come...he will elucidate for them the words of the *Torah*...and elucidate for them their errors (Gen. Rabba 98:9).

This seems to me to provide balance in regard to a Jewish understanding of Yeshua. He came to elucidate the fullness of the teaching in *Torah*, even to the point of correcting some of the errors in people's understanding of it. In that sense, the teaching of Yeshua gives both Jews and Christians a way to understand the entire Bible as a consistent revelation from Genesis through Revelation. That is why most Jewish people who deeply study the words of the Yeshua appreciate their Jewish heritage all the more!

Power Over Death   9:18-26

In the midst of the discourse, Yeshua is interrupted by an urgent situation. *An official* of the local synagogue by the Kinneret, entreated the rabbi with a desperate plea. Luke gives us the details—this was the president of the synagogue at K'far-Nachum who went by the name of *Ya'ir*/God Enlightens (cf. Luke 8:40-41). Although his daughter had just died, he expressed amazing faith that she could be resurrected if Yeshua intervened.

The fact that the other gospel accounts speak only of the daughter being gravely ill does not contradict the reality of her death, as Matthew relates. As the disciples were on their way to Ya'ir's home, they were interrupted by yet another compelling need. As Yeshua made his way through some of the crowd, a woman who had had *a hemorrhage for twelve years* made her way close to him. The fact that she approached him from behind tells us that she was sensitive to the awkward situation this might be for Yeshua as a rabbi. It was commonly understood in that day that any woman should keep her distance from a rabbi. This was doubly magnified by her ritual uncleanness due to her ailment (cf. Leviticus 15:25-27).

Before Yeshua had a chance to react, the woman reached out and touched the *tzitzit on his robe*. This detail is very important for a number of reasons. First, it tells us that although Yeshua spoke about some of the dangers of tradition, he himself followed the biblical command to wear the fringes (cf. Numbers 15:37-39). He no doubt looked like a traditional Jew of his day. Second, the fact that this woman reached out to touch the Messiah's outer garment shows her own faith. By specifically touching the *tzitzit,* she was in essence saying that it would be by the word of God (what the fringes represent) that she would receive healing. With such an action of faith, it is little wonder that Yeshua responds with a strong affirmation, "Courage, daughter! Your trust has healed you." Ultimately, the lesson to all in the crowd was that it was the woman's faith in Messiah's power, and not the garment, that brought her restoration.

After this important detour, Yeshua and the band of disciples finally arrived at the home of Ya'ir, the synagogue official. To their dismay, the crowd was in an uproar and the flute-players were already performing funeral dirges. The laws of Jewish mourning include the need for mourners to assist the grieving family. Specifically, the *Mishnah* relates that "Even the poorest in Israel should hire not less than two flutes and one wailing woman" in such cases (Tractate Ketuvot 4:4). The intense mourning period of *Shiva* (Hebrew for "Seven") marks the days immediately after burial and had not yet started, as the funeral had not even taken place yet.

It is at this emotionally charged moment that Yeshua makes a shocking pronouncement as he orders everyone out of the house. The mourners will not be needed because the girl is only sleeping. Obviously the crowd itself, by its behavior, confirmed to the contrary that the girl had already died. As the incredulous crowd left, Yeshua

took the girl's hand, clearly not concerned about any possible
defilement, and raised her up to new life. By so doing, Yeshua was
once again exerting his power in such a way as to confirm his divine
nature. News of this messianic miracle, not surprisingly, spread
quickly throughout the Galilee with many more locals joining this
growing Yeshua movement.

Power Over Darkness   9:27-38

In another dramatic encounter, two blind men approach Yeshua.
What these men communicated was quite significant as they shouted,
"Son of David! Take pity on us!" The title they used is a strong messianic
designation in many places in the Hebrew Scriptures (cf. II Samuel 7;
Psalm 110). It is likewise a common rabbinic term for the Messiah,
who needs to be a direct descendant of King David and therefore called
Mashiach ben David/Messiah Son of David (Tractate Sukkah 52a).
The men's request for pity could have a two-fold meaning, both in the
physical as well as the spiritual realm. It is interesting that they enter
the house (note the definite article), leading some to speculate that it
might even be the home of Yeshua in K'far-Nachum.

Yeshua confronts the men with the all-important question, "Do you
believe?" After answering in the affirmative, the two men received the
touch of Messiah and their eyesight was completely restored. What
happens next is astounding in light of this dramatic miracle. Yeshua
warned them to keep this incident in utmost confidence. Why this was
important, Matthew gives no indication here. From other situations,
however, it is clear that the correct time and motivation for revealing
Messiah was of the utmost importance. The crowds could be tempted
to try to install Yeshua as the Messiah-King at the wrong time or for
the wrong reasons (cf. *Yochanan*/John 6:14-15). Evidently, this was
asking too much for two men who could now see! They couldn't
help but spread the news about their dynamic encounter with Yeshua
throughout the district.

In a final incident reflecting the authority of the Messiah, Matthew records an encounter with the demonic spiritual world. Of course, it is to be expected that when the *Mashiach* comes to his people, there would be a flourish of demonic activity as a backlash. Matthew has already recorded the first confrontation with darkness in the face-to-face battle with Satan (cf. Matthew 4).

If indeed the Messiah has come to deliver his people from the present battle, it is not surprising that the forces of Satan and his emissaries (demons) would make their presence known at key junctures of Yeshua's ministry. Here, it is with a man controlled by a demon that manifests itself by causing the man to lose the ability to speak. In the Bible, demons are identified as fallen angels who rebelled along with the ruling angel, Satan. As previously mentioned, the prophets Isaiah and Ezekiel describe the rebellion of God's greatest angel and his fall from grace (cf. Isaiah 14; Ezekiel 28). In these chapters, pagan kings are described as being empowered by a greater evil force that was with God from the beginning of creation. Satan was even called the "anointed Cherub" who was at the very throne of ADONAI.

Yet, because of his pride and desire to become more powerful than God, Satan rebelled and was cast to Earth. It is in the New Covenant book of Revelation that we are told that Satan was followed by one-third of the angelic host in this evil rebellion (cf. Revelation 12:1-9). It is one of these evil spirits that had afflicted this particular man with the resultant physical manifestation. Yeshua wasted no time in casting out this demon. The crowds were amazed at this show of force over the powers of darkness. They even testified that this was an outstanding miracle. Other rabbis were known to perform some miracles within Israel, yet this particular one seemed to be beyond the reach of even the holy sages. Perhaps the crowds realized the implications of Yeshua's works in light of the predictions of the prophets who testified that "the eyes of the blind will be opened and the mute person's tongue will sing" when the days of *Mashiach* come (cf. Isaiah 35:5-6; also Gen. Rabba 95:1). Some of the Pharisees who were present expressed another opinion, however. From their perspective, it was probably because of occult power from the ruler of the demons that Yeshua could perform such dramatic miracles.

It is significant to note that the same argument is presented in the *Talmud*. There is never a denial of such public miracles by the rabbi from Nazareth, but skepticism as to the source of the power to perform them. Messiah will point out in a later confrontation the inconsistency of such a claim, maintaining that it is the power of the God of Israel who allows such displays (cf. Matthew 12:25-28). This schism between much of the crowd and some of the rabbinic leaders will continue to build in the subsequent months of Yeshua's ministry within Israel.

The final paragraph of Chapter 9 gives a summary of various signs and miracles performed by Yeshua at this point of his ministry to Israel. He traveled broadly in all the towns and villages with essentially a two-fold emphasis—*proclaiming the Good News and healing*. The Good News is the reality that the Kingdom of God is at hand because King Messiah is in their midst.

It is a tragic fact that too often in church history the news of Jesus has not been presented as good for the Jews. Yet the original context of the words and works of Yeshua should give us a fresh appreciation that it is indeed wonderful news for our people. Matthew's central theme is to present Yeshua as King Messiah, who fulfills the promises given to his people Israel and made available to believers from all nations. His healing ministry, as seen above, is the practical proof that Yeshua's words can be validated by his works. Matthew emphasizes that much of this ministry also included teaching in the synagogues. If he is the true King Messiah, then this must be proclaimed directly to his beloved people as a priority, even before the message goes out to all peoples.

That priority remains a calling and a burden on many hearts (cf. Romans 1:16). Yeshua bares his true heart as he looks upon the crowds with compassion. They were in desperate need of a shepherd to guide them into the rich pastures of the Father. Yet, because the job looked so overwhelming, Messiah challenges his disciples to pray that there will be more workers to gather in his harvest. It should be noted that from Yeshua's perspective, the problem is not with the lack of harvest in Israel, but with the lack of workers by which to get it accomplished. Indeed, as Yeshua looked over the multitude, he proclaimed that *the harvest is rich.*

The chronological details of the gospel lead many to believe that this teaching took place in the late spring around the time of the grain harvest of *Shavuot*/Pentecost. If that is the case, then the description of rich or white harvest is all the more graphic, as this would have been consistent with the visible display of the fields of Galilee at this time. As with the physical harvest, so it is with the spiritual harvest of Israel. The same prayer is valid in our day. We might ask, "How am I a part of God's plan in reaching the world? What am I doing in my life and work to show the same kind of compassion to the house of Israel?" May our generation have a fresh understanding of the Good News of Yeshua—both for Jews and for the entire world.

The Disciples of the Kingdom   10:1-42

After a time of ministry to the multitudes within Israel, Yeshua now turns his attention to his immediate disciples. Even though he is the King Messiah to lead Israel, he realizes that he cannot accomplish his messianic purpose without the help of others. In this section, Yeshua gives a mandate to his closest followers regarding the work before them and the qualities they will need to successfully accomplish this high calling as the remnant of Jewish believers.

The Program of the Kingdom   10:1-15

Yeshua now limits his focus for the moment to the *twelve talmidim* (disciples) who have responded to his call. This in itself is significant as one understands the early manner of calling a disciple. In the ancient world, it was not a disciple who signed up for a particular rabbi, but the other way around. When a rabbi could see a promising student as a possible *talmid*, only then would the rabbi himself issue the call. Those who accepted the call would enter into a time of concerted apprenticeship with their rabbi.

This was not modeled after the Greek structure of learning, which was primarily concerned with transmitting information. The Jewish model of learning was not just *transferring of information* but more of a *transformation* of life. That is why the *talmid* would also live closely with his rabbi—so that spiritual lessons would be observed in daily action, not just written on a school blackboard.

That the community had the highest regard for this mentoring relationship can be seen in the following quote: "Let your house be a meeting place for the rabbis and cover yourself in the dust of their feet, and drink in their words thirstily" (Tractate Pirke Avot 1:4). The ideal disciples would follow their rabbi so closely that his dust would swirl up against him as they walked together. We should not be too far ahead of our rabbi nor should we be too far behind.

This shows the seriousness of the call to Yeshua's discipleship. It was a strong commitment in that day and should give us all some thoughts for reflection. As the *Mashiach*, he knew that his primary purpose was to establish the Kingdom of God on Earth as well as in the hearts of people who desire that Kingdom. He now specifies the program and the means for establishing this Kingdom promised long ago through the prophets of Israel.

It would be important to proclaim the message of the Kingdom; yet with that message, it would also be imperative that the power of God be manifested to confirm the validity of the message of these disciples. They were to receive Yeshua's authority over the afflictions of mankind, whether of the body or spirit.

The names of the disciples are themselves informative, in that they give insight into the diverse character of those chosen for this monumental task. The fact that Yeshua chose twelve men is not a coincidence, as it parallels the larger community of Israel and the twelve tribes. It should be noted that the call of disciples by a rabbi was quite common in first-century Judaism. In that sense, Yeshua's actions are not all surprising. It was not his call to discipleship that was unusual, but, rather, the particular mission they were on.

The two titles of these men—*talmidim* and *sh'lichim*—tell us much about their job description. In verse one, they are called *talmidim*, that is, students or learners. The first job of any good disciple is to study closely with the rabbi in order to glean vital truths for the spiritual life. It is, in that sense, impossible to be a good disciple without concentrated study and mentoring from others. Too many self-proclaimed followers of Yeshua today are falling short of God's best because they are neglecting this imperative.

In verse two, the students are also called *emissaries* (*sh'lichim*), meaning "ones sent out." Although many people are more familiar with the Greek translation of this term (*apostle*), the original Hebrew has much to teach. We may normally think that this concept simply designates those sent out for a specific purpose. While this is no doubt true, the term also carries a deeper reality.

In the Jewish world, it is said that a *shaliach* is in fact "equal to the sender himself" (Tractate Berchot 34). In other words, a *shaliach*/apostle was not just sent out but was actually considered a direct representative of the one who sent him. Such a person has the authority of the sender. Thus, the term *shaliach*/apostle is very strong and in this context illustrates that Yeshua was designating these twelve Jewish men to be his direct representatives. It is little wonder that Rabbi Sha'ul would later appeal to this authority in many of his apostolic letters to the Messianic believers (cf. I Corinthians 1:1-2). It is this strong term that is used to describe the twelve closest followers of Yeshua.

We are now introduced officially to the earliest *sh'lichim*. *Shim'on* is listed first, as he would take prominence among the twelve. It is also noted that his Aramaic name was *Kefa* ("Rock"), which would explain the Greek translation of his name to *Petros*/Peter. He would certainly live up to his name by being a rock of the early Messianic Jewish movement. *Andrew* ("Manly") is the brother of *Shim'on*. *Ya'akov Ben-Zavdai* is named after the forefather of Israel, but his name is translated as James, the son of *Zebedee*. *Yochanan* (John) is merely noted as his brother.

Philip ("Lover of horses") also loved to share his faith in Yeshua (cf. *Yochanan*/John 1:45). *Bar-Talmai* (Bartholomew) is simply known as the son of *Talmai* and probably had the alternate name of *Natanel*. *T'oma* (Thomas) would become famous as the skeptic of the resurrection of Yeshua until given concrete proof (cf. *Yochanan*/John 20:24f). *Mattityahu* (Matthew) means "Gift of God," although as a tax collector, he must have had a difficult time convincing others of that fact. Next on the list of apostles is *Ya'akov Bar-Halfai* (Alpheus), who has the distinct position of being the half-brother of Yeshua and who would later author the New Covenant epistle of *Ya'akov*/James. *Taddia* is the Hebrew version of Thaddeus, meaning "heart" or "breast."

The next *shaliach* went by the name *Shim'on the Zealot*. This title was not meant to convey that he was merely a zealous person, but that he actually belonged to the first-century political party known by that name. The Zealots espoused the violent overthrow of their Roman occupiers, even to the point of murder and death. This fact provides an illuminating insight into the messianic agenda of Yeshua, as he purposely chooses one who is violently opposed to Rome, as well as a Roman sympathizer (Mattityahu) who was even employed by the occupying forces! It seems the kingdom that Yeshua was proposing is larger than any political affiliation here on Earth, although this certainly must have made for some interesting discussions among the disciples. The last of the apostles is the noted *Y'hudah from K'riot*, the one who would ultimately betray the Messiah into the hands of the Romans. His family name (*Ish-k'riot*) means "the man from this village."

We will learn much about the personalities and values of each of these chosen *sh'lichim* as Matthew's gospel records the events of the next three years.

Yeshua now specifies some of the details of his program to which these men have been called. True to the name *shaliach* (Greek, apostolos), these men were *sent out* with a focused purpose. It may surprise some readers that his first exhortation to them is to avoid the *territory of the Goyim (Gentiles)* and to exclusively share with *the lost sheep of the house of Isra'el.* As we know from the broader context of the Scriptures (Gen. 12; Matt. 28), this messianic message is also for all the nations and peoples of the world.

It is not that Yeshua was neglecting the call to share with all the Gentiles, but it made sense that the first priority would be to share the goods news of Messiah with those who have waited expectantly for it. The time will come when the message will go to all people, but for now the priority is to share with the covenant people of Israel the message that God has fulfilled his promise to send a redeemer. Likewise, subsequent to the earthly life of Yeshua, Rabbi Sha'ul of Tarsus would still uphold this principle even as the apostle appointed for the Gentiles (cf. Rom. 1:16).

While some modern theologians minimize the importance of this ministry strategy, I would exhort contemporary believers to consider that God still has an exceptional burden for his people, Israel. I believe the neglect of Jewish ministry and outreach in the modern church is out of balance and has brought spiritual poverty that God never intended.

The message to be shared is now clarified by the Messiah. As they go to various communities, they are to proclaim, "The Kingdom of Heaven is near." Once again we see Matthew's emphasis on the theme of Yeshua's message and ministry: The Kingdom of God is offered to Israel in the person of the Messiah. Now the message was to flow out further from the original disciples to the larger Jewish world around them. It is not only the message that is of importance, but also the resultant actions. Healing the sick, expelling demonic forces, and even raising the dead will be physical signs that the spiritual kingdom of Messiah is near. Of particular note, the cleansing of the lepers is emphasized, as this was a clear messianic miracle that could be fully accomplished only with the arrival of the true *Mashiach* (cf. Matt. 8).

The apostles are not to worry about provisions along the way. They are to give *without asking payment* and are not even to take their own *money, gold,* or extra clothing with them. The emphasis here is that they were to focus entirely upon their call to the messianic ministry without the distraction of secondary concerns. A similar point is made in the *Talmud* when it states that a man "may not enter into the Temple Mount with his staff or his sandal or his wallet or with the dust upon his feet" (Tractate Berochot 9:5). This first public ministry of the *sh'lichim* was to be a time of faith-building in many practical ways, as they were to trust that God would provide their needs from the people who would be receptive to their ministry.

As they go from town to town throughout Israel, they are to stay with *someone trustworthy* and give the familiar blessing of *shalom aleikhem,* "peace to you all." The apostles are forewarned that their message may not be welcomed by everyone. If it is not received, they are to *shake the dust* off their feet and go to where their ministry will be more fruitful. This is striking language in that it was believed that the dirt from a foreign, non-Jewish country would render a person ritually unclean (Tractate Toharot 4:5). However, such a response will not go unnoticed by God, as it will be *more tolerable on the Day of Judgment for the people of S'dom* than for that town. As bad as the rejection by the people of S'dom was in their day, the rejection of the messianic message from the apostles would carry even more judgment.

The Challenges of the Kingdom   10:16-42

The apostles should not be naïve. They are going as *sheep among wolves,* so they must be ever-diligent and wise *as snakes.* Some of their adversaries will even hand them over *to the local Sanhedrin* and administer a flogging in the synagogues. This language, of course, reflects the kinds of punishments meted out from the Jewish courts upon heretical Jews. However, the opposition will not just come from Jewish quarters, as Yeshua mentions that they will also be brought *before governors and kings* of the Gentiles.

As the apostles go throughout the land, they will also be afforded opportunities to give testimony to many non-Jews concerning this Kingdom of God. Many Gentile officials will also reject their message, and it is predicted that they will be brought to civil trial by the secular authorities. This would be fulfilled in their day, as it was not only some of the Jewish leadership that opposed the message of Yeshua, but also the pagan Roman occupiers who would drag the Messianic believers into their courts.

Through all of this adversity, Messiah assures these men that they are not to worry about having the right answer for every situation. *The Spirit* of the heavenly Father will empower them and give them all the appropriate words for the occasion. The later chapters of the gospel accounts, as well as the history in the Book of Acts, verify some of these very situations.

The opposition is predicted to become so intense that even close family members will become alienated from one another. There will be cases where *a father* will turn against his own child, and even *children against their parents.* Yet the promise is given by Yeshua that *whoever holds out till the end will be preserved from harm.* This cannot mean a guarantee of physical deliverance in all cases, as has been noted here, but spiritual redemption is the ultimate promise for all believers in Yeshua—no matter what transpires in the present age. The condition of this promise is personal endurance by the true disciple of Messiah. It is not so much that such endurance will earn spiritual deliverance, but that this endurance will confirm the reality of spiritual relationship already existing with Yeshua.

Again, the priority of sharing this messianic message with the Jewish people is affirmed in that Yeshua will not return to the people until they *finish going through the towns of Isra'el.* Commentators are divided on the exact meaning of this phrase—was Yeshua speaking of the current ministry trip, the impending judgment of 70 CE, or the latter-day events? Matthew is writing some decades after these words were spoken and certainly realized that they had not yet been fulfilled. The word used (Greek *teleo*) means "to bring to an end" or "to complete." It seems the best view is that this message of Yeshua's redemption will need to continually be presented to Israel until the day that it is finally received in its fullness in the latter-day revival (cf. Matt. 23:37-39; Rom. 11:25-27).

All these things should not catch the emissaries by surprise, as *a talmid (disciple) is not greater than his rabbi.* Yeshua would live a life of positive blessing, yet with significant opposition. The simple reality is that his followers (even today) cannot expect a different response. Some would even call Yeshua by the derogatory title of *Ba'al-Zibbul* after a Philistine god.

The usual name was *Ba'al-Zivuv* (lord of the flies), which was a part of the religious culture in II Kings 1. It seems that the name was deliberately corrupted into *Ba'al-Zibbul* (lord of dung) as a commentary on what the rabbis thought of such pagan deities. That this term would be applied to Yeshua is a statement of the contempt that some of the first-century rabbinic authorities held for this so-called messiah (cf. Matt. 13). Instead of receiving him as the promised *Mashiach*, some in the religious community attributed Yeshua's ministry to paganism or worse.

The point here is that the disciples of Yeshua cannot naively believe that they will be well received by the same people who so strongly rejected their rabbi. Nonetheless, they are *not to fear them* but to realize that the truth of Yeshua will prevail. Instead of being concerned over what people may say or do, it is better to *fear him who can destroy both soul and body*. The true followers of Yeshua are more valuable than the sparrows that God cares for.

The overriding principle is this: *Whoever acknowledges me in the presence of others I will also acknowledge in the presence of my Father in heaven.* Still today, the followers of Yeshua, especially those who are Jewish, are faced with this decision. Are we willing to stand with God and Yeshua even when it is unpopular with those around us? The implications are vast, for if Yeshua is the true Messiah sent by the God of Israel, then to reject him is in essence to reject God.

Yeshua continues to emphasize this important point as he reveals that he has *not come to bring peace to the Land.* Undoubtedly, he does not desire to bring such division and controversy. Yet, he will bring a sword in the sense that the revelation of the Messiah will naturally cause all people to choose sides. Is he or isn't he the true *Mashiach*?

It is noteworthy that Yeshua even makes this decision a part of the test of his discipleship. One must ultimately love him more than even *his father or mother* in order to be a true disciple. Yeshua's call to these twelve emissaries (as well as to anyone today) is *to take up his execution-stake and follow me.*

His call to new life actually entails a call to die to our old life and perspectives. He closes this teaching with the common principle that *whoever receives you, receives me.* This reflects the common dictum that a *shaliach* is equal to the sender himself (see 10:2). The same principle holds for a prophet as well as a *tzaddik* (righteous person). Even a simple *cup of cold water* given to a *talmid* will not be overlooked in the judgment.

As the twelve *sh'lichim* are sent forth, they certainly had to be challenged by the high calling of Yeshua's discipleship. We live in a day where there seem to be many believers, but few disciples on this level. Have you responded to Yeshua's call to follow him? Are you willing to identify with him despite the opposition and scorn of the world? While it may be costly, there is no better way to invest our lives than as committed disciples of King Messiah Yeshua! May we heed the message of our great Rabbi to find the blessing of God, both now and in the world to come.

Responses to King Messiah   11:1-30

Having described the mandate and mission of the disciples, Matthew now relates some of the responses received by the *talmidim* to his readers. As predicted in the previous chapter, there is much opposition. Even such a strong ally as *Yochanan*/John the Immerser was now having his doubts about the reality of Yeshua's claims. Nonetheless, the account continues to honestly assert that Yeshua is in fact the King Messiah given to Israel and for all nations.

The Inquiries of Yochanan   11:1-19

After Yeshua instructs his disciples about his high calling to discipleship, he proceeds to towns to *teach and preach* to the multitudes once again. At this time, Yeshua's attention is diverted to one of the vital members of his team. It was *Yochanan*/John the Immerser who had strongly proclaimed the coming of Messiah to the early seekers. He seemed to have the clear understanding at that time of the unique revelation brought through the person of Yeshua. However, after a season of persecution and imprisonment, Yochanan expresses some fresh doubts about the validity of Yeshua's mission. He had probably expected, like many other traditional Jews of his time, that the *Mashiach* would instantly bring the promised redemption to Israel.

In rabbinic understanding, *Mashiach ben David* (Messiah Son of David) must come to fulfill the kingdom of blessing and peace (cf. Isa. 2, 11). Often overlooked was the ministry of *Mashiach ben Yosef* (Messiah Son of Joseph), who was to suffer and even be rejected by many (cf. Isa. 53, Zech. 12:10 as explained in Tractate Sukkot 52a). Of course, the Son of David was the more popular, as many looked forward to the blessings and freedom of his day.

After several delays and some intense opposition, it is understandable how even Yochanan could have these questions. In this context, he sent a message asking Yeshua, "Are you the one who is to come?" Yeshua answers by drawing attention to his recent ministry among his people. Several messianic miracles have taken place through his ministry: *The blind are seeing again, the lame are walking, people with tzara'at are being cleansed* (cf. Matt. 8). To this, he adds a word of encouragement to Yochanan that the person who is *not offended by me* will be blessed.

Not only does Yeshua affirm his own calling as Messiah, but he also validates the ministry of Yochanan to those who might be wondering about it. He asks several probing questions of the crowd in order to illustrate the vital message of the Immerser. *What did you go to see? A reed swaying in the breeze?*

Yochanan, if he were the messenger predicted to prepare the way of Messiah, would of necessity be a man of strength and conviction. He may show some doubts and confusion here, but one could not call him fickle. In contrast to much of the religious establishment of the Temple, Yochanan was not a man of luxury or the status quo. In Yeshua's words, he was very much a prophetic personality and *much more than a prophet*. Yochanan was, in fact, the one to fulfill the Scripture: "See, I am sending out my messenger ahead of you; he will prepare your way before you" (cf. Mal. 3:1). Because of this high calling, there is *not anyone greater* born to the human race.

Yet, this ministry that starts with Yochanan will certainly not be easy or smooth. In his day, *the Kingdom of Heaven has been suffering violence*; that is, there would be an intensified spiritual battle over Israel as the *Mashiach* is ready to appear. This statement seems to be a reference to an important messianic prophecy that also describes two distinct personalities associated with the final redemption: Elijah the Prophet as the forerunner, then King Messiah. In the words of the prophet Micah:

> The one breaking through went up before them; they broke through, passed the gate and went out. Their king passed on before them; A*DONAI* was leading them. (Micah 2:13)

In rabbinic tradition, Elijah was considered the one breaking through (*ha-poretz*) the spiritual obstacles in order that the King (Messiah) may come to rule over the people. As it is explained in one commentary:

> When the Holy One, blessed be He, redeems Israel. Three days before the Messiah comes, Elijah will come and stand upon the mountains of Israel….In that hour the Holy One, blessed be He, will show his glory and his kingdom to all the inhabitants of the world: He will redeem Israel, and He will appear at the head of them, as is said, he who opens the breach (*ha-poretz*) will go up before them; they will break through and pass the gate, going out by it. Their king will pass on before them, the Lord at their head (Micah 2:13) (Peshikta Rabbati 35).

While there were certainly *violent ones* (e.g., Zealots, etc.) *trying to snatch it away* on their own strength, the kingdom of Messiah will come by different means. It seems to be in this sense the prophet Micah describes that Yeshua defines the place and ministry of Yochanan for the Kingdom of God. *He is Eliyahu* if Israel is *willing to accept it.* This passage also helps explains an enigma concerning Yeshua. It is sometimes asked: If Yeshua is the true Messiah, why is the kingdom not here yet? The fact is that the kingdom of Messiah will fully come only when the King is welcomed by faith. Matthew records how, for now, both the messenger and the Messiah would not be totally accepted. Therefore, there would be a delay in the kingdom until the glorious day of Yeshua's reception. It will surely come because it is the promise of God's word to us!

Having described the temporary rejection of the messengers of God, Yeshua now gives a simple illustration to bring home his point. *This generation* is compared to children sitting in the marketplace as they react to life around them. Whenever they play *happy music,* some people would not dance. Yet, when they played *sad music,* the same people would not cry either. The former is reminiscent of a joyous wedding reception, while the latter seems to allude to a Jewish funeral dirge.

In either case, the crowd refused to enter into a natural and appropriate response. Yeshua now ties that analogy to both his ministry and that of Yochanan the Immerser. When the latter came *fasting and not drinking,* he was accused of having *a demon.* Yet when Yeshua, *the Son of Man, came eating freely and drinking wine,* his enemies accused him of being *a drunkard and a friend of sinners.*

Rightly does Yeshua mock the so-called wisdom of such responses of the crowd. The simple story summarizes the folly of many who rejected not only the messenger but also the Messiah himself as they came with a message of redemption to Israel.

The Warning to Unrepentant Cities   11:20-30

Matthew now records Yeshua's response to the general unbelief and skepticism of the masses. His harshest condemnation is for the areas that had personally witnessed *most of his miracles* yet had not repented from their sins. The emotional cry "Woe to you" (Hebrew *Oy lach*!) goes out to Korazin and Beit-Tzaidah for rejecting the messianic signs done in their midst. Since three of the early disciples (Philip, Andrew, and Shi'mon Peter) were from Beit-Tzaidah, there was ample opportunity to hear and understand the messianic claims of Yeshua (cf. *Yochanan*/John 1:44). Then comes perhaps the most convicting declaration—that if similar signs were done in even some of the non-Jewish areas of *Tzor and Tzidon(Tyre* and *Sidon), they would long ago have put on sackcloth and ashes.* This refers to the ancient Middle Eastern customs associated with grief and mourning (Esther 4:3).

Another vital town of Galilee, K'far-Nachum, is to receive special judgment and be *brought down to Sh'ol.* So egregious was their rejection that even the town of *S'dom* will fare better *on the Day of Judgment* (Genesis 19). There will be great accountability to those who reject the light given to them. Many in Israel had their opportunity, as the revelation of Yeshua was spread throughout the land. The principle certainly would apply today, often to a different group of people, who have much of the revelation of God (the Bible, multiple churches, etc.) but who likewise reject the clear call of the Messiah.

In the midst of this section that recounts rejection and judgment, it is enlightening to hear how Yeshua prays to his Father. Surprisingly, he starts with a word of thanks to the *Lord of heaven and earth.* The phrase indicates Messiah's trust in the plan of God even when things don't appear to be lining up.

God is the sovereign Lord of all, and nothing, not even rejection by many of his covenant people, will thwart his ultimate plans of messianic redemption. In fact, it is ironic that part of God's plan actually includes the fact that he has *concealed these things from the sophisticated* and yet *revealed them to ordinary folks.* Yeshua finds delight in the Father's plan because it also *pleased him to do this.* This is not to say that God hid these truths from anyone, but that the messianic revelation does not come in the usual, worldly manner. What the world so often values (education, advanced degrees, etc.) does not necessarily help a person to have the spiritual discernment necessary to apprehend the revelation of God (cf. I Cor. 1:18-25). Yet, even a common person with an open heart to the things of God will be enabled to understand and receive redemption through Yeshua.

So it is in our day as well. As Yeshua continues his prayer, he exults in the fact that God the *Father has handed over everything* to his control. His own divine origin is emphasized by Yeshua himself; it is the son who *fully knows the Father* and reveals this knowledge to those whom he chooses. From these statements, it is clear that we cannot merely accept Yeshua as a good rabbi or even a prophet. He claims to have a unique knowledge of the God of Israel because he himself was in the presence of the Father from eternity past.

We also note that no one comes to the full understanding of Father unless Yeshua gives that spiritual revelation. Even to this day, a person cannot merely give intellectual assent to being a believer. Anyone who comes to a full knowledge of the Father does so only through the mediation of his son, Yeshua the Messiah. To believe in Yeshua as the Promised One is to receive the completed picture for all the previous covenants to Israel.

Yeshua now turns from his prayer of thanksgiving to the Father to a call for any potential disciples. If he is the only true mediator between the Father and his people, then the imperative to *come* is easily understood. It is a call to follow the Messiah with an emphasis on those who are *struggling and burdened.* It is significant to note that this personal call comes immediately after the prayer emphasizing God's sovereignty. In this section we have, side by side, both God's sovereignty and man's free will to respond to God. What sometimes might seem like a contradiction of terms to our thinking is evidently perfectly consistent in God's mind. He is ultimately in control, yet humanity has the responsibility and freedom to respond to his call. It is also noted here that life is filled with challenges, yet, to such a person, Yeshua promises rest.

It is not that his calling will be without its own challenges. He compares the messianic life to a *yoke* that brings to mind the picture of a beast of burden fulfilling its duty to pull a plow. In a spiritual sense, this picture was not unknown to the rabbis as they spoke of *ol ha-Torah* (the yoke of the *Torah*), which is said to be summarized in the *Sh'ma* (Deuteronomy 6:4ff) recitation three times daily in prayer. This is not a negative burden in Judaism but an acceptance of the yoke of the Kingdom of ADONAI (Tractate Berakhot 2:5).

The *Torah* presents a positive, spiritual responsibility as a Jew attempts to fulfill its commands with love (Tractate Avot 3:6). Most Jews even to this day do not consider the *Torah* a negative burden but a gift from God to be celebrated, as witnessed in the *Torah* service every *Shabbat*. After all, it is a great gift to have a roadmap on how to have a blessed life! However, Yeshua does emphasize here that he is not just calling Jews and others to merely take up the yoke of the *Torah*. He exhorts his listeners to take up his yoke and to learn from him on how to walk in the spirit of *shalom*. We will truly find *rest for our souls* when we walk in close relationship with the one who is *gentle and humble*.

In a summary statement that presents a paradox, Yeshua assures his disciples that his *yoke is easy* and his *burden is light*. While there will be responsibilities and even hardships in the messianic life, our Messiah promises to give us the strength and resources to come out victorious. Indeed, the calling of Yeshua becomes easy and light as we come to him as our source of spiritual power. It should be a delight to carry the yoke of Messiah's kingdom throughout the days of our life here on Earth. In those times when we modern-day disciples might feel stressed or frustrated, the call still goes out for us to come to Yeshua for his perspective and true *shalom* in our hearts. Are we walking in his plan today?

The Opposition to Yeshua as King Messiah 12:1-50

Up to this juncture of his ministry, Yeshua has been busy addressing the needs of his fellow Jews in Israel. There has been much support and blessing emanating from those who have been touched by his work. In some cases it is has been praise for his distinctive teaching and elaboration of the spiritual principles of the *Torah*. Others commend Yeshua for his amazing works of healing and provision.

Yet in the midst of this broad popular support, some are beginning to question the meaning of his ministry among them. Matthew records an honest assessment of both sides of the debate and now proceeds to highlight some of the details concerning those who were starting to come against the Rabbi from Galilee.

The Controversy over *Shabbat*   12:1-21

Matthew continues his account of the life of Yeshua by recording the growing controversy surrounding this one who claimed to be King Messiah. In Chapter 11, he described the philosophical· differences between many of the Jewish leaders and Yeshua on the ministry of Yochanan the Immerser. It was *during that time* of debate and disagreement that Yeshua is recorded as traveling *through some wheat fields* in the Galilee. What was discussed in a polemical manner earlier now becomes a very practical issue. Since his disciples were hungry in their itinerant travels, it is recorded that *they began picking heads of grain and eating them*. There was, of course, absolutely no problem with eating such grain at any time. This action of harvesting would normally be acceptable and even a *mitzvah* as seen from the laws of gleaning in the *Torah* (cf. Deut. 23:25).

It is significant that Matthew notes that they were picking the grain by hand and not using a sickle as is mandated by the *Torah* itself. While the Jewish farmer was obligated to leave some of his field for those in need, the harvesters were not to abuse the privilege but only pick a limited amount to fulfill their current need. Clearly, from Matthew's account, the controversy erupts not because of the legitimate harvest but because this event occurred *on Shabbat.* Since there were an entirely different level of laws in regard to the Jewish day of worship, it is not surprising that some of the Pharisees accused Yeshua's disciples of *violating Shabbat.*

Needless to say, probably the most revered commandment within historical Judaism has been the observance of the seventh-day Sabbath. It is rather surprising that for all the weight given to *Shabbat*, the Bible actually gives little definition. To this day, we light two candles on *Shabbat* evening to illustrate to us the two-fold biblical commandment to remember and observe (*zachor* and *shamor* in the two versions of the Decalogue; Ex. 20:8, Deut. 5:12).

Likewise, the biblical injunction is to refrain from all work just as God himself rested. It is unfortunate that many have misinterpreted the commandments of the Sabbath to become a burden or even bondage. While some, like the Puritans of old, made the Sabbath a time of gloom, the Jewish view emphasized the biblical perspective that *Shabbat* was in fact to be a joy and delight.

Perhaps some people who were unaware might observe the commandments of the Sabbath and conclude that they were oppressive. The traditional Jewish view, however, saw the regulations as God's gift to Israel in that they could have a consistent day of rest, free from the tyranny of daily duties. Indeed, a proper perspective of *Shabbat* should cause one to rejoice that we are not slaves to anyone or anything, whether it is the taskmasters of Egypt or the competition of modern society. This is why the *Shabbat* was to be called an *oneg*, that is, a delight and blessing (Isa. 58:13).

It is because of the importance of *Shabbat* that the rabbis of the Talmudic period carefully defined and elaborated on these biblical laws. While the written *Torah* is relatively simple in its description, the commentators developed extra laws to protect the sanctity of the seventh day. This is illustrated by the fact that an entire tractate of the *Talmud* is devoted to the consideration of what is allowed or forbidden on the holy day (cf. Tractate Shabbat). It is there that the rabbis sought to further define what constituted the concept of "work" in regard to Sabbath observance.

To clarify this issue, they came up with an ingenious definition as they drew a comparison between the work on the Tabernacle of Exodus and the modern concept of work. As they studied this example, they came up with what they called the "39 Avot" commandments (literally "39 Fathers"). Although the Bible never specified it, many actions were considered forbidden, such as sowing, reaping, weaving, baking, and even writing two letters (cf. Tractate Shabbat VII.2). If this wasn't enough, it was then expanded into what was called the *Toledot* (descendants) commandments, which were said to be almost innumerable. As the *Mishnah* itself simply notes, there are "scant Scriptures but many *halakhot* (rabbinic laws) (Tractate Hagigah 1:8). However, it must be emphasized that for the sages, this perspective was never to be considered mere bondage or legalism.

Such rabbinic laws were derived to help the common Jew define their boundaries of the blessings of *Shabbat* and thus focus on it as a delight. Yet, it was probably inevitable that in some instances the principles of joy and freedom were replaced with a structured religiosity that was more concerned about the letter of the law. At this segment of Matthew's gospel, we find the growing controversy concerning Yeshua focused not on his technical *Torah* observance but rather on his attitude toward the mishnaic elaborations of rabbinic Judaism. Historically, many interpreters have misunderstood Yeshua's attitudes as being "anti-*Torah*" but this could not be the case based on his own words (Matt. 5:17-18). Some people even believe in the Jesus who abolished the dietary laws for Jews and started eating bacon burgers!

On the other hand, it is clear that Yeshua took exception several times not to the written *Torah* but to some of the rabbinic interpretations of the *Torah*. Simply put, Yeshua never contradicted the Written *Torah* but was not afraid to oppose the Oral *Torah* (early *Mishnah*) when it was deemed necessary. In true prophetic fashion, Yeshua confronted any issue that distracted Israel from a purer form of *Torah* observance.

It is in this context of confrontation that the disciples of Yeshua are accused of breaking *Shabbat*. To answer such a strong indictment, Yeshua appeals to the original source, the Holy Scriptures. In a classic rabbinic manner, Yeshua asks the question, "Haven't you ever read the story of King David?" Knowing full well that these educated Pharisees knew of the account, Yeshua is prodding them to look deeper at the spiritual principles to be learned from the unusual encounter. Alluding to the time when David and his men were weary from battle, Yeshua notes that they *entered the House of God and ate the Bread of the Presence.* This action was highly forbidden by the letter of the Law, as the soldiers certainly were not of the Levitical descent required to partake of the ritual *hallah*/bread (cf. Ex. 25:30).

This apparent infraction is highlighted by the general principle that every *Shabbat, the cohanim profane Shabbat and yet are blameless.* In laymen's terms, Yeshua is pointing out that the priesthood not only performed work but also was commanded to serve God in this way especially on the Sabbath day. If the priests could serve God while apparently breaking some of the technicalities of *Shabbat*, how much more (*kal v'chomer*) could the *Mashiach* who is *greater than the*

Temple? In true prophetic fashion, Yeshua draws their attention to the higher principle that should govern all Sabbath observance, that God desires *compassion rather than animal sacrifice.* The Pharisees certainly would *not condemn the innocent* (his *talmidim*) if they truly realized that Yeshua, as *the Son of Man, is Lord of Shabbat.* Yet, because of the strong statement of his messiahship, the controversy surrounding Yeshua of Nazareth will only increase.

The *Shabbat* controversy now switches location from the outside field to a *Shabbat* service within *their synagogue.* It is during the main service that some of the leaders take note of a man with a medical problem manifested by his *shriveled hand.* This seems to present a perfect opportunity to test Yeshua as a self-proclaimed Messiah as they put forth the question "Is healing permitted on *Shabbat?*" It is evident that these synagogue leaders already held to the widely accepted belief that under normal circumstances, there was to be no healing unless it was a life-threatening situation.

Based on *Vayikra*/Leviticus 18:5 ("and live by the commandments"), some of the laws of *Shabbat* could be set aside under the concept of *pikuach nefesh,* literally "to save a life." Since God gave the *Torah* to bless our life, it is understood to this day that whatever is needed to save a life may be done even on the *Shabbat.* Maimonides, the great medieval commentator and physician, even calls it a "religious duty" to break the Sabbath for such a need (Yad, Shabbat 2:2-3).

Part of Yeshua's answer to this rabbinic question is actually affirmed in the *Mishnah* itself as he points out that they too would lift up a troubled sheep that had *fallen in a pit on Shabbat* (Tractate Shabbat 117b). If some of the laws of *Shabbat* can be set aside to assist a needy animal, *how much more* so in the case of a fellow human being. By using this *kal v'chomer* rabbinic principle (the lesser to the greater), Yeshua summarizes that it is permitted *to do good* on *Shabbat* any time the situation arises, not just in life-threatening circumstances. On this point, some Talmudic rabbis actually agreed as reflected in the well-known statement of the *Talmud* "The *Shabbat* has been given to you, not you to the *Shabbat*" (Tractate Yoma 85b; cf. Mark 2:27).

As a practical application of his teaching, Yeshua asks the man to hold out his hand, at which time it is *restored* completely. Upon this public healing in the synagogue, some of the *leaders went out and began plotting how they might do away* with this rebellious rabbi from Galilee. Although Yeshua could not be honestly accused of breaking the written *Torah*, he no doubt stirred up animosity among some of the people who did not agree with his *halakhah, which* seemed at variance with the rabbinic interpretations of their community. No doubt some of the leadership also felt threatened by the challenge to their authority. Although Yeshua is in fact the Lord of *Shabbat*, he leaves *that area* for a more fruitful field.

Despite the increasing opposition, it is noted by Matthew that *many people followed* Yeshua as he continued to minister to their physical and spiritual needs. While there were many healings, he also gave the warning to the crowds *not to make him known*. At first glance, this exhortation may seem confusing. After all, Yeshua had been ministering very openly and widely proclaiming his Messianic qualifications.

It seems the intention of this shift is to withhold some of the public ministry from those who were increasingly in opposition. According to the Gospel writer, this too was actually a fulfillment of prophecy from the *Tanakh*, specifically from *Yesha'yahu*/Isaiah the prophet (42:1-4). In that passage, it is noted that the Servant of ADONAI *will not fight or shout*, nor will anyone *hear his voice in the streets*. It is not that the Servant will be completely quiet, yet it is clear that there will be a point where he will not publicly refute his opposition. This will not take place *until he has brought justice through to victory* and even *the Gentiles will put their hope* in him.

While some rabbinic commentators attempt to apply this and other "Suffering Servant" passages (Isaiah 42-53) to the nation of

Israel as a whole, many other sources disagree by acknowledging that this passage solely applies to the coming Messiah (cf. Targum Yonaton, Rabbi David Kimchi). This rings true, as a close study of the Suffering Servant passages confirms that there are many results only the *Mashiach* (not national Israel) can accomplish (e.g., atonement of sins, faith from the Gentiles). As an eyewitness to those events in the life of Yeshua, Matthew uses this proof-text to show that the ministry of Yeshua will soon go through this predicted shift in emphasis as will be detailed in the encounters to come.

The Charge Against Yeshua   12:22-29

Within this tense environment after the *Shabbat* healing, some people now bring to Yeshua *a man not only controlled by demons but who was also blind and mute.* While Jewish healers and exorcists were not unknown, to confront a mute demon would present a huge obstacle that only the Messiah could overcome. When Yeshua *healed him*, the crowds are so astonished that they ask, "this couldn't be the Son of David, could it?"

This of course was a clear reference to one of the key names for the *Mashiach* who is to be the greatest descendant of King David himself. However, some of the *P'rushim*/Pharisees had an alternate explanation for this display of power. *It is only by Ba'al-Zibbul, the ruler of demons, that this man drives out demons.* The name refers to one of the most powerful gods of the Philistines. *Ba'al* (lord) reflects the ancient belief that this pagan deity controlled various aspects of local life ranging from rain and agriculture to fertility. So popular was this god that various forms of *Ba'al* worship spread through the ancient cultures of Egypt, Assyria, and Babylon.

One of the greatest judgments upon Israel was due to their incorporation of *Ba'al* worship alongside the true calling to *YHVH*. The prophets Elijah and Jeremiah were among those who warned Israel in their day of the consequences of such syncretism and idolatry. It should be noted that God sent Israel into Babylon (the land of *Ba'al*) for 70 years, which seemed to cure the nation of this form of idolatry even to the modern day. The name *Ba'al-Zibbul* (Baal-prince) was evidently an intentional corruption of the form *Ba'al-Zevuv* (lord of the fly). This was an acknowledgement of the omnipresence of the pagan deity, as flies are everywhere to be found (cf. II Kings 1:2). The Talmudic rabbis added to *Ba'al's* notoriety by stressing that *Ba'al-Zivuv* was the worst demon because he was in fact the lord of idolatry. It can't get worse than that!

This background brings to bear the seriousness of the charges against Yeshua. It should be noted that the *P'rushim* authorities here do not attempt to deny the reality of Yeshua's miraculous works. Indeed, how could they, with such powerful and public displays among the crowds? Instead of denying the miracles, they take the path of trying to discredit Yeshua as a true messenger of God.

By attributing his miracles to *Ba'al-Zevuv*, the first-century rabbis in fact are calling Yeshua the worst kind of sorcerer and idolater. In a striking parallel passage in the *Talmud*, some of the sages agree with Matthew's account. In discussing some rabbis and false teachers, it is said: "Yeshu the Nazarene practiced magic and led astray and deceived Israel" (Tractate Sanhedrin 107b). What is especially curious in the passage is that the rabbis speculate that Yeshu (their corrupted name for Yeshua which is an abbreviation for "may his name be cursed/ *yemach shemo ve-zichro*") probably acquired the special sorcery from his time living in Egypt! While coming to different conclusions than the followers of Yeshua, the rabbinic literature strangely confirms many of the details of the life of the historical Yeshua. Whatever our faith perspective, the historical traditions of the time confirm that, after spending some time in Egypt, Yeshua of Nazareth did great miraculous signs in Israel that even his opposition acknowledged.

Yeshua could not let such serious charges go unanswered. Knowing even *what they were thinking*, the Messiah had a most challenging response in the form of three statements. First, *every kingdom divided against itself will be ruined.* If he is in fact performing healing miracles by the power of the prince of demons, it would seem self-contradictory. Why would Satan want to perform a beautiful miracle by driving out himself and other demons?

Only the true God of Israel would want to build up his kingdom in such a positive manner. Indeed, such healings and deliverances are signs that *the Kingdom of God has come upon you.* Second, it is noted that other rabbis also drive out demons and Ba'al-Zibbul, which begs the question, *by whom do your people drive them out?* If they perform such healings in the Name of *YHVH,* why must Yeshua's work be attributed to Satan?

Third, he puts forth an argument that it is naturally a stronger man who *first ties up the strong man* (Satan). It must therefore be someone stronger than Ba'al-Zivuv who is able to deliver from such demonic oppression. The powerful reality is that Messiah will come to cast out the works of the Adversary (cf. Isaiah 61:1). Besides being a dynamic testimony in first-century Israel, this situation is a joyful reminder for all Messianic believers even in our day. While the Adversary still roams around seeking to devour, we are promised divine protection as we keep on the armor of God (cf. Ephesians 6:10-18). Although we have a promised victory, we also would be wise to realize that the spiritual battle will continue until the strong man is finally bound by God himself in the abyss for the 1000-year Messianic Kingdom of the future (cf. Revelation 20:1-2).

The Blasphemy of the Holy Spirit   12:30-37

This section marks a dramatic shift in emphasis in Matthew's account of the life of Yeshua. All the chapters up to this point were presented with the goal of verifying that Yeshua of Nazareth is the promised King Messiah for Israel. Through an extended time of ministry throughout Israel, Yeshua has presented his credentials both in word and deed. Yet such a life and teaching would ultimately lead to a call for a decision. His messianic claims necessitate a black or white conclusion with no room for middle ground.

In his own words, *those who are not with me are against me.* It is a matter of historical record that many thousands of Jews in first-century Israel responded positively to this call. Some today still try to make it sound as if no Jew has ever followed Yeshua, but this is ignoring first-century history.

The fact that the New Testament was written by Jews clearly testifies to this reality (cf. Acts 21:20)! However, it is just as clear that a majority of Israel, as represented by their first-century rabbinic leadership, came to a point of rejecting the messianic claims of this Galilean rabbi. It could be viewed that this encounter in Matthew 12 marked a turning point where the rabbinic leadership of the day officially pronounced their rejection of Yeshua as King Messiah.

Because of this official rejection of Yeshua, it is to be expected that there is a major change in the ministry of Messiah from that day forward. Any sin may be forgiven in God's mercy, but *blaspheming the Ruach HaKodesh* (Holy Spirit) *will not be forgiven.* Even sins *against the Son of Man* can be forgiven but whoever keeps on speaking against the *Ruach HaKodesh* will never be forgiven.

Many modern-day interpreters have put forth erroneous interpretations about this strong passage. As usual, the context is vital to its understanding. Yeshua is speaking in context of the rabbinic group rejection of his messianic claims. What the *Ruach HaKodesh* is trying to persuade, some people have rejected and, worse, attributed the work of the *Ruach* to *Ba'al!*

Our human nature and choices lead us to all sorts of sin, that is, falling short of God's holy path for us. What a blessing that our God, the God of Israel, is gracious and compassionate. Any sin can be cleansed if we have a spirit of repentance and turn from our hurtful behavior (cf. *I Yochanan*/John 1:9).

Yet, what hope is there for those who reject the testimony and conviction of the Holy Spirit in our lives? We are, in a real sense, rejecting God's only way of forgiveness and restoration. In the immediate context, these statements are a response to the national rejection of Yeshua by the first-century rabbinic leadership. Because of this official response, certain judgments would come upon that generation. While several of these judgments are unique to that time, there is certainly a personal application even for us. Likewise, for our situation, the same gracious God can forgive any repented sin. Yet, what hope is there for *olam hazeh* or *olam haba* (for this life or the world to come) if we too reject what the Holy Spirit is trying to tell us about Yeshua? If we personally reject or blaspheme the power of the *Ruach* today, we are likewise in personal danger of the judgment to come. We have also rejected the only way of receiving God's mercy and forgiveness through Yeshua the Messiah.

When all is said and done, *a tree is known by its fruit.* The words of the *P'rushim* (and even our words) are true indicators of the condition of the heart. *A good person brings forth good things from his store of good* and the opposite is likewise true. The ultimate test of this will be on the Day of Judgment when *people will have to give account for every careless word.* While this is true to a real degree in our daily lives, the context of Matthew 12 is again vitally important. Primarily, Yeshua is emphasizing the importance of our words in regard to the Holy Spirit's teaching concerning the person of Messiah. Is Yeshua the King Messiah sent from the Father or is he a false teacher representing the kingdom of Satan? It is by our words regarding this work of the *Ruach* that we will either be *acquitted or condemned.* Many in our day say that Yeshua is not our Messiah. What do you say? A fresh, historical understanding of the life of Yeshua from a Jewish perspective can help us see that he is King Messiah for our people Israel as well as for all the nations. May our words and actions testify that we believe he is our personal *Mashiach.*

The Ultimate Sign of Messiah   12:38-50

It is somewhat surprising, after such a clear rejection of Yeshua by some of the rabbis, that they would continue the discussion at this point. Yet they press on with a request *to see a miraculous sign* preformed by this self-proclaimed Messiah. Yeshua's response is strong and unambiguous. It is *a wicked and adulterous generation* that would ask for such a sign at this point of time. They are deemed wicked because of their false judgment concerning Yeshua. They are likewise called adulterous, much like previous generations of Israel who had been spiritually unfaithful to the covenant promises of God (cf. Jeremiah 3:1-5).

To such a rebellious group, Yeshua pronounces that there will be only one remaining sign, *the sign of Yonah*. All of the crowd would be well familiar with the story of *Yonah*/Jonah. It is a famous account about the reluctant prophet of Israel called to preach repentance to the evil kingdom of Nineveh. So important is this scroll that it is read every year in synagogue at the afternoon service of Yom Kippur, the most holy day of the calendar. Its theme of repentance resonates fully with this spiritually attuned time.

Many have debated what this sign of Yonah might be. Was it the fact that Yonah was swallowed by a great fish and, as it were, buried in the sea? Was it the timeframe of *three days and three nights* that is quoted by Yeshua? A close reading of Yonah in the Hebrew text seems to indicate that the prophet did not spend the three days biding his time in the belly of the fish.

Indeed, Yonah uses the language of physical death and *Sheol* (the place of the dead) to describe his experience (cf. Yonah 2). In other words, the sign of Yonah is not so much connected to the timeframe as it is to the experience of death and resurrection which Yonah himself tasted. So what is to be made of the three days and three nights? It should be pointed out that Yeshua seems to be simply quoting from the Book of Yonah (1:17) to highlight the death and resurrection experience of the prophet. Yeshua will also experience a death and resurrection as exemplified by Yonah. True, there is an interesting parallel to Yonah's three days and Yeshua's time in the belly of the earth—thus his direct quotation. However, every other time Yeshua talks of his resurrection, he uses the phrase "on the third day," not a complete three days and three nights (cf. Matt. 16:21; 17:23; 20:19; 27:64, etc.). It seems Yeshua is applying this text in a classic rabbinic parallelism and not to a wooden fulfillment of the specific details.

As we shall see in the later section of the gospel account, it seems best to accept a Friday afternoon death of Yeshua (14 *Nisan*/day 1), in the tomb all of *Shabbat*/Friday sundown to Saturday sundown (15 *Nisan*/day 2) and his resurrection before sunrise on that Sunday morning (16 *Nisan*/day 3). While it is impossible to reconcile a complete three day/three night burial with this chronology, it perfectly fits the description of his resurrection "on the third day" according to Jewish reckoning. The quote from Yonah is, therefore, not meant to lock in a detailed timeframe but it is meant to illustrate the final sign of Messiah to Israel, namely, the resurrection from the dead. For those in unbelief and denial of Yeshua's messianic claims, the final sign will come in Jerusalem on the third day of Passover. Until then, much of his public ministry will now be tempered by this official rejection of many of the rabbinic leaders of his day.

The parallelism does not stop at the sign of resurrection. Yeshua goes on to say that, just as Yonah must have been a miraculous sign to the Ninevites, so too will the resurrection of the Messiah be to all Israel. In fact, the people of Ninveh will stand up at the Judgment with this generation and condemn it. That previous generation responded in repentance to the sign and message of Yonah. How much more will the judgment be to those who ignore the one who is greater than Yonah. Another biblical parallel is mentioned in the Queen of the South. This is a reference to the famous Queen of Ethiopia (Sheba/

Seva) who came to inquire of Solomon's wisdom (cf. I Kings 10). So too, Yeshua teaches, one greater than Shlomo is here now. Why the two different biblical illustrations? The common denominator is that both events tell of Gentiles who responded favorably to the spiritual light of God. By implication, this generation of Israel is even more culpable. Nineveh and Sheba had the prophetic message of God presented to them and they both repented. How tragic that many in first-century Israel rejected not just a prophet but an even greater light, Messiah in their midst. That generation of Israel had gotten to a point where they did not need more signs but needed to respond to the light they were given.

The closing words of the chapter further describe the consequences of the decision concerning the person of Yeshua of Nazareth. The discussion about an unclean spirit aptly describes some of the spiritual dynamics involved in a person's life. There are many spiritual forces and powers with which we must engage. It is either the Ruach/Spirit of God or some of the many evil spirits from the dark side (cf. Ephesians 6:12). Even for those people who think they can get their own house in order, there is imminent danger from other spiritual oppressions if the right course of action is not taken.

The context of the statements seems to refer to some of the leaders who placed confidence in their own religious observance to put them in right relationship with God. They cleaned out some undesirable spirits no doubt, yet because they had not given a proper place to the Messiah, they would be worse off than they were before. This would be one of the resulting judgments for this wicked generation. The warning is relevant in our day as well. Many are attempting to clean up their lives with all sorts of man-made solutions and self-help philosophies. Yet without the transforming work of the Spirit of God, there is the danger of an even worse fate.

As Yeshua was still speaking to the crowd, *his mother and brothers appeared outside.* Evidently seeing a final opportunity to teach the group, Yeshua responded to their appeal with the questions: "Who is my mother? Who are my brothers?" This was not, of course, meant as disrespect toward his family members. As the sinless Messiah, he certainly fulfilled the command to honor his father and mother. However there was a greater spiritual picture to be seen in this moment. His *talmidim*/disciples were his family in a greater sense. *Whoever does what my Father in heaven wants*, this is the person who is intimately related to the Messiah. Physical family is always to be honored, but there is an even higher relationship in the Kingdom of God—not by blood but by the *Ruach*/Spirit, which ties us to the Heavenly Father. Will it be the Kingdom of God with King Messiah or our own shortsighted way?

The Mysteries of the Kingdom   13:1-52

Chapter 13 of Matthew's account marks a major transition in his biography of the life of Yeshua. The earlier events had shown the clear messianic claims and works of the prophet from Galilee. Many within Israel had become convinced that this One most assuredly was the *Mashiach* promised in the Scriptures.

However, for various reasons, there was also increasing opposition to this popular Messiah figure. Many in the rabbinic establishment had reached the conclusion that Yeshua was in fact a false messiah and a deceiver. With the accusation of being identified with *Ba'al* and satanic power, many of the leaders went on record to officially reject Yeshua as the King Messiah sent from God.

After the subsequent pronouncement of judgment upon that group, Yeshua now makes a major shift in his ministry strategy. It is at this point in Matthew's account that the teaching of Messiah takes on a new focus in response to this official rejection by some of the key leaders of Israel. The recurrent theme now will be on the mysteries of the Kingdom of God and the implications upon both believer and non-believer in Yeshua.

The Purpose of Parables   13:1-3

Yeshua starts a new trajectory of his teaching after the rejection described in the previous chapter. It is *on that day* that he departed from *the house* where many of these events took place. The crowds of people followed their teacher to a new venue at a beach in the Galilee. So large was the multitude that Yeshua got *into a boat* in order to better address the crowds who remained on the beach. His teaching reflected a new approach and focus as he spoke *in parables*.

We should not think that just because there is a new focus in Yeshua's teaching that the use of parables was an entirely new format. Many rabbis of the Talmudic age (200 BCE-500 CE) made common use of this mode of teaching. It was said of Rabbi Meir, for example, that his public discourses consisted of "a third *Halakhah* (precepts), a third *Haggadah* (stories) and a third parables (comparisons)" (Tractate Sanhedrin 38b).

Add to this the fact that a significant scroll of the Bible is called *Mishley*/Proverbs, which is actually the Hebrew root for the word parables. The Hebrew *mashal* has a rather wide range of meanings from similarity to a proverb, or even a fictional story. The common connection is that a *mashal* is used to teach an unknown reality by making a comparison with a known truth. The Greek equivalent term for parable comes from two distinct terms—*para*/alongside and *bole*/to cast. A parable is a comparison or placing alongside of similar entities.

Unlike allegories, a parable is usually focused on one significant truth. Therefore, considering a parable, one should not get too distracted by the fine details but rather look for the supreme lesson of the teaching. In the case of Yeshua, it is clear that he focuses on the use of parables at this point of his ministry to illustrate some of the mysteries of the Kingdom of God. By using familiar comparisons to nature and everyday life in first-century Israel, the hearers would be able to better understand this largely unknown part of God's universe. As we shall see, there are actually two larger purposes in Yeshua's parables. The first is to reveal truth to spiritual seekers. The second, however, is to actually conceal some truth from those who have rejected earlier light. In this sense, Yeshua's shift to the major use of parabolic teaching is both a blessing and a judgment.

In the context of Matthew 12, the lines are being more clearly defined between those who are sincerely seeking God's way and those who have rejected the earlier revelation. While Yeshua did make use of some simple parables in his earlier ministry (cf. 7:24-27), there is clearly a shift in emphasis from this point forward that is directly tied to the response of his messianic claims. In this transitional chapter, Matthew includes seven parables of Yeshua that illustrate various mysteries of his Kingdom.

The Parable of the Soils   13:3-23

The initial parable of Yeshua revolves around a familiar picture in the ancient Middle East, *a sower went out to sow.* This of course is a word-picture of a farmer planting seed in order to raise a future crop. While it might be tempting to focus on the sower or even the seed, the greater detail is actually given to the various kinds of soils that receive the planted seed. In each case the sower and the seed remain the same. It is the variation of the ground condition that dictates the differences in the harvest. The *Talmud* speaks a parallel story as it describes four kinds of disciples: "There are four qualities among those that sit before the Sages: they are like a sponge, a funnel, a strainer, and a sieve: a sponge, which sucks up everything; a funnel, which lets in at one end and out at the other; a strainer which lets the wine pass out and retains the lees; a sieve, which lets out the bran and retains the fine flour" (Pirke Avot 5.18).

In his initial presentation (v. 3b-9), Yeshua gives the basic story. Later he fills in some of the details with his explanation (v. 18-23). The first type of soil is *beside the road.* This would obviously be very hard ground that had not even been properly cultivated. Although the good seed fell on this part of the property, any farmer could predict the results. In Yeshua's description, *the birds came and ate them up.* Since the ground was so hard, it could not even receive the seed and it merely laid on the surface.

In his later explanation, Messiah equates the birds with the *evil one* who *snatches away* any potential for good. Satan is certainly stealing the good seed from many people whose hearts are hardened. The second type is *the rocky places where they did not have much soil.* This type of ground would have received at least some initial preparation and, consequently, the seed *immediately sprang up.* In fact, the seed seems to spring up quickly because there was *no depth of soil.* However because of its shallow root system, the seed was *scorched and withered away.* According to Yeshua's explanation, this soil condition reflects a man who *immediately receives* the word *with joy* yet does not have *root in himself.* Since his spiritual soil is so shallow, *when affliction or persecution arises, he falls away.* How many times has it happened even in our day that a person makes an enthusiastic confession of their faith in Messiah, only to turn away from that faith when a serious challenge comes?

The third type of soil is described as full of *thorns.* The ground evidently was properly cultivated and ideal for some growth. Unfortunately, it was also conducive to the growth of harmful weeds that *choked out* the life of any good plant. According to Yeshua, this illustrates a person who *hears the word* and yet *the worry of the world* chokes out that same word. To this he adds the hindrance of the *deceitfulness of riches* as a main thorny problem. Even though the good seed starts to grow, it *becomes unfruitful.* How tragic it is today that there are many people in this situation. They have received the seed of Messiah's life on some level yet many fail to bear any fruit as they get sidetracked by the cares of the physical world. The final type of soil is simply described as *good that yielded* a bountiful crop.

This is indicative of a true, committed follower of Yeshua as the Messiah. The soil of his life is prepared and receptive to the seed of Messiah. To prove that his spirit consists of healthy soil, a large harvest results. It is informative to note that there are various degrees of fruitfulness described for the true believer, *some a hundredfold, some sixty, and some thirty.*

The clear picture here is that of healthy soil prepared in the right way that naturally bears plenty of good fruit. Yeshua notes that this person is one who not only *hears the word* but also *understands,* meaning he applies the spiritual truth to his life in a practical way in order to bear real fruit. Certainly the mark of a true follower of Yeshua today is still the good fruit of his Holy Spirit in our lives (cf. Galatians 5:22-23). The crowd certainly could see some of the implications for their own lives as they heard this *mashal* of the Messiah. Likewise, today we would be wise to consider the various kinds of soils and to cultivate in our own life the type of soil that will bear blessings both in this age and in the age to come.

There is a further explanation between the initial teaching of Yeshua and his elaborations on the parable. In this parenthetical section (v. 10-17) the Messiah explains some of the reasons for his new emphasis on parabolic teaching. This explanation is in response to the disciple's inquiry, "Why do you speak to them in parables?" To this Yeshua responds that certain *mysteries of the kingdom* have been given to them while to others it is not given.

In fact, the one who has been open to receive some of God's knowledge *shall be given more.* In contrast, *whoever does not have, even what he has shall be taken away from him.* In this sense, Yeshua's use of parables at this point in his ministry is both a blessing and a judgment. It is a blessing of increased understanding for those who are seeking the truth of God's kingdom while, at the same time, it is a judgment of obscurity upon those who really do not want to know the full truth.

To substantiate this point, Yeshua quotes from the prophet Isaiah (6:9-10) as a precedent. In his day, Isaiah brought the message of God to a people who largely did not want to receive it. They were *hearing but did not understand.* Their *hearts had become dull.* As a consequence, many in that generation were afflicted with a judgment of further spiritual blindness. In the same way, Yeshua says he is bringing the revelation of the God of Israel to his generation. By not receiving his message, those in first-century Israel were in danger of a similar judgment.

Fortunately, there were also many in Israel who welcomed the message of the prophets and even the *Mashiach.* It is to that faithful remnant of seekers that Yeshua says *blessed are your eyes because they see.* Indeed, *many prophets and righteous men* of past generations would have been blessed *to see* what they are now seeing and *to hear* what they are now hearing. The reality is that there have always been those on both sides of the fence with God. Even among the people of Israel, there are those who want to draw close to the Heavenly Father and there are those who prefer to go their own way. On what side of the fence do you find yourself today?

The Parable of the Tares   13:24-30

Yeshua presented his next parable in which a comparison is made between *the Kingdom of Heaven* and *a man who sowed good seed in his field.* Some commentators try to make a technical distinction between the Kingdom of God and the Kingdom of Heaven. The former is sometimes portrayed as God's rule upon Earth while the latter is his reign in eternity. However, there is no reason to draw such a distinction if one knows Jewish theology on this topic.

There is simply one Kingdom of God, which stretches for eternity in every realm. Matthew, in characteristic Jewish fashion, makes a common substitution of the word heaven (*shamayim*) for the name of God. In respect to the fifth commandment (not taking God's name in vain), the name of God is never fully pronounced or written in traditional Jewish circles. Some modern substitute terms still include *ADONAI*/Lord and *HaShem*/The Name. Of course, *shamayim* is an apt word as it describes the One who dwells throughout the heavens.

This parable presents a variation on the theme of a farmer planting seed. Not surprisingly the sower would plant good seed in anticipation of a useful harvest. *But while men were sleeping, his enemy came and sowed tares among the wheat.* This is usually interpreted as a weed called *darnel* that actually resembles real wheat at first. However, as the crop matures, it becomes readily apparent that the darnel are actually weeds that are intermingled with the pure wheat.

The *Talmud* graphically describes this weed as "degenerate wheat seeds" (Tractate Kilaim 1*)*. As the present crop matured, *the tares became evident.* The obvious problem is that although the darnel would look like wheat, its fruit is worthless. Not only that, but the weeds would stifle the healthy growth of any true wheat.

Yeshua's spiritual analogy can be clearly seen. As his kingdom grows both among Jews and Gentiles, there will be false believers intermingled with the true believers. The community of the Yeshua movement, in other words, would not be a monolithic, pure entity but it would be plagued with some internal corruption by pseudo-disciples who even appear very close to the real thing.

The parable addresses an important question concerning this mixed crop: *How then does it have tares?* The saboteur is identified as *an enemy.* In the context of the parable, there certainly could be many enemies of the Kingdom of Heaven. Undoubtedly, the best candidate for the enemy of the sower would be none other than Satan himself. Since Day One of God's redemptive plan, Satan has been the adversary directly opposing all that God seeks to establish. He has unfortunately done his best at spreading evil throughout human history.

It is a sobering thought brought out in this parable that the evil one would create some of his worst turmoil in the community of Yeshua. Religious history is filled with accounts of non-believers and even pagans infiltrating the true Body of Messiah and wreaking havoc. Too often this has been perplexing to many Jews as we try to understand the existence of "Christian anti-Semitism."

A great wound and barrier has separated Jews from Yeshua because of inquisitions, crusades, and a Holocaust. In fact, it could be said that one of Satan's greatest tools has been in fact "religion." The wheat has been sown with tares and the resultant confusion is conspicuous in religious history. It continues in contemporary congregations where there is surely a mixture of true believers in Messiah mixed in with those who appear similar but do not bear real fruit.

The parable culminates with another natural question from the workers as they inquire if the owner would like them to *gather them up*. In a somewhat surprising answer, they are told not to disturb the tares for now as that would also *root up the wheat with them*. It is not until *the time of the harvest* that the separation will take place. At that future time, the tares will be gathered up in bundles and burnt because they are useless.

In contrast, the last-day reapers are told to *gather the wheat* into the owner's barn. The main point of the parable is clear. The Kingdom of Heaven will develop despite the infiltration of false religiosity. Messiah's community of true believers will continue to accomplish its called purpose. Yet, much of the confusion and evil of the world will not be removed until that final day of judgment. We would do well to ask ourselves, do we only have the appearance of a Messianic believer or are we bringing forth fruit consistent with that of a true disciple of *Yeshua HaMashiach*?

The Parable of the Mustard Seed   13:31-32

Another illustration of the *Kingdom of Heaven* is presented which related well to the everyday life experience of the Galilean crowd. In this case, Yeshua compares the kingdom to *a mustard seed*. While this particular seed is not necessarily the absolute smallest in nature, it was known as a rabbinic expression for the smallest amount possible (Tractate Berakhot 31a). Despite its small size, it is said to grow *larger than the garden plants and becomes a tree.*

Evidently, the kingdom of Messiah will have humble beginnings. It was not so impressive that a rabbi from the Galil called twelve Jewish men to be part of his religious movement. This was a small beginning even within the Jewish world. Add to that the fact that it was a rather obscure branch from a group of people (the Jews) who comprise less than one-tenth of one percent of the world's population. Yet from this tiny start would come a faith movement that would grow into a most sizable community. Yeshua quotes from the Book of Daniel to note that this tree will be large enough so that *the birds of the air come and nest in its branches* (cf. 4:12).

In the context of this verse, the birds seem to apply to the Gentile nations of the Earth. As the kingdom of Nebuchadnezzer encompassed the entire ancient world, so too will the eventual expansion of the kingdom of Yeshua encompass the world today. What starts with twelve Jewish followers will expand throughout Israel and the Nations. By the end of the present age, that kingdom will include a strong remnant of believers from all the people groups of the Gentiles (cf. Matthew 28:19-20) as well as entire nation of Israel.

This is not to be confused with universalism (all Jews from every age will be saved) but that in that last day every Jew will call on the name of Yeshua for salvation. With the prayer *Barukh habah b'shem Adonai* (Blessed is He who comes in the Name of the Lord), God will pour out his Spirit upon Israel and the Kingdom of God will come in its fullness (cf. Matthew 23:37-39). In that day, the small seed will reach its ultimate growth into an impressive tree including followers of Yeshua from every nation. How amazing that, despite its setbacks, we can now witness the growth of the Yeshua movement to virtually every corner of the earth including modern Israel. May the day come soon when all our people will welcome Yeshua back to Jerusalem as King Messiah!

The Parable of the Leaven   13:33-35

Once again, Yeshua uses a parabolic teaching to illustrate the expansion of the kingdom. In this case, the kingdom growth is compared to *leaven which a woman took and hid in three pecks of meal.* Leaven is used in many contexts in the Bible and in the *Talmud* as a symbol of evil. One of the major holy days of the calendar (*Pesach*/Passover) requires the removal of all leaven from one's dwelling place (cf. Exodus 12:18-20). The word for leaven (*chametz*) means sour, which is an apt description for the effects of yeast and its frequent association with sin. However, this is not always the case, as we also find in the *Torah* that *chametz* is actually part of the required sacrifices and Bread of the Presence used in the Temple (cf. Leviticus 7:13; 23:17-18).

Even today there is a practice where a person baking the *Shabbat* challah bread takes a portion of the dough and throws it in the oven. We are told this is to remind us of the ancient sacrifices. The context of this parable instructs us that *chametz* can also be used to teach a positive truth. The growth of the kingdom is like the leaven that permeates the dough and causes it to expand. In fact, the leaven will saturate the dough to such an extent that eventually it is *all leavened.* So despite the fact that only a little part of the dough is initially leavened, it is the *chametz* that will surely overtake the bread. By definition, *chametz* (a growing bacteria) will take over any dough if given enough time. Therefore, this parable is an encouraging description of the future of the Kingdom of God. Once again, it may at first be unimpressive in its meager beginnings, but the kingdom is destined to permeate the entire earth by the end of the age.

Verse 34 highlights the prophetic reason for the Messiah's use of parables in his teaching. Matthew sees a connection between the Psalmist and the present ministry of Yeshua. The ancient writer Asaph is quoted as saying "I will open my mouth in parables (*mashalim*)" in order to teach some of the hidden truths of God's kingdom. Asaph used his gifting to show how the history of Israel was intertwined with the prophetic Kingdom of God (Psalm 78). So too, Yeshua was teaching in his day concerning Israel's relationship to the covenants and the kingdom. Consequently, the shift in Yeshua's teaching method was also a fulfillment of prophecy and another messianic sign for first-century Israel.

The Explanation of the Tares   13:36-43

As he leaves the multitude, Yeshua is asked by the disciples to further explain the meaning of his earlier *parable of the tares*. The sower of the good seed is identified as *the Son of Man*. This is one of Yeshua's favorite titles to apply to his own life and ministry. In one sense, it is a common Hebrew term that emphasizes the humanity of a person (cf. Ezekiel 3:1, 4). Indeed, Yeshua was born as a Jew, fully human in his flesh. However, the term *Ben Adam* is also used as a term to describe the divine Messiah. Daniel sees in his vision "One like a Son of Man coming with the clouds of heaven" (7:13). The Talmudic rabbis understood that this was a reference to the unique revelation of the *Mashiach*. He was to be no ordinary person but some kind of superman coming with the clouds. In an amazing statement, the rabbis state that if Israel is worthy of the messianic redemption in the last days, the *Mashiach* will come in the clouds. If we are not worthy, he will come upon a donkey (Tractate Sanhedrin 98a; Zechariah 9:9). Either way, Yeshua's use of the term *Ben Adam* was one more way to affirm his messianic qualifications.

In this parable, it is he as the Messiah who is planting the good seed of the kingdom. In fact, the *good seeds* are specified as *the sons of the kingdom*. The Messiah is planting his kingdom in *the field*, which is *the world*, through the work of his sons. *The tares are the sons of the evil one.* The enemy is identified as *the devil*. There is a constant battle occurring between the sons of light and the sons of darkness. It is not until the end of the age that the harvest will take place. At that time, God will send for his *angels* as *reapers* to sort out the true harvest from the false. All those who *commit lawlessness* (i.e. Breaking *Torah*) and are *stumbling blocks* to God's plan will be cast into a *furnace of fire*. So intense will be the judgment of *Gei-Hinnom* that there will be *weeping and gnashing of teeth*.

The last verse of this paragraph emphasizes the contrast of the sons of the kingdom to those of the world. Once again quoting the prophetic book of the *Tanakh*, Yeshua affirms that *the righteous will shine forth as the sun* in that glorious day of the kingdom (cf. Daniel 12:3). So solemn are these truths that Yeshua exhorts those who have ears—*let him hear*. We are thus reminded in our day to give heed to the words of our Messiah. He is calling all people, Jews and Gentiles, to be part of his eternal kingdom. We have the blessed opportunity to be his good seeds sown into the world around us. Are we fulfilling our calling to be a significant part of Messiah's kingdom? Are we sowing the good seed of Yeshua's abundant life into the lives of those around us?

Three Short Parables   13:44-52

Now Yeshua shifts away from the farming parables to comparisons to other walks of life. First is a parable of a *treasure hidden in the field*. In ancient days, before the age of banks and security boxes, it was not uncommon for a person to hide or bury their valuables. Not surprisingly, several tractates of the *Talmud* deal with legal decisions of such cases when someone else's valuables are found (cf. Tractates Bava Kama, Bava Metzia). We are not told here but somehow this treasure was left buried, perhaps by death of the owner. In many such cases, the Jewish legal code essentially went by the principle of "finders keepers" if the find was made on public property.

However, the question is obviously more obscure in the case of this parable where the treasure is evidently found on private property. After finding the treasure, the man *hid* it once again and proceeded to purchase the property. The treasure is so valuable that the man is said to even sell *all that he has* in order to legally acquire these riches. The point of the parable is that the Kingdom of God is so valuable that it is well worth whatever the earthly price. The man had so *much joy over it* that he immediately restructured his priorities. May those of us who are Messianic believers today keep a clear focus on the great value of God's kingdom.

The next parable speaks about *a merchant seeking fine pearls.* Similarly to the man who found the treasure, this merchant finds one particular *pearl of great value.* Although he was in the jewelry business, he is amazed at the discovery of such a beautiful specimen. He, too, sells *all that he has* to acquire the valuable pearl. Once again, Yeshua emphasizes the immense importance of his kingdom. Perhaps the difference between these two parables is that the first man may have been poor before his find while the man in this case was a wealthy businessman. In either case, are we willing to pay the price and to even sacrifice some of our priorities in order to gain such a valuable asset?

The final parable turns its attention to the well-known trade of fishermen. The kingdom is said to be similar to a *dragnet cast into the sea.* This type of fishing got its name from the technique where a net was secured to the shore while a boat literally dragged the net over the waters. By so doing, they would ensure a productive way of bringing in a good catch. It is noted here that their catch included *fish of every kind.* This is a point of distinction between the previous two parables. In those stories, the person goes to great extremes to acquire one important object while here there is a catch of many, including both good and bad fish. The *good fish* are stored in *containers* while the *bad fish* they simply *threw away*.

In the original understanding, what would be the distinction between the two kinds of fish? Most certainly the dietary laws (*kashrut*) would be the deciding factor for the Jewish fishermen. Those that were acceptable would have the requisite fins and scales (cf. Leviticus 11:9-12) while all others would be useless for food. There are examples of both categories in the Sea of Galilee. Once again, Yeshua draws a parallel to the judgment *at the end of the age*. As with the earlier teaching of the wheat and tares, so too the *kosher and trief* (unkosher) fish will be separated for different fates. *The angels will come forth and take out the wicked from among the righteous.* The former will be delivered *into the furnace of fire* and the latter to the blessings of God's kingdom.

At the conclusion of his parabolic teaching, Yeshua asks his disciples an important question: "Have you understood all these things?" No doubt the disciples felt they had received some important new lessons on the Kingdom of God. Despite their affirmative answer one may wonder, based on their later actions, if they were truly accurate. Yeshua makes a final application to the disciples by alluding to the job of a *Torah-teacher who has been made into a talmid/ disciple.* The word used for *Torah*-teacher describes a particular kind of teacher known as a scribe (*sofer*). The *soferim* were a vitally important group of rabbis of first-century Judaism as they were the ones trained to meticulously make copies of the *Torah* and other holy writings. In so doing, they would naturally become experts in both the content and interpretation of the written *Torah*.

With this statement, Yeshua once again emphasizes a rather surprising element of his kingdom. It is the great *Torah*-teacher who humbly becomes a student who will inherit the messianic riches. Likened to a homeowner, this *talmid* will bring forth both *new things and old* from his storage room. As Matthew has highlighted before, Yeshua is the fulfillment of all the messianic promises given to Israel (things old) but with the beautiful, final piece of the puzzle in King Messiah himself (things new). When properly understood in this context, Yeshua came to complete the full revelation of the God of Israel. A Jewish understanding of Yeshua should help us appreciate the old riches found in the *Torah* and Prophets and supplement them with the greatest gift of all, the revelation of Messiah within the New Covenant.

At this time, Yeshua is said to have returned to his hometown of Nazareth. As a longtime member of the local synagogue, he once again was found teaching in such a way that *astounded them.* It was both his *wisdom* (teaching solely on his own authority) as well as his *miracles* that impressed the local crowds. Yet, his ministry raised numerous questions at this time. Where did he get these powers? Is he not from a local family of humble origins? Haven't we grown up knowing his father, *mother, brothers and sisters?*

It should be noted here that Yosef and Miryam indeed had later children after the virgin birth of Yeshua. They were, in many ways, a normal Jewish family of first-century Galilee. But it was because of this very fact that many of the townspeople *took offense at him.* Familiarity can breed contempt especially when one of their local citizens was claiming to be the divine *Mashiach!*

Yeshua summarizes the situation with an apt principle—*people don't respect a prophet in his home town.* Unfortunately, the town of Nazareth would subsequently see very few miracles because of their unjustified skepticism. It makes one wonder how often the same lack of faith keeps people from seeing the work of Yeshua in their midst? Is it God's fault or a simple reaction to our own skepticism? The prophet Yirmeyahu said it well: "When you seek Me, you will find Me, provided you seek Me wholeheartedly" (Jeremiah 29:13). The offer still stands today for the sincere seeker.

The Might of the King   14:1-16:12

Matthew now proceeds to record some of the works of King Messiah in the midst of his people. The polarity of views will increase between those who affirm Yeshua and those who reject him. His teaching will become more focused and there are still some dramatic signs for those who are openly seeking. However, the emotions and opinions of the first-century community will become intensified as Yeshua's ministry continues in the midst of Israel.

The Death of Yochanan the Immerser   14:1-14

Matthew's biography of the Messiah now turns its attention once again to the political environment of the day. Upon the death of Herod the Great (in approximately 4 BCE), the kingdom was divided among three of his political partners: Archelaus, Herod Philip, and Herod Antipas. It is the latter Herod who is mentioned here as the *regional governor* over Galilee, which was the territory where most of Yeshua's ministry took place.

As he reflected on the reports of miracles surrounding the work of Yeshua, an interesting thought came to Herod's mind. *This must be Yochanan the Immerser*, the one Herod himself had earlier executed. Matthew now gives a quick overview of the events that led to the death of this Jewish prophet. Evidently Herod imprisoned Yochanan in response to some of the elements of his teaching ministry. Specifically, Yochanan had confronted Herod about his current marriage to Herodias (the former *wife of his brother Philip*) which he pointed out *violated the Torah* (*Vayikra*/Leviticus 18:16; 20:21).

The family of Herod was indeed one of the great enigmas of first-century Israel. Because of the family's earlier conversion to Judaism from *Idumea*/Edom, they were considered technically connected to the Jewish people. But they were appointed by the Roman powers because of their allegiance to the Gentile occupiers of Judea. Since the Herods acted more pagan than Jewish (cf. the slaying of the Jewish babies in Matthew 2), there was little respect for them in the broader community.

Yet it should be noted that it was the family of Herod who also coordinated the renovation of the Second Temple in Jerusalem. All that being said, one would hope the family of Herod would have some conviction when it came to the teachings of *Torah*.

Hence, Yochanan confronts Herod Antipas about his immoral relationship with his brother's former wife. Herod, true to his family tradition, did not welcome the words of Yochanan but instead had him imprisoned, wanting to put him *to death*. Matthew informs us that Herod held back from his plans of execution largely because *he was afraid of the people* who greatly revered Yochanan as a prophet.

The stalemate changed at Herod's birthday celebration. This in itself is another indicator of Herod's Hellenistic/pagan values, as birthday celebrations are virtually unknown in ancient Jewish tradition. When *Herodias' daughter danced before the company* of people, Herod promised to give her *whatever she asked*. It is noteworthy that it was in fact her mother who sent the request for the *head of Yochanan*.

There is an irony in that Herod was said to become *deeply upset* at this request; yet, out of respect for fulfilling an oath, *he ordered that her wish be granted*. The execution was promptly meted out and Yochanan's disciples gave the body a proper Jewish burial. Upon hearing this sad news, Yeshua *left in a boat to be by himself in the wilderness*.

No doubt Yeshua was reflecting on the great loss as well as the faithful service of this prophet who prepared the way for his own messianic ministry. The quiet time did not last long, as many *people followed him from the towns by land*. In the true spirit of the *Mashiach*, Yeshua had compassion on the huge crowd and *healed those who were sick*.

Feeding the Five Thousand   14:15-21

It is at this point that a practical problem confronted the *talmidim*. It was becoming clear to them that they needed to disband the crowd as it was *a remote place* and it was *getting late*. Their recommendation was to *send the crowds away* so that they could *buy food for themselves in the villages*. To this proposal Yeshua makes his own surprising suggestion that the disciples themselves give the crowd *something to eat*. Incredulous, the disciples noted to their rabbi that they have merely *five loaves of bread and two fish* among their resources.

This was not going to be a problem according to Yeshua. After all, Jewish experience is filled with examples of God supernaturally providing for his people. It is reminiscent of the wilderness wanderings of earlier generations, which God fed with the manna from heaven. If Yeshua is indeed the true Messiah sent from the Father, there is a solution to be found. What looks impossible with man's resources becomes very possible if God is in the picture—an important reminder to modern believers, no doubt! Yeshua requests that the loaves and fish be brought to him while the disciples had the crowds seated on the grass. The actual word for "seated" is also translated "reclined" which is the traditional position of free people (non-slaves) relaxing at a banquet. It would seem that every detail of this impromptu banquet was orchestrated by Messiah to illustrate spiritual truth to his followers.

In traditional fashion, he took the five loaves and two fish and *made a b'rakhah*/blessing. Since this was a blessing over bread (symbolic of the main course of a meal), Yeshua no doubt chanted the Motzi: "*Barukh atah ADONAI, Eloheynu melech ha-olam, ha-motzi lechem min ha-aretz* / Blessed art Thou, O Lord our God, King of the universe, who brings forth bread from the earth." In the *Talmud* it is stated, "A man is forbidden to taste anything before saying a blessing over it" (Tractate Berachot 35a). The rabbis specify that the above blessing is designated whenever bread is at a meal (Tractate Berachot 6:1).

It should be noted that the prayer over meals is not to bless the food per se. The food is what it is, either kosher or non-kosher, etc. But the prayer is to bless God who has provided the meal. Matthew also notes the detail that during this *b'rakhah*, Yeshua was *looking up toward heaven*. It is interesting to acknowledge some distinctions between the mode of Christian prayer and that of Jewish prayer. While Christian tradition often calls for closing the eyes and bowing one's head, the Jewish tradition usually calls for eyes open and looking up. There are exceptions, of course, as sometimes Jews close or cover their eyes to remove outside distractions, as is often the case when chanting the *Sh'ma* (Deuteronomy 6:4) during prayer.

The Jewish context of this situation is further highlighted by Matthew as he observes that Yeshua then *broke the loaves* to distribute the bread to his *talmidim*. It is interesting to note that this is a very traditional way of sharing the bread, tearing the bread by hand rather than cutting it with a knife. Although the latter implement is allowed, there has been a longstanding custom of refraining from using a knife or other utensil, as a symbol of the day when there will no longer be nation lifting up sword against nation (cf. *Yeshayahu*/Isaiah 2:4). Hence, the common biblical and cultural phrase for this is "breaking bread/*betziat lechem*."

Curiously, some Christian traditions interpret the phrase solely as the breaking of bread to celebrate their communion service. However, the simple Jewish understanding of this phrase would mean sharing a meal together unless it was specified otherwise, as it is at the Last Passover. After distributing the bread and fish to his disciples, they in turn shared the food with the large crowd. Not only did everyone eat *as much as they wanted* but they also took up twelve baskets of leftovers. Matthew tabulates the astounding number of participants— *five thousand men, plus women and children!*

No doubt there were many spiritual lessons going on in this whole process. Besides the obvious miracle of food multiplication, one other important lesson stands out. Not coincidentally, it is the disciples (those who originally doubt that they have enough food) who are recruited to be the ones sharing the abundance with the crowds. If the *talmidim* had trouble believing such a feeding could take place, now they are part of the hands-on experience of the miracle. What a practical and unforgettable lesson in Yeshua's discipleship! If we look around us carefully, perhaps we can see a similar invitation to be active participants in Messiah's kingdom work.

Walking on the Water   14:22-36

After the massive and highly visible miracle of the feeding of the five thousand, Yeshua now turns his attention to his intimate group of disciples. In fact, it is *immediately* after the large group meal that Yeshua exhorts his *talmidim* to *get in the boat* in order to cross *to the other side* of the lake, Yam Kinneret, the Sea of Galilee. Yeshua himself is said to have retreated *into the hills* in order *to pray*. Even as *night came on*, he continued in this solo time between himself and his Heavenly Father.

Perhaps we should reflect more often on the reality of this statement. Yeshua, being clearly the Messiah, the Son of God, is also revealed as the Son of Man. In fact, the revelation of both his divine nature and humanity are often seen side-by-side as in this situation. At one point, he is multiplying the loaves by his messianic powers. Yet, immediately afterwards we find the same Messiah retreating to a solitary place for personal prayer and no doubt a physical break from the crowds. We would be wise to consider that if the *Mashiach* often had need for such a spiritual/physical break, are we in any less need?

Meanwhile, as the disciples are manning the boat *several miles from shore*, there develops a *rough sea and a strong headwind*. It is in the middle of the night (around *four o'clock in the morning*) that Yeshua comes to them *walking on the lake*. When the disciples saw this, Matthew reports that *they were terrified*. No doubt the storm conditions and limited visibility contributed to the fears of even these seasoned Galilean fishermen. "It's a ghost!" they *screamed with fear.* At this critical moment, Yeshua speaks to them, "stop being afraid." In hopes of quelling their fears, Messiah reassures them "it is I."

The modern Hebrew (*ani hu*) perhaps does not totally capture the force of the situation. In the Greek text, it is the phrase *ego eimi*/I am, which is used in Yochanan's gospel as a statement of Messiah's divine nature. In classical Hebrew it would be a form of the very name of God (*YHVH*), which is the imperfect Hebrew tense of the verb "to be." God is eternal and omnipotent, the great I AM. If Yeshua were attempting to assure his disciples that he had everything under control, this would indeed be the perfect phrase.

In response, *Kefa*/Peter comes up with an amazing sign of confirmation. If the hazy figure is really their Rabbi Yeshua, then they could ask for a miracle. Kefa is willing to express his faith if Yeshua will invite him *to come on the water* also. As the other disciples watched in awe, Kefa indeed *got out of the boat and walked on the water toward* Yeshua. What an astounding manifestation of the kingdom of Messiah! Matthew, one of the eyewitnesses, notes a dramatic change in the situation at this point. Using a word of contrast, the writer explains *but when* Kefa *saw the wind, he became afraid* again and even *began to sink* into the lake. Yelling for assistance, Kefa exclaims, "Lord! Save me!" True to his compassionate character, Yeshua *immediately stretched out his hand* to perform the emergency rescue. In the process, he gently reprimands Kefa (and the others) for doubting the Messiah by having *such little trust.* As if to confirm the Messiah's power again, Matthew observes that *the wind ceased* even as Yeshua and Kefa entered *into the boat.* Realizing the immensity of these events, the others in the boat *fell down before him and exclaimed, "You really are God's son!"* invoking a messianic term used in the *Tanakh* (cf. Psalm 2; Proverbs 30).

It is highly unfortunate, in my view, that Kefa and the other disciples sometimes are portrayed as bumbling, weak men who were constantly out of touch with Yeshua. True, they were mere men and women of their day with some of the natural challenges around them. But at least Kefa got out of the boat! This is especially praiseworthy when we reflect on the fact that the indwelling relationship of the Holy Spirit would not start until the future day of *Shavuot*/Pentecost. It is noteworthy that Kefa actually walked on the water until he took his eyes off Yeshua. Don't we also fall prey to similar temptations and distractions when we turn away from our simple trust in Messiah? Are we looking at the waves around us or at our Messiah who created the waves?

After the eventful crossing of the lake, the disciples and their rabbi *landed at Ginosar*. This would be along the northwest shore of the *Kinneret*/Sea of Galilee stretching from the town of Migdal nearly to K'far-Nachum. It is quite interesting to point out a modern discovery in this geographical area. In the 1980s a series of drought years left the lake at historically low levels. In the mud, at the shore of Kibbutz Nof Ginosar (coincidentally!), an ancient boat was discovered. It has been excavated and preserved at the modern kibbutz and dubbed the name "The Jesus Boat." If it is not the exact boat spoken of here, it certainly is a fine example of a first-century small boat that was used along the shores of Ginosar.

When the people of the ancient community of Ginosar recognized Yeshua, they sent word throughout the area and *brought him everyone who was ill*. So desperate were the people that they begged only to *touch the tzitzit on his robe*. As noted previously (Chapter 9), the *tzitzit* (fringe) on the outer garment of a Jew has long been symbolic of the covenant and commandments of God (cf. Numbers 15:37-41). In modern Judaism, many traditional Jews continue to wear the *arba kanefot*, the four cornered undergarment that contains the fringes. This is called a *tallit katan* (small prayer shawl) while the more popular version is the *tallit* (prayer shawl) worn by many Jewish men at morning synagogue services. The way in which the fringes are tied with double knots adds up to the numerical value of 613, which is the number of commandments in the *Torah*. It is especially noteworthy here that the word *kanefot* also translates as "shoulders or wings."

In this account by Matthew, we are reminded that Yeshua followed all the commandments of the *Torah* and looked very much like his *Torah*-observant, contemporaries. As a symbol of their faith in God, it was quite appropriate and very symbolic that the crowds sought to touch the outer fringe of his garment. By so doing, the multitude was affirming their belief in Yeshua as a teacher sent from God and indeed as the promised *Mashiach* according to his own testimony. Not surprisingly, *all who touched* the tzitzit *were completely healed.* Perhaps the crowds also understood this as a fulfillment of the promise from Malachi, "But to you who fear my name, the sun of righteousness will rise with healing in its wings/*kanaf*" (Mal'akhi 3:20; 4:2 English). Yeshua is the Lord who offers healing even today to those who reach out in faith to the fringe of his *tallit*.

Debate with Some of the Rabbis   15:1-20

After some of the dramatic ministry events around the Kinneret (Sea of Galilee), it should not be surprising that some of the rabbinic authorities *from Yerushalayim came to* Yeshua. Matthew verifies that it is *some* (not all) *P'rushim* (Pharisees) and *Torah-teachers (soferim)* who came to ask another one of their *halakhic* questions. What caught their attention this time was the fact that the disciples of Yeshua did not perform *n'tilat-yadayim* before they partook of a meal. This ceremonial washing of the hands is not directly commanded in the written *Torah* although there were some biblical customs alluding to the washing of the priests (*Shmot*/Exodus 30:17-21) or even the washing after a healing (*Vayikra*/Leviticus 15:13). However, the rabbis of the *Talmud* thought it expedient to broaden the application of hand washing to all Jews in certain contexts based upon the exhortation of Leviticus 11:44. In fact it is interpreted that the first part of the verse ("sanctify yourselves") illustrates the washing before a meal while the latter phrase ("be holy") speaks of the washing after a meal (Tractate Berachot 53b).

It was deemed appropriate, before tasting bread, to wash one's hands and rub them together while reciting Psalm 134:2 "lift your hands" in the sanctuary and bless ADONAI (Tractate Berkhot 46b). Before drying the hands, the person is to say the *b'rakhah*: *Barukh atah ADONAI, eloheinu melech ha-olam, asher kidshanu b'mitz-vo-tav, v'tzivanu al n'tilat yadayim* (Blessed art Thou, O Lord our God, King of the universe who has sanctified us by Thy commandments and commanded us concerning the washing of the hands). So important was this practice that the Talmudic rabbis penned an entire tractate dedicated to the fine details related to the hands (Tractate Yadaim).

All of this may have beautiful symbolism and even hygienic benefits at a time when the health habits of the pagan world were seriously lacking. It does not seem coincidental that this question is raised soon after the large meal feeding the five thousand, although the rabbis may have observed this behavior at other times as well. It is significant that the current question is why the *talmidim* of Yeshua *break the Tradition of the Elders*, meaning that they are not following this particular custom as described in the *Mishnah*. It should be remembered that from the rabbi's historical perspective, the oral law of the *Mishnah* was actually a "fence around the *Torah/se'ag la-Torah*" (Pirke Avot 1:1). A fence, when properly understood, is valuable in protecting the more important elements found inside it. Yet, it might be easy to lose perspective and start valuing the fence as equal or of even greater importance.

Yeshua's response is both simple and forceful as he posits his own question (a good Jewish tradition!), *Why do you break the command of God by your tradition?* The rabbis must have been wondering how this commandment would lead them to break the weightier commandments of the written *Torah*. Yeshua at this point gave them a specific example. A most fundamental *mitzvah* that even appears in the Ten Commandments is the one to *honor your father and mother (Sh'mot/*Exodus 20:12.) In conjunction with that *mitzvah*, the *Torah* also states that *anyone who curses his father or mother must be put to death (C'mon/*Exodus 21:17). Although these are clear *Torah* commands that any rabbi would surely respect, Yeshua points out how, by means of theological debate, they may have skirted the intent of the *mitzvah*. Yeshua refers to their own Talmudic oral law when he responds with the phrase *but you say,* in contrast to the familiar refrain "it is written."

The question continues with the debate over whether it is permissible, in certain cases, to tell one's parents that the gift that is due them is actually being offered to God as a tithe. Such a scenario, according to Yeshua, illustrates how one may rid himself of his obligation to his parents in the guise of religiosity. Such maneuvering not only could hurt one's parents but also in the process actually be making *null and void the word of God.* Messiah does not look kindly on such actions.

In fact, he sums up his perspective by calling such religious people "hypocrites." It is pointed out by Yeshua that this is actually not a new phenomenon. Such religious hypocrisy has been seen in every generation (and we should note, within other religions as well). He quotes a verse from the *Tanakh* in which Isaiah rebuked some of his generation as well, yet it can be applied to those debating with Yeshua. The people of that day as well as now "honor me with their lips but their hearts are far away from me. Their worship of me is useless, because they teach man-made rules as if they were doctrines."

We are reminded here that Yeshua came as the *Mashiach* for Israel and, as such, a prophetic voice to correct the errors of his generation. In that sense, Yeshua is once again calling our people back to a purer understanding of the *Torah* even if it means disavowing some of the man-made interpretations that have accumulated over the years. Our view in Messianic Judaism is that the Talmudic tradition is of great value and interest, especially in understanding the context of the first-century gospels. Yet, there are times when Talmudic tradition must defer to the written word of God, just as our Messiah taught in this case.

At this juncture, Yeshua turns the dialogue away from the rabbis to *the crowd* around him as he has an important lesson for them. At first glance, the Messiah's spiritual lesson could be shocking to the disciples. Since the rabbinic debate was concerning *n'tilat yadaim* (washing of hands), Yeshua broadens the lesson to a certain aspect of *kashrut* (the dietary laws). It is *not what goes into the mouth* of a person solely that makes him unclean. Of more importance, it is *what comes out of his mouth* that *makes him unclean.*

Upon hearing this, the *talmidim* point out to their rabbi that the *P'rushim*/Pharisees *were offended* by what he said. Yeshua does not back down but instead furthers his rebuke of some of these hypocritical leaders by saying that *every plant* that God *has not planted will be pulled up by the roots.* If these particular leaders are not truly of God, then God himself will ultimately deal with them. Yeshua exhorts his followers even to *let them be* for *they are blind guides.*

The analogy is striking—revered guides of the community who are actually blind themselves when it comes to the Messiah sent from the Father. In fact, much of the spiritual dynamic can be summed up with the graphic picture of *a blind man* who *guides another blind man.* The end result will be tragic, with both falling *in a pit.*

Although these parabolic pictures describe the spiritual dynamics of this encounter, Kefa still asks for a clarification. Yeshua's elaboration comes with a gentle rebuke. *Don't you see that anything that enters the mouth goes into the stomach and passes out into the latrine?* In the spiritual life, it is clearly *what comes out of your mouth,* that is, *coming from the heart,* that makes a person unkosher. While certain physical defilements may pass through the biological system, there are more serious things that defile a person spiritually. Specifically, it is *wicked thoughts, murder, adultery and other kinds of sexual immorality, theft lies, and slander* among others that truly make a person unclean. According to Yeshua, there are many larger issues to consider that are in fact more important than some of the rabbinic *halakhah.*

He summarizes his teaching by affirming that *eating without doing n'tilat yadaim does not make a person unclean.* It should be carefully noted here that Yeshua is not abolishing the dietary laws for Israel. How could this be consistent with his own words that he did not come to abolish even one letter of the *Torah* but he came to fulfill it in its fullest sense (cf. Matthew 5:17-18)? It is rather surprising that some theologies describe an antinomian Yeshua. No one should jump to such a conclusion just because Yeshua was taking issue with the rabbinic custom of *n'tilat yadaim.* We have no record that the disciples immediately went out to purchase ham sandwiches!

Even the parallel account given in the Gospel of Mark does not prove that Yeshua was abolishing the dietary laws for Jews. A careful study of Mark 7:19 will reveal that the writer says Yeshua *declared all foods clean.* But it is significant that it is not said that he declared *all things* clean (italics mine). By using the technical word "foods," any Jewish reader of the first-century would have concluded that this referred to the food list of the *Torah* as found in Leviticus 11 (e.g. cud-chewing/split-hoof mammals; finned/scaled fish, etc.). These kosher foods are not to be rendered unkosher simply because the rabbinic details of *n'tilat yadaim* were not followed.

The teaching of Messiah was simply emphasizing the priority of having a kosher heart through our words and deeds. Be assured that the sinless Messiah could never break the written *Torah* lest he forfeit his high calling. He could (and did) however break some of the issues of the traditions of the Elders as found in the Talmudic laws. For those who choose to keep kosher in their diet (including many Messianic Jews today), these lessons still remain the priority.

Ministry to a Gentile Woman   15:21-28

Having finished his dialogue with his fellow rabbis, Yeshua now takes a rare trip outside *Eretz-Yisra'el* (the land of Israel). He set his course for the territory to the north of Israel known as the *region of Tzor and Tzidon* (Tyre and Sidon) which is in modern-day Lebanon. It is worth contemplating the fact that Yeshua of Nazareth rarely traveled to non-Jewish areas in his lifetime. In fact, he seldom had a personal conversation with any persons outside his Jewish community. Yeshua sent his early disciples out solely "to the lost sheep of the house of Israel" (Matthew 10:6).

This is not to be interpreted as any form of racism or spiritual superiority but, in reality, it is quite fair and logical. After all, if the promise of the *Mashiach* was given to Israel starting with Abraham, it is only fair that the people of promise should be the first to hear of its fulfillment. Of course, the time will come when this message will go to all nations (Matthew 28:19). Yet, it is quite interesting here that Yeshua enters a non-Jewish area and ministers to a Gentile pagan woman. Matthew points out that the woman was *from Kena'an* (a Canaanite), a descendant from the ancient pagan population of that part of the Middle East.

Upon encountering this famous miracle-working rabbi, the unnamed woman cries out for mercy. By addressing Yeshua as the *Son of David*, it seems this woman had knowledge of and faith in the claim that he was the Messiah of Israel. She must have also known that the Hebrew Scriptures often promise that the blessings of *Mashiach* will not only touch the Jewish people but will ultimately bless many non-Jews as well. All the way back in Genesis 12:1-3, the promise is given that Abraham's descendants will be blessed by the provisions of the covenant. However, the covenant also holds out a day when all the Nations/*Gentiles* will also be blessed through the riches of Abraham. Of course, the greatest treasure would be the Messiah himself who would bring physical and spiritual blessing to all people who call on his name. Somehow it seems this Canaanite woman believed that moment had arrived in her personal encounter with the messianic teacher from Galilee.

Her request has a sense of urgency to it as she reveals that her *daughter* is *under the power of demons*. Undoubtedly the spiritual oppression of demonic activity was even stronger and more common in the land of paganism and idolatry. Although our contemporary society often doubts the reality of such spiritual forces, demonic activity and the reality of Satan himself are emphasized in the Hebrew Scriptures (see Job 1, Zechariah 3, etc.).

It is rather ironic that any among the Jewish community would deny the existence of Satan when his very name is in fact Hebrew (*to oppose*). Demons are described as the emissaries of the great fallen angel Satan who wreak havoc upon God's world. While Satan and his forces can do great damage to this world and its populace, believers in Yeshua take hold of the promises that "greater is he that is in you than he that is in the world" (*I Yochanan*/1 John 4:4). It is with some of this knowledge that this Gentile mother comes to the Messiah to plead for spiritual deliverance for her daughter.

Even with this critical plea, Yeshua's first response is rather shocking. After months of ministering to the needy multitudes with Israel, he *did not say a word* to this hurting woman. His own *talmidim*, having observed the situation, probably assumed that their rabbi did not have the time or desire to address the needs of the woman. They even suggested to their leader that he *send her away* because she was *pestering* them *with her crying*. On the surface it even seemed that the rabbi agreed with their assessment. Yeshua reminded them (and undoubtedly the Gentile woman) that he was *sent only to the lost sheep of the house of Isra'el.* Although the situation was bleak for the woman, she persisted, falling at Yeshua's *feet*, and begging him for *help*.

Messiah's answer still did not give the mother much hope. In fact, it must have been downright discouraging. Yeshua answers with an analogy that *it is not right to take the children's food* (Israel's blessings) *and toss it to their pet dogs* (non-Jews). As the translation here implies, he was not disparaging non-Jews with the term dogs (wild beasts) but, in an interesting twist, Yeshua refers to such people in a friendlier manner as pet dogs (in the household). Such a description was still quite shocking but it emphasizes the common understanding of the day that great treasures given to Israel were not meant to be desecrated by the pagans.

One would think that such a response from a rabbi would have put a final stop on this woman's request but, true to a woman of faith, she perseveres yet more! Somewhat surprisingly, she humbly agrees with Yeshua's statement but points out a practical exception to the case. Even the pet dogs are allowed to *eat the leftovers that fall from their master's table.* It is now abundantly clear that this woman has a sincere faith in pursuing Yeshua. Messiah finally honors her request noting that her *desire* will *be granted.* Matthew describes the answer to the request and prayer that *her daughter was healed at that very moment.*

This whole situation illustrates many fascinating dynamics in first-century Jewish culture. The responses (and even the discouragement) of Yeshua toward this Gentile woman are understandable in the context of the Scriptures. It was not yet time for the Good News of Messiah to go forth to the whole world. The Gospel is the power of God for salvation to the Jew first and also to the Greek (Romans 1:16). It should also be highlighted that this encounter is very consistent with a traditional rabbinic view of dealing with seeking Gentiles. While the door has always been open for any non-Jew to connect with Israel and their God, the rabbis did not make it very easy. Out of fear of insincere converts or pagan cultural influences, it was specified that a Gentile must clearly prove his or her commitment. The most pessimistic view stated that "proselytes are as hard for Israel to endure as a sore" (Tractate Yevamot 47b). Even the sin of the Golden Calf in the wilderness was blamed on the converts from Egyptian paganism (Exodus Rabba 42:6).

Because of these suspicions, it was understood that if a rabbi was approached by a Gentile seeker, the rabbi was obligated to initially reject the person. In a most interesting parallel to this account in Matthew, the *Talmud* notes that some key questions should be posed to a potential convert: "What is your objective?" Also, "Do you know that today the people of Israel are in constant suffering?" If the seeker says, "I know of this and I do not have the merit" then he/ she is to be accepted immediately and taught some of the precepts of the *Torah* (Tractate Yevamot 47a).

In this context, Yeshua's encounter with this pagan woman reflects a very natural response of a rabbi to a potential follower. Indeed, Yeshua rather harshly rejects the woman three distinct times—not answering, then saying his calling is only to Jews, and finally saying he cannot share the bread with a pagan. It is this commonly held tradition, along with Yeshua's grace, that results in the acceptance of this woman as a new disciple and the healing of her daughter. This should serve as a beautiful reminder to all non-Jewish followers of Yeshua that they are grafted into the Messianic faith by the amazing grace of the God of Israel and his Messiah.

Feeding the Four Thousand   15:29-39

From this encounter with a Gentile seeker, Yeshua now travels back to *Eretz-Yisra'el*. Specifically, we are told that he came back to the area of his usual ministry, to *the shore of Lake Kinneret* (Galilee). As *he climbed* a local *hill and sat down*, the *large crowds came to him* bringing many in need. Matthew observes that the group included some who were *lame, blind, crippled, mute and many others.* The supernatural power of the *Mashiach* was once again evident as *he healed them* in great numbers.

Not surprisingly, the people were amazed as they observed *mute people speaking, lame people walking, and even blind people seeing.* The crowds *said a b'rakhah to the God of Isra'el* in response to the wonders they saw with their own eyes. It is longstanding Jewish tradition to say a blessing to God after observing a wondrous event because every good thing emanates from the Creator (Tractate Berakhot 36a). This Galilean ministry time certainly qualified in their minds.

It is at this point that a potential problem develops. Yeshua expressed his concern for the large group, as they have been with them for *three days* and they were essentially out of food. It would not be right *to send them away hungry* as they might even have trouble making it back to their homes. The disciples ask their rabbi where they might find *enough loaves of bread* in such a *remote place.* As if to test their faith once again, Yeshua inquires of them, "how many loaves do you have?" The *talmidim* respond that they can only round up *seven* loaves *and a few fish.* After having the crowd seated, Yeshua took the food elements and *made a b'rakhah* as is essential before any meal (cf. Matthew 14:15f). After blessing God, he *broke the loaves* and gave it to his disciples for distribution to the large crowd. Not only did everyone present eat *his fill* but the Gospel writer points out that *seven large baskets of the leftover pieces* remained.

Some bible students have speculated if this accounting of Matthew 15 is merely a repetition of the miracle in Matthew 14. However, there are too many varying details (by the same author no less) to make these two feedings one in the same. The earlier account relates that there were five thousand men with twelve baskets of leftovers. Here we find *four thousand men (plus women and children)* along with seven baskets of leftovers. Even the types of baskets vary in each account (with two different words used), the latter describing "large" baskets which were probably made of flexible material. The most consistent view is that Matthew, as an eyewitness, gives testimony to two distinct feeding miracles with some similarities but many important differences.

This being so, one is struck by the lapse in faith of disciples who should have learned from the earlier miracle. Of course, it has happened before in Jewish history, even as the generation that walked through the sea at Passover was soon complaining about God's lack of provision! But isn't it still human nature today to have a short memory when it comes to the reality of God's presence in our midst? After the three-day hillside ministry, Yeshua *got in the boat and went off to the region of Magadan* (modern Migdal, south of Kafar Nachum).

Rejection by Some of the Rabbis   16:1-12

After the eventful ministry time around the Kinneret (Sea of Galilee), Matthew records that some *P'rushim and Tz'dukim* confronted Yeshua. Since it is now at this later phase of Messiah's public ministry, we should not expect a positive reaction from some of the religious leaders. We have already spoken in some detail of the first-century sect known as the *P'rushim* (cf. Matthew 9).

These were Jews who were very meticulous in their religious observance. Their name comes from the root *parash* meaning "to separate." The Pharisees saw themselves as religiously distinct even from many of their brothers, especially the common people known as the *am ha-aretz*. It should be emphasized that there were undoubtedly many *P'rushim* who followed their strict observances out of a sincere love for God. Certainly many of Yeshua's followers even came from the sect, including some rather high-profile rabbis such as Nicodemus and Yosef of Arimethea. But there often was a debate between Yeshua and some of the *P'rushim* revolving around their disagreements of *halakhah* and lifestyle.

Here Matthew notes that some from this group *came to trap* Yeshua with an insincere request. We know it is not with pure motives because of the many previous encounters dealing with similar issues (cf. Matthew 12). The fact that they ask for *a miraculous sign from Heaven* reveals that they were really seeking not so much the sign, but evidence to develop an argument against Yeshua and his movement. The sign is not just from "Heaven" in a generic sense, but the dialogue reflects the traditional way of substituting a word for the name of God, the One who abides in the Heavens. They were in fact asking Yeshua to confirm that he is doing his miracles from the God of Israel.

Of course, this exact scenario already came up earlier and was answered thoroughly by Messiah (cf. Matthew 12). What is even more astounding is the fact that in this particular situation, the *P'rushim* are accompanied by some religious counterparts called the *Tz'dukim*/Sadducees.

This group was in some ways the polar opposite of the Pharisees. Because they were the priests who oversaw the Temple, the Sadducees did not interact much at all with the larger community of the common people. They too were very observant Jews but with a different focus.

Whereas the Pharisees were out in the synagogue community and on the streets, the *Tz'dukim* held their lofty position as the aristocrats of first-century Judaism. While one could choose to join the Pharisees, it was only by priestly birthright (tribe of Levi) that one was included within the Sadducees.

It might surprise some modern readers that, theologically, they were considered more conservative than the Pharisees. This is because the Sadducees held strictly to the *Torah* alone (five books of Moses), seeing the rest of the *Tanakh* (Prophets and Writings) as mere commentary. The Pharisees were, in this sense, more liberal in that they accepted all of the *Tanakh* plus the rabbinic interpretations found in the *Mishnah*. Consequently, the Sadducees disavowed certain doctrines they claimed were missing from the *Torah*, most notably the belief in a future resurrection of the dead. The fact that the *P'rushim* and the *Tz'dukim* strongly disagreed on several key issues makes this particular encounter in Matthew 16 all the more graphic. Some leaders of both opposing groups came seeking another sign from this self-proclaimed Messiah. The context of this situation in itself was enough to reveal their insincere and even hypocritical intentions.

Yeshua's answer reflects the fact that he, especially as the *Mashiach*, could see through their thinly veiled request. His response consisted of a simple yet profound parable. This is consistent with Yeshua's earlier statement that, because of hardened unbelief, much of his future teaching would be in the esoteric form of parables. By so doing, seekers would glean more truth but skeptics would be judged with more confusion (cf. Matthew 13).

Here we have a common observation concerning weather patterns. Even the simplest observer can conclude that it will be *fair weather ahead because the sky is red* in the *evening*. By contrast, if the *morning sky is red and overcast*, then it will certainly be a *storm today*. These *P'rushim* and *Tz'dukim* can predict the weather based on *the appearance of the sky*, yet they *can't read the signs of the times* right around them! It is way past the time where there can be another request for a sign from God. There have been multiple messianic miracles, healings, and feedings that testify of the truth of Yeshua.

Indeed, at this point it is only *a wicked and adulterous generation* that could ask for another *sign*. Yeshua does give an answer however, which is in fact the same answer he gave to some similar skeptics. No sign will be given *except the sign of Yonah* (cf. Matthew 12). Even though every other public sign will be canceled, Yeshua reminds all that there will be one tremendous sign for all to contemplate in the days to come.

Often the sign of Yonah is associated with the three days and three nights the prophet was in the belly of the great fish. However, as we previously noted, it seems the real sign of Yonah is not the chronology of this experience but the evident fact that he died in the fish and was resurrected on the third day (cf. Yonah 2:7 where the prophet gives thanks to God who *brought me up alive from the pit*, a Jewish idiom for the grave and death). The sign of Yonah therefore is that of resurrection. As such, the ancient prophet of Israel is a perfect type of the death and resurrection of Yeshua as the *Mashiach*.

It is significant to point out that for traditional Jews, the sign of Yonah is contemplated once a year on the most high holy day of *Yom Kippur*/Day of Atonement. It is on this most significant day that the designated reading from the prophets is none other than the entire scroll of Yonah. I believe God is still giving our people a major sign of the true *Mashiach* every year as we attend high holy day services in the fall. There is no other answer that came from Yeshua to the request of some of these rabbis. The text simply records that at this point, *he left them and went off.*

Although Yeshua and his *talmidim* left the encounter with these skeptical rabbis, it continued to be a teachable moment for the disciples. After the group arrived at *the other side of the lake*, it was confirmed that they had forgotten to bring *any bread*.

Messiah saw the perfect opportunity to tie the two different situations together for a spiritual lesson. He thus warned his followers to guard themselves *against the chametz of the P'rushim and Tz'dukim. Chametz* is the Hebrew word for leaven or yeast. As bacteria it is essential for the baking of bread. However, the rabbinic tradition has emphasized that *chametz* is also an apt symbol of sin which puffs up and permeates the human soul (Tractate Berakhot 17a). It is a powerful symbol that at Passover, we Jews are commanded to remove the *chametz* from our homes as a reminder to cleanse our spiritual lives as well.

In light of the insincere questions of the *P'rushim* and the lack of bread to eat, Yeshua made the perfect connection between the two. Some of the teaching (and motivations) of these leaders is like a spiritual *chametz* that could corrupt their souls. At first, the disciples could only think of the most obvious connection, that they were in trouble for not bringing any bread. But Yeshua made the full connection for them in the form of a loving rebuke. Do they really have *such little trust?* They clearly did *not understand* that he was not strictly alluding to their lack of bread.

If nothing else, they should have had fresh on their minds the two different group meals that they recently experienced. The physical bread is not a big problem if the Messiah has already multiplied *five loaves for the five thousand* men and *seven loaves for the four thousand* men—not to mention the leftovers!

He was not talking merely about bread but about *the teaching of the P'rushim and Tz'dukim.* Some of their rabbinic doctrines (please note, not the written *Torah* itself) were like *chametz* in that they permeate and even corrupt a pure understanding of the *Tanakh.* Yeshua could be referring to both the content of their teaching (cf. *n'tilat yadaim* details in Matthew 15) as well as to the attitude of their hearts as found in the dialogue of this chapter. Either way, he warns his close followers to guard themselves against such *chametz* that may corrupt their own pure walk with the Father. We too must guard against incorrect theology and the bad spirit that often comes with it.

THE FINAL PRESENTATION
OF KING MESSIAH
16:13-28:20

"Three things come unexpectedly: the Messiah, a find, and
a scorpion"

(Tractate Sanhedrin 97a)

The New Revelations of King Messiah 16:13-17:27

Matthew's biography of Yeshua now takes another dramatic turn. Having elaborated on the preparation for King Messiah (early history) in Chapters 1:1-4:16, he subsequently spent significant time describing the program of King Messiah (his words and works) in 4:17-16:12. The final major division of his gospel deals with the latter events in the earthly ministry of King Messiah Yeshua. Not surprisingly, the writer devotes much time and energy to relating the significant events of the final months of Messiah's ministry in Israel. There are new details recorded, new revelations of the *Mashiach,* and a strong emphasis on the final week leading to *Pesach.* Matthew records a course of events that increases in intensity until reaching the final crescendo of the death and resurrection of Yeshua of Nazareth, thus fulfilling the first mission of King Messiah.

The Revelation of His True Identity   16:13-17

As he starts the final phase of his ministry to Israel, Yeshua *came into the territory around Caesarea Philippi.* This was in the very northern reaches of Israel at the foot of Mount Hermon. Since it was at the headwaters of the Jordan River, the area is striking in its beauty, with an abundance of fresh water flowing from underground springs through the impressive cliff that surrounds it.

In the first century, Herod Philip developed the area into a retreat and named it in honor of the Caesar. Later occupants named the place after the pagan god "Pan" and built multiple altars for their worship. It became known as Panias (the place of the flute player Pan). In more recent history, the Arab occupants (who have no "P" sound in their alphabet) called the place Banias as it is still known at the present time.

Because of its extreme northern location, the area of Caesarea Philippi was largely inhabited by a pagan Gentile populace and consequently was a center of idolatrous worship. In the Israelite period, the tribe of Dan settled in the area and often fell prey to the pagan influences at its border. It is a rather strange yet appropriate setting for the ensuing dialogue between Yeshua and his disciples.

As a good rabbi, Yeshua starts the discussion by posing a question: "Who are people saying the Son of Man is?" The response of the *talmidim* is informative. Some people are saying he might be *Yochanan* (John) *the Immerser or Eliyahu* (Elijah) *or one of the prophets like Yirmeyahu* (Jeremiah).

Traditional Judaism has never held to a teaching of reincarnation; however there is a belief (even in the *Torah*) that there may be a resurrection appearance of special individuals (cf. Elijah appearing again in Malachi 3:23/Hebrew or 4:5/English). In fact, common tradition reminds us that *Eliyahu* will come again to announce the arrival of King Messiah as is seen in the Cup of Elijah at the Passover *seder* every spring. It could also be that the people were looking at Yeshua as one ministering in the same spirit and power as the previous prophets. All of this is interesting but Yeshua poses a follow-up question to bring the discussion close to home: "But you, who do you say I am?"

There may be various opinions as to the identity of Yeshua in the general community but it would be most enlightening to hear the opinion of his closest *talmidim* who have lived with him these last three years. Not surprisingly, it is one of their leaders, Shim'on Kefa (Peter) who first volunteers his assessment. "You are the Mashiach, the Son of the living God."

This is rather astounding as one reflects on this declaration! Yeshua of Nazareth did many miracles in Israel, yet he is more than a prophet. He taught many beautiful truths to the people, yet he is more than an exalted rabbi. Shim'on affirms that he believes Yeshua is the promised Messiah and all that goes with the understanding of the calling and mission of the coming *Mashiach*. The Messiah was to have a unique relationship with the Father as the divine Son as described in the *Tanakh* (cf. Psalm 2, Proverbs 30, etc.).

It is vital to point out that if Shim'on was incorrect in his opinion that Yeshua most certainly would have corrected him. Not only does Yeshua let the statement stand but he rewards Shim'on for his accurate declaration. Shim'on is said to be *blessed* because *no human being revealed this* to him. In fact, it is a spiritual revelation from the *Father in heaven*, the God of Abraham, Isaac and Jacob.

Once again, we are reminded that Yeshua did not come to start a new religion but to fulfill the ancient promises given to Israel. Shim'on's understanding was that Yeshua is the promised *Mashiach* sent from our God. Someone must be the Messiah. It still is not so easy for people to see (especially for many of our Jewish brothers). Surely that is why it took a spiritual revelation in Shim'on's heart to see Yeshua for who he really is. When it comes down to it, a similar revelation (based on the clear descriptions of the Hebrew Scriptures) is needed for anyone today to understand the full identity of Yeshua of Nazareth.

The Revelation of the New Messianic Community 16:18-20

As a result of the messianic declaration of Shim'on, he is given a special blessing. Yeshua declares, "you are Kefa," which at first glance may just seem like a formal greeting. However, there is a significant word play in the original languages. *Kefa* is the Aramaic word for "rock" which is equivalent to the Greek word "petros" used in the text here. It has also been documented that Yeshua, most likely speaking Hebrew, would have used the borrowed word "petros" which also appears in other Jewish texts.

For example, there is a Rabbi Yose ben Petros mentioned (Genesis Rabba 94) as well as a Jewish market place called Petros near ancient *Lod*/Lydda (Tosefta Demai 1:11). This term literally means "a small stone" as in one that can be held in the hand. This is contrasted by the follow-up statement of Yeshua where he declares, "on this rock I will build my Community." The Greek as well as the presumed Hebrew texts make it very clear that this latter rock is not the same rock as Peter himself.

As noted, Kefa is referred to as a small stone while the secondary phrase states that upon this *rock* (Greek/Hebrew "petra") the Messianic community will be built. This latter term does not mean a small stone but rather a huge foundation stone or cliff. The reality is that a strikingly beautiful word play (*petros/petra*) comes out in any of the ancient Biblical languages: Hebrew, Aramaic or Greek (see *Biblical Archaeology Review*, "Did Jesus Speak Greek?" response letter by David Bivin, May/June 1993).

It is well known that the Roman Catholic Church has historically interpreted this phrase to mean that Peter himself would be the first pope and foundation of their church. This seems confusing since we have no biblical record of Peter ever visiting Rome and, instead, he is called in the New Testament "the apostle to the Jews" (cf. Galatians 2:7). However, it was abundantly clear to the disciples that Kefa was a rock (albeit a small stone) while the foundation of the Messianic community would be a different massive rock. It would not be Shim'on himself but it was actually the larger rock of Peter's confession that would be the foundation of the Messianic community. There is a similar *midrash* that gives some elucidation to this statement:

> When the Holy One wanted to create the world he passed over the generations of Enoch and the Flood, but when he saw Avraham who was to arise, he said, 'Behold, I have found a rock (petra) on which I can build and establish the world.' Therefore he called Avraham a rock, as it is said (Isaiah 51:1), 'Look to the rock from which you were hewn.' (Yalkut on *Bemidbar*/Numbers 23:9).

Many English Bibles translate the word *ekklesia* as "church" but this is merely an English adaptation of the Greek word which itself is derived from the Hebrew *kehilah*. Upon this inspired confession of Yeshua's messianic identity the entire community of New Covenant believers (both the Jewish and Gentile branches) would be built. In fact, the physical setting of this dialogue strongly confirms this view. One can imagine Yeshua standing at the foot of the massive cliff at Caesarea Philippi and bending down to pick up one of the many stones. It would have been a graphic object lesson as he quite logically held up a small stone as a symbol of Peter and then pointed to the massive cliff as symbolic of the foundational confession of Yeshua's messiahship.

There are more promises associated with Kefa's declaration. Yeshua also assures the *talmidim* that *the gates of Sh'ol will not overcome* this new Messianic community. *Sh'ol* within Jewish teaching was considered the place of the departed spirits, both righteous and unrighteous. It consisted of two compartments for these spirits who were awaiting the resurrection and future judgment. Subsequently, the mention of *Sh'ol* was not always bad as it was the place of hope for those who loved God (cf. Psalm 16:10; Luke 16:19-31). However, the concept was often descriptive of the kingdom of Satan and his evil inhabitants. The phrase "gates of Sh'ol" was known in some references, for example, which describe God as the one who "has power over life and death...who leads men down to the gates of Sh'ol and back again" (Wisdom of Solomon 16:13).

Of course it was wonderful news that the *Mashiach* was in their midst and would continue to accomplish his mission of redemption. However, it was also a natural reality that Satan and his forces would be diametrically opposed to the community of God's Messiah. This too would have been a graphic illustration as the disciples stood at such a place as Caesarea Philippi known for its dark idolatry. It is not difficult to imagine that traditional Jews would look at such a pagan place (especially at the edge of the Gentile world) as the gates of *Sh'ol*/Hell. Nevertheless, even the symbolism of Satan's kingdom of darkness will not prevail over the kingdom of Messiah. He has come to crush the head of the serpent and his *kehilah* will also share in that victory. Still today, followers of Yeshua are the brunt of spiritual battles and satanic opposition. Should we expect anything different? Yet, it is reassuring for modern believers in Yeshua (Messianic Jews and all Christians) to know that even today we are more than conquerors through our King Messiah (cf. Romans 8:37).

A final promise given to Shim'on at this juncture is that Yeshua would give him *the keys of the Kingdom of Heaven.* While it is Peter's confession that is the foundation of the New Covenant *kehilah*, there is also a personal promise given to this lead disciple. Keys open doors and the promise is that Kefa will have the blessing of opening new doors for the kingdom of Messiah. This would be literally fulfilled in the subsequent ministry of Kefa. In the Book of Acts we are told that the messianic outreach of the early emissaries would go from Jerusalem, Judea, and Samaria and to the ends of the earth (cf. Acts 1:8) It turns out that Shim'on was the door opener for each of these significant people groups.

It is quite natural that Shim'on is the emissary preaching the message of the risen Yeshua on the Temple Mount on the holy day of *Shavuot*/Pentecost (Acts 2). He was using the keys of the Kingdom to open the door for Jerusalem as the *shaliach* to the Jews. It is not a coincidence that months later Kefa is also present to help open the doors for the Samaritans. They were the logical next step, since the Samaritans were cousins that turned from traditional Judaism but nevertheless retained many historical connections. It is significant that the New Covenant points out that it was actually Philip who was the first emissary to take the message to the Samaritan community. Yet, he specifically requested that Kefa should come down to Samaria to confirm that this messianic salvation was legitimate.

Once again, Kefa had the keys to confirm an open door to those of Shomron (cf. Acts 8). A final door is opened in the very interesting events around the righteous Gentile named Cornelius. God arranged for this Roman Gentile to meet with Shim'on that he might be the first to officially receive the Good News of Messiah from his community. This was so radical at the time that God even had to give Kefa a dramatic dream to confirm that the Gentiles were not unkosher now. As Peter prays with this Roman seeker, it is clear that God is allowing him to use the keys of the kingdom to open up an entirely new door (cf. Acts 10-11). It is the blessing of Yeshua, in response to Kefa's messianic confession, that allows him to be the main conduit of blessing through all three doors—to Israel, to Shomron, and to the Gentiles.

There is an extra blessing included in Yeshua's promise to Kefa—a powerful ability for spiritual discernment and shepherding the Messianic flock. Undoubtedly, this new community would present unforeseen challenges to Kefa and the original *talmidim*. Decisions must be made for the good of individuals as well as the good of the larger *kehilah*.

Accordingly, Yeshua declares that whatever the leadership prohibits *on earth will be prohibited in heaven*. Juxtaposed to this, Kefa and the leaders will be able to *permit on earth* what is already *permitted in heaven*. Many translations use the terms "bind" and "loose" in this passage, which have sometimes been applied to the content of prayer. In some modern circles, it has even become a form of doctrine to "bind or loose" Satan, curses, or even blessings.

Two things appear wrong with this modern application. First, the context of Yeshua's promise is not prayer at all but the building of the new Messianic community. Part of Kefa's blessing is to be delegated insight from above on how to shepherd the flock of Messiah on Earth. It would be nice if believers had the power in prayer to "bind" Satan and all evil influences. But this is not meant to be a magical charm for spiritual warfare. If it is such a promise, one might ask how Satan keeps getting loose after being bound in prayer by so many believers! No, his binding will only come when *Mashiach* returns a second time and Satan is cast into the Abyss (cf. Revelation 20:1-3). A secondary observation based on Jewish theology clarifies the promise of Yeshua. The technical words for "bind and loose" do not come from personal prayer but from rabbinic legal decisions (*halakhah*). Quite commonly in rabbinic language, the term "bind" (Hebrew *asur*) means to forbid or prohibit something. An example is found where the rabbis could "bind/*asur*" a day by declaring it a fast day (Tractate Ta'anit 12a). Similarly, the rabbinic leadership was vested with the power to "loose/ *mutar*" something in the sense that it would be permitted within the community (Tractate Chagigah 3b). With this original context in mind, we can see that Yeshua's promise to Peter, while not dealing with prayer, is none the less a beautiful promise to grant wisdom.

The verb tense of the words (perfect tense) also bears this out as it literally says "whatever you prohibit on earth will have already been prohibited in heaven." Kefa and the first leaders are therefore given a promise that whatever is God's will in heaven regarding certain legal decisions, they will be given wisdom on how to apply it in the Messianic Kingdom of Earth. This was certainly fulfilled in the early Messianic movement as illustrated in such *halakhic* decisions as the place of *Torah* and the Gentiles in the Yeshua movement (cf. Acts 15 council).

The application comes down to this very day as spiritual leaders in the Yeshua community (both Messianic Judaism and Gentile Christianity) are promised spiritual wisdom as they sincerely seek God's will for every situation for the flock. After this amazing series of events, Yeshua does something that might seem a bit puzzling. Matthew notes that *he warned the talmidim not to tell anyone that he was the Messiah.* One would think after Peter's anointed confession that the disciples would be encouraged to pass it on to everyone they encountered. However, once again we see that Yeshua guarded his public identity at this time. Many of the rabbis had openly rejected him and perhaps many in the sympathetic crowds would misunderstand the full picture of his messianic mission. The time would come for such widespread proclamation after his work as the suffering servant is fulfilled. But for now, the disciples are warned to keep this foundational affirmation in private so that the fullness of Yeshua's latter days can unfold.

The Revelation Concerning *Mashiach ben Yosef* 16:21-27

Although the messianic revelation was to be kept private for the moment, Yeshua took this opportune time to remind his close followers of events that awaited him. It is stated very strongly that Yeshua *had to go to Yerushalayim.* As the Messiah, it was necessary for much of his work to take place in the holy city as often predicted. Although he ministered much in his home territory of the Galil, it would have to be in Jerusalem, the heart of Israel, that the ultimate climax of his ministry would take place.

Yet he reminds his disciples that the arrival of Messiah will not be as commonly expected. It will not be with great fanfare and celebration at this first arrival but with a large degree of solemnity. Yeshua predicts that he is about to *endure much suffering at the hands of the elders, the head cohanim and the Torah-teachers.* This part should not have been so surprising in that Yeshua already experienced significant public rejection from many of these rabbinic leaders (cf. Matthew 12). But the intensity of the Jerusalem confrontation would be greater than anything previously experienced.

Yeshua elaborates that he would *be put to death* by a hostile crowd. The fact that he separates the statement between the "suffering" and the "death" to follow perhaps gives a clue that it would be a larger group (not just some of the Jewish leaders but also the Romans) who would conspire in the execution of the Messiah. This would be tragic indeed if this was the culmination of the story but Yeshua reveals more vital information. He assures his disciples that *on the third day* he will *be raised to life*. Although there is coming a time of struggle and rejection, it is all part of God's prophetic plan for the Messiah's first mission as the suffering servant (cf. Isaiah 53).

It should be remembered that the rabbis also saw strong evidence of the two missions of the coming Messiah. Understandably, many focused on the King Messiah (*Mashiach ben David*/Son of David) who would overthrow all the enemies of Israel and establish the Kingdom of God on Earth (cf. Isaiah 9&11). But the rabbis also admitted that there were many descriptions of the Messiah who would somehow suffer (*Mashiach ben Yosef*) at the hands of the world (cf. Isaiah 53).

Since this picture of a suffering Messiah was so different from the promises of a coming king, some of the Talmudic rabbis came up with the view that perhaps there would be two distinct messiahs. How this could happen was debated, but one view was that Ben Yosef would come and be rejected by the world (like Yosef of Genesis), perhaps even killed in a battle (cf. Tractate Sukkah 52a, which quotes Zechariah 12:10 as the death of *Mashiach ben Yosef*)! Only then would Ben David come to rescue the first Messiah and all of Israel.

It must be pointed out that the Scriptures themselves never speak of two Messiahs but only in the singular of one redeemer. How could one person fulfill both of these contrasting pictures of the *Mashiach*? Yeshua gives the perfect answer that he, as God's only true Messiah, will fulfill both missions of Ben Yosef (by suffering) and Ben David (by resurrection). It is a most perfect way to fulfill both missions in one person!

We, of course, have the blessing of hindsight, knowing the history of first-century Israel. What seems abundantly clear to modern Messianic Jews and Christians is that Yeshua of Nazareth perfectly and uniquely fulfilled the ancient prophecies of the *Torah*. However, to those of his own day, even to his closest friends, it was not so clear. Undoubtedly, they were focused on the dynamic promises in regard to the coming King Messiah. Soon there would be deliverance from the Gentile oppressors and the paradise of God would be restored.

It is in this context that Kefa/Peter speaks up once again. Upon hearing Yeshua's words regarding his coming rejection and death, Kefa took his rabbi *aside and began rebuking him. Heaven be merciful* (common idiom "chas v'chalilah") *Lord! By no means will this happen to you!* While we can understand Peter's focus as a traditional Jew, he should have had enough revelation in his three years with Yeshua to understand his connection to *Mashiach ben Yosef*. Because of that, Yeshua *turned his back on Kefa* and said "Get behind me, Satan! You are an obstacle in my path."

Perhaps Yeshua was alluding to the thoughts of Kefa as being directly from the evil one, Satan himself. Since the Hebrew word "satan" means opposition, another option is that Peter was becoming *an obstacle* in the path of messianic redemption. Either way, Kefa is rebuked by his rabbi for thinking *from a human perspective, not from God's perspective.* Too often today, people still tell God how he should be accomplishing his plans instead of humbly listening to him! How many even reject Yeshua today as the Messiah because he does not fit their idea of what the Messiah should do? We would be wise to listen more to God and *Torah* than to our own ideas.

With some of these conflicting ideas in play, it must have been an opportune time for Yeshua to remind his *talmidim* of some of the principles of his discipleship. First, *if anyone wants to come* after Yeshua, he must say *"No" to himself.* This clearly illustrates that Yeshua's kingdom is exactly the opposite of most of our natural inclinations. We have a powerful drive for self-preservation. Even much of modern religion and psychology seem focused on "self" realization. The qualifying condition of becoming a disciple of Yeshua is to deny our personal desires and concerns. This reminder was especially striking in light of Kefa's natural human perspective in the previous discussion about the Kingdom of God. And, not only are we to deny ourselves, but Yeshua's calling is also to *take up his execution-stake and keep following* him.

It is rather ironic that such a horrible symbol as a cross or crucifix is often looked upon with such loving emotion by some. The historical reality is that the cross was indeed an execution-stake used to torture the worst criminals of the day. It should be remembered that the cross was not a Jewish means of execution but was developed by the pagan Phoenicians and fine-tuned by the Romans. The Jewish means of capital punishment stated by the rabbis (based on biblical examples) were stoning, burning, slaying, and strangling (Tractate Sanhedrin 52a-b). Even in capital crimes, the guilty party was never to be tortured; death was to be meted out in the most humane way possible.

Matthew is writing during the Roman occupation of the first century when his readers were well aware of this pagan death penalty method. It is quite striking that Yeshua would call his followers to in a sense "die" to themselves by taking up their cross. Some, undoubtedly, would actually face physical death on the execution-stake. Of even higher value was the call to put one's own soul and spirit on their personal execution-stake. To be a disciple of Yeshua is in fact to make him Lord of your life at the price of your own wishes. This is surely a high price but, then again, he is the one who has given us life and purpose. By submitting to Messiah, we are in reality merely giving back to him what is rightfully his to begin with!

Although the price of discipleship is steep, it is even steeper for those who ignore their Creator. In one of the great ironies of the spiritual world, Yeshua states that *whoever wants to save his own life will destroy it.* People throughout history have shared the common denominator of desiring a happy and full life. Yet it is those who exclusively focus on that goal who are actually in danger of missing the mark. Too many people (still today) are actually destroying the real purpose of their lives as they attempt to find life! Yet the irony applies to the opposite side of the equation as well as Yeshua states, *whoever destroys his life for my sake will find it.* He is using some poetic hyperbole here but the principle holds true in Messiah's kingdom. Those who drop their own self-preoccupation and focus on Yeshua's call are promised an abundant, fulfilling life. Nothing in this present world can fulfill the needs of the spirit. *What good will it do someone if he gains the whole world but forfeits his life?* Even the most "successful" person in this present age will be lacking greatly if he neglects his soul. The eternal kingdom is worth exceedingly more than the current temporal possessions.

In fact, there is nothing of this world that a person can give in *exchange for his life.* Whatever one's success and achievements might be in this age, there is a bigger eternal picture that we should consider carefully. As Yeshua refers to his future kingdom, he alludes to himself as *the Son of Man* who *will come in his Father's glory.*

This is supreme motivation to make sure one's spiritual focus is properly in place. The glorious *Mashiach* will return *with his angels* in order to *repay everyone according to his conduct.* We are all part of God's creation put here on Earth for a divine purpose. This is an immense promise of hope but also a sober reminder of our accountability to our Creator. Note that it is not necessarily our words that are the indicators of our spirit. Nor is it our motives or good intentions.

The ultimate measurement will be our deeds, which are a fruit of our personal relationship with God. Yeshua, as God's *Mashiach*, is the Son who is delegated the judgment of our souls. This is proper in that he is the one who became flesh and tabernacled in our midst, thus relating to our human predicament. This is why the Messiah had to come. We will all answer to God for our actions and we need all the help we can get. "If anyone does sin, we have Yeshua the Messiah, the *Tzaddik*, who pleads our cause with the Father" (*I Yochanan*/1 John 2:1).

THE FINAL PRESENTATION OF KING MESSIAH / 183

The Revelation Concerning the Coming Kingdom
16:28-17:13

Yeshua closes his teaching of Chapter 16 with an astounding statement. Since he has been clarifying some of the principles of God's Kingdom, he brings it right down to his own disciples. He affirms that *some people standing here will not experience death until they see the Son of Man coming in his Kingdom.* It is obvious that he is referring to those in his presence at that particular moment. The problem, even for many commentators, is the reference to the Kingdom of God coming while they are still living. Some skeptics point to such statements as an example of contradictions within the Bible. Clearly, the kingdom did not come in that day nor has it fully appeared even 21 centuries later.

Some attribute the statement to the over-zealous disciples who were convinced that Yeshua would bring the kingdom in the first century. If so, they were sadly mistaken. However, there is another more plausible explanation of this promise of Yeshua. It might surprise some readers that one of the big factors contributing to this controversy is simply the structure of Matthew's original scroll. As a first-century writer, he would have composed his manuscript on one, continuous "kosher" parchment without the modern addition of chapter divisions or verses. The most logical solution to the problem of Matthew 16:28 lies in the following verses of Chapter 17. The predicted coming kingdom will be revealed there in a most remarkable way.

It is not a coincidence that Chapter 17 begins with the contextual statement "six days later," thus tying the two chapters together. The promise of the revealed kingdom to the living disciples would indeed be fulfilled within the succeeding six days. At that time, Yeshua *took Kefa, Ya'akov and his brother Yochanan and led them up a high mountain privately.* These three disciples (translated Peter, James, and John) were often considered the inner circle of Yeshua's closest followers as indicated by the single definite article in the Greek. It was Kefa who had received Yeshua's blessing and the "keys of the kingdom" (Matt. 16:19). Ya'akov would be a future leader of the Messianic believers and was the first martyr from the original twelve *sh'lichim*, executed by Herod Agrippa (Acts 12:1-2). Yochanan would be next to Yeshua at the last *seder* meal, even reclining against him (Yochanan 13:23). Additionally, he is specially noted as Ya'akov's *brother* since both were sons of Zavdai (Zebedee).

It was this private group that Yeshua escorted to a secluded place on a high mountain. The exact location of the mountain has been debated, with many favoring Mount Tabor (1843 feet) just east of Nazareth. However, the context would seem to favor Mount Hermon for a couple of reasons. First, the special designation of a *high* mountain (Luke 9:28 calls it *the* high mountain) would more likely lead to this highest peak in Israel (9200 feet). Second, the previous dialogue in Matthew's account took place at Caesarea Philippi, which is at the foot of Mount Hermon (cf. Matthew 16:13).

It was at this isolated location that Yeshua's *appearance began to change form* (Greek *metamorphosis)*. Matthew seems to attempt describing something beyond the normal experience or words of the disciples. Yeshua's *face shone like the sun and his clothing became as white as light.* Both statements contain similes that indicate some kind of spiritual phenomena, not merely sunshine or even natural light. The *Tanakh* often uses such language when attempting to describe the manifestation of the *Sh'khinah*/Glory of God as in the experience of Moshe coming down from Mount Sinai (cf. Exodus 34:29).

Adding to this spectacular manifestation, the inner circle *saw Moshe and Eliyahu* speaking with Yeshua. To the average Jew, these two leaders of Israel would represent the whole history of the *Tanakh*: Moshe the representative on Mount Sinai, representing the *Torah* and Eliyahu, considered the first of the prophets, representing all the *Nevi'im*. It is also interesting to note that both men hold a special

THE FINAL PRESENTATION OF KING MESSIAH / 185

place in Jewish tradition. Despite all his great leadership, Moshe died
outside the land of Israel, yet his burial was always a bit of a mystery
(cf. Deuteronomy 34:6). Eliyahu never did taste death but was caught
up to the heavens on the chariot of fire (cf. II Kings 2:11).

Because of this mysterious exit, Jewish tradition consigns a
special place to Elijah. One example is found in the rabbinic literature
where there is often an unresolved theological problem. In such cases,
the term *Teku* is invoked, meaning that it is unresolved. According
to some, the term *Teku* is derived from an acronym in Hebrew that
translates *"The Tishbi will solve all difficulties and questions."*
Likewise, tradition speaks of a special hope that Eliyahu will reappear
at some point and announce the arrival of King Messiah (cf. Mal'akhi
3:23 in Hebrew, 4:5 English).

These promises are remembered at the Passover *seder,* as we
still set aside the cup of Elijah with the hope that he will reappear to
announce the arrival of *Mashiach*. The combining of these two special
prophets was not unknown in rabbinic thought: "Moses, I swear to
you, as you devoted your life to their service in this world, so too
in the time to come when I bring Elijah, the prophet, unto them, the
two of you shall come together" (Deuteronomy/*Devarim Raba* 3:17).
The appearance of Moshe and Eliyahu with Yeshua was no doubt a
confirmation of the central message of the New Covenant—Yeshua is
the fulfillment of all the promises to the fathers as seen in the *Torah*
and the Prophets.

With this tradition and Jewish history in mind, it is no wonder the
disciples have a strong reaction. As usual, it is Kefa/Peter who offers
the first response with the words, "it's good that we're here, Lord."
No doubt Kefa and the others presumed that the Kingdom of God had
finally arrived, thus fulfilling Yeshua's promise of Chapter 16 that the
disciples would be present at the event. If the fulfillment had indeed
arrived, then Kefa's next statement is quite understandable. He offers
to *put up three shelters*—one for Yeshua, one for Moshe, and one for

Eliyahu. Sometimes this statement is trivialized to make Kefa look naïve or lacking in spiritual discernment.

However, his offer would be a most natural response for any orthodox Jew. If the Kingdom of God had indeed arrived, then it would be time to celebrate the festival that anticipates its arrival: *Sukkot*/Feast of Tabernacles. This is the premier feast of the *Torah* that celebrates God's presence dwelling with his people. The most graphic emblem of the festival is the temporary hut (*sukkah*) in which Jews are to dwell for the eight-day celebration (cf. Leviticus 23:39-44). It must have seemed abundantly clear to Kefa that Messiah and his Kingdom had come and therefore it was quite apropos to build a *sukkah* for the *Mashiach* and these two prophets.

Although the intent was good and quite logical for Kefa as a traditional Jew, the question might still remain if this was the exact time of complete messianic fulfillment. Consequently, a correction comes in the form of a *bat-kol*/a voice from the cloud. The idea of God periodically speaking a word from heaven was not unknown among the rabbis. "After the death of Haggai, Zechariah and Malachi, the last of the prophets, the Holy Spirit ceased from Israel; nevertheless they received communications from God through the medium of the *bat-kol*" (Tosefta Sotah 13:2). Since it was too intense to consider hearing the voice of God directly, it was believed the *bat-kol* was an echoed deflection as God communicated with his people.

This voice from God had a loving correction for Kefa. *This is my son, whom I love, with whom I am well pleased. Listen to him!* The call to listen to the coming Messiah is reminiscent of the prophecy from Moses himself that there is coming a prophet like Moses to whom Israel must pay special attention (*Devarim*/Deuteronomy 18:15). At this point, the three *talmidim* took an entirely different approach. Instead of feeling the joy of Sukkot, it is recorded that *they were so frightened that they fell face down on the ground.* They had the right idea, just the wrong timing. To reassure them, Yeshua *touched them,* gently exhorting them to *get up* and not to be *afraid*. As the *talmidim opened their eyes*, they saw *only* Yeshua *by himself,* thus ending the dynamic revelation of the Kingdom of God. They would have to wait yet more (as we modern Messianic Jews wait) for the ultimate coming of *Mashiach ben David* at Yeshua's Second Coming.

Although there must have been a sense of disappointment regarding the Transfiguration event, Yeshua used it to teach his *talmidim*. It may seem a bit surprising that the disciples are exhorted *not to tell anyone* what they have just witnessed. Ironically, this was probably to curtail any rampant rumors among the masses that King Messiah has arrived.

Yes, Yeshua is the One, but it would be a matter of God's timing regarding the coming kingdom. Reporting what they had seen might actually lead the multitudes to some of the same errant conclusions. The truth of the Transfiguration would have its proper time to be made known to the general public, and that time would be *after the Son of Man has been raised from the dead.*

At that time, the whole picture of the two missions of the Messiah will be clear to understand. First, *Mashiach ben Yosef* must suffer for the redemption of the world and only then shall *Mashiach ben David* come with God's millennial kingdom. This exhortation brought a natural question to the disciples' minds: Why is it written that *Eliyahu must come first?*

Again, Yeshua affirms their basic understanding of Jewish theology but corrects some of their chronological presuppositions. *Eliyahu is coming* to restore all things, as it is written. In fact, Yeshua reveals some new information in that regard. Eliyahu has *come already and people did not recognize him.* Perhaps they remembered Yeshua's affirmation of Yochanan the Immerser as the fulfillment of a first-century Eliyahu. Yochanan, as the prototypical Eliyahu, came to prepare the way of Messiah. There was one problem however. In order for Eliyahu to fulfill his ministry completely, he must be received by Israel as a whole. Yochanan, while welcomed by many, also was largely rejected and even martyred before any final success. Yeshua applies some of these same principles to his own messianic ministry to Israel. *In the same way, the Son of Man too is about to suffer at their hands.* As the true Messiah sent from the Father, one would expect Yeshua to fulfill all the messianic promises of the *Tanakh.*

Even today, many Jews question how Yeshua can be the true Messiah if he clearly did not fulfill all the scriptural descriptions. However, the fulfillment of the mission of *Mashiach ben David* will only be realized when all Israel welcomes him to rule over them. There is a penetrating story in the *Talmud* that reiterates this belief as Rabbi Joshua ben Levi is said to be searching for the Messiah. Not surprisingly, he runs into Elijah who directs the rabbi to the *Mashiach* who is ministering among some lepers. As they greet each other, Rabbi Joshua asks the all important question:

> "When will you come, Master?" he asked. "Today," was Messiah's answer. On his returning to Elijah, the latter enquired, "What did he say to you?" "He spoke falsely to me," he rejoined, "stating that he would come today, but has not." Elijah answered Rabbi Joshua, "This is what he said to you: Today, if you will hear his voice" (Psalm 95:7 in Tractate Sanhedrin 98a).

The offer of the kingdom was given by Yeshua to first-century Israel and the same offer still stands today. But according to his own words, Israel (and the world) will not see him back in Jerusalem until our people say *"Barukh habah b'shem ADONAI/*Welcome in the name of the Lord" (cf. Matthew 23:39). In the meantime, Yeshua will actually fulfill all the promises concerning the Suffering Messiah as described for *Mashiach ben Yosef* (cf. Isaiah 53, etc.). It was then that *the talmidim understood that he was talking to them about Yochanan* *the Immerser.* The wide-reaching ministry of Messiah was coming more and more in focus for the Yeshua followers as they made their way slowly up to Jerusalem.

The Revelation of Messiah's Power   17:14-27

It wasn't long after descending Mount Hermon that the band of disciples encountered another crowd of seekers. Matthew notes that as *they came up to the crowd,* a man prostrated himself before Yeshua. The man had an urgent need to bring before the Messiah, that his son was *an epileptic* and often had fits where he even would *fall into the fire or into the water.* It is informative that Matthew uses the word "lunatic" which reflects the ancient belief that such people were literally moonstruck. The concerned father had previously approached the *talmidim* for spiritual assistance but evidently *they couldn't heal him.* Yeshua response was both a rebuke of his disciples and encouragement to the distressed man. He confronts his followers as *perverted people without any trust.* Expressing his frustration, Yeshua laments, *how long* will he have to *put up* with them?

At that point, Yeshua commands the father to bring the son to him. He immediately *rebuked the demon* and from that moment the afflicted boy *was healed.* In this case there is a clear correlation between the physical affliction of epilepsy and the spiritual powers of darkness. This, of course, is not a universal truth. There are too many exceptions where even in the Scripture, a physical affliction is totally unrelated to the curse of Satan. Rabbi Sha'ul/Paul actually praised God for his thorn in the flesh (cf. II Corinthians 12:7-10) and some afflictions are actually said to be for the glory of God (cf. Yochanan 9:1-5). This healing should not be interpreted as a guarantee of healing for all followers of Yeshua. In fact, the Messiah himself suffered great pain in order to fulfill his calling. Nonetheless, the healing of this boy's physical/spiritual affliction is a beautiful example of Messiah's power in this particular case.

The disciples must have been both amazed and perplexed. Accordingly, they came to Yeshua *privately and said "Why couldn't we drive it out?"* Yeshua's blunt retort reveals the *little trust* that the disciples had in the power of God. To drive home his point, he shares an amazing truth of the kingdom. In order to experience some of God's great power, a person doesn't need to be a great spiritual giant. Surprisingly, one only needs to *have trust as tiny as a mustard seed.* If a Messianic disciple has even this smallest amount of faith, he could potentially *say to this mountain, "Move from here to there!"* The metaphor of moving mountains is found among rabbinic expressions for accomplishing a very difficult task. The Talmudic rabbi named Rabbah is referred to an "an uprooter of mountains" (Tractate Berakhot 64a) and the arguments of Resh Lakish are described as "uprooting mountains and grinding them against each other" (Tractate Sanhedrin 24a). It was well known in the Middle East that the seed of a mustard plant is one of the smallest botanically. Yet, the seed can grow into a very large bush, even to the size of a tree.

The lesson is clear. Even with a small amount of trusting on our part, God can accomplish great things. The teaching was even more striking in the context of this encounter, as the disciples had just descended the tallest mountain in Israel, Mount Hermon. From the smallest seed of spiritual faith even *this mountain* (Hermon) could potentially be moved! Yeshua even expands the possibilities by emphasizing that *nothing will be impossible* for those who activate such faith. Once again, we must be careful to avoid interpreting more in a passage than is allowed by the context of the whole of Scripture. This statement is not license to impose our own foolish ideas over the mandate of God himself. Yeshua said in another context, "If you ask me something in my name, I will do it" (Yochanan 14:14). It is not a blank check for our own desires but answers will come, assuming we can ask according to God's will. Nevertheless, the mustard seed promise is beautiful and amazing in that it teaches us that astounding things are possible if we trust in Messiah's power.

The revelation of Messiah's power continued with a reminder that on the road to the kingdom, one must travel through a degree of suffering as well. As Yeshua and his *talmidim* traveled *together in the Galil*, he reiterated the fate of the Messiah—that he would soon be *betrayed into the hands of people*. It is at the hands of his enemies that Yeshua will be given over *to death*.

By now there was clearly opposition from many in rabbinic leadership concerning this upstart Messiah. It will not only be some of the Jewish leaders who will turn on Yeshua, but ultimately the Roman civil authorities as well. It is well documented that the Sanhedrin had to submit to the Romans in all capital cases. It is unfortunate that some today still believe "the Jews" killed Yeshua. However, it is a matter of history that he was executed on an execution-stake, which is not even part of the Jewish judicial system. In a strange way, it is prophetic that Messiah would be rejected by his own and turned over to the Gentiles for ultimate execution. All peoples are represented in his rejection so that he may turn it around and be the redeemer of all.

Despite the apparent setback, there would be good news at the end of the story, as Yeshua promises that *on the third day he will be raised*. No doubt even Satan himself thought he had conquered God's messianic redemption when Yeshua was executed as a criminal. But the true *Mashiach* will even have power over the greatest enemy of mankind, death itself! The passive verb (will be raised) is a reminder that it is the God of Israel, our Father in Heaven, who will raise Yeshua to confirm he is the true King Messiah.

It is significant to point out that even the closest disciples still did not comprehend how all these details would fit together. They could not help but be filled with sadness. Why couldn't King Messiah march into Jerusalem and establish his throne in their day? Why the suffering? It must have been difficult indeed for the disciples and others to understand how the whole plan of redemption would be completed. For now they would be filled with sadness and anxiety as they followed Yeshua.

The itinerant group ultimately made its way back to their home base in K'far-Nachum on the Sea of Galilee. It happened to be the time of year when the biblical tax was due, so not surprisingly *Kefa* is approached by some of *the collectors* since this was his hometown. Originally, this was the half-shekel fee associated with the *Mishkan/* Tabernacle in the wilderness (cf. Exodus 30:13). By the first century, this tax was applied for the upkeep of the priestly service in Yerushalayim. The collectors posed a significant question, "Doesn't your rabbi pay the Temple tax?" The contributions to the Temple were of important religious concern as seen from the fact that an entire book of the *Talmud* deals with the issue (Tractate Shekelim). While the priesthood was exempt from the payment, it was incumbent upon all others in the community.

Asking such a question in this way implies a number of things. First, they had not yet received the payment from the Yeshua followers. They may have missed their contribution because they were out of the district for several months. Now that they were back at their home base, it was time to fulfill the duty. Perhaps underlying the question is also some doubt or confusion based on Yeshua's teaching. Despite his express teaching that he did not come to erase even one letter of the *Torah* (cf. Matthew 5:17-18), some doubts may have remained based on some of his confrontations with rabbinic doctrine. It was a good question, and Kefa offered his confident opinion, "Of course he does." This is an important question still today for the modern Jewish seeker. Not only did Yeshua clearly state that his teaching was consistent with the written *Torah,* but here Kefa gives a confident affirmation to that fact. It is especially telling coming from one of Yeshua's closest disciples who had lived with the Messiah for the last three years.

The temple tax dialogue would continue as Kefa *arrived home* and was addressed by Yeshua. Evidently discerning some of the thoughts in Kefa's mind, Yeshua asks, "From who do the kings of the Earth collect duties and taxes?" In the Roman system do they tax *their own sons or others?* The obvious response in Kefa's mind is that the authorities clearly tax *others* while exempting their own family. Yeshua affirms this natural answer while drawing a larger analogy to the spiritual kingdom.

Here, too, the sons are technically exempt from even the temple tax. The *Mashiach*, who is called the Son of God, is not obliged to obey the same laws as the bulk of humanity. He even owns the *Beit-Ha'Mikdash*/Temple! But there is another spiritual principle that must be considered in this situation. By not paying the half-shekel tax, there could be even more confusion to the outside Jewish observer.

To avoid offending them, Yeshua exhorts Kefa to make their payment in a most unusual way. He is to go fishing in the Kinneret, which would have been a natural task for the Galilean fisherman. The first fish that Kefa will catch will contain the necessary payment *in its mouth*, *a shekel* to cover the tax for Kefa and his rabbi.

By making their payment in such a way, Kefa would not only fulfill the religious obligation but it would be a public testimony that Yeshua and his followers continue *Torah* observance in the most important duties. In addition, this miraculous manner of catching just the right fish was a testimony to Kefa and his colleagues.

Perhaps it was not entirely unique for a fish to swallow a shekel coin that had been dropped in the lake. But to catch a particular fish with the shekel in its mouth would defy any odds. Even today, one can lunch at the Sea of Galilee on the tilapia named "Saint Peter's Fish" in memory of this amazing sign to the disciples. The messianic signs are obvious all over the land of Israel to those who have eyes to see.

Instructions for the Messianic Life   18:1-20:34

Matthew's account of the life of Yeshua now comes to a significant transition. With the band of disciples growing numerically, it evidently became increasingly important to communicate further details on their spiritual walk to them. Once again we see Yeshua fulfilling the role of a great rabbi and the unique Messiah as he gives *halakhic* applications concerning the *Torah*. His believers will come together in spiritual communities, but this in itself will present some new challenges. In the next three chapters, we are given various details on what it means to walk the walk of Yeshua. Here we are given some very practical answers for the questions of everyday life.

Instructions for Humility   18:1-35

Since the previous chapter of Matthew dealt with the central issue of the kingdom of Messiah, the disciples pose a logical question. Matthew connects the two chapters with the opening words "at that moment." It was the current discussion after the Transfiguration experience and paying the Temple tax that focused on some of the details of Yeshua's kingdom. Who would be *the greatest in the Kingdom of Heaven?* Instead of answering their question directly, Yeshua *called a child* to himself. Those who would seek to be great in the Kingdom of Heaven would have to have a *change* in attitude and *become like little children.* In fact, one will not be able even to *enter the Kingdom* without the same kind of spirit as this young one. Ironically, *the greatest in the Kingdom is whoever makes himself as humble as this child.*

Yeshua's disciples are to focus on serving, not on being served. In the world (especially in this present age), the way to greatness is usually marked by pride, scheming, or political maneuvering. The quickest way up is often to step on someone else. Messiah's calling is to humility and self-abasement. As a child lives with simple trust in his loving parents, similarly a Messianic disciple must have a simple, abiding faith in the Heavenly Father.

These are not mere pious platitudes coming from Yeshua—he exemplified this spirit in his own life. Therefore, *whoever welcomes one such child in my name* welcomes Yeshua himself. By contrast, we are warned not to *ensnare one of these*. The judgment will be severe because of the abuse given to such a trusting child. *It would be better to have a millstone hung around his neck and be drowned in the open sea!* This strong illustration would have shocked the crowd. A millstone was the heavy round stone usually pulled by a beast of burden in order to pulverize grain into flour. It would be unthinkable to have such a massive stone tied to one's neck but such is the seriousness of causing a simple child to stumble.

Unfortunately, society has always made those stumble who would seek such child-like faith. Yeshua uses another illustration to bring home his point. *Woe* (literally *"oy!"*) *to the world because of snares!* A snare was a trap or cage that was set in order to capture an animal by stealth. Jewish dietary restrictions forbade eating any animal that is not properly slaughtered (*shechitah*) in order to remove the blood. This requires a ritual slaughterer (*shochet)* to kill the animal in such a way as to allow the draining of the blood with the required Hebrew prayers. Consequently, it was impossible to ritually slaughter a kosher animal if it was killed in the process of hunting or shooting. The logical way to capture a kosher animal alive was often in a snare or trap.

While digging a pit or setting a baited cage to catch an animal was accepted practice, it was also a picture of doing something by deceit. The world is filled with such snares and traps! Yeshua even affirms here that *there must be snares.* Maybe we can survive the direct arrows and shots, but we must watch out for the hidden traps. A special judgment is reserved for *the person who sets the snare.* No doubt this is all a sober statement of the special place children have in the eyes of God. Everyone is judged according to the light they possess, and children appear to be less culpable based on their simple trust. Yeshua is emphasizing the place of God's spiritual children. *Oy to those who cause God's own kids to stumble.*

Yeshua now turns his teaching directly to the *talmidim. A snare may be as close as your own hand or foot.* What if your own hand keeps taking you far from God? What if your feet take you to places that are destructive to your soul? In the strongest of terms, Messiah exhorts such a person to *cut off* the limb and *throw it away!* That this saying is in fact hyperbole to shock the hearers is clear. Even if a person had a problem with a sin issue, would removing a hand or foot solve the dilemma?

Although we could be tempted to blame our hand or foot, the problem is much deeper than the limbs. It is an issue of the heart. But so important is eternal life that it is better to *be maimed* to enter God's kingdom than to *keep both hands or both feet and be thrown into everlasting fire.*

Similarly, *if your eye is a snare for you, gouge it out and fling it away!* Obviously the eyes and what we choose to view can be a significant stumbling block in our spiritual walk. However, the eyes are not the real problem—it is the attitude of the heart. It is important to note the contrast and reality of both heaven and hell in Yeshua's teaching. So desirous is eternal life that if your eye is the one thing keeping you out, get rid of it. Better to be *one-eyed and obtain eternal life* than go with full vision into *the fire of Gei-Hinnom.*

Translated as "the valley of Hinnom," this area outside Jerusalem was notorious as a spot of paganism, idolatry, and even a garbage dump. As such it was constantly burning with the smell of sulfur and refuse. The Greeks later translated the Hebrew term to *Gehenna* which evolved to the English "Hell." It is easy to see how the word *Gei-Hinnom* became synonymous with a most wicked place and even the future place of the judgment of the ungodly (cf. Jeremiah 7; Matthew 7).

Although classic rabbinic hyperbole is employed here, the real lessons are clear. Eternal life is so wonderful—do all within your powers to find it. In contrast, *Gei-Hinnom* is so terrible—do all within your power to avoid it! As radical as removing limbs might be, how much more needed is spiritual repentance and a change of heart to escape the coming judgment? We must give heed to this strong lesson even today and come to the Messiah who delivers us from the judgment to come (cf. I Thessalonians 1:10). On a final thought concerning the child, Yeshua exhorts his hearers to *never despise one of these little ones.* Although it might be easy to overlook children, they have the kind of simple trust and acceptance that is needed for *olam haba* (the world to come). For this reason *their angels in heaven are continually seeing the face of my Father in heaven.*

This verse has two important truths. The first is the emphasis on the unique relationship between Yeshua as God and his personal Father. Although human beings are also called children of God, the *Mashiach* is presented here as a unique, direct, divine agent sent from the Father. Some take the second part of the statement as another indicator that children are part of God's kingdom (by his grace) until the age of accountability where they might reject God's love in Messiah. This age would vary depending on the individual but the traditional ceremony which marks such a time is the *Bar/Bat Mitzvah* at age twelve or thirteen (Pirke Avot 5:24; Isaiah 7:15-16).

Even with various views concerning the salvation of children, one thing is clear—"the Judge of all the Earth [will] do what is just" (Genesis 18:25). God has made it abundantly clear what is needed to enter his kingdom—personal faith in his way of redemption. Even a top rabbi like Nicodemus was exhorted about his personal need to have his spirit born again (*Yochanan*/John 3). Beyond that is mere speculation and uncertainty. Whatever the status of an individual (child or adult), the character of God gives us great *shalom* as we trust our Father in heaven for all things.

To emphasize this important point of teaching, Yeshua switches the analogy from children to sheep. He asks, what will be the attitude of a shepherd who *has a hundred sheep and one of them wanders away?* Even if the *ninety-nine* are secure *on the hillsides*, won't he *go off to find the stray?* Of course he will. And when he finds the stray one, the shepherd will *be happier over it than over the ninety-nine that never strayed.* So important is everyone, especially innocent children, in the kingdom of Messiah. The Father *does not want even one of these little ones to be lost.* God, as our Creator and Redeemer, desires all to share in the joys of his restored world. The great emphasis, which Yeshua places on the teaching with the young child, illustrates the degree of God's love for all his children. Such humility is a key to finding *Mashiach.*

Yeshua now turns his teaching focus to the need for humility within human relationships. It is vital to have a childlike attitude in Yeshua's kingdom. Yet, the world is filled with imperfect people in a fallen world. The spirit of humility will be especially needed in dealing with those around us. *If your brother commits a sin against you* should be understood as a given in the original language (e.g. "*when* your brother sins"). An infraction of the *Torah* will undoubtedly occur in the broken environment of the world system, but here he even alludes to the strong possibility of an offense from a fellow Messianic brother or sister. Even on our best days and with our most sincere motives, we will often fall short of God's high expectations revealed in the *Torah.* The definition of sin (Hebrew *cheyt*) is in fact a graphic picture of one missing the mark even as a warrior misses his target with a slingshot stone (cf. *Shoftim*/Judges 20:16). Such is the sad spiritual reality of all mankind as well (cf. Romans 3:23).

While the Messiah has been sent to ultimately cover the sins of those who receive his gift, here we have some practical counsel on how to deal with problem situations among his people. The first step, according to Yeshua, is to *go and show him his fault.* It is presumed

THE FINAL PRESENTATION OF KING MESSIAH / 199

here that the situation had risen to the point of personal offense that had not been unilaterally forgiven. This is always the initial step to consider, as love has the ability to cover a multitude of sins (cf. Proverbs 10:12; I Peter 4:8).

If the sin is of such a character that it is still a stumbling block to the relationship, then it should be addressed with the offending brother. By saying "go," the mandate is given to the offended party to take the initiative for resolution and not just to wait for action by the other person. It is vital to note that the situation is to be confronted with a spirit of humility (the theme of this chapter) and *privately, just between the two* individuals. This wise procedure keeps the problem on the lowest level possible. It averts the temptation of *lashon hara* (gossip), as the person is exhorted not to talk to other people before confronting the offending individual. Because this is done in private (not during the refreshments!), it prevents others from hearing something that's not their business.

Resolving issues just between the two parties involved should be done in a humble spirit because, upon further discussion, the offended party might discover their own culpability for part of the problem. Most people, especially Messianic followers, do not intend to intentionally hurt someone else, but we often do so out of ignorance or naïveté. How will we really know the truth of the situation unless we have an open and honest, heart-to-heart talk about our perspectives? This is clearly the wisest place to start when dealing with a personal sin situation. Yeshua continues by pointing out that there are essentially two possible responses to this private encounter. If the person *listens to you* and makes the adequate adjustment, *you have won back your brother.* Implied in the act of listening to the offended party is the goal of acknowledgment and *t'shuvah* (repentance).

If agreement is reached, then the situation is repaired and the relationship restored. This is another reason to take care of the problem privately. If the situation is remedied at this level, then no one else needs to be concerned or negatively impacted by it. More often than not, this is how problems are fixed within the body of Yeshua. Yet, there is another possible avenue if the confronted brother or sister *doesn't listen*. Maybe he or she does not see the sin you are talking about or perhaps may disagree about your judgment.

Yeshua's description assumes there is a real sin infraction on the part of the other person. However, it could also be that the offended person actually misunderstood the real situation. In an extreme case, it could even be the so-called offended party who has actually sinned! If the two individuals disagree on the situation, how can we know the truth? Messiah's next step answers that problem in a very practical and spiritual manner. *Take one or two others with you* to try to resolve the broken relationship. If the two brothers have not successfully resolved the problem between them, it is time for some outside assistance. Still, it is kept at the most private level possible in order to avoid unnecessary complications with other people. A qualified person outside the two parties might be able to give some objective insight toward resolution.

The fact that Yeshua is referring to one or two people of spiritual maturity and discernment is clear from his quote of the *Torah*. *Every accusation can be supported by the testimony of two or three witnesses* (*Devarim*/Deuteronomy 19:15). It shouldn't surprise us that as Yeshua addresses the issue of interpersonal relationships, he simply invokes a central *Torah* principle. Any witnesses (Hebrew *aydim*) are presumed in Jewish law to be actual eyewitnesses to the sinful situation. Their testimony concerning the sinful situation would help clear up the dispute.

However, it is also possible that the two or three people are not eyewitnesses to the original problem but eyewitnesses to the next meeting between the two parties. It is critical that the witnesses oversee and mediate the situation with spiritual maturity and objectivity. In practical terms, it would be best if these witnesses were from the spiritual leadership of the *kehilah* (*Zekeynim*/elders or *Shamashim*/deacons). Such leaders have what is needed to help resolve some of these challenging situations. In fact, an unqualified or untrained mediator could greatly complicate the entire problem. Again, Yeshua gives two options for the encounter at this point. If the person still *refuses to hear them,* there will be more dire consequences. By now, it is becoming clear what really took place between the two individuals. It is moving beyond the personal opinion of each party since objective eyewitnesses have prayerfully evaluated the evidence and interaction.

In this case, it has been confirmed that there is indeed sin on the part of one person. Because this truth was not received in the individual encounter or in the small-group confrontation, there is yet another step. *Tell the congregation* the necessary details of this sinful choice. This is a vital step toward spiritual health, but must be done with the utmost spiritual discretion. It appears that only situations impacting the entire congregation (well-known and obvious sin) must be addressed in this public manner.

Since this entire passage focuses on how to deal with any sin problem on an appropriate level with only the affected individuals, it is only in some extreme cases where the problem should rise to the level of affecting the entire local congregation. If so, it must be dealt with accordingly, always in the grace and justice of the *Torah*. Even in this case, care must be taken to share only what is necessary for spiritual purposes for the protection of the general flock of Messiah.

At this point, there is a chance of restoration if the guilty party listens to the larger body of believers. Every step, in fact, is taken with the hope that restoration (not retribution) will be the end result. But *if he refuses to listen even to the congregation, treat him as you would a pagan or a tax collector.* Please note that no indication is given here of the loss of personal salvation. The person is still a "brother," albeit, an unrepentant, sinful brother. Even at this point, there is no judgment on his eternal relationship with God through Yeshua. Such things are in God's hands. But if such a brother refuses all the attempts at reconciliation and repentance, then he is to be treated as a pagan. The lesson would be clear to Yeshua's audience. The unrepentant person was on a level with the worst person outside the covenant community. A tax collector also represented a most despicable person, essentially a traitor to the Jewish community. Such a brother must be excommunicated and cut off from the fellowship of believers. This is to protect the remaining flock from being affected by the leaven in their midst. In a strange way, it is also one last opportunity of grace for the unrepentant brother to consider his ways and perhaps still make *t'shuvah*/repentance for restoration to the Messianic community. The gates of repentance are always open, even beyond this extreme example.

Since this is a very difficult situation to deal with, Yeshua gives a special promise to those in spiritual leadership. Such mediators and counselors who seek God's wisdom on these kinds of issues are assured that there will be assistance. *Whatever you prohibit on earth will be prohibited in heaven.* This is not a blank check for our desires nor is it even related directly to prayer.

As in Matthew 16, we remember that the terminology reflects rabbinic legal decisions, not personal requests. To prohibit something (Hebrew *asur*) is to render a *halachic* decision against that action. For example, the Talmud speaks of binding a day by declaring it a fast-day (Tractate Ta'anit 12a) thus making food prohibited. The context of Yeshua's promise here must be kept in mind. Instead of talking about prayer or spiritual battle issues (as is often applied), he is speaking at length about legal decisions concerning disciplinary issues within the Messianic community.

In the Jewish community, local *halakhah* (legal decisions) are often expressed by a group of three rabbis known as a *Beit-Din* (house of judgment). In essence, Yeshua is establishing a messianic *Beit-Din* that would be able to decide important matters for his followers. Their decisions would not be an educated guess at what is right, but the Greek perfect tense strongly states that whatever is already God's decision in heaven will be revealed to the sincere leadership on Earth. Whether it is forbidden (Hebrew *asur*) or permitted (Hebrew *mutar*), God will reveal his will in such relational conflicts. *If two of you here on earth agree about anything*, the decision will proceed directly from the *Father in heaven*.

The final phrase qualifies the parameters of the promise further. *Wherever two or three are assembled* (as a *Beit-Din*) *in my name, I am there with them.* The messianic *Beit-Din* of local leaders will receive the necessary wisdom when they come together in the name of the Messiah. Reflecting a similar promise, the *Talmud* states, "If two sit together and words of *Torah* pass between them, the *Sh'khinah* abides between them" (Tractate Avot 3:2).

A first-century person's name was more than just a convenient tag to identify someone. It was often descriptive or even a prophetic picture of the person. To speak in the name of someone was to call down the full authority of that person and represent his wishes. All of this is informative in regard to this teaching of Yeshua. The binding or loosing deals with a specific decision, and those who would receive the knowledge of God's will must align themselves in the name of Yeshua first. Spiritual leaders who put Yeshua first are promised special leading into God's will. He himself will be *there with them* as they shepherd Messiah's flock.

As if to confirm the context of the teaching, *Kefa came up and said to him "Rabbi, how often can my brother sin against me and I have to forgive him?"* Note that he does not ask Yeshua about prayer, binding evil spirits, or loosing prosperity! Kefa understands that the teaching relates to the main theme of forgiveness and restoration. In his own mind, Kefa must have thought he was being gracious in his question. He could envision forgiving a brother *as many as seven times.* Some rabbinic teaching states specifically that one is very gracious if he forgives a sinning brother up to three times (Tractate Yoma 86b). However, Yeshua once again expanded the current thought on the topic from not just seven times but to *seventy times seven.* Even this high number was not meant to be the ultimate limit for God's forgiveness. The number seven is often used in biblical and Jewish metaphor as the number of completeness or an unlimited amount. Perhaps Yeshua had in mind the *Torah* passage that speaks of Lemech's unlimited vengeance in contrast to unlimited forgiveness (cf. Genesis 4:24). By saying *seventy times seven,* Yeshua is clearly emphasizing that God's forgiveness (and therefore his children's forgiveness) has no end.

Realizing that such a statement must have been almost incomprehensible to his *talmidim,* Messiah launches into another one of his enlightening parables. *Because of this* teaching on forgiveness, *the Kingdom of Heaven may be compared with a king.* Matthew's use of the term "Heaven" is a logical substitute word for "God" in the Jewish mind. Out of respect for the name of God, such words were used like *"shamayim/ heaven,"* *"HaShem/ the name"* or even *"HaMakom/ the place."*

In this story, the king has some debts to settle *with his deputies.* The first interview is with *a man who owed him many millions.* The literal translation would be "10,000 talents" which in Roman times equaled 6,000 denarii. When one realizes that a denarius was roughly one day's wages, 10,000 talents could equal the astounding amount of $3 billion! Such a high debt was impossible to repay on the spot. Consequently, the master ordered that the man and all of his *possessions be sold* including even *his wife* and *his children.*

Such a repayment sounds strange to our modern society but in the ancient Middle East, it was a viable option. The *Torah* allowed such indentured slavery as an option for those who were in extreme debt (cf. Exodus 21:1-6). This was not the abusive form of slavery that was practiced in other societies such as America in the 1800s. But this kind of biblical slavery was actually the ancient way of filing "chapter 11" bankruptcy. While it was not a desirable lot in life, often the slave would be treated more as a family member than as a hired servant. The man responsible would certainly sell his own service to repay the debt and, in extreme cases, the man's family was also affected as they were considered his property.

That this *Torah*-based slavery was not meant to be abusive can be seen in the fact that the debtor was to be set free every seven years at the *sh'mitah*/sabbatical year and could even volunteer to stay under his master's employment after the service was completed. This in itself is, by the way, a most beautiful picture of the believer's relationship with God through Messiah Yeshua. While we are technically set free by Yeshua's redemptive work, we are like slaves who desire to stay with our benevolent master.

In this parable, the servant pleaded with the master to *be patient* until he could *pay back everything*. In an amazing gesture, *the master let him go and forgave the debt.* But now comes the ironic twist of the story. As the *servant was leaving, he came upon one of his fellow servants who owed him some tiny sum* (literally 100 denarii), which translates into about $5,000. It was hardly comparable to the sum previously owed by the first servant.

Fresh from his encounter with his gracious master, one would expect a similar attitude coming from the forgiven servant. Such was not the case as he *grabbed* his fellow servant and even *began to choke him!* The blatant contrast between the large sum and the tiny sum stands out along with the extreme attitude of the servant. Instead of grace and patience, the first servant demands that the other *pay back* what is owed. The second servant begs for patience with the promise that he will pay back the debt in a timely manner. Instead of extending grace, the first servant *refused* the offer and had his debtor *thrown in jail.*

The story continues with the statement that *other servants saw what had happened* and were *extremely distressed*. They were so upset by the inconsistent actions of the slave that they immediately *told their master everything that had taken place*. As can be imagined, the master was none too happy about this turn of events. He summoned the man and strongly rebuked him, calling him a *wicked servant*. After forgiving *all that debt*, the master assumed a better attitude would be forthcoming. The logical response would be to *have had pity* on his fellow servant just as the master had pity on him. Since the servant acted in such an inappropriate way, the master angrily *turned him over to the jailers for punishment* until everything was paid back. The end result of this sad situation is both fair and just. Highlighting the main spiritual point of the parable, Yeshua exhorts Kefa and the *talmidim* that this is how the *heavenly Father will treat* anyone who cannot *forgive* their *brother from their hearts*.

The parable provides a powerful insight into the heart of God. Such forgiveness is not a mere matter of lip service but a life-changing attitude of the heart. Where the rabbis stated that forgiveness must be extended three times, Kefa had expanded it to seven times. Yet, God's own forgiveness has unlimited possibilities (seventy times seven). We must therefore be gracious and consistent in extending forgiveness to those around us. Since God through Yeshua has forgiven us a huge debt, should we not be gracious and quick to forgive those around us today?

Instructions Concerning Problematic Issues 19:1-30

After Yeshua had *finished talking* about some lessons in humility, he and his *talmidim* would now journey closer to Jerusalem. Matthew notes that they *left the Galil and traveled down the east side of the Yarden River*. In modern times since 1948, this has been the territory controlled by the country of Jordan. In biblical times, this area east of the Jordan River was still part of the tribal inheritance of Israel.

Today, there is still debate over the so-called "west bank" territory west of the Jordan. However, when Yeshua is traveling on the east side, even that area is identified as part of *Eretz-Yisra'el*. Modern political negotiations will no doubt continue, but the biblical promises stand secure. The Messianic band of believers continues until they are on the *border of Y'hudah* (the central tribe of Judah). The gospel writer records that *great crowds followed* Yeshua and he *healed* many of them at that place.

Not surprisingly, as the group draws closer to Judea and Jerusalem, they are approached by *some P'rushim*/Pharisees. Some of the rabbinic leaders had to be concerned that this maverick rabbi was once again entering their own turf. Although there had been numerous rabbinic discussions with Yeshua over the last three years, the *P'rushim* come hoping *to trap him* with a classic theological question. By now it is evident that they were not sincerely seeking new truth about this possible *Mashiach* but were merely trying to justify their own unbelief (which often happens today as well). Their question hit at the heart of a most important *mitzvah* in Judaism, marriage and conditions for divorce. So important were these issues that there was an entire tractate of the *Talmud* devoted to marriage, divorce, and remarriage (cf. Tractate Gittin).

Reflecting the most liberal Jewish opinion of the day, they ask Yeshua, "is it permitted for a man to divorce his wife on any ground whatever?" In Pharisaic Judaism there were essentially two main schools of thought in the first century. The school of Rabbi Hillel (*Beit-Hillel*) was the more lenient, often taking a less strict interpretation of social issues. The opposing school was that of Rabbi Shammai (*Beit-Shammai*), who often took a more stringent and conservative view. It is significant to note that it is only the Pharisees (and not the Sadducees) who are posing this current question. They are perhaps seeking to discover what side of the spectrum this Galilean rabbi will endorse.

The controversial question at hand centers on the much-debated phrase in the *Torah, ervat davar* (*Devarim*/Deuteronomy 24:1). The phrase alludes to a married man who has found his wife *offensive in some respect*. The Hebrew literally means "a thing of nakedness." *Beit-Shammai* took a very narrow view of the passage, interpreting it to mean sexual immorality (as the term *ervat* strongly implies). Consequently, that branch of the *P'rushim* forbade divorce in any circumstance except adultery. That there may be a more expanded interpretation is found in the *Torah* where the penalty for adultery was actually death (cf. *Devarim*/Deuteronomy 22:22).

Embedded within this particular question is an assumption that the group was favoring the more liberal *Beit-Hillel*. It was Hillel who interpreted *ervat davar* in the broadest sense, allowing divorce for almost anything that would be unpleasing to the husband. This could include such disrespectful acts as a wife not having her head covered in public or even the act of consistently burning her husband's food! (Tractate Gittin 90a).

Please know that Hillel's liberal view was not considered license for divorce based on one mistake by the wife. Instead, it required consistent and deliberate acts of disrespect that would undercut the very covenant of marriage. In contrast, it is amazing in contemporary society (even Jewish) how easy it is to get a divorce for merely "irreconcilable differences."

Yeshua's reply is most informative, not only to the people of his day but also for us. His response to the question is with a question of his own. *Haven't you read* what the *Torah* says on this issue? Messiah does not ask them for their personal view or even their rabbi's opinion. It is not what is heard in rabbinic debate but what is read in the written *Torah*. The relevant text is in the earliest chapters of *B'resheet*/Genesis where it is stated that *at the beginning the Creator made them male and female* (Genesis 1:27). Marriage, as well as any legitimate grounds for divorce, can be seen in the revelation of God.

These things are not mere sociological inventions or cultural mores but spiritual truths created by the one and only God of Israel.

Yeshua continues his quote of the *Torah* to justify God's original design for marriage in that *a man should leave his father and mother and be united with his wife, and the two are to become one flesh* (Genesis 2:24). In his elaboration of the verse, Yeshua points out that the man and woman are *no longer two but one.* The original Hebrew word *echad* is often translated "one," but perfectly reflects the concept of unity. In marriage, the two people do not lose their individuality or uniqueness but are united together in the spiritual covenant. It is this same Hebrew word *echad* that God uses to describe his own character! In the famous *Sh'ma* passage (*Devarim*/Deuteronomy 6:4), God tells us that "The LORD is our God, the LORD is One!"

However, by using the word *echad,* God seems to be telling us more about his mysterious character. While this concept may create problems for some of our Jewish brothers, it is Messianic Judaism that logically balances out these statements. The Lord, the God of Israel, is one God, a unity of our Heavenly Father (*Abba*), Son (*Mashiach*) and Holy Spirit (*Ruach HaKodesh*), all three having the divine nature of *YHVH.* A careful study of the *Tanakh* will reveal confirming evidence for these truths (cf. *Yesha'yahu*/Isaiah 48:16). Yeshua answers the rabbinic question regarding divorce with the evidence of the *Torah.* Since the man and woman are spiritually *echad*/one, *no one should split apart what God has joined together.*

This explanation from Yeshua leads to some follow-up queries from the rabbis. Why then would *Moshe give the commandment that a man should hand his wife a get and divorce her?* The term in Deuteronomy 24:1 is *"sefer kritut*/a document of cutting," which is a graphic description of what divorce is—a cutting off of a relationship and a covenant. The word *get* is the rabbinic word for the paperwork for such a religious divorce within Judaism. Even when Jews have lived outside of Israel or the Jewish community, it was not enough to acquire a civil divorce from the state authorities. For traditional Jews today, one must still receive a religious divorce through a *Beit-Din* in the written contract called a *get*. Their question is obvious. If divorce was not mentioned in the early *Torah* (*B'resheet*/Genesis 1-2), why is it that Moshe later speaks of the possibility of such an action (*Devarim*/Deuteronomy 24)?

Yeshua's answer reconciles any conflicting views. It was not God's original intention to even consider divorce but he made a concession based on human realities. *Moshe allowed you to divorce* (not commanded) because the *hearts* of people *are so hardened*. From the early covenant of *B'resheet*/Genesis, marriage was to be a lifelong covenant between one man and one woman. Divorce was *not how it was at the beginning*. This has always been God's perfect will, yet fallen human nature can often sabotage the beautiful plans of our Creator. If man and woman consistently had a soft heart toward the things of God, divorce should be nonexistent. But we all sin and fall short of the glory of God, often exemplified in breaking the *mitzvot* of the *Torah*. It is bad enough when we break the commandments, but too often we have a hardened heart about our personal choices.

In the case of marriage, things are complicated further. It has been said that it takes two committed people to make a good marriage but only one to mess it up! No doubt there is usually some degree of dual culpability in the case of a broken marriage. However, sometimes it may be the hardened heart of just one side. It is in light of this human reality that divorce was allowed later by God as a concession to make the best of a tragic sin. There are times where divorce is regrettably the best spiritual choice. However, great care must be taken not to abuse the grounds of a biblical divorce. The breaking of the covenant is only allowed, according to Yeshua, on the strictest *ground of sexual immorality*. In fact, if a man *divorces his wife* for any other reason and *marries another woman*, he himself becomes guilty of *adultery!* By his strong statement here, Yeshua is answering his rabbinic colleagues by agreeing with the conservative view of *Beit-Shammai*.

It should be noted that this is not the only place in the *Torah* or New Covenant that the grounds for divorce are discussed. Besides the sexual immorality mentioned here, Rabbi Sha'ul speaks of other possible biblical grounds for seeking a divorce. Since his primary ministry was to non-Jews, it is not surprising that Sha'ul speaks of a "non-believer" deserting a "believer." If the non-believer wants a divorce, as is evident from their departure, then the believer is actually commanded to cooperate in the divorce (I Corinthians 7:15). However, if both spouses are Yeshua followers and they end up in a divorce, then neither one of them is to remarry. The obvious hope is that there may be a reconciliation as they both keep faithful to their marriage vows and try to correct their troubled relationship (I Corinthians 7:10-11). The only other clear case for acceptable remarriage is in the case of the death of a spouse. This frees the other spouse as he/she is no longer in an earthly covenant (Romans 7:1-3).

Despite the more liberal views of Hillel or even our modern society, divorce was always considered a unique tragedy in Jewish tradition. "If a man divorces his first wife, the very altar (of the Temple) weeps" (Tractate Gittin 90b). Divorce is seldom a constructive answer to the problems in a marriage. As the rabbis lamented, "when a divorced man marries a divorced woman, there are four minds in the bed" (Tractate Pesachim 112a). If at all possible, it is much better to resolve the issues based on the principles of *Torah* and the New Covenant. Since these relationship issues can be complicated, it is essential to seek the spiritual counsel of a qualified Messianic counselor or rabbi to discern the best spiritual course of action.

Upon hearing Yeshua's interpretation of the divine laws of marriage and divorce, the *talmidim* begin to draw their own unsettling conclusions. If the marriage covenant is so strong and the problems so threatening, it might be *better not to marry* at all. This is quite a startling statement when it is considered that marriage within Judaism is one of the most important *mitzvot*/commandments. Yeshua's response reflects just how unusual it would be for Jews not to seek marriage.

Yeshua acknowledges that *not everyone grasps this teaching, only those for whom it is meant.* He seems to imply that, although this was an unusual teaching, it applies to a small group of people who may be called to a life of being single. According to Messiah, there may be a number of *different reasons* why a person chooses not to enter into the marriage relationship. Some simply are *born without the desire* while others may *have been castrated* (e.g. eunuchs). Others may have an unusual calling to abstain from marriage *for the sake of the Kingdom of Heaven.* The summary is this: Marriage is the norm for God's covenant children. In fact, it seems to take a special calling and leading *not* to enter into marriage.

It is unfortunate that later followers of Yeshua in the Middle Ages often exalted the place of singleness to an extreme through the monastic movement of Christianity. Some teaching from Christian theologians at this time even painted the sexual relationship within marriage as a necessary evil to be avoided. Judaism, on the other hand, often regarded sex within marriage as a beautiful expression of love given from God himself. It is sadly ironic that Yeshua's teaching is often interpreted as just the opposite. Here we find Messiah emphasizing the beauties of marriage even to the point of setting important boundaries on how to have a romantic covenant relationship blessed of God. Perhaps this is why Yeshua exhorts his *talmidim* to try to *grasp this* particular teaching if they are able. It is not often mentioned that there is a Talmudic debate on whether it is best to study *Torah* or to get married. Among the various views is the opinion that "because of the difficult times," it is better not to marry, especially in some troubled areas of the Jewish community (Tractate Kiddushin 29b).

It seems the gift of singleness is still an unusual yet viable calling in our day. Because of the potential consequences of divorce, one would be wise to seriously seek God's will in regard to potential marriage. Wouldn't it be wise to seek godly counsel prior to marriage in order to confirm God's will in this most important decision? Messianic Judaism has the highest regard for the marriage covenant and relationship. Premarital counseling from a spiritually qualified believer in Yeshua is the best preparation one can make in light of Yeshua's own values stated in this passage.

Matthew's account now turns to a short yet important encounter in the ministry of Messiah. At this time, some *children were brought* to him so that he might *pray for them.* By using the passive verb it is implied that these children were brought to Yeshua by their parents for this traditional duty. The act of imparting a blessing is one of the most universal customs found in Judaism. The rabbis enjoined the duty upon every Jew to give thanks continually to God for his blessings because the Earth is the Lord's and all it contains (*Tehillim/* Psalm 24:1).

Not surprisingly an entire book of the *Talmud* is devoted to the concept of blessing God (Tractate *Berakhot*). Rabbi Meir (second-century CE) concluded that it is the duty of every Jew to recite one hundred benedictions daily, not just for religious ceremonies (e.g., *Shabbat* candles, Kiddush, etc.), but for everyday occurrences such as seeing a wonder of nature, completing a successful trip, or hearing good news.

There were many blessings associated with children. The most famous is recited every *Shabbat* evening at the start of the dinner. After the blessings of candles and wine and bread, the parents place their hands on their children for the proper blessing. For the boys, based on Genesis 48:20, it is said, *"Yesimkha Elohim k'ephraim u'chim'nashe"* (May you be like Ephraim and Manasseh). The daughters receive the blessing *"Yesemeykh k'Sarah, Rivkeh, Rachel v'Leah"* (May you be like Sarah, Rebekah, Rachel, and Leah). It is not surprising, therefore, that some eager parents rush their children before the loving rabbi Yeshua so that *he might lay hands* on them for his blessing. The tradition is an ancient one, as blessing and identification were symbolically imparted by the laying on of hands. The Hebrew word (*samakh*) means to connect or draw together. For example, rabbinic ordination (*s'mikhah*) is passed on by other rabbis through the laying on of hands.

In the middle of this encounter, the *talmidim* had a different concern and even *rebuked the people* for interrupting the rabbi's schedule. Surely they had more pressing priorities than a group of children! Yeshua sees another teachable moment for his disciples (and for us) as he encourages the *children to come* to him. Such a group of trusting and simple children are actually a picture of the *Kingdom of Heaven.* Ironically, the *talmidim* are so consumed with the "bigger" issues of Messiah's kingdom that they are in danger of ignoring those who were the closest to that kingdom. How often are we too busy with important things that we miss God's will right in front of us? Matthew does not tell us much more, only that Yeshua laid *his hands on them* and *went on his way.*

At this point, the personal encounter turned from children to a particular young man. Showing his respect to Yeshua, he addressed him as *Rabbi.* This young man had a pressing question to pose to this Galilean teacher. It had to do with *eternal life* and *what good thing* must be done to secure it. The concept of eternal life has been well-established in traditional Judaism down to this very day. The rabbis drew the vital distinction between *olam hazeh* (this age) and *olam haba* (the age to come). While we so often emphasize the important responsibilities of our present life, the Scripture constantly reminds us to be prepared for the most important reality—eternal life. Besides various scriptures to this effect (cf. Isaiah 11; Daniel 12, etc.), the rabbis often emphasized the need to consider the world to come.

Maimonides even included the statement of the resurrection and the future life in his famous creed called "The 13 Principles of the Faith." The *Talmud* summarizes the teaching thus: "This world is like a vestibule before the World to Come; prepare yourself in the vestibule that you may enter into the hall" (Tractate Avot iv. 21). Unlike some modern branches of Judaism, which question the importance of *olam haba*, first-century Jews held this doctrine as an essential truth. The young man's question is apropos. He has no doubt about the concept of eternal life but questions what is actually required for admittance.

Here again, it is informative to note what the ancients said about this question. Tractate Avot also summarizes a common belief that "in the hour of man's departure from the world neither silver nor gold nor precious stones nor pearls accompany him, but only *Torah* and good works" (iv. 9). This Jewish young man sincerely desired to know Rabbi Yeshua's view of which *mitzvot* or works are needed for eternal life. Before Messiah answers the man directly, he has another detail to point out. Why did the man ask Yeshua about what is *good?* The implication is that Yeshua would be an expert of goodness and therefore, in a sense, on the same level as the *One who is good*, God himself. Some may view this question as casting doubt on Yeshua's divine nature, as he may be distancing himself from the only *One who is good*. On the contrary, Yeshua is in fact highlighting his goodness and divine nature with the young man's own words!

Having confirmed that initial point, Yeshua goes on to specifically answer the question. If the young man sincerely wants *to obtain eternal life*, he must *observe the mitzvot*. This undoubtedly sounded quite familiar to the observant man, as this would have been a common response expected from just about any rabbi. However, the young man had a very perceptive follow-up question: *Which ones* of the 613 *mitzvot* are vital to the question of eternal life?

Again, Yeshua's response is not that out of the ordinary. On the side of negative commandments (refraining from sin) there are such central *mitzvot* as *don't murder, don't commit adultery, don't steal* and *don't give false testimony.* These of course are part of the Ten Commandments (Exodus 20), which are considered a summary of all the 613 *mitzvot.* Added to these are two positive commandments exhorting us to *honor father and mother* (in the Ten Commandments) as well as to *love your neighbor as yourself* (*Vayikra*/Leviticus 19:18). By answering in such a way, Yeshua was indicating that one must perfectly fulfill all the commandments, both those relating to God and relating to our fellow man.

Because Yeshua did not specifically mention many other commandments, the young man had yet another follow-up question. He claimed, no doubt with great sincerity, that he had *kept all of these* specific *mitzvot.* Yet, the young man suspected in his heart that he must still *fall short* of God's perfect standard in some way. With discernment that only the divine Messiah could exercise, Yeshua makes a dramatic request of the young seeker. If he is *serious about reaching the goal* of *olam haba*, then he must *sell* his *possessions* and *give* them *to the poor.* After he has forfeited his material wealth, he must then *come and follow* Yeshua as his *Mashiach.* This last challenge finally revealed the spiritual barrier separating the young man from the assurance of eternal life. His response is informative as *he went away sad because he was wealthy.*

It should be clarified here that the discipleship of Yeshua does not necessarily require the surrender of all wealth. He does not put this condition on other seekers of eternal life. However, it is clear that the wealth of this particular young man was in fact the great hindrance in his relationship with God. It is commendable that the man kept many of the commandments vital to Judaism. However, Yeshua points out that he evidently missed the very first *mitzvah* of the Ten Commandments: "You shall have no other god before Me" (Exodus 20:3). In his case, he valued his material wealth even before his relationship with God. The lesson is important for us today.

Anything that would keep us from fully following Yeshua as Lord and Messiah is actually an infringement of the *mitzvot*. For us, it may or may not be wealth. It could also be a relationship, a career, even a hobby! Anything that is more important to us than God and Messiah is actually an idol. As Jews, we usually don't have a problem today with idols of stone or wood. But all people need to guard against what the prophets called any "idols of the heart" (*Yechezk'el*/Ezekiel 14:3). We should seriously reflect on the dialogue between Yeshua and this young Jewish man.

No doubt the *talmidim* had some questions of their own after witnessing this interaction. Yeshua, anticipating their thoughts, continued to elaborate these spiritual truths. As this case illustrated, it is often *very hard for a rich man to enter the Kingdom of Heaven.* We should note that it is not impossible, but Messiah points out that there are some inherent dangers to having excessive wealth.

Money itself is not evil. In fact, wealth can be used in many wonderful ways for the Kingdom of God. But the scripture delineates that it is the "love of money" that is often the fatal stumbling block in a person's life (cf. I Timothy 6:10). To illustrate just how difficult it can be, Yeshua tells a rather startling parable. It is even *easier for a camel to pass through a needle's eye than for a rich man to enter the Kingdom of God.* There are varying interpretations of this statement. In ancient Israel, it was not uncommon to have an outside entrance of a wall or courtyard built below the normal size. Even the shortest people would have to duck their heads in order to enter the small door. This was done to protect the area from attacking bands entering by horseback or camel, thus the idiomatic name "eye of the needle."

This could be a true picture of what Yeshua is alluding to regarding one who loves riches trying to enter the Kingdom of God. However, in the parallel gospel account written by Luke (a medical doctor), he actually uses the word (Greek *beloneis*), meaning a sewing or surgical needle (cf. Luke 18:25). A similar statement is made by the Talmudic rabbis in describing an impossible dream, which is compared to an "elephant going through a needle" (Tractate Berakhot 55.2). That being the case, this statement by Yeshua is best seen as a striking, rabbinic-style hyperbole to capture the attention of the students. It is so difficult for a person who loves his wealth that it is actually easier for a camel to go through an actual needle. In either case, the word-picture was shocking to *the talmidim* who were *utterly amazed.*

In light of the illustration, the disciples ask, who then could possibly *be saved* and qualify for *olam haba?* Yeshua confirms their suspicion that *humanly this is impossible.* No matter how religious or observant we may be, we all fall short of the glory of God. How much more so is the person who values the material wealth of this world above the Kingdom of God! Yet Yeshua reminds them there is always hope, that *with God everything is possible.* Granted, it is very difficult for such a person to break out of lifelong priorities, but God has done bigger miracles in the history of Israel. All of this begs the question for those committed *talmidim* of Messiah. Since they have *left everything and followed* Yeshua, what will they have in the world to come? What follows is a beautiful promise of Messiah to his twelve closest followers. *In the regenerated world,* these twelve will be seated on *twelve thrones* and even *judge the twelve tribes of Isra'el.* With the tremendous faith commitment of the original twelve comes a tremendous blessing as a reward.

Of course the number twelve is not coincidental. As the twelve sons of Jacob were blessed to head the tribes of ancient Israel, so would the twelve messianic leaders lead the spiritual renewal of Israel. Indeed, the *talmidim* had made an exceptional commitment even beyond that of any subsequent followers. They were the first ones to leave all their worldly endeavors to join this brand new Yeshua movement. What an incredible act of faith! As with their example, *everyone who has left houses, brothers, sisters, father, mother, children or fields* for the sake of Messiah will *receive a hundred times more* in return. It may not necessarily be in monetary or material reward. But if nothing else, such believers are promised blessing and *shalom* as they invest their lives in the things of the Kingdom of God. The greatest blessing of all (and the initial question of this latest discussion) is certainly in regard to *eternal life*, which is guaranteed here by Messiah himself.

The closing statement of the chapter once again reflects Yeshua's values as opposed to the commonly held values of the world system. *Many who are first* and thus enjoying preeminence in this current life (*olam hazeh*) will actually end up *last* in Messiah's coming kingdom. And yet, *many who are last* and overlooked in this current age will surprisingly end up *first* in *olam haba*. It is not only the young man or the twelve *talmidim* who should carefully heed this lesson. Contemporary Jews and non-Jews likewise should consider the spiritual implications of our values. We must all appear before God and give account for our life and our decisions. One Talmudic passage pointedly brings this to our attention as it poses various questions that we will be asked on Judgment Day:

> "Did you transact your business honestly? Did you fix times for the study of *Torah*? Did you fulfill your duty with respect to establishing a family? Did you hope for the salvation of the Messiah? Did you try to deduce one thing from another in study? Even should all these questions be answered affirmatively, only if 'the fear of the Lord is his treasure' (Isaiah 33:6) will it avail, otherwise it will not" (Tractate Shabbat 31a).

No matter how religious or sincere, we still must guard ourselves against idols of the heart that would distract us from God's core values. It will take a strong commitment to follow Yeshua today, but the benefits are tremendous both in this world and the world to come. May we continue to hope for the salvation of the Messiah!

Instructions Concerning the Kingdom   20:1-34

Matthew continues his account of Yeshua's life with a parable that elaborates on the discussion of the previous chapter. After the dialogue with the young Jewish ruler on the requirements of *olam haba,* there evidently remained some lingering questions on the part of the disciples. It seemed nearly impossible for anyone to enter the Kingdom based on Yeshua's requirements. They themselves had given up much in this present age with the hopes of the messianic redemption to come. It seems there needed to be a clarification on the justice of the coming judgment in Messiah's kingdom. Chapter 20 starts with a direct connection to this context as Yeshua gives a parabolic illustration concerning the *Kingdom of Heaven.* By nature, a parable is a comparison of what is known to something that is unknown (cf. Matthew 13). It was a common rabbinic teaching tool to teach a truth by casting (Greek *bole*) one object alongside (Greek *para*) another object. In this case, Yeshua draws the analogy between the Kingdom of God and *a farmer who went out at daybreak to hire workers for his vineyard.*

This agrarian situation was a common one in first-century Israel and would help shed some light on the reality of the spiritual world. As would be expected, the farmer and the workers agreed on the standard *wage of one denarius* for a day's labor. Accordingly, this early morning crew was sent *off to his vineyard* for their chores. The story takes an interesting turn as the farmer saw *more men standing around* the market-square at *about nine in the morning.* He immediately hired the newer group and likewise commissioned them to *go to the vineyard* with the understanding of receiving *a fair wage.* The situation gets even more complex as the owner hired two more shifts of laborers *at noon* and again at *three in the afternoon.* Adding to the interesting scenario, the farmer approached a final group of laborers *about one hour before sundown.* This group evidently had been standing around the market-square *all day doing nothing.* It was not for a lack of motivation that this last group did not work but *because no one hired* them. The owner was touched by this and immediately hired them to *go to the vineyard* even at that late hour.

Finally, evening came, which was time for *the workers* to receive their appropriate *wages.* It is noteworthy that the payday was to start with the *last ones hired* and end with the first laborers. When ones who had been hired at the last *hour before sunset* received a full day's wage, the other workers assumed their pay would surely be more. When they received the same denarius wage as the others, the full-day laborers were greatly surprised and *began grumbling to the farmer.* Their complaint at first glance seemed legitimate. The others only worked for *one hour* while they had *borne the brunt of the day's work in the hot sun.*

When the owner was questioned about this apparent injustice, he corrected their thinking. He was *not being unfair* with them in that they were paid the full, agreed-upon wage of *a denarius.* They should not be complaining if the owner chose to be generous to the last worker and to give him as much as the first. The owner reminds the worker that it is he as the employer who has *the right to do* what he wants. Ultimately it is not right to *begrudge the generosity* of the owner since he was eminently fair with all the hired hands.

The closing sentence ties the parable to the larger context of Yeshua's teaching. In the story, it is the *last ones* who are *first* and the *first last.* So, too, in the coming kingdom of *Mashiach.* Many laborers (believers) will serve with differing gifts for varying time periods. First or last, it should make no difference if we are sincerely serving Yeshua. There are many blessings in this present age *(olam hazeh)* that long-time believers enjoy. In the previous chapter, Yeshua stressed that those who serve him at this time will receive many extra benefits (cf. Matthew 19:29). Yes, it is a wonderful blessing to be assured of *olam haba.* What isn't highlighted in this parable is the fact that the last-hour laborers will have missed so many potential blessings in this present age. In this sense, the long-term servants have some extra benefits for which they can give thanks. The parable reminds us that, no matter what our personal experience, God is completely fair in how he treats his children. Instead of *kvetching/* grumbling, our energy would be better spent on enjoying the journey as we serve our Messiah!

The teaching completed, Yeshua and his followers continue on their journey *up to Yerushalayim.* Even the phrasing of this verse reminds us of the Jewish authorship of Matthew. He casually uses a common Hebrew idiom of making *aliyah* pilgrimage by going up to the Holy City. No matter where one is coming from in his travels, it is always "up" to Jerusalem. It may not always be physically "up" if one is coming from Nepal, for example. But it is certainly a spiritual *aliyah* of drawing close to God's presence.

In Matthew's account, this is the start of Yeshua's final *aliyah* on his way to accomplish his holy mission of redemption. While the *talmidim* were growing in their understanding of the coming events, Yeshua felt the need to clarify again for them what was about to transpire. As they go up to Yerushalayim, they should know that the Son of Man (a common messianic title) will not be received by all Israel. In fact, he will be *handed over to the head cohanim* (priests*) and Torah-teachers* (scribes). The phrasing indicates that it will be a larger group who will deliver Yeshua over to the religious authorities for action.

He further reveals that this group will then sentence Yeshua *to death and turn him over to the Goyim.* This reflects the accurate historical reality of the day as Israel was under Roman occupation and its civil authority. It was well known that, while the community of Israel was given a large amount of religious autonomy, many civil cases including capital punishment rested with the Roman government. Therefore, it has never been completely accurate to say, as many have, that "the Jews killed Jesus." No doubt some important

Jewish authorities rejected his messiahship and even called for his death as a so-called heretic. But the fact remained that Yeshua at this time could not be put to death within the Jewish community but would have to be turned over to the Gentiles for any capital offense. Even the mode of Yeshua's execution (a Roman cross) clearly testifies that he was not directly killed by Jews. In this passage, Yeshua notes that the Gentiles will *jeer at him, beat him and execute him on a stake as a common criminal.*

It is tragic that some people, including many anti-Semites, have inaccurately characterized the facts of the historical situation. Old perceptions are difficult to change, as illustrated by the fact that it took until 1965 for the Roman Catholic Church in Vatican II to exonerate the Jewish people (of all generations) of the death of Jesus. Thankfully, times are changing and many within various Christian denominations are realizing the grievous error of this teaching.

It must be pointed out that although there are some difficult passages in the New Testament regarding our people, an objective historical context reveals no anti-Semitism. Sadly, some of those passages have been misconstrued to sound anti-Jewish but they often forget that the book was written by fellow Jews who never lost their love for their people. It was a difficult family debate, but the writers of the New Testament are no more anti-Semitic than Isaiah or Jeremiah were in their prophetic debate.

Matthew will later specify the Jewish culpability in the religious hearing (cf. Matthew 26) as well as the Gentile responsibility at the legal trial (cf. Matthew 27). It is actually fitting that all peoples are represented in the rejection of Yeshua as King Messiah. In God's twist of irony, it will be the death of Yeshua that will open up the gates of salvation for all peoples, Jews and Gentiles alike! In the last statement of this paragraph, Yeshua gives hope to his Messianic followers. He is not merely going up to Jerusalem as another martyr but promises that *he will be raised* by God *on the third day.* Yeshua will fulfill the promises of *Mashiach ben Yosef* as he suffers to pay for mankind's redemption. He will also be able to fulfill the hope of *Mashiach ben David* as he is resurrected and thereby able to return for the completion of messianic redemption.

With all this talk of the coming kingdom, some close followers of Yeshua have a specific request. It comes from a rather unusual source, as Matthew notes that Messiah was approached by *Zavdai's sons* (Zebedee's) along with their own *mother.* In traditional humble fashion, *she bowed down, begging a favor* from him. Her request reflects her perspective on the life and teaching of Yeshua. When he becomes *king* (*Mashiach ben David*), would Yeshua be so kind as to have *these two sons* sit next to his throne, *one on the right and the other on the left?*

The mother evidently got the main lesson correct from the previous teaching regarding the reality of Yeshua's kingdom. It was so convincing for her that she wanted to reserve the leadership spots for her sons! However, she seemed to miss the part about having the humility of a child. Messiah immediately corrects her on this vital point. They *don't* even *know* what they are in fact *asking.*

Yeshua retorts with his own revealing question: *Can you drink the cup that I am about to drink?* To drink a cup is often an idiom for tasting or experiencing something. On many occasions (*Shabbats* and festivals especially), Jews bless a cup of wine and drink it as a way of connecting with the holy times. The fruit of the vine becomes part of our being.

The cup of Messiah will be more than mere wine. It will contain the whole experience of suffering, redemption, and resurrection. The request of this mother is not unwarranted but begs the further question—are they willing to suffer the same consequences as their leader?

After considering this intense question, the sons and their mother affirm that they are indeed willing and able to pay that price. Yeshua receives their affirmative response and confirms that they will indeed *drink my cup*. But the positions in the kingdom are not part of Yeshua's responsibilities. As the Messiah, he is in submission to the will of the Father who has prepared such details. He can make no such promises.

As the *other ten talmidim* heard about this dialogue, they became *outraged at the two brothers*. They did not appreciate the jockeying for position or maybe they were disappointed in themselves for not first making this request! As the internal controversy was brewing, Yeshua saw the need for some corrective teaching. He *called them* together and drew a contrast between *the Goyim*/pagans and the covenant community of God.

In the pagan communities around them the ones who are *supposed to rule* often *become tyrants*. Worst still, those who are *their superiors* quite often *become dictators*. In other words, the quickest way to leadership in the pagan world is often through the exertion of personal power and corruption. Of course, this was touching close to the very thoughts of the *talmidim* as they argued over superiority in the kingdom. Yeshua makes a simple yet powerful correction. *Among you, it must not be like that*. There are strategies for worldly success, but followers are to answer a different call in the Messianic community.

In fact, the values of Yeshua's kingdom are often *contrary* and opposite the values of this present age. If any of the disciples desire *to be a leader* in the Kingdom of God, he must actually humble himself to *become a servant*. If someone seeks *to be first* they must volunteer to *be your slave!*

These are not just rabbinic platitudes to challenge others—Yeshua holds up his own exemplary life as the ultimate model. Even he, as *the Son of Man, did not come to be served but to serve*. As the divine *Mashiach* sent from the Father, Yeshua had every right to be the top leader shouting out commands to his followers. In contrast, he would serve them in so many ways, from washing feet at the future Passover *seder* to even giving up his life at the Roman execution hill. Yeshua's entire life was one of serving, giving, and blessing those around him.

The crowning example would be in his death that would serve *as a ransom for many*. The idea of a ransom in Judaism is most informative. There were *Torah* laws to offer the option of buying back a personal slave who had been previously sold. Israel itself was a nation of ransomed slaves through the Passover experience. Our people were in bondage but purchased for freedom through the price paid by the Father. The ancient Passover lamb slain to symbolize the price of the ransom prefigured the future death of the Messiah.

While some only see the tragic death of a sincere, albeit misled, rabbi, Yeshua confidently makes the spiritual connection to the transcendent effects of his execution. It would all be the perfect will of the Father to offer the Messiah (*Mashiach ben Yosef*) as the appropriate payment for the ransom of Israel and the whole world. While the price of redemption is adequate for the whole world, Yeshua notes that the ransom will only be realized by many and not all.

Of course, there is a condition for anyone (including us) to enjoy the benefits of that ransom. We must be willing to specifically receive the gift of Yeshua. God's love will only be experienced by our reciprocal faith and trust, as Yeshua confirmed in his conversation with Rabbi Nicodemus: "For God so loved the world that he gave his only and unique son, so that everyone who trusts in him may have eternal life, instead of being utterly destroyed" (*Yochanan*/John 3:16). Because of our personal sins and folly, we are in slavery without hope. Our people have long waited for the arrival of King Messiah to bring national and personal redemption.

Yeshua of Nazareth is that one who has come to pay the price of our ransom, to buy us back to our Father, the God of Israel. Do you believe? Have you personally received this gift of love? Thanks be to God for his indescribable gift! (II Corinthians 9:15).

Chapter 20 closes with another personal encounter between Yeshua and some needy individuals of first-century Israel. Matthew records that the messianic group was *leaving Yericho* when a *large crowd* gathered around the popular rabbi from Galilee. Some commentators see a contradiction between Matthew's account (leaving Jericho) and Luke's account (arriving in the city).

The Jewish historian Josephus actually gives us an answer, noting that in the first century there were in fact two cities, the ancient settlement and the much newer Roman town (War 4:459). It is quite possible therefore that Yeshua was traveling between the two centers when the next encounter took place. Jericho was a bustling town on a major road leading up to Jerusalem. It is quite natural that Matthew notes a large crowd of pilgrims traveling through the area as Passover was approaching. The city is located on the banks of the Jordan River in a fertile valley that takes advantage of the low elevation and warm weather. Its name *Yericho* (perfumed) describes the fragrant fruit trees and crops that were commonly grown there.

As Yeshua and the crowd were passing by, *two blind men sitting by the side of the road heard* the commotion. Mark's gospel account names one of the blind men who was the most vocal. *Bar-Timai/* Bartimaeus is indeed a descriptive name adding to the drama of this encounter, as it means "son of the unclean"! (Mark 10:46). We can imagine this sad couple of blind beggars who would strategically place themselves along the road in order to collect alms. Their opportunity had come to be blessed by the famous rabbi and they *shouted* for his attention.

What they called out gives an insight into their spiritual perception and hope as children of Israel. Addressing Yeshua as the *Son of David*, they cry out for *pity* and help. The title is common for the Messiah who would be the greatest descendant of King David, thus the messianic title *Mashiach ben David* was often used (Tractate Sukkah 52a). The fact that the needy souls used this exalted term shows their hope that Yeshua was the mighty Anointed One who would have miraculous powers of healing. The tumult and noise from these outcasts was more than the crowd could tolerate. Some told the beggars *to be quiet* and strongly *scolded them* for interrupting the important rabbi and the entire procession. But this only served to urge them on and *they shouted all the louder.*

Their next exclamation is even more powerful than the first as they address Yeshua this time as "Lord!" The Hebrew could be *Adon* and thus taken in a common fashion, addressing one as "sir." But the context of their exalted respect for Yeshua as *Son of David* indicates the secondary understanding of ADONAI/Lord, that is, the divine Messiah sent from God. They reiterate their request that the miracle-working rabbi would *have pity* on them. Their petitions got the attention of Yeshua who *stopped* and asked the beggars an important question: What did they *want?* As the divine Messiah, he undoubtedly could detect what they desired but perhaps the question was more of an opportunity for the needy men to verbalize their own faith. They responded with a rather obvious request as they ask Yeshua, "Open our eyes.*"

Building on the names by which they address Yeshua, the beggars evidently are alluding to the promises of the *Tanakh* where Messiah is said to bring a great healing even to the blind (cf. Isaiah 35:5 in Genesis Raba 95:1). Their logic is simple: If Yeshua is indeed *Mashiach ben David,* then healing the blind will be part of his messianic miracles.

Revealing the heart of Yeshua, Matthew observes that Messiah was *filled with tenderness* as he saw the plight of these men. Accordingly, he *touched their eyes* even though one was called "son of the unclean!" Some other rabbi and even most of the crowd would not have reached out to bother with such a motley crew. But Yeshua is the *Mashiach* sent from the Father, revealing God's heart for his beloved world. The gospel records that *instantly they received their sight.* Not only were the physical eyes of the beggars opened, but the spiritual eyes of many in that Jericho crowd.

The encounter closes with the healed blind men instantly following Yeshua as ADONAI and Messiah. We might suspect that the crowd of disciples grew larger that day on their way to Yerushalayim. This messianic sign and encounter can still speak to us today. Has Messiah opened our spiritual eyes?

The Aliyah of King Messiah   21:1-23:39

Matthew's historical account of the life of Yeshua now turns the corner toward the final days. This last segment is vitally important to Matthew; the final nine chapters of his biography trace the last seven days of Yeshua's ministry in Israel. All of this parallels the most holy week of *Pesach*/Passover, which was the busiest time of the year in ancient Jerusalem. As we shall see, the *Pesach* season is also an amazing prophetic picture of the significance of Messiah's ministry to Israel and to the Nations as well.

The Welcome of the Crowds   21:1-22

The messianic ministry of Yeshua and his *talmidim* had taken a rather circuitous route in the previous months. From the northern Galil to the ancient city of Yericho, crowds continued to gather to hear the popular rabbi from Nazareth. Yet in the midst of the many amazing encounters, one thing was becoming increasingly clear. Their route must take them to the Holy City, Yerushalayim. As the group travels from lowlying Yericho, the road takes them to the eastern approaches of the city, most notably through the area of *the Mount of Olives.*

The writer records that as they came to the village of Beit-Pagei (House of Unripe Figs) that Yeshua *sent two of the talmidim* on an important task. Before they proceeded further, these two should *go into the village* and *find a donkey* with *its colt* for a particular purpose.

Yeshua commands his disciples to *untie them* both and to *bring them* to the rabbi.

Of course such an action might bring some objections from the owner or his neighbors. If anyone should happen to inquire, they are instructed to merely reply that "the Lord needs them." Yeshua assures them that this response will satisfy the owner and he will let the livestock *go at once*. No doubt, these beasts of burden were meant to assist the group in their travels. But Matthew notes that there was a much larger meaning to this situation. It was all evidently orchestrated by Yeshua to fulfill two specific messianic prophecies in the *Tanakh*:

> "Say to the daughter of Tziyon, Look! Your King is coming to you, riding humbly on a donkey, and on a colt, the offspring of a beast of burden!" (Isaiah 62:11 combined with Zechariah 9:9).

The rabbis debated the many possibilities by which *Mashiach* could come to Israel. The following quote stresses two distinct ways the Messiah might appear:

> "Rabbi Alexandri said: Rabbi Yehoshua ben Levi cast together two verses: It is written: 'And, behold, one like a son of man came with the clouds of heaven,' and it is written: 'Humble, and riding on an ass'! If they merit [he will come] 'with the clouds of heaven'; if they do not merit [he will come] 'humble, and riding on an ass.'" (Tractate Sanhedrin 98a).

We gather from Yeshua's manner of entry into Jerusalem that King Messiah is coming when Israel does not merit his salvation (do any of us merit?). But we also get a glimpse here of the belief that there might actually be two appearances of the *Mashiach*. This is consistent with the convictions of Messianic Judaism that Yeshua has come the first time to bring us redemption and yet will reappear for the final completion of the Kingdom of God. Some people may complain that Yeshua was manipulating the circumstances to make it appear that he was the long-awaited *Mashiach*. However, even though this particular prophecy was fulfilled in a directed manner, we should also keep in mind the dozens of messianic predictions that Yeshua had no control over (e.g., he couldn't have picked his place of birth at Beit-Lechem). Actually, from another angle, this situation must have spoken to the *talmidim* about the divine power of Yeshua. Only the omniscient Son of God could know the exact details of the donkey and its colt, as well as the future response of the owner.

Every detail worked out as their rabbi had predicted; the disciples *went and did as* Yeshua *had directed them.* They made the donkey and colt ready by adorning them with *their robes.* What a contrast! King Messiah was not arriving on the victorious white horse of an army general or with the pomp and circumstance of an earthly king. He was a king, yet riding on a humble beast! This was a perfect picture of the entire life of Yeshua as the Messiah/Servant.

Crowds of people began to take note of the unusual occurrences in their village. Some were carpeting *the road with their clothing* to welcome Yeshua as the King Messiah. Others *cut branches from trees and spread them on the road* in a similar gesture of adoration. This is reminiscent of the festival of *Sukkot*/Feast of Tabernacles. In that holy day celebration, Israel was told to take branches and palm fronds as part of the worship ceremony (cf. *Vayikra*/ Leviticus 23:40). In modern Judaism, we take up the *lulav* (palm branch) and wave it before the Lord, saying certain blessings, as an acknowledgment of God's presence at the festival. Not surprisingly, the eight-day festival of *Sukkot* became synonymous with the coming of *Mashiach* and his kingdom.

Adding to this messianic processional were the confirming words of the multitude. As Yeshua approached the holy city, the adoring crowds shouted, "Please! Deliver us!" This is not merely a personal prayer for help; it is a specific quote from the Hallel Psalms (*Tehillim*/Psalms 113-118). These are the liturgical Psalms chanted on the joyful holy days of the calendar and in particular on the eight days of *Sukkot*/Tabernacles. Because of their theme of rejoicing, the Hallel is omitted on the more somber holy days of Rosh Hashanah and Yom Kippur.

In this case, Matthew observes that the multitude is chanting a particular part of the Hallel, Psalm 118:25-26, which in Hebrew says *hoshia na*. This is often transliterated in the English as "hosanna" meaning "Please, save!" It is significant to note the play on words in Hebrew—the root word for *save/hoshia* has the same root as the name of the one entering Jerusalem (Yeshua). With cries of joy, the crowd welcomes Yeshua as *the Son of David* with the famous greeting, "Blessed is he who comes in the name of *ADONAI/Barukh habah b'shem ADONAI*" (Psalm 118:26). This phrase was used often as the priests addressed each other in their Temple service. Here it has larger messianic implications as the crowds acknowledge Yeshua as the Messiah able to bring about the ultimate deliverance of Israel.

The multitude cries out again, this time directly to the Father *in the highest heaven, "hoshia na"!* When the processional finally *entered Yerushalayim*, Matthew records that *the whole city was stirred*. With such a commotion, many are asking, "Who is this?" The crowds offer a simple yet profound response. *This is* Yeshua *from Natzeret*. Yet they add an amazing detail that Yeshua, in their estimation, is also *the prophet* (note the definite article). This is not just a general acknowledgment that the Galilean rabbi was like many of the prophets of Israel. But this seems to be a specific designation that he is also the particular prophet predicted to come as the anointed one, the *Mashiach*. This is an allusion to the words of the *Torah* that exhorted all Israel to be on watch for a special prophet who would be even greater than Moshe himself:

"I will raise up for them a prophet like you from among their kinsmen. I will put my words in his mouth, and he will tell them everything I order him. Whoever doesn't listen to my words, which he will speak in my name, will have to account for himself to me." (*D'varim*/Deuteronomy 18:18-19).

In the context of this entrance into Jerusalem, it is clear what the Jewish multitudes are saying with both their actions and their words. Yeshua is our promised King Messiah! The Messianic Kingdom has arrived, so let's break out the *lulavim* and chant the *Hallel* as we celebrate the fulfillment of *Sukkot*! This is all the more powerful when we realize that these events were not taking place during the Feast of Tabernacles but during the days approaching Passover. It mattered little to this crowd of believers. They were welcoming Yeshua as the King of Israel irrespective of the date on the calendar!

From Matthew's perspective, it is vital that the last earthly days of Messiah be lived out during the preparation time of Passover. Yeshua's first mission is to fulfill all the promises regarding *Mashiach ben Yosef*, the suffering Messiah. With this in mind, even the exact date of this processional is highly significant. On the church calendar, this is usually called the "Triumphal Entry" into Jerusalem. Normally this is placed on Sunday of the week before Passover, "Palm Sunday." However, a close chronological study of these last chapters of the gospel reveal that this took place not on a Sunday, but more likely on the Monday of that week.

Of course, the Roman days of the week are not authoritative here, as they are not mentioned. But in backtracking from the clear statements in relationship to the Jewish calendar, we can conclude that the date of this entry into Yerushalayim was on the 10th of the month *Nisan*. Internal evidence from the gospel accounts indicates that there were five full days from this procession to the execution of

Yeshua on the Roman cross. Sunday or Monday is not the important issue, but the 10th of *Nisan* is a vitally important day in the biblical calendar. While Passover was to be celebrated on the 14th of *Nisan*, the *Torah* teaches that it is on the 10th of the month that the Passover lamb is to be chosen by every family (Exodus 12:3).

Consequently, we begin to see some of the amazing prophetic details being fulfilled in the life and death of Yeshua. He most certainly died on the afternoon of the first day of *Pesach* (15 *Nisan*), which was the very day of the paschal offering in the Temple. Not only did Yeshua die on the exact day of the national Passover lamb, but even at the exact hour. As we shall see in the details of Matthew 27, Yeshua gave up his physical spirit at 3 p.m., the exact time of the *minchah* national offering for Israel!

Backtracking to the entry into Jerusalem, we find it took place on the very day that Israel was to choose the lamb for Passover. According to the specifications of Exodus 12, the lamb must be inspected to insure that there were no defects, impurities, or broken bones. The lambs were chosen on 10 *Nisan* and then given four days of close inspection to confirm that they were in fact the best of the kosher offerings. How amazing, yet not coincidental, that Yeshua made his entry into the holy city on the very day that the lambs were being chosen! With his public presentation to Israel on that day, it was as if to say, "See if I am the kosher Lamb of God, your Messiah."

First-century Israel would have one more public opportunity to inspect this Lamb and draw its own conclusions. Sadly, most would reject him at this first appearance. But we should emphasize that there were large crowds of Jewish people who welcomed this Yeshua as their King.

It is inaccurately portrayed that "the Jews" rejected Jesus, as if not one Jew followed him in the first century. If that were true, we would like to know how we even got the New Testament? Who were the *talmidim,* Sha'ul, and the tens of thousands who called on his name (cf. Acts 21:20)? Quite frankly, these were not "Christians" converting to a new religion, but they were all Jews who followed Yeshua as King Messiah.

Opinions were divided in the Jewish community, and they remain so even to this day. Certainly, many of our people today still reject Yeshua, but it must be noted that there are hundreds of thousands of modern Jews who follow him. For many today, the life account of Yeshua is just another story or even mythology. We Messianic Jews and Messianic Gentiles cannot overlook the amazing prophecies fulfilled that last week before *Pesach*. What part of the crowd do you stand with today? Have you personally welcomed Yeshua into your life with the words *"Barukh habah b'shem ADONAI!"*?

As the messianic group entered the city, they went directly to the center of God's spiritual universe, *the Temple* Mount. This was a bustling hub of activity for the tens of thousands of Jews who lived in the vicinity. It was even more crowded as the major festivals approached. There were sacrifices to be purchased, pagan money to be exchanged for Jewish currency, and other necessities to be acquired for the religious services in the *Beit-Ha'Mikdash* (Holy Temple). When Yeshua entered the outer courts, he was visibly disturbed by some of the proceedings, so he drove out some of the *merchants and their customers.* Matthew observes that he specifically *upset the desks of the money-changers and knocked over the benches of those who were selling pigeons* for sacrifices.

Too often modern readers of this account assume that the terrible offense was doing any kind of business in the Temple precincts. Quite the contrary, the *Torah* even mandated that the needs of the pilgrims coming for the festivals must be met in order that they could properly worship. It was a requirement for all Jewish men not only to come to the Temple for the three main *shalosh regalim (*foot festivals, or pilgrim festivals)—*Pesach, Shavuot,* and *Sukkot*—but to bring their tithe from their labors. Obviously, this could be a hardship if one was trying to travel from abroad in the first century with several carts of produce! In the *Torah*, God provided a logical adaptation:

> "If the distance is too great for you, so that you are unable to transport [your tithe], because the place where ADONAI chooses to put his name is too far away from you; then, when ADONAI your God prospers you, you are to convert it into money, take the money with you, go to the place which ADONAI your God will choose and exchange the money for anything you want...." (*D'varim*/Deuteronomy 14:24-26)

It must be emphasized that these money-changers and sacrifice merchants were in the outer courts (*Temple grounds*) and not in the sanctuary proper. The problem was not the presence of such vendors per se, as they fulfilled a *mitzvah* and a vital function for all pilgrims. The money-changers especially fulfilled an important job for all traditional Jews who came from abroad with pagan money, often with images of idols and Caesars minted on the coins! Such graven images could not be used to pay a temple tax or to purchase a kosher offering. The money-changers' service was necessary to convert pagan money to Jewish currency (Tractate Bekorot 8:7).

Yet something was terribly wrong that day in the Temple courts as Yeshua confronted the merchants. His quote of the *Tanakh* clarifies why he is so upset: "My house will be called a house of prayer," speaking of the main purpose of the *Beit-Ha'Mikdash* (Isaiah 56:7). Not a problem so far. Yet, they had made it *into a den of robbers*. Here is the heart of the issue: These vendors were evidently gouging the worshippers and charging exorbitant prices for the required religious articles. This problem, interestingly, is confirmed by the outside source of the *Talmud* where a rebuke is issued to the sons of Annas who had corrupted the Temple and Sanhedrin with similar injustices (Tractate Pesachim 57a). Apparently Yeshua himself had witnessed a vendor extorting from a fellow Jew and it did not sit well.

It is not coincidental that Yeshua enters the *Beit-Ha'Mikdash/* Temple on the very day of his arrival into Jerusalem, the 10th of *Nisan.* As mentioned above, this is the very day of choosing and inspecting the lamb for each home to celebrate the upcoming *seder* on the 15th of *Nisan.* In these final days of preparation, every home would need to be meticulously cleaned and koshered for the holy day. In the case of Passover, this requires the removal of all leaven from our dwelling places. In a spiritual sense, the removal of leaven is a picture of removing sin from our presence as well. How appropriate and prophetic that Yeshua enters the House of God on this all-important date! Everything must be made *kosher l'pesach* (kosher for Passover) as the holy day approaches.

Messiah's experience in the Temple is not just relegated to Passover cleaning. Besides removing some leaven from the community, Yeshua also desires to bring a positive blessing. While he is yet in the *Beit-Ha'Mikdash,* it is not surprising that some *blind and lame people* approach Yeshua. Their obvious need is for physical healing, something for which the Messiah was always eager. However, the conflict was growing stronger as the epicenter moved into Jerusalem. Some of the *cohanim and Torah-teachers* took exception to not only what he was doing but also to what the children were *crying out.* As with the entry into the holy city, the children called out for the Messiah with the quote from the *Hallel* Psalms (Psalm 118:25-26) *"Ana ADONAI hoshia na/*Please [Lord] deliver us!"

What especially infuriated the religious leaders was the title given to Yeshua as *the Son of David*, a clear messianic reference. It must have been in a state of shock and indignation that they confronted Yeshua about the tumultuous scene. When questioned if he is hearing *what they're saying*, he calmly replies, "Of course!" Not only does Yeshua understand what was proclaimed, he affirms it as part of the prophetic picture of the coming *Mashiach*, for *from the mouths of children and infants you have prepared praise for yourself (Tehillim/*

Psalm 8:2). It seems a rather consistent theme that the messiahship of Yeshua was questioned and rejected by the religious establishment yet affirmed by those (like children) who take an honest and simple look at him. Such is often the case to this day. *With that, he left them and went outside the city to Beit-Anya* (Bethany), a village on the east approach to Jerusalem. Yeshua spent that night there, closing the 10th of *Nisan* and a most eventful day as the sun set.

The next morning (now the 11th of *Nisan*), Yeshua returned *to the city*. Matthew reports that, as he was passing *a fig tree by the road,* Yeshua *felt hungry* and decided to check for some fruit. Some interpreters question why Yeshua would expect fruit so early in the season. If it was impossible to expect fruit, then this would still serve as a graphic object lesson regarding Israel and the lack of fruit. Others say because it was approaching Passover week and springtime, he had every right to expect that there would be some early fruit on this common Middle Eastern tree. When he found no fruit at all, Yeshua expressed a judgment that the tree may *never again bear fruit.* The disciples were eyewitnesses to the fact that *immediately the fig tree dried up.*

Some might question if Yeshua was not overreacting or even lashing out in anger. Two things are noteworthy here. First, something was defective in the tree that should have had plenty of early figs in the spring season. It would be commonly expected that if a fig tree had leaves, then it would at least have some early edible fruit. Second, the fig tree is an apt symbol of the Jewish people, as the prophet said:

> "When I found Isra'el, it was like finding grapes in the desert; when I saw your ancestors, it was like seeing a fig tree's first figs in its first season. But as soon as they came to Ba'al-P'or, they dedicated themselves to something shameful; they became as loathsome as the thing they loved" (*Hoshea*/Hosea 9:10).

God's loving covenant with Israel is beautifully portrayed as finding the best fruit of the early harvest. In Hosea's day, the prophet lamented that Israel did not have the fresh spiritual fruit that God rightly expected. The cursing of the fig tree by Yeshua was a graphic illustration of the spiritual predicament of Israel. Perhaps it took such a dramatic event to express the dire problems of Israel, God's fig tree that was not producing fruit, especially in relationship to the arrival of Yeshua as King Messiah. The *talmidim were amazed* as they witnessed all of this. Even if they did not grasp the full meaning of the Messiah's action, they wondered out loud just how the fig tree could *dry up so quickly.*

Yeshua used the incident not only as a prophetic picture of national Israel but also as a lesson in personal faith. Such personal faith is a prevalent theme of the entire Scriptures, but especially of the New Covenant where "faith/*emunah*" is mentioned 243 times and the verb "to believe" 241 times. If a person can *trust and not doubt* the power of God, even greater things could be done. It will even be possible to *say to this mountain, "Go and throw yourself into the sea!"* This was a powerful visual lesson as they stood on the Mount of Olives, overlooking the Dead Sea to the east. Anything is possible with God in the picture.

Yeshua affirms this omnipotence of God and the power of prayer as he promises that believers can *receive everything* they may *ask in prayer, no matter what it is, provided you have trust* (that is, *emunah/* faith/). This is a tremendous promise and truth but it must also be tempered with what God says about the details of prayer. God cannot sin and will not endorse any activity that breaks the laws of his moral universe (James 1:12-16). Likewise, we are told by God that we will receive such answers to prayer when we ask for things according to his will and not necessarily based on our own desires (*I Yochanan/* I John 5:14-15). What's the point? Yeshua is clearly giving a practical picture of first-century Israel as well as a teaching on the power of prayer. For the record, there is no mention of the *talmidim* or Yeshua himself ever moving a literal mountain.

There are rabbinic expressions used in the Talmudic literature to teach similar truths. The "rooting up of mountains" is a phrase used to describe something impossible (Tractate Sanhedrin 24a; see Matthew 17:20). In this sense, we must look at Yeshua's statements as a common form of rabbinic hyperbole to express an important point. There are many mountainous challenges that face all of us at different times, yet with God's presence in our lives, there is power for change and victory. The disciples took careful note of the implications. We, too, can see amazing answers to our prayers when they are aligned with the will of God through Yeshua our Messiah.

The Skepticism of the Religious Leaders   21:23-22:14

Matthew's account now moves further along as he records the details of the final rejection of King Messiah. While many in Israel welcomed Yeshua during his entrance to Jerusalem, it is clear that a majority of the community still had questions. The controversy heightens as some of the religious leaders in the holy city confront and question the maverick rabbi from Galilee.

The Question of S'mikhah   21:23-27

It is not surprising that after the dramatic Passover cleansing of the Temple, some of the *head cohanim and elders approached* Yeshua. This could have been an impromptu meeting of various leaders or possibly an official delegation of rabbis representing the Sanhedrin to investigate some of the messianic controversy. They had two pressing questions for this Galilean rabbi: "What *s'mikhah* do you have?" and "Who gave you this *s'mikhah*?" It has long been common practice within Judaism that one must have some kind of rabbinic ordination to establish one's religious authority. It was never enough to merely quote one's own views. A qualified teacher would need to substantiate his opinion with references to other scholars who hold such a view as well. The Hebrew word *s'mikhah* literally means "to connect or draw close," thus, the ordination ceremony of kings, priests, and rabbis was symbolized by the laying on of hands (connecting) by other leaders affirming the call to duty of the newly ordained. By implication, the question arose early in his public ministry when it was perceived that Yeshua taught in a different manner than other rabbis. It was not the content that stood out, but his manner of speaking authoritatively on theological issues that would normally need the affirmation of other rabbis (cf. Matthew 7:28-29).

With all that had transpired in the three and a half years of Yeshua's ministry, the question of *s'mikhah* still followed him. The present questions arise in light of Yeshua's cleansing of the Temple and disruption of the corrupt practices in the courts. His was an action of tremendous zeal, and the local priests wanted to know by what authority he could *do these things.* This demand came from a group of rabbis who already had authority over the Temple precinct. Yeshua's response comes, again in classic Jewish form, by posing another question. If they sincerely answer his question, he will be more than happy to reciprocate. Yeshua takes them back to the ministry of Yochanan and his *t'vilah*/immersion. Was his immersion *from Heaven (God) or from a human source?*

This is not an unrelated question, as Yochanan was one of the leaders who endorsed the authority of Yeshua as the true Messiah. This seemingly simple question, however, presented an unusual conundrum for the religious leaders. They reasoned that if they answered, "from Heaven," Yeshua would challenge them on why they themselves rejected Yochanan. Yet if they answered, "from a human source," they would be going against the widespread sentiment that Yochanan was *a prophet* sent to Israel. After pondering the consequences, the leaders answered Yeshua with a simple "we don't know." Since they are unwilling to take a stand one way or the other, Yeshua responds that he doesn't need to tell them the answer to their question either.

Three Parables of Messiah 21:28-22:14

One might think the unresolved question in the previous encounter could be the end of the story. But Yeshua proactively challenges the Temple leadership with some rabbinic style parables. We should remember that parables, by definition, are stories of real-life scenarios meant to shed light on things that are not so well known (cf. Matthew 13). In the context of this challenge to Yeshua's authority, the next three parables give an insight into spiritual truth. The first *mashal/* parable is about *a man* who *had two sons*. The man approached the first son and exhorted him to *go and work today in the vineyard.* Despite the direct command, the first son made it clear that he did *not want to* toil on the land. To his credit, he *later changed his mind and went* to the vineyard for his work. There is a clear spiritual allusion here, as the phrase *changed his mind* is the same as the common word for repentance (*t'shuvah*).

The story continues with the father going to the *other son* with the same exhortation. Responding in the opposite manner to his brother, this son answered affirmatively, "I will, sir." Yet his words did not match up to his actions and *he didn't go* into the vineyard. Having painted a contrasting picture of the two sons, Yeshua now asks a thought-provoking question: "Which of the two did what the father wanted?" It was clear to these *cohanim* and elders that *the first* son was the one who pleased the father. Although he had started reluctantly, he ultimately responded with obedience. Yeshua affirms the answer of these leaders as correct, yet he has a surprising application that is relevant to them. According to Yeshua, the story is an illustration that even *the tax collectors and prostitutes* would make it *into the Kingdom of God ahead* of these religious leaders!

He then makes a direct application to his previous question regarding Yochanan. The Immerser came to them *showing the path to righteousness* and yet they *wouldn't trust him*. Some of the leaders were like the son who had said "yes" to God by their religious observance yet, in reality, did not follow through, as they rejected the *Mashiach* sent by the Father. It is a great paradox that many "non-religious" people in Israel had simply put their trust in Messiah and would be welcomed into the Father's kingdom.

The door of repentance is always open, but Yeshua has a sober warning for the religious leaders. They are in danger of judgment because *even after* they saw the mercy of God, they still *didn't change* their *minds later and trust him*. Evidently there will be surprises in the Kingdom of God. Even as we observe people around us today, we must not be too quick to judge before the final fruit is obvious. The gates of repentance are always open, yet God is the final gatekeeper. According to this *mashal*, it is not so much where we start but how we finish. It matters little what we say—more important is what we actually do. How does God look at us at this moment?

Yeshua now calls on the group to give heed to another *mashal/* parable. This story refers to a vineyard scenario once again (Isaiah 5), but with significantly different details. Instead of a father and two sons, this account revolves around *a farmer* and some *tenants*. The farmer *planted a vineyard* and meticulously developed it by putting *a wall around it,* digging *a pit for the winepress* and constructing *a tower.* Every feature was important for protection (the wall and tower) and for the harvesting of the crop (winepress).

After renting it to some tenants, the farmer *left* the area and delegated the responsibilities of his vineyard to the tenants. As *harvest-time came* the farmer sent some of his servants to the property *to collect his share of the crop.* This would normally be a simple transaction as part of the agreement between owner and tenant.

However, in a major twist in the story, the tenants rebel against the servants (and thus, against the owner).

Such a dispute was not unheard of. In fact, the *Talmud* addresses a similar case where some tenants could actually claim ownership of a property if they could prove their undisputed possession of it for three years (Tractate Bava Batra 3:1). In this story it is evident that the tenants were attempting to make the vineyard their own in such a way by challenging the owner and his dispatched emissaries. *One* servant is *beat up, one they killed,* and *another they stoned* to death. Frustrated and no doubt infuriated, the owner *sent some other servants*, even *more than the first group*, but the tenants treated them in *the same* way.

Figuring he must take extreme measures, the farmer sent his very own *son* thinking they would certainly *respect* him. But the evil tenants in the parable actually see this as an opportunity as they plot to *kill him and to take his inheritance.* When they saw the son, *they grabbed him, threw him out of the vineyard and killed him.* Evidently this rebellious group, in the midst of murder, was still concerned about the *Torah* laws against desecrating the property with death, so they attacked the son outside the boundaries (Tractate Oholot 2:1).

Once again, as he comes to this climax of the *mashal,* Yeshua asks a penetrating question: "When the owner of the vineyard comes, what will he do to those tenants?" The answer of the *cohanim* and elders is revealing. In their opinion, the owner would naturally be outraged and *will viciously destroy those men.* Not only that, but the owner would probably *rent out the vineyard to other tenants* who would give the right share of the crop when it was due. The sharecroppers should not only have respected the owner's representatives but should have paid the crop due the owner to begin with.

The answer of the religious leaders is self-incriminating, as it illustrates their own current spiritual attitude. Israel (including its spiritual leaders) was called to be God's special vineyard, an analogy given much earlier by the prophets (cf. Isaiah 5). Using the commonly known story found in Isaiah, Yeshua makes some points to his current generation. In the Isaiah passage, God is said to have checked his vineyard (Israel) for the expected fruit, but he was disappointed at the lack thereof. He had expected to find good fruit (like justice) but instead found bloodshed and distress (5:7). Yeshua's parable adds a new wrinkle.

The original tenants are destroyed, and the vineyard is subsequently rented out to other tenants. As the group ponders the meaning of this statement, Yeshua emphasizes that this unfortunate rejection by the first tenants also has a biblical basis *in the Tanakh*: "The very rock which the builders rejected has become the cornerstone! This has come from *ADONAI*, and in our eyes it is amazing" (*Tehillim*/Psalm 118:22-23). Once again, as in the earlier part of this chapter, the quote is from the *Hallel* Psalms chanted at the major festivals.

Messiah's application of this final quote was shocking indeed. In his estimation, *the Kingdom of God* (the vineyard) *will be taken away* from the current leaders and *given to the kind of people that will produce* good fruit. We should carefully note here that this is not a passage that teaches "replacement theology," that the Kingdom was taken from the Jewish people and given to the Gentile church. Although this is a popular teaching in many church circles today, it cannot be justified based on the entire context of Scripture. There are too many verses in the New Covenant affirming that while Israel may be largely in unbelief regarding Yeshua, the promises of God stand firm in regard to his covenant (cf. Jeremiah 31:31-36; Romans 11:1-5, 25-29).

How can one reconcile these verses with the theory of replacement theology? The obvious reconciliation of all these passages is for us to be the "kind of people" who produce good fruit, not as the Gentile branch of the church, but with the faithful remnant of Jews who receive the beauties of the New Covenant by their personal faith in Yeshua as Messiah. No doubt there will be many from the Nations who will also embrace Yeshua as the message goes out to them.

The immediate context of this parable is that the vineyard applies to Israel. The message is not about a replacement of Israel here, but a postponement of the fulfillment until all Israel is ready to receive the true King Messiah. In particular, Yeshua seems to focus the statement on the religious leaders (the builders of Judaism) who ironically rejected the very cornerstone of the faith (Yeshua as King Messiah). The analogy is striking. One can imagine an entire building (probably the Temple itself) built up as walls, roofs, pillars, etc. Yet it is all glaringly missing the very cornerstone of the foundation!

As has been emphasized through the generations, Messiah is the very foundation of the Jewish faith. Rambam (Maimonides) stated this doctrinal truth in his famous "13 Principles of the Jewish Faith," which is in the daily prayer book to this day: "I believe with perfect faith in the coming of the Messiah, and though he tarry, I will wait daily for his coming."

The *cohanim and the P'rushim* leaders must have been shocked as they now realized that Yeshua was *speaking about them*. But the decision had already been made in their ranks. All the way back in Chapter 12, most of the leaders had pronounced Yeshua as empowered by *Baal Zevuv*/Satan himself. In these final days of Yeshua's journey to Jerusalem, the lines were drawn even more deeply. They now set about to arrest him but are constrained because the crowds consider him a prophet.

This is another reminder that the official rejection of Yeshua as King Messiah was in no way unanimous. True, many rejected his claims, but this same passage reminds us that a great many of our people also received Yeshua as the promised One. How tragic that many of the spiritual leaders confronting Yeshua in this passage undoubtedly had a zeal for their faith and tradition, yet missed the very foundation stone of that tradition! This sad truth still applies to many of the religious of the world, both Jew and Gentile, even in our day. Are you a tenant in God's vineyard? Do you have Yeshua as the cornerstone of your personal faith in God? Are you bearing the kind of fruit that is pleasing to the landowner, our Father in Heaven?

At this point, Yeshua elaborates his teaching with a third *mashal/* parable. This time the Messianic Kingdom is compared to *a king who prepared a wedding feast for his son.* In the spirit of a *mashal*, Yeshua uses a commonly understood event (a Jewish wedding) with something not so well understood (the coming Kingdom). Much preparation needed to go into this joyous event. In biblical times, it all started with an arrangement (*shiduchin*) by the parents. How much more would the King of an empire make a special selection for his own son? As the children grew into young adults, the next step of the ceremony (*erusin*) would take place. This was the public ceremony, under the *huppah/*canopy, that would officially set the engagement of the couple.

After culminating this beautiful ceremony, a one-year engagement period would elapse where the bride would prepare her dowry and garments while the groom would prepare the future home for the couple, often as a room addition on the father's house (cf. *Yochanan/*John 14:1-3). At some point, at the discretion of the father of the groom, the *shofar/*ram's horn would sound and the wedding procession would start for the groom to gather his bride. This would lead to the second step of the wedding ceremony (*nisuin*) where the couple would gather once again under the *huppah* for the blessings of full marriage. After this meaningful gathering, the family and guests would be invited to a joyous wedding feast to celebrate the occasion.

It is in this context that the parable of Yeshua takes place as he describes the king sending *his slaves to summon the invited guests.* All would seem to be going well until a surprising element is introduced—the guests *refused to come!* This of course would be considered a great insult and totally unexpected. In response to this first rejection by the invited guests, the king comes up with an alternative plan. *He sent some more slaves* to impress upon the guests the extreme importance of the celebration. The banquet was already prepared with the *fattened cattle* and all the details that must have gone into such a big event. With an urgent plea, the slaves were to appeal to the guests: *Come to the wedding!*

The shock factor of the parable continues as the guests still *weren't interested* and even *went off* to their own activities. One guest returned *to his farm; another to his business.* Their apathy is striking. However, what follows is even more alarming. According to the parable, the rest of the guests *grabbed his slaves, mistreated them, and even killed them.* The king finally reached his threshold and was *furious* about the situation, so much so that he *sent his soldiers who killed those murderers and burned down their city.*

The spiritual picture of this parable of Yeshua was both shocking and abundantly clear to the listening crowd, which mainly consisted of the head *cohanim* as well as the *P'rushim* (Priests and Pharisees) cf. Matt. 21:45. Clearly, the children of Israel are the invited guests to the kingdom celebration. That being the case, the first invitation could well be considered the call of the prophets who came many times with to appeal to our people. The second invitation of the parable would logically apply to the other servants of God, *Yochanan the Immerser* and to Yeshua himself. Both came to our people with a second invitation to join the kingdom, only to be rejected by many of the Jewish leaders. Sadly, the strong reaction of the king (God himself) will be to judge those ungrateful guests even to the point of burning down their city, no doubt an allusion to the coming judgment of 70 CE upon Jerusalem. This is the story within the parable that tragically became historical reality for our people.

The parable continues with some important details. The king now is faced with a dilemma: *The wedding feast is ready but the ones who were invited didn't deserve it.* Who would attend this wonderful occasion and celebration? The surprising, yet logical, solution would be to *go out to the street-corners and invite to the banquet as many as you find*. The slaves did just that and gathered a mixed multitude— *the bad along with the good*. It is noteworthy that many different kinds of people are invited. Some are classified as "good," referring to God-fearing Jews (and later non-Jews), thereby reminding us that not all leaders or religious people rejected God's revelation. As the parable illustrates, the decision was divided among good people. Many no doubt rejected Yeshua and his claims, but many others (even rabbis like Nicodemus) gladly received the invitation. On top of this, many "bad" people were now invited to the kingdom party. This is also at the heart of Yeshua's message and the entire Bible. Most of us are undeserving and unrighteous, yet we have been graciously invited to the feast. Good news for many people indeed!

One final surprise is revealed in the parable, as the king discovered a guest at the festivities who *wasn't dressed for a wedding*. This, of course, was common courtesy when attending such a special event. The natural question from the king followed—*how did you get in here without wedding clothes?* It is customary at Jewish weddings for all to be dressed in festive clothes, often with men in the ancient world commonly wearing the white robe called a *kittel*. When the man could not provide a good answer, the king admonished his servants to *bind him* and put him *outside in the dark*. It is a terrible result, as it is a place where the outcasts will *wail and grind their teeth* in grief. This is a fearful fate indeed, with some clear spiritual lessons as well. It is a dangerous thing to reject the invitation of the Heavenly Father. Yet, so many in our present day are doing just that!

People too often fail to respond to God's clear invitation to be in relationship with him, even advancing such excuses as illustrated in this parable. Even those who respond to the invitation of the Father face an additional challenge. What if we show up at God's kingdom without the proper wedding clothes? Won't he let us in with our own choice of attire? This is a common mistake and a warning to all, even today. First, we are wise to RSVP to the wedding of *Mashiach*. Then we should consider that it is not by our own garments that we attend, but by those provided through Messiah himself. "I am so joyful in *ADONAI*! My soul rejoices in my God, for he has clothed me in salvation (root word for *Yeshua*), dressed me with a robe of triumph, like a bridegroom wearing a festive turban, like a bride adorned with her jewels" (*Yesha'yahu*/Isaiah 61:10). *Barukh HaShem*/Blessed be His Name who has provided the wedding *kittel* to those who sincerely desire to attend the joyous feast! *Many are invited, but few are chosen.* Have you responded to Yeshua's call? Have you received the garments that he offers all of us?

Questions from Three Jewish Groups   22:15-46

The Question from the Herodians   22:15-22

The previous wedding feast parable certainly served as a clear indictment of many of the *P'rushim*/Pharisees. Sadly, instead of receiving the truth of the parable, many of *the P'rushim went away and put together a plan to trap* Yeshua. Yet their plan had a twist. Some of the Pharisees teamed up with *some members of Herod's party*. The irony of this new alliance should not be overlooked.

The Pharisees were certainly no lovers of Rome and its iron fist to keep the Jewish religious authorities in line. Certainly most Pharisees, as orthodox Jews, would pray daily for the restoration of a Zion free from the occupation of any pagan nation. The Herodians, by contrast, were staunchly pro-Rome as they were the political party specifically appointed by the occupiers. What a strange sight it must have been when representatives from such opposing parties approached Yeshua with some questions. Among other things, it verifies the depth of the conflict with Yeshua's message that these two vastly different groups would unify against the one claiming to be the Messiah.

At this point of the conflict, we would not expect sincere questions. The group starts with what sounds like a patronizing statement: "Rabbi, we know that you tell the truth and really teach what God's way is." If the group sincerely believed their own words, why were they constantly opposing Yeshua's teaching? Something didn't sound right. The next part of the statement likewise sounds like a set-up: "You aren't concerned with what other people think about you, since you pay no attention to a person's status." Once again, the statement is true in itself, yet something seems awry since both parties have taken strong exception to Yeshua. Nonetheless, they continue the inquiry with the hope of tricking Yeshua into a self-incriminating response.

The heart of their question could indeed be a minefield of controversy: "Does *Torah* permit paying taxes to the Roman Emperor or not?" This would have been a tricky enough question in itself, but it took on double the weight considering who was posing the question. It seems that a simple "yes or no" answer would be a major problem for Yeshua before either of the political parties.

If he responded positively, then the *P'rushim* would have had a major accusation against Yeshua as one who placed the pagan empire above obligation to God. Yet, if he responded negatively, no doubt the Herodians would have verifiable evidence of one who advocates political rebellion. They thought they had this self-proclaimed Messiah painted into a corner with no viable way out.

However, since Yeshua is the divine *Mashiach*, he can see through their disingenuous questions. *Knowing their malicious intent*, Yeshua gives an answer they could not have predicted. He first exposes their true colors by calling them *hypocrites*. The term comes from actors of the Greek theater who would wear various masks as they pretended to portray a character. Here, it is a strong term revealing the playacting of the Herodians. Yeshua next responds with a question of his own: "Why are you trying to trap me?"

Again the term is revealing. The concept of trapping an animal was well known in the Jewish world, as it was necessary to first catch a kosher animal so that it could be ritually slaughtered in the correct manner. Since a dead animal could not be koshered, a trap/ snare was often set to catch a kosher animal first. This was often done by digging a pit and setting bait to draw the animal to its capture. It is this graphic picture that Yeshua uses to expose the motives of his questioners. So, what is his actual answer? Yeshua simply asks to see *the coin used to pay the tax.*

As they *brought him a denarius,* little did they know a most profound answer awaited them. First, Yeshua queries, "Whose name and picture are these?" The simple answer—it was the Emperor's picture on the Roman currency. It is significant to note that Yeshua (as with most Jews) would be reluctant to even carry or acknowledge a pagan coin with a human image on it. Not surprisingly, Yeshua has to ask for such a coin because he does not have one available. Yet, because the Emperor's image is on the coin, the first part of the answer is obvious: "Give the Emperor what belongs to the Emperor."

It must have pleased the Herodians to hear this first part of the statement, just as it must have shocked the *P'rushim.* However, the second part of the answer certainly would have offended the Herodians while pleasing the Pharisees, as Yeshua adds, "and give to God what belongs to God!" It is not an either/or proposition but both/and. Yeshua clearly affirms that allegiance to *HaShem*/God takes precedence over everything else. It is the very first of the Ten Commandments!

Yeshua also affirms that it is not a contradiction for *Torah*-observant Jews to submit to government authority as long as their moral boundaries and responsibilities are obeyed. Yeshua's view is that one can and should be a strong follower of God and, at the same time, be a good community citizen fulfilling such obligations. The Herodians and *P'rushim* could not have envisioned such a complete answer and were truly *amazed.* They had no choice at this point but to leave him and *went away* to ponder their next move.

The Question from the Sadducees   *22:23-33*

Having recorded the confrontation of the Herodians, Matthew's account continues with dialogue from another adversarial group. He notes, *that same day, some Tz'dukim/Sadducees came* to Yeshua. There had been several encounters with this religious party during the ministry of Messiah (cf. Matthew 16:1ff). The Sadducees consisted of those of priestly descent who were primarily in charge of the Temple worship in first-century Jerusalem. As such, they were quite different from the Pharisees, who were essentially the orthodox Jews in the synagogue community.

By contrast, the *Tz'dukim* were more of an aristocratic and aloof sect of Judaism. Even their given name means "Righteous Ones," which was an assumption based on their high calling. Matthew reminds his readers that one of the main theological distinctions of the *Tz'dukim* was that *they said there is no such thing as resurrection.* How could this be? It is well known that the *Tz'dukim* were the conservatives among the religious parties, meaning that they only accepted the *Torah* (5 Books of Moses) as divinely inspired. While having respect for the later prophets and writings, the Sadducees based their theology solely on the written *Torah*. They found no concrete evidence concerning the doctrine of resurrection, so they claimed.

Some representatives from this group now approach Yeshua with a *sh'eilah*/theological question. True to form, they ask about a teaching from the *Torah*: "If a man dies childless, his brother must marry his widow and have children to preserve the man's family line." This was the important law of levirate marriage, which was a vital protection to women in the ancient Middle East. In many societies, if a woman was widowed and childless, she was in danger for her life with no outward means of support. The *Torah* stipulated that a man's family was then responsible to care for the widow through this arrangement (cf. Deuteronomy 25:5ff). So far so good, but there is a distinctive twist with their hypothetical story. There were *seven brothers* who, at their own time, had a certain woman for their wife until each one died. A rather bizarre case, no doubt, which leads to a most bizarre question after the widow herself *died*. The *Tz'dukim* posit: "Now in the Resurrection—of the seven, whose wife will she be?" Again, as with the previous dialogue with the Herodians, the question is clearly a calculated one. How strange for some of the *Tz'dukim* to even mention the idea of resurrection in the context of their question!

As King Messiah, Yeshua answers their question with such clarity and conviction that they must have been put on the defensive. He first notes that they are mistaken and *gone astray* because they are *ignorant*. In fact, they are ignorant of two vital areas—the teachings of the entire *Tanakh and of the power of God*.

The source of their theological confusion is ignorance of the scriptures (not unlike many people today!). These are priests serving in the Temple in Jerusalem who were no doubt highly educated in many areas. Yet their own theology has created a blind spot in regard to the full revelation of God's truth. Yeshua could have had various scriptures in mind when he rebukes their ignorance, since the doctrine of the resurrection of the dead is clearly taught in dozens of scriptures (cf. Daniel 12:1-2; Isaiah 26:19; Psalm 16:10, etc.).

It is noteworthy that later Judaism affirmed *t'chiyat ha-meytim* (resurrection of the dead) as a vital doctrine within Maimonides' 13 Principles of the Jewish Faith, as still found in most daily prayer books. The *Talmud*, reflecting the Pharisaic doctrinal stand, said it succinctly: "All Israel have a share in the World to Come....And these have no share in the World to Come: He who says, 'There is no resurrection of the dead from the *Torah* and the *Torah* is not from heaven'" (Tractate Sanhedrin 10:1-3).

There was, therefore, an inherent problem with Saducean theology: They did not give authority to some of the vital portions of the Hebrew Scriptures. However, that is not their only problem, according to Yeshua. The *Tz'dukim* also minimized the power of God to accomplish the Resurrection. To them, this hypothetical example presented an impossible conundrum. Yeshua rebukes them by asserting that the power of God trumps any other challenge before us!

That said, Yeshua elaborates why they are incorrect in their conclusions. First, it is affirmed that *neither men nor women will marry* in the world to come. We will be in a whole new dimension with glorified bodies through the Resurrection. Relationships will be changed, and the earthly marriage covenant will not be needed. But why are some of these *Tz'dukim* even posing such a question when they don't even believe in the Resurrection? Once again, it appears that they want to set a trap for Rabbi Yeshua in order to discredit his ministry to Israel. Yeshua refocuses on the main issue of their *sh'eilah*. It is not about a woman or seven husbands—the central issue is resurrection itself.

With this in mind, Yeshua challenges them with a text they would surely believe and respect. In the spirit of true rabbinic *pilpul*/dialogue, it comes in the form of a question. "Haven't you read what God said to you?" Realizing that quotes from the scrolls of Daniel or Isaiah would fall on deaf ears, Yeshua quotes a passage that was central to the theology of the *Tz'dukim:* "I am the God of Avraham, the God of Yitz'chak and the God of Ya'akov" (Exodus 3). This is a quote from the middle of the *Torah* from a passage of God's revelation to Moses himself! But what's the point? On the surface, one may wonder, but the use of the present tense of the verb highlights the fact of the Resurrection. Many generations after Avraham, why does God speak of our forefather as if he is still alive?

The logical rabbinic inference is pointed out by Yeshua: "He is God not of the dead but of the living!" The resurrection of the dead is taught in the *Torah* itself and the *Tz'dukim* have erred. Once again, some of the strong critics of Yeshua must back away, realizing his logical and anointed answers. Even the crowds *were astonished* at how he responded to such tests.

The Question from the Pharisees   22:34-46

A third group now jumps into the fray. After witnessing the dialogue of Yeshua with the Herodians, and later with the *Tz'dukim*, it is now the turn of the *P'rushim*. Matthew notes how some of the Pharisees *got together* to construct their own rabbinic challenge to this rabbi from the Galilee. They chose from among them one *who was a Torah expert* to pose his own *sh'eilah*/rabbinic question. Once again, It becomes evident that this group of leaders, like the others, wished *to trap* Yeshua into somehow incriminating himself. By so doing, perhaps they could discredit his claims of messiahship. Their representative brings a central question to Yeshua: "Rabbi, which of the *mitzvot* in the *Torah* is the most important?" Nothing could be more important in a discussion between two rabbis!

The question had no doubt been asked countless times in the *Yeshiva*/rabbinical school, with various answers given. The rabbis considered many angles to the question, taking into account the concept of lighter and weightier *mitzvot*. In a lengthy but intriguing quote from the *Talmud*, we can glean some perspective.

> "613 commandments were addressed to Moses—365 prohibitions corresponding to the number of days in the solar year, and 248 positive commands corresponding to the number of limbs in the human body. David came and reduced them to 11 principles, which are enumerated in Psalm 15. Isaiah came and reduced them to 6, as it is said, 'He that walks righteously, and speaks uprightly; he that despises the gain of oppressions, that shakes his hands from holding of bribes, that stops his ears from hearing of blood, and shuts his eyes from looking upon evil' (Isaiah 33:15). Micah came and reduced them to 3, as it is written, 'What does the Lord require of you, but to do justly and to love mercy and to walk humbly with your God?' (Micah 6:8).

Isaiah subsequently reduced them to 2, as it is said, 'Thus says the Lord, Keep justice and do righteousness' (Isaiah 56:1). Lastly came Habakkuk and reduced them to one, as it is said, 'The righteous shall live by his faith' (Habakkuk 2:4)." (Tractate Makkot 24a).

It is not a coincidence that a later rabbi, Sha'ul of Tarsus, would answer the question with this familiar teaching (cf. Romans 1:17). The concept of living by a personal faith, while forgotten by many people today, has always been a central tenet of Judaism. Yet, how would Yeshua answer this pressing question? His response focuses on the most central prayer in the liturgy—the *Sh'ma* (Deuteronomy 6:4-9). Three times daily, traditional Jews have chanted the proclamation "Hear O Israel, the LORD our God, the LORD is One." Since the first verse (6:4) is a declaration of our faith in God, Yeshua addresses the commandment that immediately follows: "You are to love *ADONAI* your God with all your heart and with all your soul and with all your strength" (Deuteronomy 6:5).

Of all the possibilities, it is most beautiful that Yeshua draws our attention to the value of the entire Scriptures—love. God certainly has revealed his love to Israel and the entire world in a most concrete way. Besides our daily blessings of life, provision, and purpose, God revealed his love for us by sending the Son, the *Mashiach*. It is actually not just a command for us to love God, but a response to God's attitude toward us.

As another New Testament writer says, "we ourselves love now because he loved us first" (*I Yochanan*/1 John 4:19). Not surprisingly therefore, as Yeshua elucidates his response, the greatest *mitzvah* goes all the way back to Moshe—love God. Our personal, loving relationship with our Heavenly Father is to be top priority in Yeshua's call to discipleship, and this is to be with the entirety of our being. With all our heart (*lev*), meaning our spiritual being. With all our soul (*nefesh*), meaning our personal humanity. With all our strength (*meod*), meaning with all that we have. Like the Talmudic quote above, one must show his love for God by performing the 248 positive *mitzvot* over the entire 365-day year, adding up to 613. There can be no higher calling and sign of faithfulness to God.

Yeshua now points out that there is *a second mitzvah* that is *similar to it*. It is not just a religious connection to God—there is also the call to *love your neighbor as yourself* (Leviticus 19:18). This would seem to be a clear command on the surface, but other details may arise on further examination. Most notably, the rabbis questioned the exact meaning of "neighbor" in the *Torah*. Is it one close to you or any fellow Jew?

Yeshua answered this issue in another discussion where he gave the parable of the Good Samaritan (Luke 10:25ff). How beautiful that the Messiah highlighted that anyone, even someone outside our community like the Samaritan, is our neighbor in God's eyes. All humanity is created in the image of God. The rabbinic answer of Yeshua covers our whole existence in this present world and in the world to come. Love God and love all humanity, even as you have love for yourself. Accordingly, *all of the Torah and the Prophets are dependent on these two mitzvot.*

In the true spirit of *pilpul* (rabbinic discussion), Yeshua now turned to the *P'rushim* and countered with a *sh'eilah*/question of his own. His question would cause them to consider some important details *concerning the Messiah.* It is a question phrased in familiar language to these first-century rabbis: *Whose son is he?* It is important to point out that the teaching of a "son of God" is found numerous times in the *Tanakh* as well as in Talmudic commentaries. Psalm 2:12, Isaiah 9:5 (Hebrew) or 9:6 (Christian), and Proverbs 30:4, among others, are scriptures that mention the concept of God having a son who is often equated with the coming *Mashiach. Tractate Sanhedrin 93b* states that the government will be on the shoulders of the Messiah, who is also called *a son* in the same passage. Of course Judaism never understood this idea in the same sense as pagan Greek mythology, where a "god" could give physical birth to a son. Yet in Hebrew idiom, a son is also one who is a direct representative in a spiritual sense.

Of course, God is spirit and cannot physically father a son! Nor does God have literal wings, hands, or eyes. However, God often helps us mortals understand some of his eternal nature through familiar terms. The term "son of God" would help us understand the unique relationship between God and his son, the Messiah. The rabbis here answer Yeshua's question with another familiar teaching, that the Messiah would be the Son of *David.* Several passages speak specifically of a son coming from the house of King David who would rule over all Israel (cf. II Samuel 7:12-16). Consequently, a common rabbinic designation for King Messiah is *Mashiach ben David* (Messiah Son of David) (*Tractate Sukkah* 52a).

This being an established belief, Yeshua asks his rabbinic friends a deeper question. How is it that David *calls* the Messiah "Lord" if he is merely a physical descendant of the family? The scripture under discussion is the well-known Psalm which makes this strange statement about a son of David (*Tehillim*/Psalm 110:1). Some have argued that the passage only applies to King David himself as a son of God. But other details present problems for this view. Was David ever called a priest by God (v. 4)? Did he have a priesthood that would last forever (v. 4)?

While there are various rabbinic views, there are clearly some references applying this Psalm to the greater Son of David, the Messiah (cf. Midrash Tehillim 2:9; 18:29). If that is the case, then it is Messiah who is invited to sit at the right hand of God, which is not surprising. What is especially unusual about the passage is that *YHVH/ADONAI* speaks to *adonee/my lord or sir.* Yeshua's follow-up question is penetrating: *If David thus calls him "Lord," how is he his son?* At a minimum, it seems David is affirming that this son, the Messiah, therefore will be greater than himself. Not only that, but Yeshua also poses a technical question based on the Hebrew text. How do we account for two instances of the root word *Adon* in the same verse? Is it just a statement of David's respect for a human son or is it in fact God's affirmation that the Son of David is really the divine *Mashiach, ADONAI* revealed to Israel? In classic *midrash* form, Yeshua challenges his fellow rabbis to consider the unusual double use of the title *Adon* to lead them to the latter conclusion.

So deep was this question that the rabbinic representatives could not *think of anything to say in reply*. The lines were drawn even more deeply, and *from that day on, no one dared put to him another sh'eilah.* It is sad to note that in contemporary Judaism it is often claimed that there is no doctrine about the "son of God." It is often relegated to some supposed pagan aspect of Christian doctrine. Consequently, many Jews automatically reject the possibility of Yeshua being the Messiah because our modern Jewish thought says it cannot be so.

The challenge of this passage is to listen carefully to the Yeshua and to realize that the concept of the "son of God" is indeed found in many Jewish sources. The only real question should be, "Is Yeshua of Nazareth that promised Son of God, the Messiah?" May *ADONAI* open our eyes to hear the spiritual words of Yeshua to the rabbis of his own day. May we, Jews and non-Jews, all welcome him for who he says he is: *Mashiach ben David*!

The Seven *"Oys"* 23:1-39

Matthew continues his biography of the life of Yeshua, noting Yeshua's final conflicts with some of the religious leaders of first-century Israel. In the previous chapter, the writer had recorded some of the specific questions in the dialogue between Yeshua and some of his contemporaries. Having answered their most recent questions in Chapter 22, Yeshua now gives a strong, straightforward teaching to those who knowingly reject him. Since this teaching takes place close to his last Passover in Jerusalem, it represents Yeshua's final indictment against some of the dysfunctional and contrary attitudes of some *Torah*-teachers and *P'rushim*. In the spirit of the prophets of Israel, Yeshua issues seven *"oys"* (woes) to emphasize the religious problems of his generation.

Warning Against the Attitudes of the P'rushim   23:1-12

Yeshua now addresses *the crowds and his talmidim* regarding some of the implications of his recent questions. There will not be many questions but a plethora of observations from the One who can see the hearts of men. He first starts with an acknowledgement of the position of *the Torah-teachers and the P'rushim*/Pharisees. Since they *sit in the seat of Moshe*/Moses, they should command a certain amount of respect and attention. The architecture of the ancient synagogue was as appealing as it was instructional. Separate seating was required for men and women as is still practiced today in Orthodox Judaism.

Synagogues have been arranged since ancient times where the ark and the *Torah* scrolls are situated at the point of the compass closest to Jerusalem. In synagogues in the east, this meant facing west to acknowledge the importance of the holy city for Jews, as Daniel did while in Babylon (cf. Daniel 6:10). For Jews in the west, this meant facing east as is practiced by Jews in America today. If a synagogue is in Israel proper, then the ark faces Jerusalem at whatever direction needed. If the synagogue is in Jerusalem itself, the ark would face the Temple Mount. Obviously, Jerusalem has long been acknowledged as the center of Jewish life and spiritual hope. It is informative to contrast this with Islam, whose adherents, even if they are praying in Jerusalem, face away toward Mecca in modern Saudi Arabia.

In the first-century *Beit-Knesset*/synagogue (house of assembly), there was also a visible place of honor for the teaching rabbi or scholar. It was from the *seat of Moshe*/Moses that the rabbi would issue his authoritative teaching and *halakhah*/rulings concerning the

Torah. Yeshua begins his lengthy teaching of this chapter with what may be a surprising affirmation for some people. *Whatever they tell you, take care to do it.* This would be a common policy among the community; however, Yeshua adds an important condition to this call to obedience. *Don't do what they do, because they talk but don't act!* Their teaching is often correct and to be respected, but the apparent problem is their inconsistent lifestyle. They were not practicing what they were preaching.

This verse must be the lens by which the following teaching is judged. The manner in which Yeshua addresses many of the traditional customs in the subsequent verses has led some interpreters to conclude that he is attacking Judaism itself. This cannot be accurate in light of his exhortation to do whatever the rabbis accurately teach.

Clearly, the main problem addressed in Matthew 23 is not any Jewish custom per se but a hypocritical attitude associated with some spiritual leaders. We have seen, in fact, that Yeshua observes some of the very customs that he addresses, e.g., wearing of *tzitziyot*/fringes. It should also be kept in mind that this chapter is not a wholesale condemnation of every *Torah*-teacher or Pharisee. As with any other religious group, there are good adherents as well as bad adherents. It is unfortunate that some have used these verses to justify their own anti-Semitic attitudes by broadly condemning Jews and Judaism. We must take a fresh look at Yeshua's important teaching with these realities in mind.

Messiah challenges the attitude of the *P'rushim*, as *they tie heavy loads onto people's shoulders but won't lift a finger to help carry them.* It is easy to give authoritative teaching with the wrong attitude. What should be done in humble reliance upon God can become a burden to place on sincere people. In a strong rabbinic hyperbole, Yeshua paints a picture of the common person burdened with a huge pack while the religious teachers stand by and watch. He exposes a fundamental problem with some of the teachers when he says *everything they do is done to be seen by others.* Not only do they put unnecessary religious burdens on others, but they often perform their own religious actions merely to impress those around them. This, of course, misses the original motivation for performing a *mitzvah.* Whatever the impact upon the people around us, we are to find joy in simply serving God through the *mitzvah.*

Yeshua expounds on a practical example of such errors. Some of these leaders were known to *make their t'fillin broad.* This is the ancient custom of wearing leather prayer boxes on both the arm and forehead to fulfill the biblical commandment of the *Sh'ma* passage (Deuteronomy 6:4-9). Here Israel is commanded to remember the commandments of the *Torah* by tying them in this way so they may be a sign. Historically, this was fulfilled by wearing *t'fillin* during the morning prayers of the Jew. Within the leather boxes are tiny parchments handwritten with the *Sh'ma* passage and other parallel verses (Deuteronomy 6:4-9; 11:13-21; Exodus 13:1-10, 11-16) It is a most literal way to fulfill this commandment.

It must be noted that Yeshua never condemns the use of *t'fillin.* In fact, he himself undoubtedly prayed with *t'fillin* as he fulfilled all the commandments of the *Torah* as the sinless Messiah. What he does condemn is the practice by some to broaden their prayer boxes. Such is the tendency of some religious people to expand a commandment to the point where it actually annuls the original intent! If *t'fillin* are good, how much better and spiritual would be *t'fillin* that are bigger? Perhaps prayer boxes from Jerusalem are more holy than *t'fillin* from Galilee or even the USA! Yeshua warns the crowd not to lose perspective on the pure intent of this beautiful Jewish custom.

In the spirit of the prophets of old, Yeshua also rebukes those who would make *their tzitziyot long. Tzitziyot* is the Hebrew term often translated as "fringes," which were to be placed on the corner of the outer garment of every male (Numbers 15:37-41). Over the centuries, this has been observed in one form or another. The most ancient application was simply to put a fringe on the outer garment worn by a man. Since the command is spoken "to the sons of Israel" (*b'nai Yisra'el*), it has been historically interpreted that the commandment is only incumbent upon the men of the community. It should be noted that in some modern denominations of Judaism, the term *b'nai Yisra'el* is more broadly interpreted as "children of Israel;" that is, it also includes women. It is not uncommon today for many Jewish women to also wear a *tallit* with the symbolic fringes during synagogue services.

Over the years, there has been some beautiful symbolism incorporated within the *mitzvah* of the fringes. In more modern times, Jews often did not wear the fringe on the outer garment out of fear of persecution. An adaptation called the *tallit*/prayer shawl was developed, in which the *tzitziyot* are connected to the four corners of the garment. The fringes themselves are very symbolic, as there are four strands attached to each corner of the *tallit*. These in turn are threaded twice within the corner, thus creating eight strands. These eight strands are then tied with five double knots as they hang from the corner of the garment. The symbolic numerical value of this is 13. Add to this the numerical value of the Hebrew word *tzitzit,* which is 600. The total is 613, a graphic picture of the 613 commandments of the entire *Torah*! In this fashion, the *tallit*/prayer shawl is a literal reminder to keep the commandments God has spoken.

Since this is a biblical commandment, we know that Yeshua cannot be condemning the custom of wearing *tzitzit* (singular). In fact, it is clear that he himself diligently followed this commandment as a traditional Jew (cf. Matthew 9:20). Once again, it is not the *use* of a Jewish custom but the *abuse* of that custom that is problematic. He warns against the practice of some who make their fringes excessively long. If *tzitziot* are good, how much better and spiritual would be *tzitziot* that really stand out? Such is often the logic of religious people, but ironically, it can cause them to lose perspective on the original intent of the commandment. Yeshua gives the crowd some food for thought in their approach to observing even the biblical *mitzvot.*

Messiah continues his exposure of some of the extreme attitudes of the religious leaders. The next topic does not deal with a Jewish ritualistic custom but with their attitude of seeking honor. He warns that some *love the place of honor at banquets and the best seats in the synagogues.* As mentioned above, the rabbis were also afforded a great deal of respect for their position. This would be fine as long as the respect was coming from the larger community. However, when leaders lose focus and start seeking that respect and honor for themselves, something is amiss. There is a midrash that reminds us to take a lowly seat at a banquet so perhaps we may be invited to take a better seat of honor. Some of these particular leaders were showing their true colors by seeking public recognition and exaltation. It is all about attitude.

In a similar manner, some of these leaders *love being greeted deferentially* by being *called "Rabbi."* Once again, we should realize that there is nothing inherently wrong with the term *rabbi,* or pastor or priest for that matter. *Rabbi* simply means teacher, and these leaders were the designated rabbis of their community. The problem develops, as Yeshua points out, when such leaders *love* such greetings and titles. What should be a title of respect received in humility had become a source of pride for some of the rabbinic teachers. How subtle are the attitudes within our religious walk! A bad attitude in any one of these areas can nullify the good that was originally intended.

The fact that Yeshua is not issuing an outright condemnation of such titles can be clearly seen in the following verses. He admonishes the crowd not to let themselves be *called "Rabbi" because you have one Rabbi.* In context, Yeshua is clearly warning against using this title in the arrogant, even hypocritical manner exemplified by some of the *P'rushim*. Believers are admonished to be careful not to love this or any other title that would distract from the spiritual reality. Believers ultimately understand that we have one perfect teacher in Yeshua himself. Consequently, we are all brothers of equal value and respect. Of course, this must be taken in the context in which it is given, for elsewhere in the Scripture we are told that God himself establishes certain teachers and leaders within the Body of Messiah (cf. Ephesians 4:11ff). Yeshua is certainly not advocating radical independence for his disciples but wariness of leaders with bad motives.

In similar fashion, Yeshua exhorts the crowd to *not call anyone on earth "Father" because you have one Father, and he is in heaven.* Is there something innately evil about the term *Father*? Of course not, for the *Torah* and Yeshua himself command us to honor our father and mother (cf. Matthew 15:1-5). No one is sinning by calling their earthly dad by the term!

The entire context of this chapter is about bad attitudes and the abuse of titles. It is noteworthy that the term *Av/*Father was quite commonly used in the rabbinic circles of Yeshua's day. In fact, the top officers of the Sanhedrin of the first century were the *Nasi/* President and, sitting at his right hand, the *Av Beit-Din* (father of the court). This was obviously a title of respect and honor for one of the top rabbis of the community who served as the vice-president of the Supreme Court.

Yeshua reminds his listeners that, with all due respect to earthly leaders, we ultimately have only one true Father in heaven. Use of the term *Av* becomes wrong only when it distracts us from our Great Abba who watches over us. Yeshua also warns against the abuse of the term *leader* because *you have one Leader, and he is the Messiah!* While it is true that the term is used of earthly leaders (cf. Ephesians 4:11ff), one must guard against the temptation to arrogantly exalt an earthly leader above the *Mashiach* himself. Some may attempt to exalt themselves through their position of spiritual leadership, but in Yeshua's kingdom "the greatest among you must be your servant."

Yes, there is a proper place for spiritual leaders and even for the use of the terms of honor and respect, but it is the arrogant attitude of some of these leaders that must be guarded against. Those who are Yeshua's disciples will prove their leadership abilities by serving others in the world and his kingdom. This is so contrary to the normative thinking of the world yet is a beautiful principle of Messiah's kingdom to come. In the spirit of true justice, Yeshua assures the crowd that *whoever promotes himself will be humbled, and whoever humbles himself will be promoted.* How contradictory is this philosophy to those of the corporate world and even the religious world of some of these rabbinic leaders! Yet, it rings with the truth of our Heavenly Father. It is not enough to merely observe the religious customs of our people. We should listen to the words of Yeshua and examine our attitudes as well.

Warning Against the Practices of the P'rushim   23:13-36

Messiah now turns to the heart of his teaching in exposing unbalanced religious views. His focus is still on the *P'rushim/* Pharisees, as it is some of their high-profile leaders who are guilty of such offenses. Yeshua prefaces each of his seven rebukes with an emotional *woe!* (literally, *oy* in Hebrew). This is an expressive Hebrew (and later Yiddish) word connoting a wide range of emotions from extreme joy to shock or dismay. It is obvious in this context, as Yeshua condemns some of the inconsistent and hurtful practices of this group. The reader is reminded that, as strong as this passage is, it is directed to a limited group in the immediate context. There undoubtedly were sincere, godly Pharisees mixed in with the hypocritical. Some have even accused Yeshua (or Matthew) of blatant anti-Semitism with these harsh words. However, Matthew 23 is not much different than Isaiah 1, where the Hebrew prophet goes even further in judging his own generation. We must view Yeshua in the same spirit as the prophets of Israel, speaking as a concerned Jew to fellow Jews, not as an outsider with an anti-Jewish grudge.

It is important to note that the *Talmud* itself honestly describes seven different kinds of Pharisees in the first century, many of which are problematic in their own estimation. In *Tractate Sotah 22b*, the following seven types of *P'rushim* are listed:

The Shoulder (*shikmi*) Pharisee who performs the action of Shechem (cf. Genesis 34). It should be remembered that Shechem pretended to convert to the God of Israel, performing good deeds visibly (worn on his shoulder) that were limited to outward appearance. This seems to be part of Yeshua's reference in Matthew 23:4, as they lay burdens on men's shoulders.

The Stumbling (*nikpi*) Pharisee who walks in an exaggerated manner to draw attention to his humility. How sadly ironic!

The Bleeding (*kizai*) Pharisee who is so concerned about looking upon a woman that he causes his own bleeding by bruising himself against a wall.

The Pestle *(me-dukiya)* Pharisee who publicizes his own holiness as his head is bowed like a pestle in a mortar.

The Reckoning *(ma chovti)* Pharisee who constantly asks, "What is my religious duty?" as though he has fulfilled every *mitzvah*.

The Loving *(me-ahavah)* Pharisee who has a balanced understanding of the *Torah* and his walk with God.

The Fearful *(me-yareha)* Pharisee whose relationship with God is not based on reverence but on actual fear and trembling.

As we study Matthew 23 and Yeshua's exposé of the Pharisees, we can't help but notice the parallels. It is significant that, even by their self-examination, the Talmudic rabbis describe only one sect in a fully positive manner. Messiah's words, while appearing harsh in some ways, are nonetheless consistent with the prevailing views of his day.

The first *oy*/woe is directed to those *hypocritical Torah-teachers and P'rushim* who obstruct others from the *Kingdom of Heaven*. How could this be? Were not the Pharisees very concerned about religious observance in order to enter that Kingdom? On the surface the answer is "yes," but the reality could be quite different. Their very name, *P'rushim*, implies the problem. They were separatists who sometimes made it even more difficult to enter the Kingdom of God. It was not so much the written *Torah* that they zealously observed (although that would make it difficult enough!)—a major part of their rabbinic/Talmudic doctrine added an extra fence around the *Torah*. These consisted of innumerable man-made interpretations of how to apply the *Torah* as illustrated in the oral tradition of the *Mishnah* and *Gemara*. These would often amount to a maze of extra commandments and obligations that would actually keep many people further away from a personal relationship with God.

In contrast, Yeshua said just the opposite as he emphasized the simplicity of coming into the kingdom, even stating that we must become like little children (cf. Matthew 18:3). Consequently, such actions deny entrance to both *yourselves* and, sadly, *those who wish to enter* as they are in danger of confusing the pure message of the Scriptures. A question for us: "Are we making our relationship with God more complex than it really needs to be?"

Another *oy* described in Matthew 23:14 isn't formally counted in this list of seven *oys* but is worth discussing. Verse 14 is included in some of the oldest manuscripts of Matthew, but omitted in others. This *oy* is a strong rebuke for the lack of social justice. Yeshua exposes the *hypocritical* action of some of the leaders who make quite a show of *davvening/praying at great length.* Prayer is always good, but, as usual, Messiah tries to draw us to a proper attitude toward prayer. *Davvening*, in the Jewish sense of the word, is good. No one should doubt the sincere devotion of Jews who pray with such zeal.

The problem arises when such prayer is going forth yet the person is obviously disobedient to other, more important aspects of *Torah*.

In this case, Yeshua charges some of the *Torah-teachers* with the sin of *swallowing up widows' houses*. We can only speculate what is meant by this, but clearly it is a reference to the neglect of one of the highest values of *Torah*—social justice. Some were overlooking the helpless widows of the community, perhaps even defaulting on loans and endangering their housing. The *oy* is pronounced out of shock that such seemingly religious people could infringe upon a more weightier *mitzvah* of the *Torah*. Their *punishment will be all the worse* because they are putting up a façade of spirituality. A question for us: Are we clearly applying the values of our faith in our local community?

The second *oy* (if one excludes verse 14 because of the textual questions) gives an interesting historical insight into the work of the P'rushim in the first century. Yeshua shares his warning with those *hypocritical* leaders who *go to great lengths to make one proselyte*. This verse might sound strange to 21st-century Jews, who often point out that Judaism is not a religion that practices outright proselytizing. But there is no doubt that the Judaism of the Second Temple period still had an aggressive outreach campaign as part of the call to be a light to the Nations (cf. Isaiah 49:6).

Besides the many Gentiles of the Roman Empire who converted to Judaism, we can essentially add an entire nation called the Edomites, who were forcibly converted in the first century BCE. This was the home community of the notorious Roman convert by the name of Herod the Great. He was therefore the ideal choice of the Romans for a leader who could, in a superficial way, relate to the Jewish community of first-century Israel.

Such proselytizing would soon come to an end in the Roman Empire, as the oppressors felt threatened by such religious movements and eventually outlawed any conversion to Judaism. So why the rebuke of this practice by Yeshua? The problem is that the Pharisees were making converts to their way of life that would actually lead many away from the simple purity of the *Torah*. In the strongest terms, Messiah warns that such converts are actually *twice as fit for Gei-Hinnom as you are!* A question for us: "Are we drawing people to the pure message of the Scriptures or converting them to something else?"

The third *oy* is a rebuke of the spiritual blindness of some of the *Torah-teachers and P'rushim.* In highly ironic language, Yeshua calls them *blind guides!* Those who prided themselves in being spiritual guides to the common people were, in fact, not able to see the full spiritual reality for themselves. He points out several egregious examples of practices that prove this principle. Yeshua first speaks of the true-to-life example of a religious person who might swear by the Temple in the process of taking an oath.

The practice of taking an oath was quite common in the biblical narratives, as well as in rabbinic discussion. So important was it that an entire Tractate of the *Talmud* is devoted to the details of taking an oath (Tractate Shevuot). Again, there is nothing inherently wrong with taking an oath or vow, as it was common practice and could be quite beneficial in establishing an agreement. If people needed to strongly verify their promises, they could swear by something or someone greater than themselves. In this case, some of the rabbis could solidify their word by swearing *by the Temple*, the great House of God.

Such an oath was considerably strong, but there could be a way to circumvent even such a promise. Yet if that same person were to *swear by the gold in the Temple, he is bound* to fulfill the promise. Even though there were religious exemptions allowed in such cases, how is this logical? Yeshua rebukes such logic as coming from *blind fools!* Isn't it *the Temple that makes the gold holy?* And yet a person could *swear by the altar,* only for that promise to later be considered non-binding. Yet, if the same person takes an oath invoking the name of *the offering on the altar,* it is considered binding. Again, the rebuke is forthcoming—*blind men!* It makes no sense that the offering is regarded as more important than the holy altar on which it is presented. In reality, anyone who *swears by the altar* actually *swears by it and everything on it!* Likewise, if someone swears *by the Temple,* the person *swears by it and the One who lives in it.* And if someone takes an oath in the name of heaven, he also *swears by God's throne and the One who sits on it.* A question for us: "Are we consistent in speaking words that are true and that bring the blessings of God to those around us?"

The fourth *oy* directed at the *Torah-teachers and P'rushim* exposes some of their misplaced priorities. They pay their *tithes,* which is in fact a commendation as this is part of the *Torah* requirements incumbent upon every Jew (cf. Genesis 14:18-20; Deuteronomy 14:22-29). The importance of tithing is exemplified by the fact that an entire tractate of the *Talmud* is devoted to such details (Tractate Ma'aser). *Ma'aser*/tithe is reflected in the word *tenth,* so the amount spoken cannot really be doubted. Every Israelite male was required to give 10% of his earnings to the worship of God and the upkeep of the Tabernacle or Temple.

It is a misnomer and inaccurate to say one is giving a 2% tithe. A 2% offering would be more accurate. The spiritual discipline of giving had many important lessons for sincere Jews, as it does today for all believers today. It is perhaps the most practical exercise in faith to dedicate 10% of one's income to the Kingdom of God. Many times we may think of how we need that investment for our own personal needs. But faith enables us to give, even our first fruits, and to trust that God will provide for all our needs according to his riches. Some of the biggest lessons in faith come when we trust God with that last frontier—our finances!

The Pharisees strongly believed and applied the entire teachings of *Torah,* so it is not surprising that they were known for their scrupulous tithing. Yeshua even notes that they followed this *mitzvah* right down to the smallest spices—*mint, dill and cumin*. It is significant that the Messiah never condemns the practice (how could he if it is in *Torah*?), but in fact affirms that *these things you should have attended to*. Their tithing is not the problem, rather it is that they have *neglected the weightier matters of the Torah*.

The *P'rushim,* while attending so meticulously to the fine details of *Torah,* had lost perspective on the more important elements of the *Torah—justice, mercy, and trust*. It is not a matter of "either/or" but "both/and" when it comes to the 613 *mitzvot*. It is noteworthy that Yeshua alludes to the principle of weightier and lighter commandments. Not all are of equal importance, and some are prioritized over others. What ultimate good is it if we keep track of all our spices and yet neglect to show mercy to others when it is called for?

Again, Yeshua rebukes some of the religious teachers with a highly ironic term—*blind guides!* Those who should be leading Israel and the Nations in the light of God are acting like they are blind. Yeshua ends this fifth *oy* with a shocking and humorous analogy. The P'rushim, whose very name means "separatists," were *straining out a gnat while swallowing a camel!*

The picture is of people so worried about keeping kosher (insects obviously are forbidden) that they strain their soup to make sure it is pure. Good so far. But for the main course, they are having a whole camel. Not only is this *treif*/non-kosher, but a shocking hyperbole that would be sure to draw the attention of the crowd. The warning is clear: No matter what our religious observance level, don't miss the most important values of the Scripture. A question for us: "Have we been sidetracked by lesser important commandments to the neglect of more important ones?"

The fifth *oy* has to do with an overly concerned focus on external appearances. Some of the *P'rushim* are said to be *hypocritical*, similar to an actor in a Greek drama. The word hypocrite was not originally used in a pejorative sense but merely meant "actor." In this particular denunciation, Yeshua points out some obvious inconsistencies in some of the practices of these leaders. They were quite meticulous in keeping the outside of the cup and the dish strictly clean and kosher. There is nothing wrong with this practice. The word itself (kosher) implies cleanliness, both ritually and literally. Not surprisingly, there is a vast number of commands (such as what animals are considered food, how to kill them, how to cook them, and what to keep separated) reflected in the fact that an entire tractate of the *Talmud* is dedicated to utensils and *kashrut* (Tractate Kelim).

Obviously, attention must be paid to the condition of the kitchen vessels if dietary laws are to be maintained. The problem, however, lies with the hypocritical actions of some who keep their kitchen kosher yet let unkosher actions creep into their lives. These very leaders are accused of living a lifestyle *full of robbery and self-indulgence.* These obvious infractions of the spirit of the *Torah* lead Yeshua to call such a person a *blind Parush.*

Messiah's exhortation to such a person is to *first clean the inside of the cup, so that the outside may be clean too.* While it is commendable to have a pure outer life, care must be taken to make the inner life match up to that same standard. A question for us: "Even while admitting our imperfections, is our inner life basically consistent with our outer behavior?"

The sixth *oy* emphasizes the danger of having inconsistencies between our religious life and our practical lifestyle. Switching the word-picture from the kitchen to the cemetery, Yeshua makes a striking comparison. Some of the *Torah-teachers are like whitewashed tombs.* Whitewashing was a common practice in Israel, especially at the holy season of Passover when this dialogue takes place. *Pesach*/Passover is a holy time that places great emphasis on cleaning (cf. Exodus 12). The home must be thoroughly cleansed of any items containing *chametz,* and the *kosher l'Pesach* products must be brought in. *Matzah* replaces bread and the usual flour. Utensils are switched out or koshered with boiling water or fire. In order not to compromise the ritual purity of the season, special care is taken to mark areas that might create a problem. A cemetery was a good case in point, as unnecessary contact with a tomb could render one ritually unclean. To avoid this possibility, it was customary to clearly mark all tombs with a fresh coat of whitewash paint.

Again, all of this is well and good in itself. But Yeshua points out a problem, as he describes some of these teachers with this analogy. They are like such good-looking tombs yet *inside are full of dead people's bones and all kinds of rottenness.* Their appearance on the outside is vastly different from the spiritual reality of the inside. Some would *appear to be good and honest,* but inwardly, they are actually *far from Torah.*

Messiah is clearly not belittling any religious practice of Judaism here but directs our focus to the dangers of hypocrisy. Yeshua reserves some of his harshest criticisms not for "sinners" who admit their need for help, but for those who put on a religious show by playacting. While they claim to be the teachers of *Torah,* they are actually missing the main point of the *Torah!* A question for us: "Are we merely concerned about the letter of the *Torah,* or are we also focused on the spiritual intent of the *Torah?*"

The seventh and final *oy* speaks to the ultimate hypocritical behavior of some of these *P'rushim.* Continuing his thematic teaching, Yeshua points out that they *build tombs for the prophets and decorate the graves of the tzaddikim.* This has always been a common practice in Jewish history, as one can still witness today in a walk through modern Jerusalem. It is a respectful custom to honor our religious forefathers. Many of the prophets who came to Israel were ultimately appreciated for their important words of guidance, even if their message wasn't fully received at first. Jeremiah was cast into a cistern (Jeremiah 38), and Isaiah was sawed in two by King Manasseh

(Tractate Yevamot 49b). Also worthy of honor are various *tzaddikim/* righteous ones who lived exemplary lives and blessed our people.

The strange thing is that many of these same prophets and *tzaddikim* were rejected and experienced opposition in their own lifetimes. What becomes the greatest of ironies is that, according to Yeshua, some of his fellow Jews were denying that they would have had the same attitude as their fathers. Indeed, they say, "Had we lived when our fathers did, we would never have taken part in killing the prophets." In true prophetic fashion, Messiah uses their own words to connect them to the ungodly behavior of the past. They testify against themselves that they are *worthy descendants of those who murdered the prophets.* They may try to disassociate themselves through their words, but their own actions speak louder than their confessions. A question for us: "Are we merely continuing some bad decisions by our forefathers (even our own families), or are we evaluating our relationship with God for ourselves?"

Yeshua speaks out now with a general denunciation of all such leaders who fall into this trap of hypocritical religious behavior. At this climax of his teaching, Messiah withholds nothing, by addressing them with the indictments "you snakes" and "sons of snakes!" Strong terms, indeed, that are not directed at every rabbi or leader but clearly at those who are as deceptive as serpents.

Their judgment is sealed as they will not escape *being condemned to Gei-Hinnom.* Regardless of what any previous generation did, this current generation is in danger of many of the same godless actions. Yeshua, speaking for God, says, "I am sending you prophets and sages and *Torah*-teachers" who are the Father's representatives. How interesting that he uses the same term (*Torah-teachers*) used earlier to refer to some of the false teachers. Again, we are clearly reminded that Yeshua's rebuke is in no way against all religious leaders (whatever their affiliation), but against those who live in a world of spiritual hypocrisy.

Some of these designated representatives of God *will kill,* having Yeshua's followers *executed on stakes as criminals.* This is a clear reference to those leaders who handed over righteous people to the Romans for criminal crucifixion. In addition to that, these leaders will authorize Jewish authorities to *flog them in your synagogues.* This was an acceptable *Torah* practice as punishment for heretics or criminals. Such sentences were to be meted out with due process and even with mercy, as seen in the practice of withholding one lash from the full punishment (39 lashes when 40 are due—Deuteronomy 25:3). The leaders are rebuked because they will be so consumed with opposing God's true messengers that they will *pursue them from town to town.* Because of their rebellious behavior against God and his messengers, they will be *guilty of all the innocent blood that has ever been shed on earth.* This is a rabbinic hyperbole but, nevertheless, indicative of the seriousness of their transgressions.

In a sense, the long history of righteous men illustrates this truth, from *the blood of innocent Hevel/Abel to the blood of Z'kharyah/ Zechariah Ben-Berekhyah.* Abel represents the first homicide in history as recorded in the first book of the *Torah* (Genesis 4:8), whereas Zechariah represents the last of the leaders in the last book within the Jewish order of the *Tanakh* (II Chronicles 24:20-21). The last murder is especially egregious, as it occurred in the Temple compound. As a result of the first-century parallel actions, a strong judgment *will fall on this generation.*

Yeshua's Burden for Jerusalem 23:37-39

Matthew culminates this strong exhortation by recounting one of the most emotional and heartfelt events in the life of Yeshua. As if it were a final call to receive him, Messiah beckons to the holy city *"Yerushalayim! Yerushalayim!"* The repetition shows great emphasis. The burden of Yeshua is portrayed by the ensuing words and, lest anyone think he is simply angry, Luke's scroll records Yeshua weeping as he overlooked the city a few days prior (Luke 19:41). The source of this grief is the rejection of God's true messengers, of those in the history of the *Tanakh* as well as of God's *Mashiach* standing in their midst. How tragic that many in the holy city had not received the very ones that brought the message of life for the people. Instead, some had even decided to *kill the prophets* or to *stone those who were sent*. With such a hostile reception in those cases, we might expect Yeshua to thunder the righteous judgment of God. On the contrary, he speaks in the first person: "I wanted to gather your children, just as a hen gathers her chickens under her wings."

This is a profound statement for two reasons. First, it must be understood that God has always had compassion for his beloved covenant people. Sadly, the message of the prophets was often interpreted as a negative judgment from the God of our fathers. From Yeshua's perspective, however, it was more like a mother hen wanting to protect her children from harm. The Father gives us all instruction and even correction out of love for us. Second, it is amazing and shocking to realize that Yeshua is saying he is the one who was calling Israel through the Prophets. It is not just the Father in Heaven who has been seeking his children, but Yeshua himself as the eternal *Mashiach*! Whether it was the mysterious *Malakh Adonai*/Angel of the Lord who appeared to Abraham or the message of repentance by Micah the prophet, it has been Messiah who has desired to gather his people together for blessing.

God's compassion for us is so beautiful and compelling, yet the response was—*but you refused!* Jewish history is filled with many mysteries. Why have so many tragic events taken place? Or in the words of the *Haggadah*/Passover Guide, why is it that "in every generation there are those who rise up against us?" Yeshua's answer is not meant to be simplistic, but it does hold a great part of the answer from God's perspective. It is not that God has abandoned us, but that we, as a people, have too often abandoned God. He has desired to protect and bless us, but we have refused to accept his offer. From God's perspective, it is not so much that God has judged Israel so harshly, but that we have removed ourselves from God's protective grace in this hostile world.

The *Talmud* discusses this same issue, as Rabbi Joshua is said to have asked the Messiah, "When will you come, Master?" "Today" was his answer. In explaining this encounter to Elijah, Rabbi Joshua showed his disappointment as he said, "He spoke falsely to me, stating that he would come today but has not." To this Elijah answered, "This is what he said to you: Today, if you will hear his voice" (quoting Psalm 95:7 in Tractate Sanhedrin 98a). Too often the problem is not with God or Messiah but with our lack of response. This does not answer every question and every tragedy, but it must be considered as part of the eternal puzzle.

Yeshua continues to explain some of the immediate ramifications of his rejection by most of the religious leaders. He asserts in the strongest terms, "Look! God is abandoning your house to you, leaving it desolate." Messiah is not just announcing the judgment upon their own personal dwelling places but upon the great "house" of Jerusalem, the Holy Temple. This would have been more clearly understood in the original Hebrew, which Yeshua undoubtedly spoke with these leaders. The magnificent Temple of Jerusalem was called the *Beit-Ha'Mikdash/* The Holy House. In fact, so common was this term that the Temple was often simply referred to as *Ha-Beit/*The House.

This is an important statement for all to consider, even to our own day. The Second Temple was destroyed by the Roman armies on the *9th of Av* in the year 70 CE. While no one can question that historic fact, it is still debated as to why the *Beit-Ha'Mikdash* was destroyed. Was it not God himself who commanded Israel to build this House in the Holy City? Why would God allow this important element of biblical Judaism to be torn to the ground? And why in the year 70 CE/AD? Why not 300 BCE or 750 CE? Among the

280 / YESHUA, KING MESSIAH

various theories as to why all of this happened, it is stated in the *Talmud* that whereas the First Temple was destroyed because of our idolatry, the Second Temple was destroyed because of *sinat chinam*/gratuitous hatred among the brothers (Tractate Yoma 9b). This is no doubt a grievous sin, but an important question must be considered: Is the sin of gratuitous hatred a strong enough sin for God to then destroy the center of Judaism?

While the Talmudic rabbis and even modern scholars have discussed this question, Yeshua gives a perspective that deserves our serious attention. Let me put it this way: If the real Messiah came to Israel and was rejected by the majority, would we be surprised if there was a strong reaction from God? It would seem that the total destruction of the Holy Temple would necessitate a most serious sin such as the rejection of God's greatest messenger, the *Mashiach*. It should be noted that this judgment is localized to a particular time and space. It is *you* (that generation only) who were eyewitnesses to the life of Yeshua and who personally rejected his visible offer.

Yeshua is not speaking judgment upon every Jew who ever lived, as some anti-Semitic theologies have taught in history. Thankfully, even the Roman Catholic Church finally renounced such teachings in its Vatican II decisions of 1965 (better late than never!). It must also be emphasized that this judgment is not applicable to every house but only the one Holy Temple at 70 CE. While there are some important qualifications to this judgment, this watershed event of Jewish history still draws us to consider its relevance today. For those who have an open mind and spiritual eyes to discern, the destruction of the *Beit-Ha'Mikdash* stands as a sign from God and perhaps the greatest testimony to help us ask the question, "Could Yeshua be the true Messiah?"

The final statement of this passage reminds us that all is spoken with the spirit of hope and God's deep love for his people. It would be extremely sad if the chapter ended with the previous sentence, but there is a beautiful promise in the midst of these troubling events. Yeshua proceeds to tell the crowd that they *will not see* him *again until* something dramatic happens. It is a blessing that he does not say the first-century rejection has nullified all covenants. He does not threaten to totally stay away from his people. What he actually reveals is that he will be leaving them for a certain amount of time, but they will indeed see him again! Messiah will be separated from his people by his impending death, but will then be resurrected and appear again. This would be partially fulfilled in the 40 days from his resurrection until his ultimate ascension to the right hand of God. But many in Israel did not see him within that short time. The ultimate fulfillment will be after his longer separation from Israel (now nearly 2000 years!) when another miraculous event will take place.

Jerusalem will see Yeshua again when they say, "Blessed is he who comes in the name of *Adonai*." This famous phrase is part of the Hallel Psalms (113-118) that are chanted at several major Jewish holy days, including *Pesach* and *Sukkot*. This particular segment of the Psalms is highly messianic, speaking of *Adonai*'s return to Zion and the days of messianic redemption. The Hebrew is most beautiful: *Barukh Habah*, literally "Welcome" (Psalm 118:26). The entire phrase evokes a time when, instead of rejecting Yeshua, all Israel will welcome him in the name of *Adonai*. Yeshua makes this statement just a few days before the entire Jewish community will be chanting the Hallel at their Passover *seder* meals! It would have been a great blessing for all Israel to welcome Yeshua as King Messiah at that Passover season, but it will have to wait for a later generation.

Despite the national rejection at Passover, his acceptance is predicted at the other major holy day called *Sukkot*/Feast of Tabernacles. How fitting that Passover is the feast of redemption and Sukkot is the feast of God's kingdom. For those of us in Messianic Judaism, Passover perfectly prefigures the death of Messiah, whereas *Sukkot* is a sign of Messiah's return. It is no coincidence that Yeshua died exactly on 15 *Nisan,* the very day of *Pesach*! It seems his return as symbolized at Sukkot is guaranteed. This vital phrase of the Hallel is said to contain the very words that all Israel will speak when Yeshua returns. To many people, Jews and Christians alike, this promise is so big it seems impossible. All Israel will call out for *Mashiach*? However, it is not just an affirmation of Yeshua but a promise of the Hebrew prophets as well. "I will pour out on the house of David and on those living in Yerushalayim a spirit of grace and prayer; and they will look to me, whom they pierced" (Zechariah 12:10). This will clearly be a miracle from God. After nearly 2000 years of separation from Yeshua and even persecution in his name, God will pour out his Spirit and every Jew living at that point in history will look to him in faith. Their faith will be exemplified in the famous prayer of the Hallel, as they all call out *"Barukh habah"* for the deliverance of Yeshua as our King Messiah. When will these things occur? The next chapter of Matthew's account will give us more details.

This has practical implications for all modern-day followers of Yeshua, both Jew and non-Jew. No doubt, every true believer looks forward to the promise of Yeshua's return. But we should ask the deeper question: "What are some of the prerequisites for his return?" We have the strongest one here.

Quite simply, Yeshua is not returning to planet Earth until all Israel welcomes him back as Messiah. What does this mean to the average believer? Is your congregation actively involved in loving outreach to the Jewish community? Our people are the key to the messianic redemption. Are we personally following the mandate to share with our Jewish family and friends about the Good News of Yeshua? May God use us to be a light for Messiah in our world!

Predictions of King Messiah 24:1-25:46

Having completed the exposé in Chapter 23, Yeshua continues his teaching concerning future events. His special focus, according to Matthew, is the centrality of the Jewish people (worldwide) and the nation Israel in the Middle East. These two chapters have a wealth of information and give the hearers insight into the very last days just before the coming of the messianic age. It will be both a time of great darkness as well as emanating light as God winds down the clock on human history. Since Yeshua is the Messiah sent directly from God, he has insight that no mere man or even rabbi could have. His teaching here is not meant only for futuristic speculation but to make a practical impact on the personal lives of his hearers, including us.

The Prophecy Concerning the Temple 24:1-2

Matthew continues to record the dialogue with the crowd, which was intently listening on the Temple Mount. As seen in Chapter 23, the backdrop of the entire conversation is The House of God in Jerusalem. Having mentioned the future desolation of that House in 70 CE, Yeshua fields some logical questions from his *talmidim*. The text notes that as he *left the Temple,* his disciples *called his attention to its building.* No doubt it was an impressive sight around the year 32 CE.

The Second Temple compound started with humble origins with the return of Ezra and the remnant after the captivity in Babylon. With the appointment of Herod the Great as a puppet Jewish government leader, the buildings received a major renovation. Intent on leaving an impressive legacy, Herod built many amazing projects around Israel including the Herodian retreat and his desert palace Masada. At this juncture of Matthew's account, the Temple Mount renovation had been underway for about 50 years and would not be completed until 64 CE. By all accounts, it was one of the most splendid and impressive projects of the ancient world. Its massive Herodian stones (some weighing 60 tons!), imported woods, and inlaid gold caused the Temple to gleam with a special glory much of the day. We can imagine the disciples, after hearing Yeshua's statements about the tenuous future of the *Beit-Ha'Mikdash*, pointing to the glorious colonnades as they departed through the courtyards.

At this point, Yeshua elaborated on his earlier statements concerning the future of this House. It was indeed hard to believe as the disciples heard their Messiah say, "You see all these? Yes! I tell you, they will be totally destroyed." Even to his own disciples, this must have seemed incomprehensible. All the years of labor by a Roman/semi-Jewish King could in no way be destroyed!

Yet, that is exactly what Yeshua predicts in the true manner of the Hebrew Prophets. It is a word that seems so ludicrous that it is either patently false or, in fact, a divine revelation from the God of Israel. The ancient test for a true prophet as found in the *Torah* may be applied in this case (cf. Deuteronomy 18:20-22). Simply put, a prophet is sent from God if his words are proven true. This is just one more detail that should cause everyone, even in our generation, to carefully consider the entire message of Yeshua of Nazareth. This very specific prophecy was fulfilled within a generation, as the Romans destroyed the Sanctuary in 70 CE.

Yeshua adds one more astounding detail to this word when he predicts that *not a single stone will be left standing* from the Temple. It is one thing for the magnificent structure to be totally destroyed, but this extra description adds even more to the prophetic word of Messiah. First-century historian Josephus also made an amazing observation of this event. As Titus and his Roman troops seized the Temple, we are told that they set fire to much of the structure. This was a common practice but, in this case, resulted in a curious effect. Josephus describes how much of the gold used to line the Temple rooms actually melted in the intense heat and flowed in between the Herodian stones. The net result was that the soldiers, in their desire for that valuable gold, literally tore apart the stones of the Temple in order to collect their riches (Wars of the Jews IV-VI). In this way, the prophecy of Yeshua was fulfilled down to the finest detail.

The recent archaeological excavation of the south side of the Temple Mount provides a modern validation of the truth of Yeshua's word! At that current site lays an impressive pile of stones that once stood on the Temple. This is not to be confused with the retaining wall of the Temple Mount known as the *Kotel*/former Wailing Wall, still standing on the west side. Jews continue to gather at the western wall for prayer and celebration, as this is the surviving part of the entire compound but not part of the Temple building itself. Sadly, the magnificent *Beit-Ha'Mikdash* was completely destroyed and literally torn apart by the Romans. There are no coincidences in God's world. The events of 70 CE would be a sign from God to that unbelieving generation and to our people to this very day. It is another strong proof that Yeshua is the true *Mashiach* of our people Israel.

The Sincere Questions   24:3

The declaration of Yeshua regarding the destruction of the Temple leads to some logical questions from those who were listening to him. Matthew points out that the inner circle of twelve disciples had retreated with their rabbi to the east side overlooking the Temple Mount. While he was *sitting on the Mount of Olives, the talmidim came to him privately* with their follow-up questions. In light of the difficult times predicted for Jerusalem, the most natural issue for clarification would be about the timing. They ask their rabbi/Messiah *when will these things happen?* They must have wondered if these tragic events were to come upon them immediately or in the distant future. The response could have direct implications for their lives as Jews living in first-century Israel. There is also a secondary question posed by the disciples. It may be related to the destruction of the Temple but is expanded out to the very end of the current age.

With that in mind, the disciples also seek to know *what will be the sign that you are coming.* It seems they were beginning to understand the reality of the two separate missions of the Messiah through their years of following Yeshua. The rabbis also affirmed this scriptural teaching in various ways. The most intriguing is perhaps the rabbinic doctrine that possibly two different Messiahs may be coming to Israel. *Mashiach ben David*/Messiah Son of David was the Messiah who must come as the King to rule over Israel and the Nations. This was based on such scriptures as Isaiah 11 and II Samuel 7, which speak about the messianic age of blessing and prosperity through a descendant of King David. However, the rabbis also noted many other passages of the *Tanakh* that speak of a suffering Messiah to whom they gave the title *Mashiach ben Yosef*/Messiah Son of Joseph.

That the Messiah is also to suffer somehow and even be killed is taught in such passages as Isaiah 53 and Zechariah 12:10. The latter passage uses the exact phrase and is quoted in the *Talmud* as the title for this suffering Messiah (Tractate Sukkah 52a). The name of Yosef is given, as it aptly describes the sufferings and rejection of our forefather from Genesis who was considered a type of the coming Messiah. With this background of understanding, the disciples seem to be seeking clarification on how Yeshua would fulfill both aspects of the messianic promise. He is with them for now but had already taught that he would be rejected and killed after his final trip to *Yerushalayim.* If this is so, it would necessitate a Second Coming to fulfill the remaining prophecies of *Ben David.* It seemed logical to the disciples that there would be a clear sign of this glorious return to Zion, but what would it be?

To this question they add: What would be the sign *that the olam hazeh is ending?* The Hebrew phrase is a common rabbinic term for "this present worldly age." By contrast, the future messianic age is called *olam haba* (the world to come). It is directly related to the previous question and is indicated with the conjunction "and" in the text. It is really two ways of asking the same question—"When will *Mashiach* come?" When he comes, *Mashiach* will usher in the end of the present age and subsequently establish his eternal kingdom. So, we can distill them down to two main questions. The first deals with the particular sign of Messiah's arrival in Israel, whereas the second seeks to know the various signs that will be manifest toward the end of this current age.

Note the comparisons to the account of these questions recorded in Luke's gospel (Luke 21:5-7), where he adds the specific question as to the sign of the Temple's destruction. To this, Luke gives an expanded description of the events leading to the tragedy of 70 CE (cf. Luke 21:20-24) as he focuses on that time when *Yerushalayim will be surrounded by armies*, undoubtedly referring to the Roman destruction of that generation. This phrase must refer to something different than the end of the age since it predicts the dispersion of Jews *into all the countries of the Goyim*/Nations, as opposed to the regathering of Israel in the latter days. While those details are important, Matthew puts his entire focus on the events preceding the last-day return of Yeshua as *Mashiach ben David*. Yeshua's answer is both fascinating and vital to our understanding of God's plan for Israel in the latter days.

The Signs of the End of the Age   24:4-26

The First Half of the Great Tribulation 24:4-8

Matthew now records Yeshua's answers to the two main questions of his *talmidim*. The first segment focuses on the start of the time of trial that will be centered in the Middle East and, in particular, in Israel. The fact that there would be a time of turmoil just before the coming of Messiah is well documented both in the Hebrew Scriptures as well as the Talmudic commentaries. Among the many passages of *Tanakh* that describe this tumultuous time, the Prophet Jeremiah offers perhaps the most succinct summary:

> "These are the words ADONAI spoke concerning Isra'el and Y'hudah: Here is what ADONAI says: 'We have heard a cry of terror, of fear and not of peace. Ask now and see: can men give birth to children? Why, then, do I see all the men with their hands on their stomachs like women in labor, and every face turned pale? How dreadful that day will be! There has never been one like it: a time of trouble for Ya'akov, but out of it he will be saved.'" (*Yirmeyahu*/ Jeremiah 30:4-7)

The rabbis noted that the prophet is predicting a unique time in Jewish history. It is said to be a time of trouble for Jacob (*tzarah hee l'Yaakov*) that at first glance may not seem so unusual. Israel has known plenty of *tzuris* (Yiddish for troubles) in its tumultuous history! But this is said to be a day like none before in history. It was commonly understood that before the glorious day of Messiah, there must come a time of extreme darkness and tribulation.

So unique is this description by Jeremiah (e.g., the paleness of men) that the rabbis titled those days "the birth pains of the Messiah" (Tractate Sanhedrin 98b; Tractate Ketuvot 111a). In this graphic description, the events immediately preceding the coming of Messiah will be reminiscent of a woman in her final days of labor. The pains become more intense as well as closer together before that moment of new birth. So, too, will it be with the world events just prior to *Mashiach's* arrival. It will be an increasingly intense time but will culminate with the glorious birth of the messianic age.

Elsewhere in the Scripture, we are told the timeframe of this season of Jacob's Trouble. If one takes the commonly held interpretation of Daniel's 70 weeks (cf. Daniel 9:24-27), then the prophet is speaking of 490 years. The Hebrew phrase often translated "weeks" cannot mean the standard seven-day week, as the word used is *shavuim*/7's and not *shavuot*/weeks. Daniel seems to be alluding to 70 periods of 7's, be they weeks, months, or even years.

As one studies the historical context of the book of Daniel, it seems that the interpretation of "years" makes the most sense given Daniel's focus on the coming of Messiah after the first 69 7's. This would translate into 483 years from the issuing of the decree to rebuild Jerusalem, the decree of Xerxes in 444 BCE. When one makes the necessary calendar adjustments (e.g., Jewish 354-day year instead of the Roman 365 days, no year "0," etc.), Messiah's arrival would be around the year 32 AD. That being so, the focus on the "70th week" would perfectly fit the last time of Jacob's Trouble and would correspond to the last seven years immediately before Messiah's appearance. The final scroll of Revelation, in which Yochanan speaks of 1260 days as the length of half of the Great Tribulation (cf. Revelation 11:3; 12:6), also confirms this reckoning.

In this regard, Yeshua's teaching about the last times closely parallels the Jewish understanding of his day. Messiah starts his teaching by highlighting some of the events predicted for the first half of the seven-year period of Jacob's Trouble. His first exhortation is for his disciples to *watch out* and *not to let anyone fool* them. The perilous times to come will include the possibility of spiritual deception. The disciples must keep alert and vigilant, as there will be many conflicting spiritual dynamics at that time.

The most serious is that *many will come* in the name of Yeshua saying, "I am the Messiah!" It has been highlighted by many that, at least in Jewish history, the first person to clearly claim to be the promised Messiah was Yeshua of Nazareth. Before him, there were some minor political rebels but none that unequivocally claimed to be the messianic deliverer. It is logical, therefore, that one of the signs of the last days is that many messianic pretenders will come and stir up religious fervor. This will be especially true as one considers the dark times that will come upon Israel, thus creating a ripe climate for a renewed messianic hope, even if false.

Yet because of the great need for physical and spiritual deliverance, such pseudo-messiahs *will lead many astray.* This reminds us of an important truth. Many of our brothers have either given up hope of a coming messiah or forgotten the criteria for recognizing him when he comes. If God promised Israel a coming Messiah, he would also give information on how to recognize him. There are scores of messianic prophecies in the *Tanakh* that make a certain identification of the *Mashiach.*

Such prophecies as Micah 5:1 in Hebrew (Messiah's birthplace), Genesis 49:10 (his lineage), and Isaiah 53 (his suffering and resurrection) give us a detailed picture of who to look for. Yet the sad reality today is that many would have a difficult time identifying the true Messiah because we are unaware of what the *Tanakh* says on this issue! There have been many false messiahs in our history (cf. Bar Kochba in 135 AD and Shabbetai Tzvi in 1660), and the stage is set for many in the Jewish community to be deceived.

Along with the appearance of latter-day false messiahs, there will be *the noise of wars nearby and the news of wars far off.* A sad testimony of human history has been the consistent conflict between peoples and nations. Yeshua predicts that the wars will continue and even escalate as the day of his return draws near. Since Yeshua is addressing his Jewish disciples on the Mount of Olives, the *wars nearby* are certainly a reference to the Middle East and Jerusalem in particular.

On one hand, it is rather surprising that tiny Israel would even be mentioned in a discussion of world wars. Yet because it is the spiritual center of God's plan, no one should be surprised when Jerusalem is the focus of world attention. The time of climactic warfare (Jacob's Trouble) will be preceded by multiple international conflicts. Those who have eyes to see today can easily understand why the conflicts of the Middle East (Hamas, Hezbollah, Iran, Iraq, al-Qaeda, etc.) are building in our generation as the stage is set for the last world war known as Armageddon/ *Har Megiddo.*

Yet, Yeshua's exhortation at this point is that his disciples *don't become frightened.* As bad as these conflicts are, they are part of the inevitable march of world history. *Such things must happen but the end is yet to come.* Because of mankind's fallen nature, there will be ongoing disputes and wars. *Peoples will fight each other,* which means smaller-scale conflicts will be part of life. Yet, as one of the signs of the end of the age, a unique period will suddenly come when entire *nations will fight each other.* It has been noted by historians that it wasn't until the 20th century that the usual tribal and local conflicts escalated into entire nations fighting alliances of other nations (World War I & II). Add to this the development of unthinkable weaponry as we have moved from crossbows to nuclear missiles! The rabbis put it this way: "If you see the kingdoms contending with each other, look for the steps, i.e., footsteps, of the Messiah" (Gen. Rabba 42:4).

Even with the growth of these local wars, Yeshua teaches that *the end is yet to come.* There will be great tragedy in everyday life with the report of *famines and earthquakes in various parts of the world.* While the existence of such catastrophes is part of history, it has been documented that the number and strength of these events has multiplied in recent decades.

As extreme as these things are, they are *but the beginning of the "birth pains."* As the rabbis stated and Yeshua affirms, the events of the last days will increase even more in number and intensity. The time of Jacob's Trouble/The Great Tribulation will be the culmination of centuries of conflicts manifested in unique ways just before the revelation of King Messiah.

The Last Half of the Tribulation 24:9-26

Matthew now records the words of Yeshua as he addresses some details of the second period of three and a half years within the time of Jacob's Trouble. The first half of the Great Tribulation, though containing a great degree of turmoil, will seem somewhat tame compared to the second half. The birth pains will surely get more and more intense. Messiah turns his attention to the future experience of some of his disciples, who will undergo an *unprecedented degree of persecution.* Since the context is speaking of Israel, the reference seems to be to the future experience of Jewish followers of Yeshua in particular. Of course, the application of this truth would make it relate in theory to all believers (including non-Jewish Christians) who embrace Yeshua as the Messiah. At the time of the Great Tribulation, they will *be arrested and punished* or even *put to death.*

Since the first coming of Messiah, there have been those who have strongly opposed him and his followers. Even martyrdom was not unheard of as seen in the case of the first Messianic Jewish martyr Stephen (Acts 7). Persecution will increase from the peoples of the secular world and possibly from the religious community. Yeshua warns that the time is coming when *all peoples will hate you because of me.* This could include persecution from secular governments as was seen historically by Rome in first-century Israel. In a world that is increasingly pluralistic or even pagan, the believers in Yeshua will represent an intolerable threat. Even some of the zealous from various religious communities will arise with their opposition.

It is significant that the opposition is not based upon merely the personal life of any believers but upon their affiliation with the unique Messiah. This is obvious today when people like us personally until they find out we are followers of Yeshua! Clearly, they do not have a problem with us as people, but they are more often wrestling with God and Messiah. So bad will the latter-day persecution be that *many will be trapped into betraying and hating each other.* Such intense persecution of believers will lead many to turn away from the community and even betray those within it. This may seem incomprehensible to some, but there are examples of such betrayal in other times, such as the Inquisition and the Holocaust. Severe persecution will test the strength of each person's faith at the time of Jacob's Trouble.

Another unique aspect of the Great Tribulation will be an *unparalleled apostasy,* or falling away from the faith. Building on the previous mention of false messiahs, Yeshua now predicts that *many false prophets will appear and fool many people.* A prophet is one who is to proclaim the word or revelation of God. Yet, along with true prophets whom God sent to his people there were also false imitators who would twist the truth of God.

While there have always been people who fall away from God, in the last days the numbers will reach new proportions. False prophets with false words will multiply, and we indeed already see the multiplication of false teachers expanding in our day. How doubly tragic that so many of our own brothers have fallen away from *Torah* and into the grasp of eastern religions, philosophies, and even false teachers who are agnostics! Yeshua says this will only increase in the days of the birth pains, as *many people's love will grow cold because of increased distance from Torah.*

Love fulfills the *Torah,* so it is logical that love will decrease as we turn away from our Father in Heaven. It is not God who has brought problems into the world; it is largely because we have fallen away from God that we see such bad fruit. We live in a day when many people (including Jews) have turned away from the revelation of God to all sorts of man-made speculations. Again we are reminded that Messiah is especially addressing his Jewish brothers who have the *Torah.* One must have the *Torah* in order to distance oneself from the *Torah*! The pagans and modern agnostics do not have a *Torah* to turn away from. But the warning is especially relevant to Israel in the last days, as so many have forgotten about their call to a relationship with the God of our fathers. The time of Jacob's Trouble will be bleak in this regard, but Yeshua gives a promise to the believing remnant—*whoever holds out till the end will be delivered.*

In context, this would naturally apply to the physical deliverance of those whose life is spared at such an intense time. Of course, it is not a universal promise that no one will be killed in this time. Yeshua had just addressed the reality that some of the righteous would die during the period of persecution. But the promise is given nonetheless that those who endure and remain strong in their faith will see the deliverance of Messiah.

This promise undoubtedly also applies to the spiritual deliverance of the faithful remnant. Even if people are physically killed during the persecution, their spirits are guaranteed salvation because of their personal trust in Yeshua. This is a wonderful truth for all believers in all ages. No matter what physical affliction we experience in this life, *olam haba* (the world to come) is guaranteed through the completed work of Messiah.

Matthew now records Yeshua's comments about another activity occurring in the time of Jacob's Trouble—intensified world outreach. The latter days before Messiah's return will be among the darkest in world history and unique in many ways. But in the midst of the increasing darkness will be a ray of light. *The Good News about the Kingdom will be announced throughout the whole world as a witness to all the Goyim* before the arrival of the Messianic Kingdom.

This is another hint by Yeshua that his messianic mission has a two-fold audience. It would have been assumed by his disciples that this message of Good News was first for the chosen people of Israel. Earlier in his ministry, Messiah even directed his followers not to go outside of Israel to non-Jews, as the first mandate was to share with the "lost sheep of the house of Isra'el" (Matthew 10:6). This was logical, as it is the Jewish people who have the long history of previous covenants. Shouldn't the people of the covenant have the first opportunity to hear the Good News of his arrival?

Yeshua shares the expanded vision of his messianic calling. The message is for all peoples, since there is only one God who created them all. Israel was to share with all, as they were commissioned to be "a light to the Nations [*le-ohr goyim*] so my salvation can spread to the ends of the earth" (*Yesha'yahu*/Isaiah 49:6). While Israel would have the high privilege of being the conduit for the true light of God, all nations would be benefactors as they would be invited to share in the messianic blessings. There are those who would say that Israel failed in fulfilling its mission, but the facts speak otherwise. True, most of Israel did not receive the Messiah at his first coming, but how did his message spread after his death? Clearly it was through the twelve Jewish *talmidim* and the thousands of Jewish believers who not only shared the Good News with the world but actually wrote the entire New Testament Scriptures (Romans 3:2).

Many of the later Gentile believers also picked up the mandate and faithfully spread this message to the outer corners of the earth. But it is clear that believers in Yeshua must actually trace their spiritual heritage back to the faithful Jewish believers who first fulfilled their commission. At our time in history, the message of Messiah and the one true God has reached virtually every people group, especially with the help of the amazing capabilities of modern technology. Yet there are still some to be reached even in the 21st century. Yeshua teaches here that the Good News of the Kingdom will continue to expand in the last days as a prerequisite for his return to Jerusalem. He affirms that after that last great push of outreach, *the end will come.* In a strange way, the fact that so many Gentiles believe in Jesus today is a testimony that he is the true Messiah of Israel!

Yeshua now turns his attention back to the events surrounding the holy city of Jerusalem just before his return. One of the obvious signs of the approaching messianic redemption will be *political turmoil around the ancient Temple Mount.* He is clearly speaking to his disciples when he says *they will see the abomination that causes devastation* predicted by Dani'el. Messiah has already given some details in regard to the destruction of the second Temple and subsequent scattering of Israel. The same passage in Daniel 9:24-27 not only speaks of Messiah's first appearance but also of some important events before his second appearance. The prophet predicts that within the last period of seven years, *the desolator will come and continue until the already decreed destruction* (Daniel 9:27).

Based on the scroll of Daniel, commentators have applied this time of devastation to the upheaval surrounding the later Maccabean Revolt (167-164 BCE). It was during this time of the Greek occupation that the infamous Antiochus IV invaded Jerusalem in his attempt to destroy the Jewish people either through the sword or by conversion to Hellenism. *Shabbat* was outlawed. *Kashrut* observance was impossible. All traces of Jewish life were forbidden.

The culmination came when Antiochus invaded Jerusalem and desecrated the Holy Temple by sacrificing a pig on the altar! Just to make his point clear, he also took the title *Epiphanes,* meaning "god revealed." It was at this point that a heroic priestly family arose to fight against this desolation. Mattityahu and his sons (later called the Maccabees) rallied the troops and, after a three-year military campaign, saw the miraculous overthrow of the Greco-Syrian army. This history is celebrated every year with the holiday of *Hanukkah,* the eight-day festival in the winter, when we light the *menorah* to commemorate the rededication of the *Beit-Ha'Mikdash/* Holy Temple (cf. the apocrypha scrolls of I and II Maccabees; also *Yochanan/*John 10:22ff).

It is logical that Dani'el's amazing prediction would indeed apply to the story of *Hanukkah,* as Israel fought off this pagan king who desecrated the holy place. However, Yeshua makes it clear that there will be another replay of these events just before the return of Messiah to Jerusalem. The Jewish nation will again see a similar event as a Temple is rebuilt in the holy city. The Scriptures teach that, ironically, it will be this pagan political leader who will somehow assist Israel in the rebuilding of the Temple, as it is noted that *he will make a strong covenant with the leaders* for the last seven-year period of time (Dani'el 9:27). Yet this leader will ultimately be the very one who becomes the desolator. The latter-day leader will defile the Temple and even proclaim himself as God (cf. Epiphanes; also see II Thessalonians 2). It is this tumultuous time in history that Yeshua clearly refers to in his teaching, and he even exhorts his listeners to *understand the* allusion.

Another sign of the latter days will be an *unprecedented military attack upon the state of Israel.* Yeshua notes that at the time of Jacob's Trouble, *those in Y'hudah* will need to *escape to the hills.* Judah is the ancient tribal name for the southern kingdom that includes the holy city of Yerushalayim. With the outbreak of intense persecution and war, many will be forced to run for their lives. Even *if someone is on the roof* (a common patio area in Middle East homes), *he must not go down to gather his belongings from his house.* Similarly, *if someone is in the field, he must not turn back to get his coat,* which was a necessity for daily survival. These statements underscore the urgency of that moment and the emergency responses that will be necessary. It will be an especially *terrible time* for *pregnant women and nursing mothers!* One can only imagine the incredible difficulty of undergoing this military attack while needing to care for children.

As challenging as this situation will be, there will be further complications. Messiah exhorts his listeners to *pray that they will not have to escape in the winter or on Shabbat.* The winter is the main rainy season in Israel and thus presents some distinctive challenges. It is not uncommon for heavy rains in the hill country to flow down previously dry river beds (wadi) in the desert lowlands. In a matter of minutes, there can be a flash flood roaring through the ravine, destroying roads and most anything else in its path. The winter flash floods would present a daunting hurdle for those needing to flee from war. Yeshua also points out a distinctive challenge at that time, the need to travel on *Shabbat*. Although traditional *halakhah* allows for emergency vehicles on *Shabbat*, the norm is that private and public transportation are not allowed on the Sabbath, especially in modern Jerusalem. By considering the Yom Kippur War of 1973, we can see the devastating impact a military attack can bring on a *Shabbat*. Thankfully, Israel recovered from that attack but only after some terrible loss of life. How dangerous it would be trying to flee the city when most everything is shut down for that day!

A theological point must be highlighted in regard to the above statements. Some interpretations of Matthew 24 have Christians (meaning non-Jewish believers) going through these events of the Great Tribulation. It is true that some of the earlier teaching could equally apply to the Gentile branch of the Church internationally, as many of the catastrophic events extend beyond the geographical borders of Israel. However, it becomes completely confusing if one ignores the immediate context of Matthew 24.

Yeshua is addressing his disciples in the city of Jerusalem. On top of that, he warns them about the dangers of fleeing on *Shabbat*. It is such an obvious Jewish context that is only understandable when applied to Israel and the Jewish people. In other words, Matthew 24 is largely dealing with warnings to the latter-day generation of the Jewish community and not to the Church. This has vast implications for our reading of this chapter. Some Christians are storing power generators and extra food because they believe Matthew 24 is speaking directly to them. Some theologians may continue to debate the issue of the Great Tribulation and the Church's presence in it, but Matthew 24 does not support the view that the Church will have to endure this period of great trial. Some Christians could save themselves a lot of worry and trouble if they reconsidered the Jewish context of these words of Messiah.

The next statements of Yeshua affirm that his warnings are primarily to the Jewish community of the last generation. He quotes passages in the *Tanakh* that emphasize that this will be a unique time of *trouble* for Israel (cf. Jeremiah 30:7). In fact, it will be a time that will be *worse than there has ever been from the beginning of the world until now* (cf. Daniel 12:1). So destructive and unique will be this time of Great Tribulation that unless the *time had not been limited, no one would survive!* But it is *for the sake of those who have been chosen* that its time will be cut short. Some interpreters have been tempted to apply this last phrase to the "chosen" in the Gentile branch of the Church, but the context dictates otherwise.

Certainly Israel and the Jewish people are the original chosen and elect ones. While there is always some application to a broader audience of believers, the quotes from the Scriptures confirm that the immediate application is to Israel's part within the Great Tribulation. It is virtually a direct quote of what the Prophet Daniel spoke in regard to his people that *there will be a time of distress unparalleled between the time they became a nation and that moment. At that time, your people will be delivered, everyone whose name is found written in the book* (cf. Dani'el 12:1-2). Although the time of Jacob's Trouble will be a unique time of testing upon Israel, Yeshua's promise is that a believing remnant of the nation will be rescued both physically and spiritually.

Matthew now records further details spoken by the Messiah regarding the *dangers of spiritual deception* at that time. Some will come to the Jewish community with the proclamation, "Look! Here's the Messiah!" The fact that Yeshua must repeat this warning (cf. Matthew 24:4-5) underscores that this will evidently be one of the preeminent dangers of that day. The temptation to follow any pseudo-messiah at that time will be overpowering as Israel tries to survive the Great Tribulation of the last days. In the enveloping darkness around Israel, there will be many calling out for the last hope of the

Jewish people. Some will say, perhaps out of their spiritual hunger, *there he is!* But Yeshua warns all those of the last generation—"don't believe him." It is part of the birth pains of Messiah that there will be imposters even *performing great miracles* and many *amazing things.*

It is a sobering reminder that believers cannot ultimately trust even signs and wonders. One must ask the deeper question "Is this from God?" During this time, there will be miracles but they will be false signs so as *to fool even the chosen, if possible.* The true measurement of a God-given sign or miracle must be the *Torah* and the entire Word of God. It is too easy to be deceived by man-made (or satanic) false signs. Yeshua warns that generation to be discerning in the midst of the spiritual dynamics of the last days. If they are told that *he's out in the desert, don't go.* Some will even entice them by saying, *"Look! He's hidden away in a secret room!"* Again they are exhorted to be discerning and not to believe such stories. How can one distinguish between such intriguing rumors and the legitimate appearance of the true *Mashiach*? The teaching continues with some of the indisputable signs that will be manifested just before the return of Yeshua to Jerusalem.

The Signs of the Second Coming of Messiah 24:27-31

Matthew continues to record this discourse of Yeshua as he teaches about the details of the Great Tribulation. As has been noted, there are numerous signs that will indicate the imminent return of Yeshua to establish the Messianic Kingdom. Among these are increased wars and natural disasters, as well as the rebuilding and subsequent desecration of the *Beit-Ha'Mikdash*/Temple in Jerusalem. The disciple now records Yeshua's response to the second big question posed by the *talmidim* at the start of this chapter.

Verses 9-26 answer many parts of the first question, "When will these things happen?" The second question is now addressed: "What will be the sign that you are coming?" (both questions are posed in Matthew 24:3). Instead of being some secretive event in the wilderness, the return of Messiah will also have some public and dramatic elements that will be self-evident.

Using one of the famous Jewish titles for the Messiah, Yeshua asserts that *when the Son of Man does come, it will be like lightning that flashes.* The title is a common one in the rabbinic writings based on the phrase as it is found in the *Tanakh* (cf. Daniel 7:13; Tractate Sanhedrin 96b). The Son of Man/*Mashiach* will not be hiding from Israel and the world but will return in such an obvious fashion that it will be like a dramatic flash of lightning. This could be describing both the visibility and the suddenness of Messiah's appearance.

Yeshua is not literally speaking of an electrical lightning strike. The most obvious comparison would be to the *Sh'khinah*/Glory of God that is often manifested at crucial times of God's revelation (cf. Sinai in Exodus 19).

He adds to the description the detail that this flash will come *out of the east* and even *fill the sky to the western horizon.* This is more consistent with the *Sh'khinah* that will be so intense on that last day that it may be visible even worldwide. The fact that this Glory of God shines from the east to the west is consistent with the revelation of *Mashiach, which* is said to come out of the east.

While it is true and often quoted that Messiah will stand on the Mount of Olives in Jerusalem, the prophets confirm that is not his first place of return. Among other things, one must factor in Messiah's battle in the valley of Megiddo (cf. Zechariah 12:10-11) and his appearance to the Jewish remnant in the wilderness (cf. Isaiah 63:1-6). The latter passage seems to describe the very first place of Messiah's Second Coming in an unusual way: "Who is this, coming from Edom, from Botzrah with clothing stained crimson...? It is I, who speak victoriously, I, well able to save [Hebrew root Yeshua]. I have trod [the peoples] in my anger...so their lifeblood spurted out on my clothing" (63:1-3).

302 / YESHUA, KING MESSIAH

Botzrah is in southern Jordan and includes the ancient hiding place that the Greeks called Petra. This would be the wilderness hiding place of the remnant of Jews who will flee from Judah in that day of attack. The prophet sees the Redeemer appearing but is shocked that his garments (even *tallit*) are stained with blood.

Messiah had already been doing battle in the campaign of Armageddon as he fights off the nations who have attacked his people Israel. Accordingly, Messiah comes from the wilderness in the east, through the valley of Megiddo and onward due west until his victory ascent at the Mount of Olives (cf. Zechariah 14:4). In that manner, the flash of lightning from east to west is representative of Messiah's path of victory in the last day.

The next statement of Yeshua may seem strange at first glance but, in the context of this battlefield description, it makes sense. Since there will be a tremendous death toll at the last battle, *that's where you find the vultures*. It will be an incomprehensible time of warfare among the nations, especially as they attack Israel. The picture of death and vultures is a sobering description of the dark season of Jacob's Trouble.

It is at this darkest moment of Jewish history that the greatest light breaks through. Just as it appears that the destruction of Israel is imminent, some unique signs will indicate Messiah's approach. *Following the trouble of those times, the sun will grow dark.* This could be a solar eclipse or some other supernatural phenomenon. At that moment on the opposite of the globe, *the moon will stop shining and the stars will fall from the sky.*

This could be a lunar eclipse and the proliferation of meteorites. However it is fulfilled, there is one common result; the sky will be abnormally darkened, which will accentuate all the more the sign of Messiah's return. The *Sh'khinah* brilliance will be that much brighter as all the inhabitants of the earth witness this unique event. This is *the sign of the Son of Man, which* appears *in the sky.*

The response to this climactic event will be mixed. On one hand, *all the tribes of the Land will mourn* at the appearance of King Messiah. Like so much of the New Testament material, it is really nothing new, as Yeshua invokes the details spoken of in the prophets (cf. Zechariah 12:10-14). No doubt it will be a most troubling sight to the rebellious world when the King of the Universe, *Mashiach ben David*, arrives! Many will grieve over the realization of lost opportunities. It will also strike fear in many hearts as the *Son of Man* comes *with tremendous power and glory.*

There will be no excuses on that day of Messiah's return, as every mouth will be shut. In contrast to the rebellious of the world, the godly remnant of Israel and all remaining believers in Yeshua will realize their ultimate hope of redemption. On that last day, Messiah will *send out his angels with a great shofar and they will gather together his chosen people.* It is a well established tradition in both *Tanakh* and rabbinic sources that a great *shofar*/ram's horn will be sounded at the coming of *Mashiach* (cf. Isaiah 27:13). A Jewish commentary from the Middle Ages has these intriguing details:

> "Elijah of blessed memory will come and give good tidings to Israel, to those who will be alive and to the dead.... Messiah ben David, Elijah, and Zerubbabel, peace be upon him, will ascend the Mount of Olives. And Messiah will command Elijah to blow the shofar....All will come to the Messiah from the four corners of the earth, from east and from west, from north and from south. The children of Israel will fly on the wings of eagles and come to the Messiah" (Midrash Ma'ase Daniel p. 225-26).

We must be reminded again of the total Jewish context of this entire discourse of Yeshua. Some teach that the "church" (usually for them meaning Gentile believers) will go through the Great Tribulation because they are the new "chosen people." Too many scriptures conflict with this idea of replacement theology in which the Gentile church usurps all the promises previously given to the Jewish people. Rabbi Sha'ul/Paul responded strongly to this notion: *Chas v'chalilah/* Heaven forbid! (cf. Romans 11:1). In fact, it is just the opposite, as the Gentiles are invited to become "partakers/sharers" with the Jewish believers in the riches of the Olive Tree faith.

This is a classic illustration the rabbi uses to show how all believers in Yeshua, whether Jewish or non-Jewish, are grafted into the same root of the biblical faith. It is striking that even in the first century, Sha'ul must warn some Gentile believers not to be "arrogant" toward the natural branches by thinking that they somehow have replaced the branches of Israel (cf. Romans 11:17-18).

This idea (supersessionism) has had tragic results in much of Church history for both the synagogue and the church. In the context of Matthew 24, we again are reminded that the chosen people must be the Jewish nation to which Yeshua is speaking in this teaching. The Gentile branch of the Church has many beautiful promises but should not use this passage to teach that Messiah will gather them and leave out his Jewish people.

There are actually two different times when the *shofar* will be sounded in the future. Rabbi Sha'ul confirms that there will be a first resurrection of Messianic believers from the last 2000 years as we are called to meet the Messiah in the air (cf. I Thessalonians 4:13-18). It is debated when exactly this will take place. There are views that place it before the seven-year Tribulation, in the middle of that time, or even at the very end. I hold the view that the catching up of believers will take place just before the time of Jacob's Trouble.

Though there is much scriptural evidence for this pre-Tribulation rapture view, perhaps the best evidence is seen in the model of the holy days. *Rosh Hashanah/*The Feast of Trumpets takes place on the first day of the month *Tishrei* and is followed by a ten-day period of repentance (analogous to the call of repentance of the seven-year Great Tribulation). This is culminated with *Yom Kippur*/Day of Atonement on the 10th day of *Tishrei,* known in tradition as the Day of Judgment. This day of fasting and repentance is culminated with the Last Shofar, the *tekia gedolah*/one great blast. With this chronology in mind, it is consistent that Messianic believers are called out by the first shofar, followed by the final ingathering of Israel at the last shofar when Messiah comes back to Jerusalem.

Yeshua here confirms that, at his return, there will be a great shofar sounded for the re-gathering of the Jewish remnant that has survived. Add to this the return of the messianic remnant that comes with Messiah. These two main groups (Messianic Jews and non-Jewish believers in Yeshua as well as the last-day remnant of Israel) will be the first inhabitants of the restored Messianic Jerusalem. Later resurrections include the faithful remnant that lived before Messiah Yeshua came the first time. Together, these groups will make up the amazing and wonderful family of God who enters the kingdom of Messiah!

Parables of the End-Times   24:32-25:46

The Parable of the Fig Tree   24:32-36

After this lengthy discourse about the end-times, Yeshua turns to some parabolic illustrations to help his disciples better understand these coming events. His first illustration comes from a common tree of the Middle East as he says to *let the fig tree teach its lesson.* Besides being a ubiquitous crop in Israel, as any disciple would know, when the fig tree *branches begin to sprout and leaves appear, summer is approaching.* The fruit is plentiful in the summer months in Israel, so the first signs of flowering are an accurate indicator of the soon-coming summer season.

This word-picture would have been especially timely as the disciples were just a few days away from the annual spring feast of *Pesach*/Passover. No doubt they could see some sprouting fig trees even on their journeys that very week. Messiah makes the spiritual application in classic rabbinic fashion using the parable. In the same way, they should make the comparison between that which is obvious fact (the fig tree harvest) and the spiritual lessons of Yeshua as taught in the coming prophetic events. When they *see all these things,* it should be obvious that the end *time is near.*

The parable is apt, as the fig tree was a commonly known symbol for the nation of Israel (cf. Hosea 9:10). Here the prophet recalls God's description of Israel as *a fig tree's first figs in its first season.* For too much of Israel's history there was limited spiritual fruit, but Yeshua specifically predicts here that the Jewish people and the nation of Israel will blossom just before the coming of Messiah.

Our present generation has witnessed the physical restoration of the modern state that occurred in May 1948, as well as the reunification of Jerusalem under Jewish control in June 1967. The fig tree is beginning to sprout in a physical sense! Add to this a spiritual renewal that is taking place, as thousands of Jews are embracing Yeshua as Messiah and continuing to live within our rich heritage through the expression of Messianic Judaism. These lessons of the fig tree are thought-provoking.

The next statement has been interpreted in various ways. Many translations read the Greek word *genea* as "generation." If that view is taken, then Yeshua is saying that a particular generation of Israel will be eyewitnesses to the prophetic events of the last days. Even within that translation are at least two different options.

He could be referring to "that generation," meaning the first-century disciples who heard and recorded this teaching. This interpretation has led some to discount that the first-century generation of Jewish believers passed away without seeing the return of Messiah. Some blame the accuracy of the New Testament, but maybe the real problem is that they have the wrong interpretation! A secondary view could refer to "that generation" who sees these prophetic signs, meaning the last generation of Israel. This is a more preferred view and would fit with the reality of a 2000-year gap in history.

A third view is even better, as many have pointed out that the word *genea* often means "race" in the sense of an ethnic group (cf. Abbott-Smith Lexicon, p. 89). If that view is taken, then Yeshua is affirming that *this people will certainly not pass away before all these things happen.* It is not about the chronology of a last generation but a promise that the Jewish people will survive and thrive all the way until the coming of *Mashiach.*

This seems to be a fitting promise and interpretation, especially in light of the terrible time of Jacob's Trouble to come (in addition to the long history of persecution, crusades, and even the *Shoah/* Holocaust against the Jewish people). In this regard, it is a wonderful and essential promise to those who may fear for the survival of Israel. To add to the strength of the promise, Yeshua affirms that while *heaven and earth will pass away*, his *words will never pass away.* The truth is evident today, even in the traditional Jewish song "*Am Yisra'el Chai*/The People of Israel Live!" It is said that the Queen of England once asked her court for a proof of God's existence, to which the reply was: "Your Majesty, the Jews!"

With all these prophetic signs, especially as related to Israel and the Jewish people, Yeshua gives a word of caution. Some might be tempted to specify the exact time of Messiah's return, but *when that day and hour will come, no one knows.*

Although there were periodic warnings against it, messianic speculation was not uncommon among the rabbis. As previously noted, the idea of a time of trial (birth pains of the Messiah) was well established in the discussion of the *Talmud.* Some even pushed further to guess the exact time of *Mashiach's* arrival. One theory states that, according to the model of the spiritual week, there will be 6000 years of world history and then the sabbatical millennium will come with King Messiah (Tractate Sanhedrin 97b).

At the time of this writing, it is the year 5771 on the Jewish calendar, 5771 years since the creation of mankind. This calculation is based on the strict genealogical evidence in the Bible. This being so, history could very well be close to the 6000 years predicted until Messiah comes. Another calculation predicts that "the world will endure for at least 85 Jubilees and in the last Jubilee the Son of David will come" (also Tractate Sanhedrin 97b). This equates to 4250 years based on the fifty-year *yovel*/jubilee (cf. Leviticus 25:8-13). The rabbis thus place the date between 440-490 AD.

Yeshua claimed to fulfill part of the *yovel* as he commented on the *Haftarah* section of the traditional reading at his home synagogue in Nazareth (cf. Isaiah 61:1-2; Luke 4:14-22). This was just one more way in which Yeshua openly proclaimed his messiahship to our people. Although there will be many signs and indicators of Messiah's return, Yeshua warns his disciples not to enter into speculation. Both Jews and Christians have been guilty of this, often resulting in great disappointment and even tragedy.

The fact is, *no one knows* the exact time—*not the angels in heaven, not the Son, only the Father.* If no one knows, that must mean no one knows! There is a very interesting analogy hidden within these words as well. The words perfectly fit the word-picture of the traditional Jewish wedding ceremony in biblical times. A wedding ceremony for an engaged couple would take place only upon the initiation of the father of the groom. Even the groom did not know the exact time of the ceremony until his father announced its arrival with the sounding of a *shofar*/ram's horn. In keeping with the Jewish custom of the day, Yeshua acknowledges that even he as the Son does not know the exact time of the wedding ceremony, that is, his return for his bride. Only the Father has such information, and we should leave it at that.

Analogies for Watchfulness 24:37-44

The next word of exhortation recalls the lessons from the ancient patriarch Noah and the Flood in his generation. There will be parallel events because *the Son of Man's coming will be just as it was in the days of Noach*. The historical account is well known from the *Torah* and holds many spiritual lessons regarding the coming of *Mashiach*. As in those days, the time just before Messiah's return will in many ways be surprisingly normal. *Back then, before the Flood, people went on eating and drinking, taking wives and becoming wives*. This is a rather amazing contrast to the other details concerning the time of Jacob's Trouble. There will certainly be some shocking and unique events in those last days, yet in some ways, the arrival of Messiah will catch people off guard because of the normality of the times. Life will be moving along as usual, just as it was in Noach's generation.

It was, no doubt, an unusual sign for a man to be building a huge boat before there was ever substantial rain! But evidently, most people simply ignored the signs and went about their busy lives. That is, until it was too late. When *Noach entered the ark, they didn't know what was happening until the Flood came and swept them all away*. Yeshua affirms that it *will be just like that when the Son of Man comes*. Those living during that final generation will similarly be preoccupied with their own concerns. So much so that they will miss being prepared for the greatest concern of life—the state of their own souls! As with the Flood of Noach's day, the judgment of God will come like a flood in the day of *Mashiach*. On that day, many will be swept away to spiritual judgment because of their lack of attention to their own relationship with God and his redeemer Yeshua. Are we paying attention to these vital matters for our own lives?

Another word-picture is presented by Yeshua to illustrate the need for watchfulness in the latter days. At that time, *there will be two men in a field—one will be taken and the other left behind*. Similarly, *there will be two women grinding flour at the mill—one will be taken and the other left behind.* At first glance, it is tempting to interpret these pictures in a positive sense. Historically, some have interpreted these passages as describing the rapture/catching up of believers (cf. I Thessalonians 4:13-18). In that view (popularized in *Left Behind,* the recent Christian book series), the ones taken away in this passage are those blessed enough to be caught up to Messiah's presence in the clouds. The others are left behind for the judgment of the Great Tribulation and the last war. However, a careful study of the context would dictate differently.

In the previous paragraph, it is noted that Yeshua warned about the similarities between the last days and the former days of *Noach.* In that account it was just the opposite, with *Noach* being left behind for God's kingdom while the others were taken away, not for blessing, but for judgment. The men and women left behind in the latter day will be left to enter the blessing of the Messianic Kingdom on Earth. It is those who are taken away that will have to contend with the impending judgment of God.

There is one more parable/analogy that Yeshua uses to elaborate these lessons of the last days. The main purpose of all of these word-pictures is to motivate his listeners to *stay alert.* It is obvious in light of the fact that his exact time of arrival is uncertain. Messiah's appearance is never said to be "immediate," but it is "imminent." It is not promised for today, but it can take place at any time. How can we know that we will not be caught by surprise? Always be ready! Even if we were alert and prepared yesterday, there is the potential for danger. If believers stay alert at all times, we will be ready whenever Messiah Yeshua returns. The discerning believer may even know the approximate season of Messiah's return based on the analogy of the fig tree.

We live in a day that points to the season (late springtime) of Messiah's advent. But since we cannot know the exact hour, the prudent policy is to always be ready! Yeshua uses a picture of someone who failed to stay alert at a crucial time. *Had the owner of the house known when the thief was coming, he would have stayed awake and not allowed his house to be broken into.* Obviously a thief does not announce his arrival in advance but comes when not expected. The application is made by Messiah to his *talmidim: You too must always be ready, for the Son of Man will come when you are not expecting him.* Most of the world is slumbering in a spiritual coma. Many are "busy" with the chores and responsibilities of life. But *Mashiach* is at the door! Those who await the messianic redemption must be alert and not distracted by any other thing. Are you ready for his imminent return?

Parables Concerning the Future Judgment of Israel 24:45-25:30

The Faithful Servant 24:45-51

Matthew now records the words of Yeshua as he continues with his teaching in parables. In the previous section, he had illustrated some of the details of the latter days just before Messiah's return to Jerusalem. Yeshua now makes some personal applications to his listeners.

The application of the teaching applies in some way to all readers of every age (including us). Yet the immediate context is once again vitally important. Yeshua is still talking to his disciples about distinctively Jewish themes in the entire chapter of Matthew 24. The Jewishness of the context is clear from such references to the Temple (verses 1-3), the province of Judea (verse 16), and even the travel challenges on the Jewish *Shabbat* (verse 20).

We must keep this context in mind as we consider the connected parables. They must be speaking directly about the experience of the Jewish people at large and the people of Israel specifically since there is no indication of a change in context. Again, this is important for modern readers to understand, as Yeshua here is not addressing non-Jews or the Gentile Church (as he does in other passages) but his brethren according to the flesh. The fact of a unique day of judgment concerning Israel is not a new teaching but is revealed many times in the prophets (cf. Ezekiel 20:36-38). Messiah's teaching here adds some important details and perspective that are especially relevant to his brothers and sisters.

After the numerous warnings and challenges in the earlier teaching, Yeshua now calls his listeners to consider the implications for their own lives. *Who is the faithful and sensible servant?* It was commonly understood that Israel is the first servant of ADONAI (cf. Isaiah 41:8). Our people were called to be priests among the Nations (cf. Exodus 19:6) and to share the light of the true God with the Gentiles (cf. Isaiah 49:6). This is the historic call of every Jew and our nation Israel. Yet, Messiah gives a parable that poses a penetrating question: What kind of servants are we? Too often, many have fallen short of this divine mandate, but God is looking for faithful servants. Such trustworthy ones will be put *in charge of the household staff.* There is a calling upon every Jew to serve ADONAI as his representative, and this will only magnify in the last days of Jacob's Trouble. Yeshua assures them that *it will go well with that servant if he is found doing his job when his master comes.* What a blessing it will be for our Father in Heaven to see the faithful Jewish remnant—especially in those most troubling times.

A reward is promised if they stay faithful to God and Yeshua. But there is another option, as he illustrates with an account of a *servant who is wicked.* Mankind in general and Israel in particular have a choice regarding how we spend our days. This servant is not faithful but is instead neglecting his God-given responsibilities. Part of his problem is his impatience with God's plan, as he *says to himself, "My master is taking his time."* Because of his perception that the master is far away, the wicked servant even starts *beating up his fellow servants and spends his time eating and drinking with drunkards.* These blatant acts of rebellion will not be overlooked for long. It will surprise and shock the wicked servant when the master comes *on a day he does not expect, at a time he doesn't know.* The servant was indeed foolish both in his behavior and in his vision of life. He not only deeply transgressed the wishes of his master but also did not have a clue as to the time of his return. So grievous are these sins that the master will *cut him in two and put him with the hypocrites.*

The parable is clearly alluding to the common Jewish doctrine of judgment in the world to come (*olam haba*). How sadly ironic that some of God's covenant servants (Israel) will be so far from God in that day that they will experience this tragic judgment. The reality of *Gei-Hinnom* is not to be taken lightly, as it is described as a place where *people will wail and grind their teeth.* Such is the warning of this parable of Messiah. Many of the children of Israel will be in danger of losing their blessing as they fail to live up to their calling. Whether we are Jewish or non-Jewish, believer or skeptic, the parable should give us pause to consider our current ways. Now is no time for us to be distracted or rebellious. Are we faithful servants eagerly awaiting the return of our Master?

The Ten Bridesmaids   25:1-13

Although there is a chapter division artificially inserted here, Matthew continues with the parables of Yeshua concerning the judgment of Israel. The first of these teachings dealt with Israel as a servant and her responsibility as such. The next word-picture calls up a familiar event in the first-century Jewish community—a wedding feast. The concept of a parable is implied within its name. The Greek word *para*/alongside and *baleo*/to cast remind us that it is a word-picture comparing a familiar event with something less understood. In this case, it is a Jewish wedding being compared to the coming kingdom of Messiah. Yeshua continues his teaching by affirming that *the Kingdom of Heaven at that time* will be analogous to parts of this most joyous celebration. Once again, we are reminded of the Jewishness of Matthew's account as Yeshua refrains from using the actual name of God but chooses instead the substitute term "Heaven," which was commonly employed.

We also note here that the parable relates to Israel in the last days, specifically, the day of judgment immediately after the time of Jacob's Trouble. Israel at that time will be *like ten bridesmaids who took their lamps and went out to meet the groom.* Some of the customs of the Jewish wedding ceremony in biblical times have been pointed out in previous chapters (cf. Matthew 22). After the arrangement (*shiddukhin*) by the parents, the young couple would at some point make a public statement of their engagement (*erusin*). They would come under the wedding canopy (*huppah*) and profess their intentions while blessing the first cup of wine.

In biblical times, the engaged couple would not cohabitate despite the fact that they were indeed considered married. It was during this one-year period of *erusin* that the couple would take care of their individual responsibilities. The bride would need to arrange her dowry and garments in preparation for the upcoming wedding, while the groom would have to prepare the future living space for the couple. As the year drew to a close, all the participants in the ceremony were to be on high alert because only the father of the groom could make the official announcement to commence the ceremony. This call to preparedness was especially important for the wedding party.

Yeshua's teaching offers fresh insight into the coming messianic age. The bridesmaids were preparing to meet the groom to start the wedding ceremony. Of the ten bridesmaids in the parable, however, only five were *sensible* while the other five were *foolish.* What was the difference between them? *The foolish ones took lamps with them but no oil.* This would be a serious problem, as the oil-burning lamps were an essential ingredient for an evening event. Indeed it would be the height of folly to run out of oil at such a crucial time. By contrast, *the others took flasks of oil with their lamps.* These bridesmaids came prepared by bringing not only the needed clay lamp but also extra olive oil in case they ran low. In a situation that was not totally uncommon, *the bridegroom was late.*

In ancient times, there was usually an element of surprise as to when the groom's father would actually announce the start of the ceremony. He would pick what he considered to be the opportune time and, with the blast of the *shofar*/ram's horn, the wedding processional would begin. With great joy, the wedding contingency would travel to the residence of the bride to literally "carry" her (*nisuin* from *nasa* in Hebrew) to the place of the second cup and the marriage *huppah*. In the current parable, it is the late arrival of the groom that creates a bit of a problem. In fact, the hour was so late that all the bridal attendants *went to sleep.* They were suddenly awakened in the *middle of the night* when the traditional *cry rang out, "The bridegroom is here! Go out to meet him!"* Since it was in the darkness of night, it was imperative to have the light of the oil lamps available.

Consequently, all the girls *woke up and prepared their lamps for lighting.* The wise maidens were not caught off guard, as they had prepared extra oil in case of just such an emergency. However, the foolish attendants were caught without enough oil due to their lack of planning. They made an urgent request of their fellow attendants, *"give us some of your oil, because our lamps are going out."* The wise bridesmaids could not meet this request, as they had only enough oil for their own lamps. Therefore, they exhorted the needy ones to *go to the oil dealers and buy some* for themselves. They proceeded to run this errand at the worst possible time, just as the *bridegroom came.*

The bridal attendants *who were ready* and waiting were invited to go with the groom *to the wedding feast.* With great joy, they entered into the special *simcha*/celebration as participants in the wonderful ceremony. But a problem developed for the attendants who had left the area to buy more oil, as *the door was shut,* making it impossible for them to join the festivities. Even their cries and appeals of "let us in!" were unsuccessful. Their exclusion was confirmed, as the groom declared, "I don't know you."

The close of the wedding parable is short but profound. Yeshua exhorts his listeners to *stay alert because you know neither the day nor the hour* of the groom's appearance. He himself is the coming groom. He had taught on several occasions that the exact time of his appearance in Israel was unknown by everyone except his Father. If that is the case, then it is of utmost importance that his disciples always be ready for his return. No one would want to be caught unprepared and lacking the necessary requirements to attend the messianic wedding. We must be reminded here once again that the parable was taught specifically to Yeshua's listeners concerning the condition of the people of Israel.

Some interpretations have erred by mistakenly applying this parable to the Gentile church, meaning non-Jewish believers. Some have anguished over the apparent teaching that some Christians will enter the kingdom while others will not! What is the distinguishing factor? As the interpretation goes, the ones who have the oil of the Holy Spirit will enter, while some well-meaning believers will be left out because they didn't have the Spirit of God.

The context of the passage clears up such angst and confusion. Besides the immediate context of Matthew 24, Israel's relationship with God is often compared to the picture of a marriage or wedding (cf. Isaiah 54:5; Jeremiah 2:1-3). As Yeshua is speaking about the judgment of Israel in the last day, he is clearly addressing two kinds of Jews within the household of Israel.

Quite simply, there will be some Jews who will be excluded from the messianic wedding while other Jews will be allowed to enter. The former ones are invited to the wedding based on the earlier covenants between Israel and God. Yet if they don't have a personal relationship with our God through the work of the *Ruach*/Spirit/oil, then the invitation will be in vain.

The Jewish remnant that has the oil of the Spirit as a reality in their personal lives will, by God's grace, be able to join the wedding feast. The parable is not about some Gentile Christians losing their salvation but about two different kinds of Jews and their relationship to our Heavenly Father. The final exhortation is clear: Stay alert, as we don't know the time of *Mashiach's* return. Are we alert and ready? Whether we are Jewish or non-Jewish, believer or skeptic, this parable is a wake-up call to carefully consider our relationship with God. Before the door of the kingdom shuts, we want to make sure we have entered in.

The Lesson of the Talents   25:14-30

Continuing his teaching on the future judgment of Israel, Yeshua now invokes a lesson from the business world. In this parable, the Kingdom of Heaven is compared to *a man about to leave home for awhile.* His extended trip necessitated that he *entrust his possessions to his servants.* Here again, Messiah uses a very common analogy of Israel being the servants of *ADONAI* (cf. Isaiah 41:8). That being so, the context of the teaching is again clearly about the situation of the Jewish people in the latter days.

The details of the parable reveal different levels of responsibility for each servant. *To one he gave five talents*, the equivalent of a huge amount—*a hundred years' wages.* The term *talent* is not to be confused with our modern term depicting an ability, as it referred in first-century Israel to a sum of money. The man gave the other servants *two talents* and *one talent,* respectively. Why the differing amounts of responsibility? Evidently, the owner felt compelled to delegate a specific amount of his possessions *according to the ability* of each servant.

In the parable, although the entrusted amounts differ, the corresponding actions result in proportional results. *The one who had received five talents immediately went out, invested it and earned another five.* The servant was faithful in his stewardship. *Similarly, the one given two earned another two* and thus also served his master in a commendable way. The servant who was given a single talent is a different story altogether. He *went off, dug a hole in the ground and hid his master's money.* Some people might regard this as a prudent move, but the story will reveal the problem with this servant's actions (or lack thereof!) The interpretation of Yeshua's parable so far is not too complex to discern. If Israel and the Jewish people are the servants, then the master is clearly a picture of ADONAI our Father. The interesting twist thus far is that different people are given differing degrees of stewardship. Likewise, these different people respond with different actions. People come from so many experiences and perspectives, especially in regard to the things of God.

The parable continues with some more relevant details. Yeshua tells his disciples that *after a long time, the master of those servants returned.* This is consistent with the teaching of Yeshua and elsewhere that the Messiah will have two distinct missions. The first mission, as *Mashiach ben Yosef,* will be to accomplish redemption through his suffering and death (cf. Isaiah 53). After his resurrection, Yeshua would depart, as illustrated within this parable. It also offers an accurate picture of the period of time during his trip (so far about 2000 years) and of his sudden return to establish his kingdom (cf. Isaiah 11).

In this story, the master returns for a particular reason, primarily to *settle accounts* with the servants. The first servant approached the owner and pointed out that he had earned *five more talents* with the five he invested. The owner was obviously pleased with such wisdom and commended him as a *good and trustworthy servant.* Since he was faithful with this relatively small amount, the servant is promised *a large amount.* The fruitful servant is invited to *come and join in his master's happiness.* Similarly, the servant who received a lesser amount reported to the master that with his *two talents* he had *made two more.* His master was quite pleased by this and exclaimed, "Excellent! You are a good and faithful servant." Even though this servant had received less than the first servant, he was still a *good and trustworthy servant* in his master's eyes. He, too, will be put in charge of *a large amount* of the master's property and is invited to *join in* his *master's happiness.*

In Yeshua's parable, it is the last servant who receives the bulk of the attention. His words and attitude are quite different from those of the previous two servants. Although he had received only one talent, one would expect him to have at least matched the amount given him but he did not do so. He starts his explanation on shaky ground, as he addresses the master as *a hard man.* In addition to this negative salutation, the servant continues by denigrating the master as one who would *harvest where he didn't plant and gather where he didn't sow seed.* Because of these perceptions, the final servant admits that he *was afraid* of the owner, so much so that he hid his *talent in the ground.* With an obvious attitude, this servant offers to give his talent back to the owner, with no profit or labor to show for it.

The master is not at all pleased with these actions or attitudes, and he rebukes the man as a *wicked, lazy servant.* He marvels at the unfair observations made by the servant. The owner actually has the right to *harvest* wherever he desires on his property and to *gather* where he didn't *sow seed.* After all, he owns the place! Since the servant knew this, it makes all the more sense that he should have at least *deposited his money with the bankers.* That way, when the master returned, he *would have gotten back interest* with his investment.

Because of these irresponsible actions, the master directs others to *take the talent from him and give it to the one who has ten.* According to Yeshua's teaching, this is fair and just. He elaborates on the earthly principle and how it relates to the spiritual truth within this parable. The master is quoted as saying, "Everyone who has something will be given more so that he will have more than enough." The faithful servant will be blessed even beyond his immediate added responsibilities.

And this blessing will come in a rather surprising way. Yeshua said, as *anyone who has nothing, even what he does have will be taken away*. Even with this great loss, there are even more ramifications for the untrusting worker. The master commands others to apprehend the *worthless servant* and *throw him out in the dark*. In parabolic metaphor, this seems to be an allusion to the judgment of *Gei-Hinnom*/the place of judgment. The terrible consequences of the servant's bad choices are emphasized as he is cast into the place *where people will wail and grind their teeth*.

The lessons of the parable of the talents are both encouraging and sobering. In general terms, all people are given the gift of life by the Master in Heaven. We are also given certain personal gifts which we are to use in the service of God with the corresponding accountability. These lessons apply to the broader audience of Yeshua's message, Jew and Gentile alike. However, the specific context of Matthew 25 reminds us that these lessons were originally intended to describe the experience of Israel and our people. Jewish people, believers and skeptics alike, are called the servants of ADONAI. We as a people have been given a special stewardship and corresponding responsibility. It is our people (and even we as individual Jews) who are to be a light to the Gentiles and a testimony for God (cf. Isaiah 49:6).

In this historic context, the parable is a strong teaching about different kinds of Jews and their relationship to our calling. Some are given much and do much good with their blessings. Others are given a lesser amount but are just as faithful with what they have. Note that in God's eyes, it is not the amount of the gifts but our *faithfulness* to use what we have that is most important. Sadly, many people completely ignore their gifts and callings. The ultimate price will be heavy, as some fail to fulfill the very purpose for which God created them. In the future day of judgment, Israel and all of our people will give an account for that holy stewardship. What does all of this mean for us today? Have we discovered the purpose of God in our lives? Are we faithfully fulfilling that vital calling? May our Heavenly Father and Messiah say to us in that future day: "Excellent! You are a good and trustworthy servant. Come and join in your master's happiness!"

Parables Concerning the Future Judgment of the Gentiles   25:31-46

After an extensive teaching about the future of Israel, Yeshua now addresses a different topic. Chapter 24 of Matthew's account tells of the prophetic events that will transpire as birth pains just before the Second Coming of *Mashiach*. As we saw, these details clearly speak of Israel in those last days (e.g., *Shabbat*, the rebuilt Temple, etc.) and not the Gentile branch of the Church. Even the first part of Chapter 25 speaks in parabolic terms about the status of the Jewish people in the days just prior to Messiah's arrival.

Now attention is turned to the large percentage of the world (roughly 99%) that is not Jewish or related to the nation of Israel. Although the Gentiles of the world may have various religions and philosophies, they will also be directly impacted by the return of the only true Messiah, Yeshua. When this *Son of Man comes in his glory*, the Nations will realize that there is only one God, the God of Israel. This will be unquestioned as they witness Yeshua surrounded by the *Sh'khinah* glory of God. Yeshua adds that he will be accompanied by all the angels, which would include not only the angelic armies of God but, evidently, the returning raptured believers (cf. *Y'hudah*/Jude 1:14). His ultimate destination at that time will be to *sit on his glorious throne* as the Judge and messianic King. As such, Yeshua reveals that *all the nations will be assembled before him* for the final judgment.

This is a change in context, as it is no longer Israel being addressed but the Nations (Hebrew *goyim*), meaning all non-Jews. In his previous parables of Chapters 24:32-25:30, Messiah never alludes to the Nations, so we are alerted to the fact that this parable is addressed to a different cultural group. The theme itself is not new here, as the distinctive judgment of the Gentiles is addressed several times in the *Tanakh* (cf. *Yoel*/Joel 3:1-2 English). In that context, part of the judgment weighs the actions of the non-Jewish nations in regard to their part in scattering Israel and even dividing the Land that God assigned to his chosen people. The United Nations and other countries might want to take note of that in our day! In this parable, Yeshua adds some other issues that will be raised in the final judgment of the Gentiles.

As the non-Jews are gathered together at Messiah's throne, we are told that he will *separate people as a shepherd separates sheep from goats.* In the Middle East, shepherds often watch over a mixed group of these two kinds of animals. Sheep are a familiar symbol for those who follow God as their true Shepherd (cf. Psalm 23; *Yochanan*/John 10). This is both good news and bad news. Sheep are known to have terrible eyesight, so much so that they rely heavily on following the crowd in front of them. And that crowd may or may not be going in the right direction! Because of their limited vision, they rely most heavily on their keen sense of hearing. A good shepherd will take advantage of this fact and develop a unique voice to call his sheep together (cf. *Yochanan*/John 10:27).

Goats, on the other hand, tend to have a strong sense of independence. They will wander from the herd even at their own peril. With this in mind, one can see why goats are often a typological picture of unbelievers. They have a mind of their own and are often in rebellion against any shepherd that would try to guide them. Yeshua's parable becomes intriguing as he notes that *the sheep will be placed at his right hand and the goats at his left.* We learn, therefore, that at the judgment throne of Messiah, the Gentiles will be separated into two distinct categories with two different destinies. We can predict which group is more favored than the other, as the right hand is often symbolic of strength and blessing—a fact that bodes well for the sheep of this parable (Psalm 118:15-16).

The word-picture continues with a consistent theme in Matthew's gospel: Yeshua is King Messiah. Yeshua continues to teach that *the King will say to those on his right, "Come, you whom my Father has blessed, take your inheritance."* It is the Gentiles on the right hand of the throne who are blessed for their faith and obedience. Their inheritance includes the most wonderful experience of all, their participation in and enjoyment of *the Kingdom prepared for you from the founding of the world.*

These blessings include, but are not limited to, eternal life, the removal of all pain and death, and fellowship in the presence of the Heavenly Father forever. This Kingdom with Messiah as King has always been the major focus of God's plan for his creation. What was lost in the Fall of early Genesis will ultimately be restored by the work of *Mashiach*. There have been many dark periods in human history, yet none have taken God by surprise. Everything ultimately transpires to fulfill God's plan of redemption and paradise restored.

Although this is not so much a new teaching of Yeshua's, certain details about the judgment of the Gentiles might have surprised even his disciples. Messiah elaborates that their judgment will be based on how they helped people in great need of food, drink, and housing. Further, Yeshua personalizes this basis, noting that it is he himself who *was hungry, thirsty,* and *a stranger* in their midst.

These issues have always been of utmost importance in Judaism. We were redeemed physically from Egypt as a nation of slaves, so our people have always related to the plight of the less fortunate. Helping those in need is often mandated by *Torah* commandments, including leaving part of one's harvest field to feed the needy (Leviticus 23:22). Similarly, confiscating any outer garment of a Jew, even if he or she owed a large amount to a debtor, was prohibited (Exodus 22:26-27). One of the highest *mitzvot* is that of *hachnasat orchim*/hospitality to strangers. This was not just a nice gesture in ancient society, but often served an important function in a time when there were no local hotels for distant travelers. In addition to these *mitzvot*, Yeshua adds the other humanitarian endeavors of caring for the *sick* and visiting those *in prison*. It is important to care for anyone in society in all of these ways, yet how much more so when it is the Messiah himself who has such great need.

While these *mitzvot* were commonly known, those among the "sheep" (from the previous discussion of sheep and goats) are rather surprised to hear that it was Yeshua himself who was in such need. Indeed, they ask, *When did we see you hungry and feed you, or thirsty and give you something to drink?* They couldn't remember a time when they brought Messiah in as a *guest* or when he was *sick* or *in prison*. Nor could they recall when they responded by providing clothes or visiting him. Yet on the final judgment day, *the King will say to them, "Yes! I tell you that whenever you did these things for one of the least important of these brothers of mine, you did them for me!"*

Again, we should pay close attention to the original context of this parable. Often, people have applied these verses to everything from feeding the downtown homeless community to helping orphans in Africa. Of course, scripture does exhort us to address such concerns. And though this parable may be broadly applied to these communities, it does not directly speak to them. Rather, this parable refers to judgment of the Nations based on how they treated the "brothers" of Yeshua. It is not about Gentile Christians helping other Gentiles, here, but about them helping an outside party. In this context, the "brothers" of Yeshua refers specifically to the Jewish brothers of Yeshua.

This fits the broader context of Matthew 24-25, where certain teachings are addressed directly to the Jewish community and others are intended for the Nations. This being so, the parable is a powerful teaching about the important relationship between true Gentile believers and the Jewish people. This should not be confused with the idea that one's salvation is based merely upon his or her works. It is abundantly clear in the entire Scriptures that spiritual redemption is attained only through the love and grace of Messiah's work on our behalf (cf. Isaiah 53; Ephesians 2:8-9; *Yochanan*/John 14:6).

However, it is equally true that God weighs our works as evidence of whether we indeed know him personally. In other words, works/ *mitzvot* are not the basis of spiritual salvation but are indeed an indicator of that salvation (cf. Ephesians 2:10). Yeshua is not saying that the salvation of Gentile believers is based on their humanitarian acts, but that such acts will be an accurate reflection of their authentic relationship with God. The parable emphasizes that one of the best fruits of salvation for non-Jews will actually be their treatment of the Jewish people in their daily lives. Since the days of Abraham, God has given both promise and warning regarding how the Nations treat Israel (cf. Genesis 12:1-3). Clearly, the fruit of one's salvation may be evident in many ways, but it is reasonable that the proper treatment of God's *own* people will be a direct manifestation of that fruit.

History is filled with much suffering and tragedy for the Jewish community—persecutions, pogroms, and holocausts. Too often, the Nations either promoted such actions or neglected to intervene to assist God's people. The most egregious cases occurred when Jews were persecuted in the name of "Christ." We know from Yeshua's own definition that such people have a questionable or nonexistent relationship with God (Matthew 7:20-23). There are, however, many notable cases of righteous Gentiles who risked their own lives to help the brothers of Yeshua. With awe and respect, many Jews appreciate the Corrie ten Booms and Raoul Wallenburgs, and even the Oskar Schindlers, of the world.

It is fitting that this parable weighs the actions of the Gentile nations in the last days, immediately after the time of Jacob's Trouble. It will be a most dark and dangerous time for the Jewish world, and it is thus understandable that the Gentiles will be judged on how they reacted in their own day. They will be the ones who enter the blessing of Messiah's Kingdom because they showed the true fruit of salvation in their treatment of Yeshua's relatives.

Messiah now turns his attention to the goats standing *on his left*. We can anticipate his words of judgment as, traditionally, the left side is not the side of blessing. Indeed, the goats are exhorted to *get away* from Yeshua because they *are cursed*. It is important to note that the goats have several things in common with the sheep. They are part of the same original flock even though they are ultimately separated. Both groups appear before the judgment seat of Messiah to give account for their actions. Similarly, both the sheep and goats are given opportunities to bless Israel in a great time of need. Here is where the similarities end.

The sheep are commended by Yeshua for their actions in life and brought into the blessings of the Messianic Kingdom. The goats, by contrast, merit a different response and subsequent judgment. They are told to *go off into the fire prepared for the Adversary and his angels*, a clear reference to Satan and his rebellious followers. The place of eternal judgment is undoubtedly Hell. Yeshua says that this is the eternal fate of the goats because of their pagan rebellion against the things of the true God, the God of Israel.

Yeshua specifies some of the exact actions (or lack thereof) responsible for such a terrible fate by noting that he *was hungry* and they gave him *no food*, *thirsty* and they gave him *nothing to drink*. This is the same Yeshua in the same circumstances who was encountered by the sheep. He also cites the other circumstances such as being *a stranger, needing clothes*, and being *sick and in prison*. Unlike the sheep who assisted those in need, these goats provided no help. Nonetheless, the goats are greatly surprised by Yeshua's examples, as they also do not recall seeing him in such need. They inquire, "Lord, when did we see you hungry, thirsty, a stranger, needing clothes, sick or in prison?" Perhaps they would have taken action if that were the case. But Messiah's shocking answer is that whenever they refused to assist the "least important of these people," they "refused to do it for me!"

Because the context for the parable has not changed, the "least important… people" must still refer to Yeshua's Jewish brothers. Gentiles from both the "sheep" and the "goat" categories were faced with the same situation to test the reality of their professed faith. The sheep pass the test by having assisted the Jewish people in their time of great need, especially in the last days of the Great Tribulation.

The goats, although presumably professing a similar faith, fail the practical test of that faith. They did not help Israel because they do not have the reality of God's love in their hearts. Accordingly, Yeshua says *they will go off to eternal punishment, but those who have done what God wants will go to eternal life*. It must be emphasized that their actions do not earn their judgment (punishment or blessing), but, rather, prove the reality of their relationship with God through Yeshua the Messiah. It should be reinforced that this condemnation is not on all Gentiles, per se. Rather, it's on how those Gentiles treated the Jews.

With this, Messiah's teaching regarding the judgment of both Israel (24:45-25:30) and the Gentiles (25:31-46) ends. Although some new details are taught here, it is not an entirely new teaching, as the prophets speak often of such a time of judgment (cf. Israel in Ezekiel 20:36-38 and the Gentiles in Joel 3:1-2). This future judgment is both sobering and comforting. It is sobering in that all people should live in light of their future appearance before their Creator. By contrast, it is comforting in that God will correct all injustices on that last day.

Without a doubt, this is the most important question you must ask yourself today. Are you a faithful servant? Do you have the oil of the *Ruach*/Holy Spirit in your life? Are you being faithful with the talents that God has given you as one of his own? With respect to the parable of the Nations, are you a sheep or a goat? Is your faith real

328 / YESHUA, KING MESSIAH

enough to be lived out in difficult times? For both Jew and non-Jew, the essential key is a personal relationship with Yeshua as redeemer and *Mashiach*. May we all have confidence that we will hear him say on that day, "Come and join in your master's happiness!"

The Redemption of King Messiah   26:1-27:66

Matthew now turns his attention to the last few days of Yeshua's earthly ministry in Israel. The past three and a half years of teaching, mentoring, and healing are now coming to a close. Yet it is not a sad ending when properly understood. All along, Yeshua has made it clear that the apex of his time on Earth would be his death and subsequent resurrection. It was for this very purpose that Messiah came into the world, as these events would hold the key to Israel's salvation and the restoration of God's Kingdom. The glories of the Messianic Kingdom through *Mashiach ben David* can only be attained by the sufferings of *Mashiach ben Yosef*. It is this phase that Yeshua now enters in his dramatic last days living in first-century Israel. The timing of these events cannot be coincidental, as the most holy week of *Pesach*/ Passover is approaching. It is God's perfect will to accomplish the spiritual redemption for Israel and the Nations during the historic annual feast that celebrates the physical redemption of Israel.

Celebrating the *Seder*   26:1-30

A major transition now takes place, as Matthew notes that Yeshua *finished speaking* about Israel's last days to focus on the immediate. He is still addressing *his talmidim* as he reveals that *the Son of Man will be handed over to be nailed to the execution-stake.* He had spoken of this reality several times before in his teaching, but it becomes all the more crucial. *Pesach is two days away. Pesach*/Passover is the great celebration of Israel's deliverance from slavery during the time of the Pharaohs. The Hebrew word means "to spring or jump over."

It is an appropriate name for the time that the angel of death "passed over" the Children of Israel as a nation. This refers to the tenth and final plague that came upon Egypt in that generation. It was a horrible judgment upon all those who oppressed Israel. Since Pharaoh had been killing Jewish baby boys in the Nile, it is appropriate that the last plague would result in the death of all firstborn sons in Egypt.

However, as usual, God also provided a way of escape from the coming judgment. Any household (Egyptian included) could take for itself a lamb and have it slain, applying the blood of the innocent animal to the doorposts of the house (cf. Exodus 12). The *Torah* makes it clear that when the angel of death saw the appropriate sacrifice, it would "pass over" that house and spare it of judgment.

One can see that Israel was set free by the vicarious death of the kosher lamb, most certainly a picture of the work of the coming Messiah. As the children of Israel are later led to Mount Sinai to receive the *Torah*, they are told to always remember this day of redemption, the 14th day of the Hebrew month Nisan. An annual dinner was mandated so Israel would never forget God's great miracle in this spring season. Added to this were seven more days of *matzah/* unleavened bread during which only pure bread is permitted to be eaten (cf. Leviticus 23:5-8). In subsequent times, these two feasts (Passover and Unleavened Bread) were considered so connected that to this day they are usually referred to as one feast, the eight-day Passover holiday.

Yeshua gives additional details at his last Passover seder. Not only will he be executed as a criminal, but a broad-based conspiracy will arrange for his death on *Pesach*. Matthew points out that some of *the head cohanim and elders of the people* will initiate some of the arrest proceedings. This would encompass some of the top Jewish religious leaders of the priestly party (*cohen*), as well as synagogue elders (*zakeyn*). The former speaks of the aristocratic Sadducees, whereas the latter alludes to some of the Pharisaic rabbinic leaders.

330 / YESHUA, KING MESSIAH

The fact that they *gathered in the palace of Kayafa/Caiaphas, the* reigning *cohen hagadol,* or High Priest, speaks loudly regarding the depth of the opposition to Yeshua. The Roman leaders will, of course, jump into the fray soon enough, but at this point Matthew focuses on the Jewish side of the issue as *they made plans to arrest* Yeshua.

Of concern would be the imminent holy day and the Jewish community's tenuous relationship with their Roman occupiers. It is important to point out that this relatively small group of Jewish leaders is concerned that the people will riot. While it is well known that much of the establishment opposed Yeshua and his messianic claims, many thousands of his fellow Jews followed him as the *Mashiach.*

Too often, emphasis is put on the "Jewish" rejection of Yeshua while forgetting the fact that it was an area of disagreement *within* the larger Jewish community. The same could be said today, as many—both Jews and Christians—seem to forget that there are many thousands of contemporary Messianic Jews! In the first-century context, some of the leaders feared that if a riot took place in Jerusalem, the Romans would crack down even harder on the community. If the arrest could be avoided *during the festival,* then many of Yeshua's Galilean supporters would be out of town and traveling back to their homes. With this, their plan is set in motion.

Matthew points out that Yeshua was still in the Jerusalem environs at an outlying village called Beit-Anyah/Bethany. This was both close in proximity to the Holy City and *the home of Shim'on, the man who had had tzara'at*/leprosy. It is most probable that Shim'on had been healed of this dreaded affliction, perhaps even through the ministry of Yeshua himself (cf. Matthew 8:1-4). He now welcomes his Messiah to stay at his home in these final days before Passover.

As if to get an early start on the *seder* preparation, *a woman who had an alabaster jar filled with very expensive perfume approached* Yeshua. In the ancient Middle East, it was considered a natural part of hospitality to welcome guests by offering them anointing oil or perfume. In the days of minimal bathing and much travel in dusty areas, this would be more of an expected obligation than a luxury. As the woman *began pouring it* on Yeshua's head, Matthew and the other disciples *became very angry*. The woman's action went well beyond the accepted custom, as it was a most costly perfume in an elaborate container.

Evidently, the simple band of disciples was not expecting this, as the perfume, seemingly more appropriately, *could have been sold for a lot of money and given to the poor*. We are told in Yochanan's account that the estimated value of the perfume was 300 *denarii, which* was almost a year's wage, as a *denarius* was a day's wage (cf. *Yochanan*/John 12:5). Even though he had taught many times on the need to help the poor, Yeshua does not stop this particular action.

Instead, he affirms that the woman *has done a beautiful thing* by, in essence, preparing his *body for burial*. Messiah points out that her action is not just an extravagant welcome for a houseguest, but fulfillment of a *mitzvah* associated with burial customs. Since the days of the *Torah*, Jews have not allowed the body of the deceased to be tampered with. Other peoples of the ancient world allowed embalming and other practices.

Based on the principle in Genesis 3:19, Judaism has long held that the body is best left unchanged after death so it may go "from dust to dust." Although Jews have not used embalming historically, the body was always treated with the utmost respect. This included washing the body, clothing it with proper burial garments, and anointing it with oil or spices. It is this point that Yeshua brings out. The woman performed this prophetic action, anointing the Messiah (play on words) with a most costly perfume because she understood his impending death. Not only does Yeshua deem this appropriate, but also he makes a rather astonishing promise that *throughout the whole world* this *mitzvah* will be remembered *in her memory*. How amazing that we are fulfilling that promise even as we read this account today!

Matthew records another significant event leading up to the last *seder*. As some of the Jewish leaders were considering how they might implement their plans for Yeshua, it must have occurred to them that they needed some inside assistance. That seemed possible by obtaining help through *one of the Twelve, the one called Y'hudah from K'riot*. It was this one (usually translated Judas Iscariot, literally in Hebrew, *Y'hudah, ish*/the man from the town of *K'riot*) who *went to the head cohanim and asked, "What are you willing to give me if I turn* Yeshua *over to you?"*

Ever since he appeared on the stage of human history, Judas has been an unending source of speculation. How could one of Yeshua's own inner circle turn against the Messiah? What were his motives? Some have suggested that he was simply disenchanted with the direction of Yeshua's ministry. If he was the true Messiah, he should overthrow the Romans and establish his kingdom immediately. When Yeshua started talking more and more about the delay of the earthly kingdom, perhaps Y'hudah decided to give up any previous commitment to Yeshua.

Some have countered that Judas' betrayal may have been for financial reasons. This would be strange, however, as Judas was evidently a very trusted disciple who was given charge of the group's meager income. The former argument seems to be the best, as it fits with a Jewish understanding of Matthew's account. Y'hudah was simply a zealous Jew, like the others, hoping for the messianic redemption to be accomplished by Yeshua in his day. When it became clear that it would not happen according to his own plan, Y'hudah gave up and was self-deceived (with Satan's assistance) to the point of betraying his former master.

Some of the priestly leaders responded, appreciative of Judas' offer to help them and offered him a fee of *thirty silver coins*. The amount is not coincidental. It is the same amount of monetary compensation for a slave who was killed (cf. Exodus 21:32). In the latter prophets, Zechariah uses the analogy of casting thirty shekels into the sanctuary as a sign of his grief over the rebellion of Israel in his day (cf. Zechariah 11:12). Sadly, the amount paid to Y'hudah in the gospels is an apt symbol of the rejection of Yeshua by many, even devaluing him to the price of a dead slave. Matthew points out that Y'hudah received the payment and began looking *for a good opportunity to betray* Yeshua.

With some of these preliminary events fulfilled, Matthew now records one of the most important gatherings in history. The "Last Supper" of Yeshua was no doubt a full Passover *seder*. All of the first-century elements are present, and the fine details confirm this fact. The synoptic Gospels (Matthew, Mark, and Luke) clearly state that it is the very night of the first *seder,* whereas *Yochanan*/John, in characteristic fashion, portrays it as a dinner not occurring on the holy day (cf. Yochanan 13:1). For centuries, theologians have speculated as to why Yochanan's gospel is so different regarding many of the fine details of Yeshua's life. Skeptics have charged that it contains some glaring contradictions and even errors. It seems unlikely, however, that Yochanan would be that ignorant, as he was at the same dinner as the other disciples!

This has commonly been called the "Synoptic Problem" by scholars. Many of them have also offered possible reconciliations of the apparent issues. A rather recent solution is contained within the astounding collection of the Dead Sea Scrolls, discovered in 1947. These Scrolls confirm that first-century Judaism was very diverse, with a variety of sects each with their own distinctive practices. Included in the many religious insights found in the Scrolls is the confirmation that the Qumran community had its own unique calendar. Since they were rebels against the Pharisaic/Jerusalem establishment, it is not surprising that they developed their own 364-day solar calendar as opposed to the typical lunar calendar used within mainstream Judaism (cf. DDS, 4Q317). This could be the logical reconciliation of the Synoptic Problem. Simply put, the Synoptic Gospels were written to mainstream Jews within the Pharisee and Sadducee tradition, whereas John could have been written to Jews from the Qumran or some other sectarian tradition. For Yochanan's account of the same dinner, he thus must note that "it was just before the festival of *Pesach*" (13:1).

Matthew, on the other hand, specifies that it was *on the first day for matzah* that the disciples inquire of Yeshua *where they should prepare the seder*. The final preparations were critical for this most important feast. Three elements were required for the first-century Passover *seder*—lamb, *matzah* (unleavened bread), and *maror* (bitter herbs). These three continue to be central elements of the modern *seder* meal, with many rabbinic additions over the centuries.

The disciples are seeking to know where the *seder* dinner will take place for their group. The room and food area would have to be specially cleansed to meet the more stringent kosher requirements of *Pesach*. All leaven would be removed and all utensils either boiled in water or temporarily replaced with some that are *kosher l'Pesach/* kosher to/for Passover. A kosher, ritualistically pure lamb would need to be purchased from the kosher markets of Jerusalem. Upon the ritual slaughter of the lamb on the late afternoon of 14 Nisan, the lamb portions would be brought to the home and cooked so that an entire family or group could eat it (cf. Exodus 12). It was also important to prepare the special *matzah* and *maror* for the celebration of the *seder* meal.

Passover was always (and continues to be) a most busy holiday in the Jewish community, and the disciples had their work cut out for them. In reply to their question about location, Yeshua exhorts them to *go into the city, to so-and-so and tell him that the Rabbi* desires to *celebrate Pesach at his house*. Matthew points out that the disciples would know the man, probably a Jerusalem disciple by a certain name. Other accounts add the detail that the man would be carrying a jar of water (cf. Luke 22:10). Although it was quite common to see people carrying water necessary for the ritual requirements of *Pesach*, it would normally be a woman's chore. Water was an element of every *seder,* as seen in the two different hand washings (*natilat yadaim*) included within the *haggadah*. In the first century, this would have also included the requisite foot washing to welcome the guests (cf. *Yochanan*/John 13:1-17).

The foot washing at the last *seder* was nothing new or unexpected, but what was highly unusual was the way in which it was administered at the dinner. Normally, one would expect a servant to assist with this menial task. After all, the Passover is a celebration of our newfound freedom, and every Jew can recline to enjoy the meal. But it was at this very time of *natilat yadaim* that Yeshua arose, took the water and a towel, and began to wash the disciples' feet, thus providing a living model of the priority of serving in Messiah's kingdom.

This action made an indelible impression upon the twelve at that *seder* and continues today at Messianic *seders* worldwide. In the bustle of overcrowded Jerusalem on that day, a confirming sign of the *seder* location would be this known male believer carrying the water jar. The man himself would have been most amenable to the disciples' request, as it has long been a special *mitzvah* to invite guests to your home *seder* (Tractate Yoma 12a). The *talmidim* did as requested and completed the necessary preparations for the last *seder* of Yeshua with his followers.

When evening came, Yeshua *reclined with the twelve talmidim as they were eating*. There has been and continues to be a major debate on the exact dating of the last *seder*. This stems back to the phrase in the *Torah* that describes the slaying of the Passover lamb as "between the evenings/*beyn ha-arba'ayim*" (cf. Exodus 12:6). The Hebrew wording has led to some historical debate whether this refers to the evening of 13 Nisan or the evening of 14 Nisan. The traditional view (as adopted by the Pharisees and modern Judaism) is that the phrase refers to the lamb being slain on the late afternoon of 14 Nisan entering into 15 Nisan. Consequently, the best view in Matthew is that Yeshua's last *seder* took place after dark at the beginning of 15 Nisan.

Matthew's identity and knowledge is evident even in the finest details of his account of the dinner. The fact that Yeshua was reclining at the dinner table is quite authentic for first-century Jerusalem. There were no high tables or chairs as we use today (with all due respect to Leonardo Da Vinci), and participants would stretch out on the floor with their head facing a low table, thus enabling them to reach the food by hand. Since the days of Moses, it has been a requirement to not only have a Passover dinner but to retell the story of our redemption at that time. Throughout the centuries, the written story called the *haggadah* (the telling) was compiled and has been read every year to fulfill the commandment to "tell your son" about the events of that great day (cf. Exodus 13:8). It is in the *haggadah* that we are told specifically to recline at the table, as this was also a sign of our newfound freedom. In the ancient world, only the free people had time to relax in such a way. What a beautiful picture this portrays, as the Messiah is relaxing before his ultimate act of redemption!

Interwoven with the symbolic foods of the *seder* is a full meal that is usually nothing short of a feast. As the disciples *were eating* the meal with its various symbolic elements, Yeshua shares a shocking revelation: "I tell you that one of you is going to betray me." As previously noted, Y'hudah had already struck his deal with some of the leaders who wanted to have Yeshua arrested. But now Messiah brings up this pending reality to the entire group in the middle of the celebration dinner. It is no wonder that *they became terribly upset and began asking him, "Lord, you don't mean me, do you?"* It must have seemed utterly impossible that one of the inner circle would turn against their Master, especially considering all that they had been through in the last three and a half years together. Who could possibly fall to such depths? There was even self-doubt manifested.

Yeshua lets them know that *the one who dips his matzah in the dish with me is the one who will betray* him. This seems to be a clear reference to the part of the *seder* meal in which a piece of the unleavened bread is dipped into the *maror* as a reminder of the bitterness of our past slavery. In Yochanan's account, it is reported that Ycshua dipped matzah in the *maror* and gave it to Y'hudah, thereby identifying his betrayer (cf. Yochanan 13:26). It was also a very symbolic act, reflecting the bitter deed about to be performed by this disenchanted *talmid*.

Even with these bitter events about to take place, Yeshua affirms that it is all part of God's great plan of redemption. *The Son of Man will die just as the Tanakh says he will.* Yet, at the same time, Judas is held accountable for his personal choices, as Yeshua warns *woe to that man by whom the Son of Man is betrayed!* At this point, Y'hudah asks, as if still in denial, "Surely, Rabbi, you don't mean me?" But Yeshua strongly affirms that Y'hudah is the one by emphasizing that "the words are yours." The stage is set, but nothing is out of the control of the sovereign God. Yeshua will soon be betrayed, but he clearly understands that no one will take his life but that he will give it voluntarily to fulfill the great purposes of messianic redemption (cf. Yochanan 10:18).

As the meal and reading of the *haggadah* continued, Yeshua *took a piece of matzah.* The entire meal would include only unleavened bread/*matzah,* as this is one of the strict requirements of the holy day. Matthew's wording here implies that Yeshua took a particular piece of matzah on the table. From ancient times to the present day, Jews have celebrated the *seder* by focusing at one point on a special *matzah tash*/pocket. This is a ceremonial container that may have a variety of artistic shapes or sizes, anything from a plate to a linen case. What is especially distinctive is that the *matzah tash* always has three separate compartments, each with one piece of the unleavened bread. Anyone familiar with the details of the Passover *seder* knows that this ceremonial plate is one of the key items placed at the table every year.

Even more amazing is the focus on the middle piece of *matzah* within that *matzah tash*. At the beginning of the *seder*, the middle matzah is taken out of the container and broken in half. From there, half goes back into the *matzah tash*. The other half becomes very important and is even given a particular name, the *afikoman*. This broken piece of matzah is then wrapped in a napkin or pouch and subsequently hidden by one of the *seder* participants from the sight of the others.

In the festivities after the supper, during the part of the haggadah called *Tzafun*/Hidden, those at the meal search for the hidden matzah. To this day, the search for the *afikoman* is one of the highlights for grandchildren at the *seder*. It has become customary to reward the one who finds the *afikoman* (usually with something from Grandpa's wallet). The spiritual symbolism can still speak to us today, as the person who finds the hidden one is still rewarded. Messianic Jews believe this is part of the "hidden" truth that upon closer observation is revealed in the traditional *seder*.

At that point of the *seder*, the *afikoman* is distributed to everyone present, each partaking of a bite-size portion of the same matzah. It must be this particular piece of matzah that Yeshua took up, given the context of all of these details. Likewise, Rabbi Sha'ul confirms that it was "after supper" that these actions occurred, which is exactly the right time for the *afikoman* (cf. I Corinthians 11:23-25).

Our people continue to celebrate this most beautiful feast every year, with all of the symbolic elements and a wonderful dinner included. Besides being an important religious holiday for modern Jews, it serves as a great time to join with family and friends.

However, maybe all of us should take a deeper look at the symbols of Passover.

Scholars are not absolutely sure of the etymology of the word *afikoman,* although it is usually translated "dessert" or "it comes last." According to contemporary Jewish scholar David Daube (formerly of the University of Oxford and UC Berkeley), the word has messianic implications. It evidently comes from two Greek words, *afi* + *komenos,* which can mean, "it returns" or, if personalized, "he comes" (cf. Daube, *Collected Works of David Daube*, p. 425). Significantly, a similar form of the word is used in Matthew 3:11, where Yochanan calls his followers to look for the "one coming/*erkomenos*" after him, Yeshua the Messiah. Either way, the *afikoman* is broken early in the *seder* and makes another appearance at the end of the *seder*.

While rabbinic scholars admit they are not quite certain of the meaning of *afikoman* or how it was incorporated into the *haggadah*, one clue is within the word itself. Its Greek origins at least tell us that it was developed in the Jewish community during the Greek period, which encompasses the New Testament times. One possible explanation as to its origins is that it was an established tradition previous to the first century. One rabbinic interpretation is that the three *matzot* of the *matzah tash* represent a unity (three in one) of our forefathers Abraham, Isaac, and Jacob. Another interpretation is that it represents a unity between three kinds of bread—the *lechem oni* (bread of affliction) and the double portion of manna. There is also an ancient interpretation that the middle matzah is to remind us of the Passover lamb since it is the last thing tasted that night (Tractate Pesachim 119b-120a).

If the *afikoman* was already established as a traditional element of the *seder* prior to the first century, then Yeshua was using a well-known ceremony to illustrate some new truth about his work as *Mashiach*. On the other hand, it is entirely possible that Yeshua took some matzah and created the ceremony for the first time at this *seder*. This might explain how it is that such a key part of the Passover meal is somewhat mysterious in origin. It could be that Yeshua and the disciples developed this part of the ceremony, which was later celebrated at other first-century *seders* in which many participants would not fully know the messianic meaning of the *afikoman*. Whatever its origin, the *afikoman* ceremony no doubt illustrates the full ministry of the Messiah—his appearance (leaving the *matzah tash*/Micah 5:2), his death (broken for our iniquities/cf. Isaiah 53:5), and his resurrection (reappearance at the end of the *seder*/cf. Isaiah 53:10).

After the full dinner, Yeshua immediately makes the direct connection between himself and the ceremonial elements of the *seder*. Matthew notes that Yeshua *made the b'rakhah*/blessing while he *broke* the matzah and *gave it to the talmidim*. The disciples probably did not regard this as anything different than what they had celebrated every Passover as Jews. Perhaps it evoked pictures of the forefathers or the unity of the Jewish people, but the next statement of their rabbi/Messiah must have been shocking as he exhorted them to "Take! Eat! This is my body."

At first glance, this is both astounding and perplexing. Certainly Yeshua was not advocating cannibalism, as this is entirely contrary to the *Torah*! It shouldn't even be a topic of discussion, as the *matzah* could not literally be his body since he was reclining right there with them.

To the Jewish mind, all the elements (wine, *matzah, maror,* etc.) were strictly symbolic elements representing the important truths of *Pesach*. One line in the *haggadah* states, for example, that "this is the bread of affliction which our ancestors ate in the land of Egypt." Clearly, we are not to think that the *matzah* on the table is more than **3500** years old! It is, however, an important symbolic element of the *seder*. Add to this the analogy of the *afikoman* as a remembrance of the Passover lamb, which did have a body and was eaten.

Yeshua's statement was no doubt astounding to the disciples, but it was not contrary to some of the spiritual pictures associated with the *seder*. It is important for all Christians to also understand the context of the ceremony. Denominations have split and even wars have been fought over the debate about the meaning of Communion (or the Eucharist, or Lord's Supper).

First, it should be noted that Yeshua did not technically create a whole new ceremony, as is often portrayed. Communion is not something new but a completion of something very old! It is simply the fulfillment of the details of the Passover *seder*.

Second, the spiritual/literal interpretation of Yeshua's words is often questioned. In the Reformation era of Christianity, Protestants took exception with the Roman Catholic view that the *matzah* (today known as a "wafer") is somehow mystically transformed into the actual body of Jesus (a process that theologians call transubstantiation). Protestants, led by Martin Luther, took a modified view that the communion bread is literal bread but "contains" the presence of Jesus in a spiritual sense (consubstantiation).

It is interesting that John Calvin took a third approach that was different from both the Catholic and Lutheran views and argued that the bread was only a symbolic representation (see Grudem p. 994-995 for a good overview). With all due respect, these views could benefit from taking a closer look at the meaning of the matzah at Passover, where the unleavened bread is representative of an important spiritual reality. This would be more in line with the understanding of the symbolic nature of the *seder* elements.

The transubstantiation view also led to some bizarre misunderstandings among medieval Christians, some of whom even accused Jews of "Host desecration," asserting that Jews were desecrating the communion elements and thereby physically attacking Jesus! Many Jewish communities were attacked by angry mobs because of such slander and misinformation.

Other significant points in relation to Christian communion are the actual elements used. Since the ceremony took place at a *seder*, Christians should consider what type of bread they use for communion. Though the bread is symbolic, the symbolism is significant. There was only *matzah* on the table because it is required for Passover, but it is also the perfect symbol of the Messiah's body. Being unleavened, it is a reminder of the sinless life of Messiah, which is the perfect payment for our redemption. How strange it would seem to a Jewish disciple to see the Savior's body represented by fluffy leavened bread (again with all due respect to Da Vinci!). Yeshua did not use just any kind of bread, but the *matzah* of Passover, the perfect symbol of our pure Messiah who is therefore qualified to be the perfect payment for the sins of Israel and the entire world.

Yeshua continued with the next chronological element of the *haggadah* after the *afikoman*. Matthew records that *he took a cup of wine, made the b'rakhah/blessing, and gave it to them*. Over the course of the entire Passover evening, participants partake of four cups of "the fruit of the vine." This would normally be *kosher l'Pesach* wine but could also include kosher grape juice. The former was most prevalent, as Rabbi Sha'ul even admonishes the believers in Corinth not to overindulge at their Messianic *seder* (cf. I Corinthians 11:21). Indeed, it would be difficult to become intoxicated with grape juice. The four cups of the *seder* are quite beautiful and spiritually instructive. They are based on a rabbinic application of the four promises to Moshe as he is on the verge of delivering the people of Israel (cf. Exodus 6:6-7).

The first cup is based on the promise from the Lord that "I will bring you out/*hotzeyti*." In the *haggadah*, the cup is called *Kadesh*, or the Cup of Sanctification. The Hebrew word implies separation, or being set apart, and is an apt word for the first step of the redemption from Egypt. At the very first part of every *seder*, the *b'rakhah* is chanted: "*Barukh atah ADONAI, Eloheynu melech ha-olam, borey p'ri ha-gafen*/Blessed art Thou O Lord our God, King of the universe who creates the fruit of the vine." The cup of wine or grape juice is partaken of to thank God for bringing us out of Egypt.

The second cup is based on the promise from *ADONAI* that "I will deliver you/*hitzalti*." This is a step beyond the calling out of the first cup to celebrate the deliverance from our former lives as slaves. It is called the Cup of Plagues, a remembrance of the ten plagues upon Egypt. Although this cup represents the freedom of the Jewish people, we have been told from ancient times that we are not to rejoice in the misfortunes of the evil (in this case, the Egyptians). That's why the cup is emptied by dropping ten drops, one for each plague, on our plate rather than by tasting and enjoying the wine.

The third cup of the Passover is called the Cup of Redemption because it comes from God's promise that "I will redeem you/ *gaalti*." This has always been the cup taken right after the main meal, immediately after the *afikoman* search. The Hebrew term *gaalti* implies buying back something that was in the possession of another. It is the same verb used in the redemption of a slave at the Year of Jubilee (cf. Leviticus 25:47-55). Every year at our *seders,* Israel is to remember that the Father paid a price for the physical redemption of his people. In biblical times, it was clearly understood that it was by the death of the Passover lamb (and the blood applied to the door of our home) that we were bought back by our God. We were slaves but now are free. The Cup of Redemption is a wonderful symbol of God's love for us! With great joy, we sing the *b'rakhah* and partake of the third cup in remembrance of our deliverance.

At the very end of the *seder,* we celebrate the final promise whereby the Father says, "I will take you for My people/*lakakhti*." This Cup of Praise (also called the Cup of Acceptance) occurs at the recitation of the second part of Hallel (Psalm 115-118) and is the climax of the previous cups. The blessing is chanted again and the cup is shared, followed by songs of praise in celebration of our full redemption.

Added to these four cups was one more symbolic cup, not drunk from even though it's on the table. The Cup of Elijah is a reminder of the promise that this prophet will come "before the Great Day of the Lord" (cf. Malachi 4:5 in English). The hope is that *Eliyahu*/Elijah will appear at our *seder* and announce the arrival of King Messiah!

While they illustrate tremendous historical lessons, the four cups of the *seder* contain vital spiritual lessons for us as well. For believers in Yeshua, both Jewish and non-Jewish, the cups describe our spiritual journey. At some point, we were set apart for a purpose. We were also delivered from the foolishness of our old life, not just in Egypt, but also in the world around us. Likewise, we experienced Messiah's redemption through our personal trust in him. No wonder it was this very cup that Yeshua highlighted at the last *seder* and presented to his disciples when he said, "This is my blood which ratifies the New Covenant, my blood shed on behalf of many, so that they may have their sins forgiven." How full of meaning it must have been to them! Their Messiah was about to fulfill the ancient promises depicted by the symbols of the *seder*!

Clearly, the first three cups of the *seder* were celebrated at that last *seder,* but Yeshua said something surprising as he and his disciples approached the end of the evening. The disciples would have naturally expected to partake of the Cup of Praise at the end of the *seder,* as they would have done all of their lives. But at that point, Yeshua says he will *not drink this "fruit of the vine" again until the day I drink new wine with you in my Father's Kingdom*. He was referring to the final and fourth cup, which he clearly did not partake of at that last *seder*. How strange, but, at the same time, how significant!

The Cup of Praise is symbolic of the completed redemption in the Kingdom of God. Although we as believers in Yeshua know we have tasted our spiritual redemption, we must also acknowledge that we still await the ultimate fulfillment of the Messianic Kingdom at the return of Messiah. Thus, Yeshua refrains from drinking the last cup at that time but anticipates the great messianic Passover feast when he returns to establish his kingdom. That will be one *seder* you won't want to miss, as believers will rejoice in the fullness of our spiritual redemption in the restored Jerusalem, praising God!

Yeshua's last *seder* with his *talmidim* concludes in the normal way, as Matthew points out that *after singing the Hallel, they went out to the Mount of Olives*. Some translations say that they sang a "hymn" (based on the Greek *humneo*), but this could be misleading. Although there are many beautiful Christian hymns, many people forget that there are also Jewish hymns within the liturgy. In this context, Matthew is obviously referring to the Hallel, which is sung at the end of every *seder*. How appropriate this hymn would be, as it includes such messianic verses as, "This is the day [of redemption at Passover] the Lord has made" and "Blessed is he [the Messiah] who comes in the name of the Lord" (cf. Psalm 118:24-26). The band of disciples concluded the *seder* with their rabbi, singing about the prophetic events soon to be fulfilled before their eyes.

Before we leave the teaching on the last *seder,* we must address a couple more issues. The first concerns the timing of celebration of this remembrance meal. Church history is filled with discussions on how often believers should celebrate what they call "communion/ the Eucharist/the Lord's Supper." Is it to be celebrated every month, every week, or even every day? The debate will no doubt continue, but it is always helpful to consider the original context of Yeshua's teaching. While he does not seem to assign a specific time for the remembrance meal, we must not forget it is a Passover *seder*! It was not just any bread that he took up, so it is a particular piece of *matzah* (*afikoman*) that is celebrated exclusively at our *seder* meals. Similarly, he did not pick up just any cup of wine, but the highly symbolic Cup of Redemption, the third cup of the *seder*.

What can we learn from this Jewish background? Although there can be some flexibility as to the times of the Lord's remembrance

(God must certainly appreciate any time his people celebrate him), it seems that Yeshua assumed that his followers would certainly remember his redemptive work on the holiday of *Pesach*. Churches and denominations will probably continue in their own interpretations regarding the time of communion, but how ironic that many do not celebrate the *seder*, the very meal during which so many spiritual lessons were taught! I am happy to say that many Christian groups are now showing their appreciation for their Jewish roots by having an annual Passover *seder*. The exact times will continue to vary (even among some Messianic Jews), but it seems most natural to remember the redemption of Messiah at the Jewish holiday celebrating our historic redemption.

The second consideration is personal. Where do we stand in relationship to Yeshua and his teaching at his last *seder*? Even if we understand all of the cultural and historical details, we must not miss the vital spiritual truths. Yeshua gave himself as the Passover lamb for Israel and all peoples. As commanded in the *Torah*, have we personally tasted of the lamb? Have we received the gift of redemption sent by the Father? Are we walking as the redeemed remnant of God's people? May we all join the celebration of the coming *seder* of Messiah and sing the Psalms of Praise together!

The Arrest of Yeshua 26:31-56

Matthew now records the events of the hours immediately following the *seder* in the Upper Room. Upon the disciples' arrival at the Mount of Olives, Yeshua gives them a somber prophecy as he predicts that *tonight you will all lose faith in me*. As with their encounter at the *seder* a few hours earlier, it must have seemed inconceivable that any or all of them would desert their rabbi. Yet not only would this happen, but, according to Yeshua, it is actually part of God's larger prophetic plan. It is in *the Tanakh* that God himself states, "I will strike the shepherd dead, and the sheep of the flock will be scattered" (cf. Zechariah 13:7).

The prophet, who has much to say about the appearance of *Mashiach* in Chapters 12-14, predicted a most unusual occurrence in the life of the coming Messiah. In the original Hebrew, Zechariah says it is ADONAI himself Who calls for the strike against "the man close to me/*amiti*,"a fitting description of the close relationship to the Father. While many interpret this verse as pertaining to the kings of Judah in the days of their calamity, Yeshua applies it to himself as the unique representative of the Father. In the typology of the *Mashiach ben Yosef*/ suffering Messiah concept, God himself will strike the Messiah.

This reminds us that the events leading up to Yeshua's death were not tragic turns in man-made history, but, rather, were directly initiated by God as part of his divine plan of redemption. Yet in the process of striking the Shepherd, the flock will be scattered. Yeshua predicts the direct fulfillment of God's plan, as one of the twelve has already arranged to betray him and the other eleven will surprisingly deny their association with him in the hours to come. The twelve sheep will be scattered temporarily, and yet we should not overlook the larger implications. The entire flock of Israel will be scattered in the tragic Diaspora in 70 CE, just one generation after these events. If this verse was the last word, it would be a sad commentary on the Passover events, but there is more. Yeshua adds that after he has *been raised*, he *will go ahead* of the disciples *into the Galil*. The death of the Messiah is both unavoidable and essential, but the ultimate victory will come as he conquers death through the Resurrection. In response to Yeshua's statements, Kefa/Peter boldly proclaimed, "I will never lose faith in you even if everyone else does."

Although Kefa's faith and commitment are commendable, Yeshua reveals that even this key disciple *will disown me three times before the rooster crows*. The statement is both literal and yet filled with spiritual lessons. In the Talmudic world, there was much speculation

about the reality of the spirit world, both good and evil. The rooster
was just one animal regarded by some as representative of the power
of darkness as it crows in the dark (Tractate Sanhedrin 63b). Yeshua
predicts that sometime before morning dawns, even Kefa will deny
him, which is aptly symbolized by the rooster crowing. But Kefa
protests Christ's statement, claiming that "even if I must die with
you, I will never disown you!" *All the talmidim said the same thing,*
although Yeshua knew better.

At this point, Yeshua *went with his talmidim to a place called
Gat-Sh'manim*/Gethsemane. This location is identified as a place to
press (Hebrew *gat*) oil (*shemen*). It could also have had the appearance
of a garden or orchard, as there were olive trees growing nearby.
Specifically Yeshua chooses the place for some of his last prayers before
his arrest. In this sense, it is appropriate, as he himself will endure great
agony (crushing the oil) at the place well known for that task.

The location of the oil press on the Mount of Olives is quite
symbolic as well, as this hill east of Jerusalem is to play a vital role in
the appearance of the Messiah (cf. Zechariah 14:4). Yeshua bids his
disciples to *sit over there* while he goes nearby to *pray*. He did take
Kefa and Zavdai's/Zebedee's two sons with him, as *grief and anguish*
start to press on his soul. It is in these dark hours of the first night of
Passover that Yeshua comes to this special place for prayer.

Matthew testifies that Yeshua was *filled with sadness* even to the
point of death. Because of his tremendous trial, Yeshua requests that
his inner circle *remain here and stay awake* with him. He went on
to the hilly slope a little farther, where *he fell on his face praying*.
Matthew records the earnest prayer of Messiah, no doubt overheard
by the other disciples.

His first request was that, *if possible*, to *let this cup pass* from
him. The idiom of "a cup" is often symbolic in Judaism of tasting a
certain experience. This would be fresh in the mind of Yeshua and his
talmidim, as they had just partaken of the cups of the *seder* that very

evening. Certainly Yeshua was beginning to anguish over the reality of his impending physical suffering and death. And how much more so given that he knew his death would be at the hands of the Romans on a torturous execution-stake. But Yeshua also would have realized the even larger implications of his cup of suffering, namely, spiritual separation from a Heavenly Father whom he had always known!

Despite all of the anguish of body and soul, Yeshua adds a remarkable statement to his prayer—*Not what I want, but what you want!* Messiah's love and commitment for all people is revealed once again in these words. Even though in his humanity he would have gladly passed on the suffering ahead of him, Yeshua also knew that by his suffering, the world's redemption would be purchased! He therefore gladly submitted his prayer and attitude to the Father since he knew he had to fulfill his purpose.

As Yeshua broke away from the first part of his sincere time of prayer, *he returned* to find the *talmidim sleeping*. How disappointing to him, as he rebuked them by questioning, *were you so weak that you couldn't stay awake with me for even an hour?* Of course the hour was very late and they had just partaken of a full *seder*, not to mention four cups of wine. Nonetheless, it was a crucial hour in Yeshua's life, and he needed his disciples' support. He exhorted his disciples to *stay awake and pray* that they would *not be put to the test*. They, too, needed much prayer at this critical time, for even if *the spirit indeed is eager, the human nature is weak*.

Having awakened his close disciples, Yeshua now returned for *a second time and prayed*. It is interesting to note that he essentially repeats the same prayer request, saying, "My Father, if this cup cannot pass away unless I drink it, let what you want be done." As with the first time, Yeshua *returned and found* the *talmidim sleeping because their eyes were so heavy*. Even with this disappointment (or maybe because of it!), Messiah left them again and went off to pray *a third time*. Matthew reports that Yeshua prayed *the same words* this time as well. He finally rouses the disciples with some sobering words, as he proclaims "for now, go on sleeping, take your rest… Look! The time has come for the Son of Man to be betrayed into the hands of sinners." With that startling statement, a group of Jewish religious leaders and assistants approached, being led by *Y'hudah/ Judas*, to make their arrest of the Messiah.

Based on Matthew's description, this is not just a mob from the streets, but, no doubt, official representatives of the Sanhedrin akin to the Temple police. Matthew describes the group as *a large crowd carrying swords and clubs, from the head cohanim and elders of the people*. In an interesting side note from the *Talmud*, it is written that the House of *Chaniyah/Annas* (the High Priest) was so corrupt because its members were known "to beat people with clubs" (Tractate Pesachim 57a). *Y'hudah* had *arranged to give them a sign*al in the form of a deceptive greeting. It is the one he greets with a *kiss*, often a sign of a disciple's respect for his rabbi, (cf. Tractate Rosh Hashanah 2:7), whom the leaders will want to detain. Although the full moon of Passover would have made the sky brighter, they would still need exact identification of this person in the middle of the night.

At this point, a strange mix of words and interaction between Yeshua and his betrayer were heard and observed. Unabashedly, *Y'hudah went straight up to* Yeshua and greeted him by saying, *"Shalom, Rabbi!"* While Y'hudah is kissing him, Yeshua responds with an acknowledgment, *"Friend, do what you came to do."* It is one of the great enigmas of history that Yeshua would be betrayed by one of his closest disciples and, at the same time, receive that betrayal as a sovereign work of God.

What on the surface seems to be a great tragedy to many is actually a fulfillment of the Father's plan of eternal redemption. And yet, Y'hudah is not just a pawn in God's plan but is also held accountable for his actions. In situations like this, that we cannot fully comprehend, believers find comfort in the confession of our forefather Avraham that "the Judge of all the earth will do what is just" (Genesis 18:25). With this dramatic act of betrayal, the officials *laid hold of* Yeshua *and arrested him.*

Even the disciples fail to comprehend the enormity of the unfolding situation. One of them (identified as Kefa in Luke's account) even *reached for his sword and struck at the servant of the cohen hagadol, cutting off his ear.* At the time it must have been a most natural response, but it was not a response of one who could discern the entire spiritual picture.

Yeshua thus gently rebukes his follower and exhorts him to *put the sword back where it belongs.* His Kingdom will not come by the force of man. In fact, the *one who uses the sword will die by the sword.* If it was God's will, Yeshua could call on the Father to *instantly provide more than a dozen armies of angels* to deliver him from this distress. But the amazing plan of messianic redemption must include this betrayal and the ultimate death of Yeshua. Indeed, numerous *passages in the Tanakh* are *fulfilled* when all these things *happen this way.*

At this point, Yeshua turns to the crowd members and challenges them with some convicting questions. Why are they coming against him *the way they would the leader of a rebellion?* He and his followers were not seeking the violent overthrow of the Romans, or anyone else for that matter. Why didn't they arrest him in the openness of the *Temple court* where he was *teaching* on a daily basis? Even the unusual manner of Messiah's arrest was orchestrated so that *what the prophets wrote may be fulfilled* (cf. Zechariah 13:7; Isaiah 53; etc.). Even the minute details of Messiah's betrayal came to pass, as *the talmidim all deserted him and ran away.* Yeshua is about to fulfill all of the required events associated with the mission of the suffering Messiah, *Mashiach ben Yosef.* He is now alone, forsaken by his disciples, and yet prepared to complete the final chapter of his earthly ministry for the salvation of Israel and the Nations.

The Legal Trials of Messiah   26:57-27:26

The Preliminary Hearing Before Caiaphas   26:57-75

After his arrest by some of the religious authorities, Yeshua is led to *Kayafa*/Caiaphas, who was the reigning *cohen hagadol*/high priest. Matthew records the fact that there will be, in essence, two distinct legal hearings for Yeshua—one by the Jewish authorities and the other by the Romans. The former had jurisdiction over the religious matters of the Jewish community and, as such, could mete out appropriate punishments for any guilty defendants. In first-century Israel, there was one major exception—carrying out the death penalty. Although the Romans were known generally to respect the decisions of the local communities under their rule, they took control of any capital punishment issues. This was viewed as the prerogative of the state.

Matthew here gives us details of the first part of the legal proceedings against Yeshua. It is perhaps better understood as not an official trial, as many of the requirements for such are missing and there are several inconsistencies regarding Jewish legal decorum. It was more likely considered a preliminary hearing by some of the religious authorities to examine the case against Yeshua and subsequently make a recommendation to the Roman leaders. Because of this political reality in the first century, the hearing would naturally seek evidence that would be of greater concern to their Roman oppressors. As for the details of the hearing, the *Talmud* Tractate that specifically deals with such legal issues says the following about capital offenses:

> "They hold the trial during the daytime and the verdict must also be reached during the daytime. A verdict of acquittal may be reached on the same day, but a verdict of conviction not until the following day. Therefore trials may not be held on the eve of the Sabbath or on the eve of a Festival day" (Tractate Sanhedrin 4:1).

It must be pointed out that this meeting with *Kayafa* took place in the middle of the night, after Yeshua's *seder* with his disciples. According to the legal discussion in the *Talmud*, all capital cases must be tried during the daytime, presumably to ensure a fair and open hearing of such important cases. Similarly, it is mentioned that any verdict for a capital case can only be issued during the daytime hours, which may also serve as a metaphor for all Jewish legal decisions being "in the light." Likewise, this meeting with Yeshua could not be a full trial, given that any guilty verdict must be delayed at least until the next day.

Adding to the questions regarding Yeshua's hearing is the fact that it occurs on a *Shabbat* or Holy Day (both in this case). This would normally present a legal obstacle although there are cases where such a meeting could be held if it was considered an emergency (Tractate Sanhedrin 45b).

All of these indicators, along with other internal evidences, lead many to view this first step by some of the Jewish authorities not as a "trial" but as a preliminary hearing in an emergency situation. We must add to these facts that some high-profile Sanhedrin members, such as Nicodemus and Yosef of Arimethea, missed the meeting (cf. *Yochanan*/John 19:38-39)! Matthew specifies that some *Torah-teachers and elders were assembled* for this hearing, and it is noted that *Kefa followed* the group into *the courtyard of the cohen hagadol* with the hope of seeing *what the outcome would be*.

In this setting and context, it is no surprise that the Jewish leaders would examine the evidence against Yeshua. Matthew here notes that the meeting included some of the *head cohanim and the whole Sanhedrin*. For the reasons stated above, plus the fact that this meeting took place at the home of the High Priest (and not at the usual Temple court), we must still understand this as referring to representatives from these two groups and not the entire convened religious court. Undoubtedly, the group would represent a legal quorum (minimum of

23 out of 71 members), so the writer uses this phraseology (Tosefta Sanhedrin VII.I).

Consistent with the role of a preliminary hearing, the leaders move forward in their examination of the actions of Yeshua. Matthew makes it clear that the group was forced to seek *false evidence*. This was not to say that they were blatantly overlooking any real evidence, but that the real evidence did not support their preconceived ideas. After the last three and a half years of dealing with the words and works of Yeshua, this group of leaders had decided that he was guilty of religious crimes. Since they could not confirm any legitimate arguments against Yeshua, they needed to seek some kind of weighty evidence elsewhere so they might carry out their wishes to *put him to death*.

After unsuccessfully interviewing several false witnesses, the committee finally comes up with *two people who came forward* with a controversial claim. According to them, *this man* (Yeshua) *said, "I can tear down God's Temple and build it again in three days."* The statement itself seems to be taken out of context.

Indeed Yeshua made such a public statement, but the gospel writers interpret it in an allegorical way as referring to Yeshua's own death and resurrection on the third day (cf. *Yochanan*/John 2:19). Likewise. the integrity of the two witnesses could be questioned, as they refer to Yeshua as "this man," apparently a title of contempt when one wanted to avoid even the mention of a name. With this formal charge, the High Priest *Kayafa* stands up and cross-examines Yeshua, asking for his response. It came as a surprise to the group that Yeshua *remained silent* and said nothing. This could be for two reasons. Messiah surely realizes that any answer to such charges could actually backfire and give the leaders more misinterpreted evidence. The silence of Yeshua is also a fulfillment of the prophetic description of the Messiah under duress (cf. Isaiah 53:7).

This must have been aggravating to Kayafa, as it posed a major obstacle to the proceedings. Because of that, the High Priest boldly moves forward by putting Yeshua officially *under oath,* even using a traditional formula as found in the *Talmud* (Tractate Shevuot 4:3). The oath is intensified, as it is administered in the name of the *living God*. Kayafa pushes the issue to what is really the most salient point: "Tell us if you are the Mashiach, the Son of God!"

At this juncture, Yeshua feels it is good to answer a straightforward question as opposed to the previous false accusations. His response is both powerful and challenging, as he first points out that "the words are your own." This is probably the perfect answer, as it focuses not on Yeshua's own interpretation of the question but on the words of the inquirer. In essence, Yeshua is affirming that whatever the views of Kayafa about the concept of *Mashiach*, he fulfills it! As such, he has a unique relationship with God as his son (cf. Psalm 2; Proverbs 30).

But just to be totally clear, Yeshua adds the detail that one day everyone *will see the Son of Man sitting at the right hand of HaG'vurah and coming on the clouds of heaven*. To these educated rabbis and priests, the phrase would invoke a clear image of the appearance of the Messiah. In *Tehillim*/Psalm 110, the Messiah is invited to sit at the place of honor (*HaG'vurah* being a Hebrew term meaning "the Power," a common substitute for the actual name of God). In Daniel 7, the writer speaks of his vision of the coming *Mashiach* from the clouds of heaven. Both phrases were shocking and deeply thought-provoking. It became quite evident that this Yeshua of Nazareth was claiming to be much more than a good rabbi or even a prophet. He clearly claimed (although it is surprisingly denied today in some quarters) to be the unique Messiah sent from the God of Israel.

Although some modern theologians might seek to downplay the life of Yeshua, the response of the Jewish leaders who actually heard him face to face is quite compelling. Not only did this confirm their own misgivings about Yeshua, but it provided a perfect basis for taking this case to the Romans for adjudication. The claim of messiahship was indeed controversial within the Jewish community,

356 / YESHUA, KING MESSIAH

but it would have been explosive to the Roman leadership that was always fearing a political uprising.

Upon hearing Yeshua's straightforward response, *the cohen hagadol tore his robes* and declared his religious opinion— "Blasphemy!" It is another enigma of the preliminary hearing that the High Priest Kayafa tore his robes, an act strictly forbidden in the *Torah* (cf. Leviticus 21:10). This was to maintain an atmosphere of objectivity while seeking legal justice. The tearing of the garment (Hebrew *kria*) is still in Judaism today a sign of utmost grief and despair, usually reserved for the mourning ritual at a funeral.

For the High Priest or any judge to show such emotion at a legal hearing would be inexcusable, as it would clearly influence the other members making these important decisions. *Kayafa*/Caiaphas lost control at this seemingly preposterous statement by Yeshua. Surely this rebel rabbi from the Galil could not be the powerful Messiah? Of course there are two possible answers to this question. If Yeshua of Nazareth is not the Messiah, then his own statements about his divine origins would constitute blasphemy. But if Yeshua is in fact the divine Messiah, there is no blasphemy but, rather, a profound declaration of this spiritual reality.

Kayafa now asks two vital questions of his rabbinic colleagues: "Why do we still need witnesses?" and "What is your verdict?" The answers were clear and unequivocal: Yeshua is *guilty* and therefore *deserves death!* If the quorum of the council was convinced of this verdict, then the logical sentence would indeed be death since blasphemy was one of the most egregious sins in the *Torah* (cf. Leviticus 24:16). Although it is not specifically mentioned here, one definition of blasphemy in classical Judaism was the pronouncing of the Divine Name (Tractate Sanhedrin 7:5). Could this be related to Yeshua's unusual earlier statements before the religious authorities?

At this point, things seem to get out of hand. Matthew records that *they spit in his face and pounded him with their fists,* both actions of contempt and rejection (cf. Isaiah 50:5-6). These actions could have been those of overzealous leaders or, as Luke notes, were taken by the military guards who were present at the proceedings (cf. Luke 22:63). Either way, the aggressors would have thought themselves justified in light of the outrageous claims of this rabbi. They capped their mockery by striking Yeshua and even beseeching him as *"Messiah"* to *prophesy* as to *who hit you that time?*

Matthew now turns his attention back to another important person, also named Kayafa, of that Passover late night. Kefa (same root word as Caiaphas) is still *sitting outside in the courtyard* of the priestly home. It is here that *a servant girl* comes up to him and accuses him of being *with* Yeshua *from the Galil*. Peter had tried to keep a low profile in this potentially dangerous situation. He desired to know the fate of his master but, as predicted, was about to be severely tested.

Once again, Kefa shows some faith and chutzpah, as he at least stays close to his rabbi when all others had fled. But Kefa strongly *denied* this statement *in front of everyone by saying, "I don't know what you're talking about!"* With this first plea of ignorance, Kefa undoubtedly hoped that the suspicion would end. But *another girl* sees him and says, "This man was with Yeshua of Natzeret." With this second accusation, *Kefa* even swears (in the sense of an oath) that he doesn't even *know the man*. However, even the religious oath is not enough to quell the suspicions of some.

After a little while, some *bystanders approached Kefa and said, "You must be one of them—your accent gives you away."* This is a most intriguing statement that reveals some cultural differences between the local Judeans in Jerusalem and any visiting Galileans. These two Jewish groups were known to have differences, not only in some religious customs, but in their dialects as well (cf. Tractate Eruvin 53a). It was probably comparable to a Mississippi Jew, with his southern accent and simpler ways, visiting a New York Jew, with his New York accent and more sophisticated ways!

This time Kefa took another oath and even invoked *a curse on himself* by saying, "I do not know the man!" The depths of his denials were confirmed by the prophetic sign, as *immediately a rooster crowed.* At that dramatic moment, *Kefa remembered what* Yeshua *had said* about his denials and the subsequent sign of a rooster. Luke also includes the detail that Yeshua looked directly at Kefa at that moment (cf. Luke 22:61). Peter must have felt such a weight of conviction that he left the courtyard and *cried bitterly.*

It must have been a moment of indescribable grief when Peter realized what he had just done, but his words of remorse also indicate a spirit of repentance in addition to that grief. It would be a difficult couple of days for Kefa, but his faith (and leadership in the Messianic movement) would soon be restored after the events of the third day.

Perhaps many of us can relate to the experience of Peter. We surely have our moments of doubt and, sadly, disappointment. However, it is most encouraging to see Yeshua's mercy and love toward this wayward *talmid,* as it reminds us of his great patience with us even today! Would we have stood with Yeshua at his moment of great need? We would all like to say most certainly. But our fallen human nature is quite unpredictable. One thing is for sure: We should all be thankful for God's great love expressed to us even when we fail him. Sadly, Yeshua was not fully received by all of our people when he came the first time. Yet, we know that in God's unfathomable plan, redemption was being accomplished for Israel and the whole world. We, like Kefa, may have fallen in our faith at times, but the real question is "where are we in our relationship with Yeshua?" His hand reaches out to us even this day.

The Inquiry Before the Sanhedrin   27:1-10

Matthew continues to document the events of the last hours of Yeshua's earthly life. Having recorded the details of the late night arrest and hearing before Kayafa, the disciple now tracks the events of that early morning of the first day of Passover. According to Jewish reckoning, it is still 15 Nisan since the biblical day starts at sundown the previous day. We are told that *early in the morning, all the cohanim and elders met to plan how to bring about Yeshua's death.* This description seems to indicate that this is not just a preliminary hearing as took place earlier, but an official meeting at which at least a quorum of Sanhedrin leaders was present to decide the next step regarding the rabbi from Galilee. This would be in line with the policy that such major decisions should be made only in the daytime hours on a day after the initial hearing (cf. Tractate Sanhedrin 4:1).

It had already been determined that there were sufficient charges (blasphemy) to warrant the death penalty. The problem with the first-century religious structure was that it did not have the power under Rome to unilaterally carry out that punishment. Consequently, some of the religious leaders meet here to consider the further step of determining how they might hand Yeshua over to the Romans and convince them of the need for their intervention.

Strictly religious charges like the messiah issue would not necessarily get the attention of the secular Roman authorities. However, if Yeshua's claims of messiahship could be interpreted as a potential enthroning of a "king," then the Romans would have a vested interest in dealing with this case. The last thing the local Roman leaders needed was another Jewish riot or rebellion, as this could have a ripple effect throughout other regions of their empire. With this in mind, the Jewish leaders put Yeshua *in chains* and hand him *over to Pilate*, the ruling *governor* of Judea.

Sometimes readers of the New Testament underestimate the negative description of Pilate. Certainly the details of the Gospels are accurate in recording his unstable spirit in dealing with the Yeshua situation. But those living under his rule in first-century Israel were well aware of his extreme wickedness and iron fist. The historian Josephus records, for example, how Pilate once pilfered funds from the Jerusalem Temple treasury in order to fund one of his aqueduct projects. When there was a strong protest against this injustice, Pilate ordered hundreds of his troops to dress as civilians and infiltrate the Jewish crowd. Hidden under their garb were clubs and when the signal was given, many Jews were brutally beaten to death (cf. Antiquities 18:55-62).

We must keep in mind that it was before this unscrupulous puppet of Rome that Yeshua would appear in the next stage of his trial. Pilate should not be regarded as a sincere political leader whose hand was forced by a group of Jewish leaders. That would be a ridiculous show of weakness on his part and inconsistent with the historical reality of Rome's power. To the contrary, Pilate had all the power to do whatever he desired with this volatile situation, and he should be judged based on his own chosen actions. While some people may overlook the brutal Roman governor (and even blame the Jews!), the New Testament clearly delineates that Pilate is culpable for his part in these proceedings (cf. Acts 4:27).

Matthew describes an important interlude before the encounter with Pilate. Early in the morning, the betrayer *Y'hudah saw that* Yeshua *had been condemned and* Y'hudah *was seized with remorse.* We have already spoken about some of the enigmatic issues revolving around this close follower of Yeshua. Was he disenchanted with the apparent delay in Yeshua's kingdom? Did his definition of the Messiah not match up to Yeshua's later words? Whatever his reason, we should view Y'hudah as a sincere and even most trusted member of Yeshua's inner circle who, for his own reasons, decided to turn away from the Messianic movement. It is significant that the word "remorse" is used to describe Judas' feelings, as opposed to the different word that would be translated as "repentance." This will be verified in the context of the passage, as well as by Y'hudah's actions. His first action was to return *the thirty silver coins to the head cohanim and elders.* As recorded earlier, this was the amount paid to

Judas for his cooperation in the arrest of Yeshua. The amount perhaps also makes a prophetic statement about the attitude of the leaders and Y'hudah, as thirty pieces was the *Torah* compensation given for a dead slave (cf. Exodus 21:32; Zechariah 11:12)!

Y'hudah was feeling such grief over his recent actions that he now felt compelled to return the payment. He condemns his own actions by confessing, "I have sinned in betraying an innocent man to death." The Jewish leaders, for their part, were not sympathetic to Yeshua's plight or to Judas' feelings, as they answered, "What is that to us…that's your problem." Y'hudah's spirit was in such turmoil at this point that he hurled *the pieces of silver into the sanctuary and left* the religious leaders. The weight of guilt was clearly overwhelming for this wayward disciple—even to the point of death, as Matthew records that Judas *went off and hanged himself.*

Though it is tragic that Judas felt compelled to take this ultimate action, only God knows the depths of his heart. But here we also see a distinct difference between being "remorseful" and being truly "repentant." Y'hudah clearly felt badly about his actions, yet did not turn to God in the spirit of *t'shuvah*/repentance. Kefa also failed Yeshua in a sad way with his threefold denial of his Messiah. Yet, even with that terrible sin, Kefa truly repented and was ultimately restored to Yeshua. Tragically, Y'hudah never displays the true fruit of *t'shuvah,* and his life ends accordingly. Some have noted an apparent discrepancy between Matthew's account of Judas' death and Luke's account in Acts 1:18-19. They are not irreconcilable, however. One viable interpretation is that Y'hudah hanged himself, and his body subsequently fell when the rope gave way. Whatever the details, the enigma of Judas remains, and it is best to leave the ultimate judgment of these matters to God himself.

The *head cohanim* now found themselves faced with a religious dilemma. They realized that it would be *prohibited to put* the shekels *into the Temple treasury because* it would be considered *blood money.*

Since they had used this money to facilitate the arrest and death of Yeshua, it would not be proper to use it for any sanctified purpose. Evidently, they were totally convinced that it was best to turn Yeshua over to the Romans, even if the reasons for doing so might be highly questionable. And yet these same leaders were concerned about the proper allocation of the returned money!

Matthew holds nothing back, even when he must reveal some of the darkest aspects of human nature. In order to assuage their own conscience, the leaders decided to use the returned shekels *to buy the potter's field as a cemetery for foreigners.* Apparently, it was their way of trying to turn a shady moral dilemma into a religious *mitzvah.* The place was given the name "Field of Blood" and was evidently used for the burial of those who either could not afford one or who would present a *halakhic* problem for a Jewish cemetery. Y'hudah himself would be a classic example as one who committed suicide, which is expressly against Jewish law.

Matthew concludes his description of this situation by once again drawing the reader's attention to its prophetic significance. The *thirty silver coins* and the resultant purchase of a *potter's field* are both said to have been predicted by *the prophet Jeremiah.* In various passages of that scroll, there are references to potters (18:2-3) as well as purchasing a field (32:6-15).

It is interesting and yet quite logical that Matthew includes some details from Zechariah's scroll in this quote as well. In the rabbinic list of the prophets, they are often grouped together with the first scroll being Jeremiah, which is also the longest text. In classic Jewish fashion, Matthew combines a number of prophetic passages and puts them under the heading of the main scroll. We are thus reminded once again that so many amazing messianic details from the *Tanakh* were minutely fulfilled in the life of Yeshua of Nazareth. It should be a sign even to us today!

The Trial Before Pilate   27:11-26

After the sad events associated with Judas' death, Matthew focuses on the next stage of Yeshua's legal proceedings. The Messiah had been arrested and charged by some of the leaders of his own community. In hopes that the Romans would be amenable to the wishes of the Sanhedrin committee, they had delivered him to the secular rulers. On that morning of the first day of *Pesach*/Passover (15 Nisan), the Romans brought this young rabbi *before* Pilate, *the governor.* The fate of the man they viewed as a rebellious, self-proclaimed king would now be entirely in the hands of this insecure Roman leader.

Pilate opens his interrogation with a pointed question: "Are you the King of the Jews?" This, of course, reflects the governor's uneasiness with the idea that there may be some political competition coming from a Jewish religious leader. Perhaps the Sanhedrin leaders had paraphrased their own language regarding the question of Yeshua's messiahship when they contacted the Roman authorities. In the Jewish understanding, the *Mashiach* was to be a king, and it was this aspect that would most likely get the attention of the civil authorities. In his account, Luke adds that Yeshua was also accused of sedition against Rome (cf. Luke 23:2).

To this direct question, Yeshua gives a direct answer: "The words are yours." While the response might seem evasive to some, it is actually the most appropriate way to affirm his claims. To respond with a direct "yes" would imply that Yeshua was seeking an earthly kingdom at this time. A "no" answer would deny the fact that he is in reality a king. Yeshua's exact response would cover all interpretations of the question; in essence, he is the king of Israel but not in the sense that Pilate may envision.

Matthew now turns his attention to a most unusual interchange. With the arrest of Yeshua by the Romans and their interrogation of him, another legal detail is now highlighted—*it was the governor's custom during a festival to set free one prisoner.* This gesture would be doubly symbolic for the festival of Passover, which, at its core, is a celebration of freedom from slavery. Undoubtedly, the Roman leadership followed this custom with hopes that the benevolent action would encourage a good relationship with their citizens.

Because *Pesach* is a festival of freedom for all Jews, it is not surprising that the *Mishnah* specifies that a Passover sacrifice could be offered "for one whom they have promised to bring out of prison" (Tractate Pesachim 8:6). This could very well be an early allusion to the Roman practice described here. Matthew adds the detail that the prisoner could be *whomever the crowd asked for,* so Pilate turned to the small assembly for their opinion. Some might think it is a coincidence that the *notorious prisoner* under consideration was named *Yeshua bar-Abba* (literally, "Yeshua son of the father")! While some early manuscripts record the name as simply *Bar-Abba,* significant manuscript evidence exists for the fuller name given here.

Pilate wanted to expedite the situation as quickly as possible, so he simply asked the crowd which man they wanted to *set free—Bar-Abba*/Barabbas *or* Yeshua, *called the Messiah?* Matthew now explains some of Pilate's thoughts on the issue, noting that the governor perceived that it was *out of jealousy that they handed over* Yeshua. Another strange occurrence took place as Pilate was sitting in court. His wife sent him a message to "leave that innocent man alone" because she had an agonizing *dream* concerning this so-called messiah. On the surface it might thus seem like an easy case to adjudicate, but *the head cohanim persuaded the crowd to ask for Bar-Abba* to be released and Yeshua to be *executed on the stake.*

This is a reference to the most torturous form of execution in the ancient world, first developed by the Phoenicians and later perfected by the Romans. When we think of a "cross" today, we might think of the religious symbol illustrated by two perpendicular beams. Archaeology has shown, however, that more often a cross consisted of a single stake or diagonal beams on which the victim would be nailed.

It was not just the pain of having nails driven through the wrists and ankles (although that would be bad enough), but also the resultant physiological effects on the entire body that made this execution so feared. Sometimes death would come by heart failure after such trauma. Most often, the victims would die of slow suffocation as their own body weight would make it impossible to breathe adequately. The Romans even adapted this execution method by placing a foot beam so that the condemned could push up to catch their breath, though only temporarily until their strength gave out.

Even before execution on a cross, brutal guards were known to inflict upon their victim an assortment of beatings and tortures. The first-century historian Josephus testifies that he witnessed some prisoners being "flayed to the bone with scourges," as they were often whipped with multiple leather thongs, each laced with pieces of metal or bone (War 6:304). The end result was an excruciating and prolonged experience of unspeakable magnitude. In the pagan world, virtually anything would be allowed in the treatment of the prisoners.

It should be noted that the *Torah* and Jewish values strongly condemned such actions. Even in the Jewish court cases in which 40 lashes might be fairly meted out, the religious authorities often held back one symbolic lash to reflect the *Torah*'s call for mercy (cf. Deuteronomy 25:3; II Corinthians 11:24). In the most extreme capital cases, the *Talmud* stipulated (based on the *Torah*) only four possible means of execution—stoning, burning, strangling, or slaying by sword (Tractate Sanhedrin 52a). Furthermore, these could be used only if they did not desecrate the physical body since all people, even criminals, are created in the image of God. They were just a means of execution. Even burning was usually done only after the person had already been executed. There could be no cruel or unusual punishment, a value carried over in our Western society today.

Since capital punishment was such a serious practice, ultimately the Sanhedrin stopped implementing it altogether, as reflected in the declaration of Rabbi Tarfon and Rabbi Akiva that, "Had we belonged to the Sanhedrin, during Judea's independence, no person would ever have been executed" (Tractate Makkot 1:10). Of course, under the first-century Roman occupation, the right to carry out capital punishment was taken from the Jewish authorities.

It is important to note that the execution of Yeshua was not physically carried out by Jews, for two clear reasons. First, they lacked the authority to carry out such an execution, and, second, the torturous death by crucifixion was never a Jewish means of execution. How ironic and inaccurate that some still say today (even in sermons!) that "the Jews killed Jesus." Clearly there was a plan by some leaders to hand Yeshua over to the Romans, and for that they must be accountable. But it would not be Jews who drove the nails into the execution-stake.

The narrative continues with some follow-up questions from Pilate to the group of Jewish leaders before him. He pressed the question as to *which of the two* criminals they desired *to set free*. With a unified voice, the small crowd called out, "Bar-Abba!" That being so, Pilate asked the next logical question: "Then what should I do with Yeshua, called the Messiah?" Again the group's decision seemed unanimous, as they responded, "Put him to death on the stake!" It seems that Pilate was still unclear about the full situation regarding Yeshua and was somewhat perplexed as to the crowd's choice. When he inquired as to *what crime* Yeshua had committed, the crowd *shouted all the louder* that they desired his execution. The governor could see that the crowd was convinced of its decision and was even at the point of starting *a riot*. What follows next is one of the more graphic events in world history.

As stated earlier, we must remember that Pilate had total control of the situation in Jerusalem and could have easily commanded the release of Yeshua if he so desired. He evidently could not have cared less about this issue in the Jewish community and simply wanted to do what was politically expedient. Given his cruel history, what was the death of another Jew? In a self-serving gesture, Pilate *took water* and publicly *washed his hands, declaring that "My hands are clean of this man's blood; it's your responsibility."* Pilate could say whatever he wanted to, but the fact is that God would hold the Roman leader accountable for this great miscarriage of justice (Acts 4:27).

In response to Pilate's action and declaration, the crowd makes an emotional statement, "His blood is on us and our children!" Here is another highly charged statement that has been taken out of context innumerable times in history, right down to the present day. In fact, it wasn't until 1965 at Vatican II that the Roman Catholic Church finally rendered the decision that all Jews are not corporately responsible for the death of Jesus (followed more recently by several other denominations within Christianity). Much ugly history had transpired until then, with some residual misunderstandings continuing in some quarters of the modern Church.

So what happened here? There is no denying that this particular Jewish group made this declaration, but a few things must be clarified in this context. First, the physical location of the meeting with Pilate must be taken into account. We know it was at a place called the "Pavement of Judgment" within the famous Antonio Fortress complex, which served as military housing for the Romans guarding the Temple Mount area of Jerusalem. From a naïve reading of Matthew's account (not to mention some Hollywood portrayals of the event!), one might think there were tens of thousands of Jews appealing to Pilate. Recent archaeological discoveries have confirmed, however, that the courtyard for these proceedings was large enough to hold perhaps only 300 people! Again, there is no denying Matthew's account, but it helps us understand the situation when we realize that "the crowd" that was vehemently opposed to Yeshua was a relatively small group and certainly not representative of every Jew in Jerusalem, much less the entire Jewish world.

A second consideration is of the statement that this group makes. It is believable that perhaps 300 Jewish leaders and supporters would have made such a statement in the heat of the moment. Even if we assume that they correctly want to hold themselves accountable for their choice to reject Yeshua, does their statement bind all Jews everywhere? We would do well to remember that actually most Jews in this time had not yet even heard of Yeshua, and thus could not have rejected him, as they lived outside the land of Israel in places like Babylon. Just because this small group made such an oath, is it automatically binding even on their children?

The *Torah* has always taught the importance and blessing of individual responsibility. Every man answers for his own choices, irrespective of what others may think or say (cf. Ezekiel 18). Certainly the statement made by the group before Pilate cannot be applied to every subsequent generation of Jews. Again, believers must guard against such erroneous statements as "the Jews rejected Jesus." Such statements are not only inaccurate but cause much hurt and misunderstanding.

Of course it can be said that some (even many) Jews rejected Yeshua at this time. But what about the thousands of Jewish followers who embraced Yeshua, not to mention the tens of thousands of Jews who would soon be joining the Messianic Yeshua movement (cf. Acts 21:20)? From the first century to the present day, there has been a divided opinion in the Jewish community regarding Yeshua of Nazareth. In response to the crowd's request, the wavering Pilate *released Bar-Abba*. In accordance with Roman sentiment, he had Yeshua *whipped* and *handed him over to be executed on a stake*.

The Roman Execution   27:27-56

Matthew provides some of the graphic details of what transpired next on that first day of Passover. From the Pavement of Judgment where Pilate's interrogation took place, *the governor's soldiers took*

Yeshua *into the headquarters building* (Greek *praetorium*) in the Atonio Fortress overlooking the Temple Mount. A larger group (the whole battalion) gathered around this self-proclaimed "Jewish king" and proceeded to mistreat Yeshua as they so pleased. First, the soldiers humiliated Messiah, as *they stripped off his* clothes presumably down to his inner garment. To further amuse themselves, the soldiers *put on him a scarlet robe,* which was evidently their way of giving him kingly garments. Matthew also records how they continued by weaving *thorn-branches into a crown and put it on his head.*

Again, this was their way of mocking this rebel; yet, unbeknownst to them, they were also modeling an amazing spiritual truth. Yeshua indeed came to Israel and the entire world to be king and also to reverse the curse on the fallen world. At the Fall of mankind recorded in the early chapters of the *Torah*, God brought a judgment upon his rebellious creatures as he commanded the earth to bring forth thorns for the first time (cf. *B'resheet*/Genesis 3:18).

Much is said in the Prophets about one of the main works of the *Mashiach* being his restoration of the fallen paradise. The crown of thorns was at the same time a physically painful reminder of the ultimate work of messianic redemption that Yeshua will accomplish! The Romans continued their mockery as they *put a stick* in Yeshua's *right hand* and *kneeled down in front of him,* proclaiming "Hail to the King of the Jews!" Through it all, Messiah suffered in silence, knowing that through their great defiance, God was actually working his plan of redemption.

The soldiers weren't done yet, as *they spit* on the Messiah and even *used a stick to beat him about the head.* It was not unusual for a convicted criminal to actually die from the torture even before reaching the point of execution on a cross. Yeshua's condition must be what the prophet Isaiah had in mind in his description of the suffering servant (*Mashiach ben Yosef*) as "so disfigured that he didn't even seem human and simply no longer looked like a man" (Isaiah 52:14).

Matthew curtly notes that *when they had finished ridiculing* Yeshua, *they took off the robe, put his own clothes back on him and led him away to be nailed to the execution-stake.*

It is recorded that *as they were leaving* the Roman compound, the execution party met a certain man by the name of *Shim'on*. Matthew points out that *Shim'on* was from the area of North Africa called Cyrene. Undoubtedly, he would have been one of the many pilgrims in Yerushalayim fulfilling the mandate of Passover. Little did he know that he was about to become part of the most important *Pesach* since the days of Moses.

It would not be unusual for the Romans to recruit help from the general public when needed. One can only imagine why Yeshua needed assistance beyond his own human resources. He had been up all night—first at his *seder* and then at the place of the oil press (*Gat-Sh'manim*). From there, he was forced to attend two different legal hearings, which ultimately included the physical abuse by the Roman soldiers. On the march to the place of execution, it became evident that this Messiah from Galilee would need extra assistance. It was customary for criminals to carry their own execution-stake in their final death march. It was in this context that the Romans conscripted *Shim'on to carry* Yeshua's *execution-stake*. What a life-changing experience this must have been for this man! In his parallel account, Mark lists the personal names of Shim'on's sons, thereby implying that the whole family became Messianic Jews after this face-to-face encounter with the suffering Yeshua (cf. Mark 15:21).

The somber processional ultimately reached its destination, a place called *Gulgolta* (which means "place of the skull"). It is unclear whether this name is a reference to the shape of the hillside (as seen in the modern Garden Tomb) or simply to its purpose as a place of execution. *Gulgolta* was later translated into the Latin word for skull, *Calvary*. The exact location of Gulgolta has never been definitively proven, though the site is preserved at the current Church of the

Holy Sepulcher, where Western church tradition acknowledges the execution and burial of Yeshua. This is west of the Temple Mount, whereas the much later Garden Tomb (Protestant tradition) is located north of the Temple Mount. Very few have even considered the east side of the city (Mount of Olives area), although this was a vitally important place in tradition. We shall see that compelling biblical evidence exists for considering that possibility.

Wherever the exact location of Gulgolta, the soldiers set up Yeshua's execution-stake and prepared him for his last rites. Matthew notes with great interest that they gave Yeshua *wine mixed with bitter gall to drink*. This is consistent with a passage in the *Talmud* that states: "When one is led out to execution, he is given a goblet of wine containing a grain of frankincense, in order to benumb his senses, for it is written, Give strong drink unto him that is ready to perish, and wine unto the bitter in soul" (Tractate Sanhedrin 43a quoting Proverbs 31:6). As a well-educated Jew, Matthew saw many fulfillments of the *Tanakh* as he witnessed the death of Yeshua, even though it was carried out by the Romans.

It seems significant that Yeshua, upon *tasting* the sedative, declines to *drink it*. Could this be a way of embracing his death to the fullest extent since it would be the means of world redemption? The writer uses the shortest language possible to describe this horrendous means of execution, simply noting that *they nailed him to the stake*. The death of Yeshua as *Mashiach ben Yosef* is indisputably of central importance to the message of the New Testament, but it was considered unnecessary to delve into the gruesome details of that death.

The Roman soldiers then *divided his clothes among them by throwing dice*. Matthew points out that they specifically kept *watch over him* during his hours on the execution-stake. This probably reflects the fact that it was the responsibility of the soldiers (normally four of them per execution) to guarantee the death of the one in their custody.

It was common to place a statement of the charges over the head of the criminal, so in this case the soldiers *placed the written notice* stating: "This is Yeshua—The King of the Jews." This is a logical charge from the Roman perspective, as the Romans were more concerned about political sedition than a religious messiah. However, the charge was broad enough to also cover the accusations coming from some of the Jewish leaders that this Yeshua claimed to be King Messiah.

The Romans undoubtedly kept a busy schedule of executions, so it is not surprising to read that *two robbers were placed on execution-stakes with* Yeshua, *one on the right and one on the left.* Because this event was so public, various groups of people were beginning to notice the proceedings. Some people passed by while they *hurled insults at him, shaking their heads.* Their insults were both shocking and misinformed, as they confronted Yeshua with questions such as, "So you can destroy the Temple, can you, and rebuild it in three days?" Of course Yeshua never said he would literally destroy the Temple but, in rabbinic *midrash* form, used similar language to describe his own death and resurrection (cf. *Yochanan*/John 2:19).

The second provocation is even more ironic and startling, as some people called out, "Save yourself, if you are the Son of God, and come down from the stake!" As the true Messiah, Yeshua could have delivered himself if it was in fact the will of the Father. It is also recorded that some of the religious leaders joined in the derision during Yeshua's final earthly hours. Some of the *head cohanim along with the Torah-teachers and elders* are quoted as saying, "He saved others, but he can't save himself! So he's King of Israel, is he?" The irony of their statement should not be missed, as they challenge Yeshua to *come down from the stake* so that they would finally *believe him.* It must have seemed impossible that a rebel rabbi hanging on a Roman cross could be the true Messiah. Surely, the curse of such a death could not be put on the real King Messiah (cf. Deuteronomy 21:23: "A person who has been hanged on a tree is cursed by God").

The passersby, as well as these leaders, could not see that it was actually Yeshua's very presence on the execution-stake that was fulfilling the messianic redemption within God's mysterious plan.

These religious leaders even offer a scriptural principle to support their skepticism as they question Yeshua's predicament: "He trusted God? So, let him rescue him if he wants him!" (cf. Psalm 22:8 English). Did this rabbi not claim to be the *Son of God?* The logic must have seemed airtight (at least on the surface), proving that Yeshua was not the messiah but instead one with a curse on his head. The superficial evidence seemed so compelling that even *the robbers nailed up with him insulted him in the same way*. Luke adds that these criminals even called out for their own deliverance as proof of his messiahship (cf. Luke 23:39). With the true disciples momentarily scattered, the consensus was that Yeshua was a sad deceiver who was meeting his just reward.

The intensity builds as Matthew continues his description of the last hours of Yeshua's earthly life. The writer specifies the events starting *from noon* of that first day of Passover (still 15 *Nisan*) until the *three o'clock* hour. The times are significant both in a natural sense and in a traditional sense. It is obviously striking that at high noon, *all the Land was covered with darkness*. One might be tempted to attribute this to an eclipse; however, that would not be possible given the full moon of the first day of Passover. Certainly, the Heavenly Father was making a statement using supernatural means. It is not without precedent, as one need only recall the first Passover and the plague of darkness that came over the land of Egypt (cf. Exodus 10:22). Subsequently in the Scriptures, darkness is often associated with the judgment of God (cf. Amos 8:9; Joel 3:14-15).

Anyone in Jerusalem on that ominous day, whether Jew or non-Jew, could not escape the conclusion that the God of Israel was making a statement! Messiah was paying the price for mankind's sin as he hung on that execution-stake. From the traditional perspective, it was most obvious what was happening if one looked deeper. About three o'clock in the afternoon was the common time for the *minchah* prayers, and, in those days, the communal offering by the priests in the Temple. How much more so on this holy day of *Pesach* as the *levi'im* were preparing the annual sacrifice of the national Passover lamb! Of course tens of thousands of lambs had been koshered and eaten at *seders* on the previous night, as families recalled the redemption from Egypt. But it was also a vital tradition to offer this single *minchah* lamb, which was offered up on behalf of the entire nation of Israel. It is not a coincidence that Matthew notes the approaching death of Yeshua at the very time of the lamb offering.

The details of Yeshua's final words are recorded simply, yet very powerfully. *At about three,* Yeshua *uttered a loud cry, "Eli! Eli! L'mah sh'vaktani? (My God! My God! Why have you deserted me!)"* The call to God is in Hebrew, whereas the latter statement is in Aramaic, the common language of the day. It is manifestly clear that Yeshua quotes directly from Psalm 22 because of its messianic associations. While rabbis, both classic and modern, have various interpretations of this Psalm, one interpretation is that King David was travailing over the suffering of the future Son of David, King Messiah. "It was because of the ordeal of the Son of David that David wept, saying 'My strength is dried up like a potsherd'" (cf. Psalm 22:16 as quoted in Pesikta Rabbati 36:2). Yeshua's words, therefore, are not coincidental; rather, he is directly connecting his death with the prophetic suffering of the promised *Mashiach*.

Some of the *bystanders*, perhaps hearing from a distance, speculated that Yeshua might be calling out for the help of *Eliyahu*. The Hebrew phrase could have been easily misunderstood, and it was quite reasonable to hope for the intervention of the beloved prophet of Israel. Because he never experienced death, Elijah has long been the focus of such prayers as it is part of Jewish tradition that *Eliyahu* might appear to help those in need. To this day, we set a place with a special cup at our Passover *seders* with the expectation that the prophet might visit us and announce the arrival of King Messiah.

As some of the bystanders debated Yeshua's situation, *one of them ran and took a sponge, soaked it in vinegar and put it on a stick for him to drink.* Matthew's attention to this detail seems to underscore his association with this drink and another Psalm of a suffering person (cf. Psalm 69:21 English). The *Talmud* records that as a comfort to condemned criminals, a mixed drink would often be offered. "Give strong drink unto him that is ready to perish, and wine unto the bitter in soul" (Proverbs 31:6). It has been taught that gracious women in Jerusalem used to provide this potion voluntarily, but if they failed to provide it, it was supplied from the funds of the community" (Tractate Sanhedrin 43a).

Others at the execution-stake wanted to wait and see if *Eliyahu* would *come and rescue him.* Although Yeshua had not tasted the last cup of the *seder* on the previous night, it is clear here that he was willingly tasting the terrible death on the execution-stake or the Father's divine purpose. His cry to God must have been from the incomprehensible depths of his spirit, as his suffering was unique among mankind. Certainly there have been others who have suffered terrible fates in this earthly life. But none of these individuals was in the unique relationship with God as the Son of God, the Messiah, and all that implies. For the first time in eternity, the Son would be separated from the Heavenly Father as he took upon himself the sins of all humanity.

Yet within that incredibly dark moment, the cry of Yeshua reflects his ultimate faith in the Father. In his flesh, it may seem that he has been deserted; however, in his spirit, he has the firm conviction that the Father is still "my God." He then cried out a second time *in a loud voice* and *yielded up his spirit.* Even here, the language reflects the true reality of Yeshua's death. No one took his life from him; rather, he himself ultimately offered it up in order to fulfill the Father's amazing plan of world redemption. From Yeshua's messianic perspective, the is not a surprising tragedy but a divine completion of his calling—so much so that his final words are "it is accomplished!" (*Yochanan*/John 19:30).

Matthew now gives testimony of some astounding things that took place at the moment of Yeshua's death. As Messiah gave up his spirit, *the parokhet in the Temple was ripped in two from top to bottom.* This is the Hebrew name for the veil that separated the Holy Place from the Holy of Holies in the Jerusalem Temple. Even to this day, much of the ancient Temple format is present within the architecture of the modern synagogue. The Bema (raised platform) is usually the place where the Ark is situated on the east side of the building in synagogues in the Western world. This is to remind us of the place of the messianic hope, the city of Jerusalem. The modern Ark (a large cabinet) contains one or more *Torah* scrolls. Between the doors of the Ark and the scrolls is usually a curtain that is still called a *parokhet,* which is reminiscent of the massive curtain in the *Beit-Ha'Mikdash*/ Holy Temple.

The immensity of the Temple and its furnishings is well documented in Jewish literature. We are told that the main *parokhet*/ veil before the Holy of Holies was some 40 cubits long (60 feet) and 20 cubits (30 feet) wide. It consisted of a pattern of 72 squares, and the veil was the thickness of the palm of the hand. The statement that it took 300 priests to manipulate the *parokhet* (cf. Tractate Yoma 54a; Ketuvot 106a) may reflect some artistic exaggeration (but maybe not). With this in mind, we can better appreciate the miraculous event of the tearing of the *parokhet*! Matthew does note *an earthquake* at that very moment, which could have been a contributing factor to the tearing, but there seems to be more to the event. Not only were the veil's dimensions overwhelming, but it is recorded that it was torn from the top where no man could even reach. This stresses both the physical miracle, as well as the spiritual result. God was telling all

Israel and the world that the way into his presence had now been opened by the death of Messiah Yeshua.

Given such an astounding event described by the writers of the New Testament, we would expect some corroboration from other Jewish sources. Once again, the *Talmud* gives us a rather esoteric description of some strange events at exactly this time in Jewish history.

> "Our Rabbis taught: During the last forty years before the destruction of the Temple, the lot (For the Lord) did not come up in the right hand; nor did the crimson-colored strap become white; nor did the western-most light shine; and the doors of the *Hekal* (Temple) would open by themselves, until Rabbi Yochanan ben Zakkai rebuked them, saying: '*Hekal, Hekal,* why wilt thou be the alarmer thyself? I know about thee that thou wilt be destroyed, for Zechariah ben Ido has already prophesied concerning thee: Open thy doors, O Lebanon, that the fire may devour thy cedars'" (Tractate Yoma 39b).

This is an intriguing description of certain occurrences that started about 30 CE/AD (forty years before the destruction of the Temple in 70 CE)! The rabbis describe some changes in the Yom Kippur ceremony of the two goats (cf. Leviticus 16). Whereas the lot would always come up in the correct way, this changed in 30 CE. Likewise, the crimson strap on the scapegoat, which would normally turn white on Yom Kippur, suddenly ceased to change. The light of the *Menorah*/Lampstand representing the light of God's presence had some problems as well. All of these manifestations are not surprising to us Messianic Jews, as we know that Yeshua's death had vast implications for our relationship with God.

What is especially relevant to the current verses in Matthew is the description of the mysterious opening of the Temple doors. The Talmudic rabbis interpret this as a harbinger of the coming destruction of the Temple in 70 CE. It is as if the Temple doors (made from cedars from Lebanon) were opening to receive the destructive fire of the Romans. Our point here is that all of these things must be based on some sort of historical occurrence. If so, then this passage could very well be the Talmudic way of describing an incredible opening of doors (tearing the *parokhet*) in about 30 CE. It was actually a very well witnessed event, as we must remember that hundreds of Levites must have been on duty offering the *minchah* lamb for the nation at that very hour of 3:00 p.m.! If so many priests were eyewitnesses to this dramatic event, it would also logically explain why a large segment of the Levites were among the first Messianic Jews (cf. Acts 6:7). There were many signs given to our people on that unique day in history.

Matthew records more miraculous signs that took place at the hour of Messiah's death. After taking note of an earthquake that shook the region, Matthew says that many *graves were opened and the bodies of many holy people who had died were raised to life*. Of course, this could not be the final resurrection of the end time, as we continue to wait for that upon Messiah's return. But short-term resurrections that took place during some unusual junctures in Jewish history have been recorded. Elijah raised the son of the Shunamite woman (cf. II Kings 4), Rabbi Sha'ul raised his fallen yeshiva student (cf. Acts 20), and Yeshua raised his friend *Elazar*/Lazarus (cf. *Yochanan*/John 11). However, all of these persons died again and now await the Messianic Resurrection of the end time. And so it is here where Matthew documents that many were raised as a sign (albeit temporary) that the *Mashiach* has come and conquered death! It is another amazing sign to that generation, as these risen ones *went into the holy city where many people saw them*—a miraculous event no doubt.

Matthew cannot leave this subject without pointing out that even *the Roman officer* and his pagan soldiers were struck by the events around them. They *saw the earthquake* and *were awestruck* by the happenings. It seems significant that Matthew describes the soldiers as "seeing" the earthquake and not just "feeling" it. This seems to imply that the Romans were actually eyewitnesses also to the splitting of the veil and the opening of the Holy of Holies in the Temple. Something stood out to them in the spiritual world as they declared, "He really was a son of God."

This gives us an interesting insight when we realize that the Romans were standing right at the execution-stake at Gulgolta at the moment of Yeshua's death. Wherever Gulgolta was located, it was clearly outside the city or, as the *Torah* says, "outside the camp." However, the internal evidence of the gospels seems to indicate that the soldiers witnessed the effects of the earthquake east of the Temple Mount, where they could look directly at the torn veil in front of the Holy of Holies. If this is so, then the more likely location of Gulgolta would be on the Mount of Olives just east of the Golden Gate.

Perhaps it is significant that the only place of sacrifice outside the Temple area was on the Mount of Olives for the most central offering, the sacrifice of the Red Heifer. The ashes of this most vital sacrifice in the *Torah* were used to cleanse the entire Temple and its altars (Numbers 19). As if to highlight its importance, there is an entire Tractate of the *Talmud* (*Tractate Parah*) devoted to the details of this sacrifice during the Second Temple period.

One interesting statement notes that it was on the Mount of Olives that the priest immersed himself, killed the heifer, and sprinkled the blood of the sacrifice toward the Temple (Tractate Parah 3:6-10). The writer to the Messianic Jews of the first century makes a direct connection between the death of the Red Heifer and the death of Yeshua as the Messiah (cf. Hebrews 9:13-14). This information not only gives us some details to consider when speaking of the location of Gulgolta, but also helps reveal the spiritual meaning of the execution-stake. Indeed, the death of Yeshua provides cleansing for the sins of Israel and the whole world, for all those who receive his gift.

Our attention is now drawn to some of the other witnesses on that dramatic Passover day. It is significant to Matthew that *there were many women there, looking on from a distance.* It would have been difficult for any women to get close to the place of such an execution, but evidently this group of women felt compelled to stay close to their Messiah. They were most certainly Jewish believers, and we are told that *they had followed* Yeshua *from the Galil, helping him.*

It is not unheard of that a rabbi would have some female disciples, but it is nonetheless noteworthy. They would not have had all of the responsibilities of the male *talmidim,* but they certainly assisted the rabbi and the Messianic band with some of their necessary needs, especially with their itinerant lifestyle (cf. Luke 8:1-3). Two different Miryams are mentioned, one *from Magdala* (Migdal) and the other who was identified as *the mother of Ya'akov and Yosef.* Also included in the list is *the mother of Zavdai's/*Zebedee's sons, who is identified as *Shlomit* in Mark's account (cf. Mark 15:40). It is informative to know that Yeshua not only had many faithful disciples who were women, but that they were so committed to him that they stayed close to the very moment of their rabbi's death.

The Burial of Yeshua   27:57-66

A most amazing situation develops immediately after the passing of Yeshua. It is now late afternoon, *toward evening*, and the timing of Yeshua's burial is becoming a pressing issue. This means, according to our chronology, that the first day of Passover (15 *Nisan*) is coming to a close. It was also approaching a high Sabbath (double Shabbat of Passover and the seventh day together), as it was Friday afternoon moving into the weekly *Erev Shabbat.* The Romans often tried to cooperate with their subjects by allowing them to follow their local customs. In this case, Jewish tradition dictated that any dead body, even of a criminal, could not be left out in the open overnight (cf. Deuteronomy 21:22-23). Matthew sees here again prophetic fulfillment from the ancient prophecies of the *Tanakh,* as he notes it is *a wealthy man from Ramatayim named Yosef* who asked to assist with the burial of Yeshua (cf. Isaiah 53:9 "in his death he was with a rich man"). Not only was this man a prominent member of the Jerusalem community, but the other Gospels point out that he was, in fact, a member of the Sanhedrin (cf. Mark 15:43)!

Perhaps as a surprise to some, Matthew explains that Yosef was *a talmid*/disciple of Yeshua. This significant footnote reminds us that Yeshua drew disciples from every sector of the Jewish community, from fishermen to rabbis, street people to the wealthy. It is also a reminder that not everyone in the Sanhedrin voted to deliver Yeshua up to the Romans, but it was an area of disagreement even among some of the top rabbis. Because of his status, Yosef was able to approach Pilate and ask *for* Yeshua*'s body.* Matthew's language is simple and to the point that *Yosef took the body and wrapped it in a clean linen sheet.*

This is no doubt a summary of the very elaborate details of traditional burial in first-century Israel, many of which continue to this day. Upon death, the body of a Jew is treated with the utmost respect. Because we are created in the image of God, it has long been considered inappropriate to make any changes to the body or to embalm it, as was done in pagan cultures. The *Torah* states simply that we all came from dust and therefore will return to dust (cf. Genesis 3:19). The implication is that the body must not be altered, and burial should be in the earth. The body is clothed with a white robe or shroud called the *takhrikhim.* It is significant that the garment has no pockets, illustrating the reality that we can take nothing with us from this life! Often a male is buried with his *tallit*/prayer shawl as well, with one adaptation: The fringes are cut to illustrate that the person is no longer bound to the commandments. There are various other traditions for burial, which are usually carried out by a local *Chevra Kaddisha* (Holy Society).

No doubt Yosef of Ramatayim saw to it that these customs were followed in the traditional burial of his Messiah. We are told that Yosef laid the body *in his own tomb*. Burial space close to Jerusalem has always been in high demand, and it makes sense that Yosef, as a rich man, could afford such a precious commodity. Consistent with first-century custom, he had the cave/tomb sealed by *rolling a large stone in front of the entrance*. The two Miryams were left there, *opposite the grave*, to begin sitting *shiva* (the seven days of mourning that commence at the burial of a loved one).

Matthew's account of the burial of Yeshua concludes with a most interesting detail. We are told that the *next day, after the preparation, the head cohanim and the P'rushim went together to Pilate* with an unusual request. Since the Preparation Day alludes to Friday (preparing for the weekly Shabbat), the next day would mean that some of the religious leaders met with the Roman governor on the evening or day of Shabbat (now 16 Nisan, or the second day of Passover).

This was one more aspect of the death of Messiah that was highly unusual in a most unique way. It is greatly ironic that those opposed to Yeshua were stronger believers in his possible resurrection than were his own close disciples! In that regard, these leaders tell Pilate that *that deceiver said while he was still alive, "After three days I will be raised."* While these individuals did not personally believe in Yeshua, they nonetheless were fearful that somehow his words would come to pass.

It is intriguing that in some later passages of the *Talmud*, Yeshua (code name "Ben Stada") is accused of deceiving Israel through some magic he learned in Egypt (Tractate Shabbat XI.15; Shabbat 13d). The *Talmud* actually confirms that Yeshua worked miracles in Israel (and that his family visited Egypt at one point) but simply attributes those miracles not to God but to the dark side. With similar logic, these first-century leaders speculated that some of Yeshua's *talmidim may come and steal him away* as their ultimate act of deception. They could take no chances of this possibility in the religious community, and the governor would certainly not want such a controversy breaking out in the secular community under his jurisdiction.

Their practical recommendation was *that the grave be made secure till the third day.* They felt it would be wise to have a Roman military guard keeping close watch over this potentially volatile situation, so Pilate allowed them to have the *guard.* In addition to that precaution, the religious leaders are told to *go and make the grave as secure* as they know how. This they did by *sealing the stone and putting the guard on watch.*

Little did they know that even these extreme measures would not be able to stop the events of the third day that was quickly approaching. In fact, the precautions taken here by those who opposed Yeshua (even professional military guards) will actually give more validity to the claims of the disciples that he has risen. The stage is set for the greatest revelation of God's power as Yeshua conquers mankind's greatest enemy, death itself.

The Victory of King Messiah   28:1-20

Matthew, as an eyewitness to the traumatic events of those last hours of Yeshua, now turns his focus to the apex of it all. What started as a joyful yet contemplative *seder* meal had turned into a series of overnight legal hearings. Religious leaders had expressed their dismay over this one who claimed to be the unique Messiah sent from God. Political leaders showed little patience for this renegade rabbi, who seemed to have issues with the Roman occupation.

The followers of Yeshua, both men and women, had witnessed the torturous execution of their leader and undoubtedly began to question their own place at this juncture. Yet through it all, the writer records his account of the greatest (and most controversial) event to ever be reported in world history.

The Resurrection of Yeshua   28:1-15

Jerusalem must have been filled with an incredible range of emotions on that Shabbat of the Passover week. There was surely tremendous joy as the multitude of Jewish pilgrims filled the city for this most wonderful holy week. The *seder* was celebrated with family and friends, not to mention the wondrous services at the *Beit-Ha'Mikdash*/Holy Temple. Some were well aware of the controversial events surrounding the arrest and execution of the rebel rabbi from the Galil. But most were ignorant or unconcerned, as they had their own religious duties to attend to.

The tranquil spirit of Shabbat permeated the Holy City, and, appropriately, Yeshua's body rested in the tomb on that day of rest. In the midst of it all, the disciples of Yeshua were both perplexed and downhearted, as their messianic ideals seemed suddenly dashed. It seems as if virtually all of the *talmidim* had accepted the apparent reality that their leader was dead and gone. Matthew recounts how, *after Shabbat, as the next day was dawning, Miryam of Madgala and the other Miryam went to see the grave.*

It had been reported that Yeshua received a traditional Jewish burial just before the commencement of Shabbat. It was no doubt a hurried burial in the tomb owned by Yosef of Ramatayim, but all had been completed before sundown Friday. The two women here were part of the team of disciples and desired to show respect to the late rabbi. Of course this was nearly impossible on Shabbat itself, especially in the middle of the night after the close of the holy day. It is clear that these women took their first practical opportunity to visit the grave at the first light of the first day of the week (Sunday morning). Matthew actually uses the plural word (Sabbaths), which reminds us of the exact timing after the Sabbath of Passover (Thursday sundown to Friday sundown) and then the Sabbath of Unleavened Bread and the weekly Shabbat together on the same day. It was now the third day of Passover, the exact time of the important prophecies of Yeshua concerning his own resurrection.

What happened next shocks the women to their core, both physically and spiritually, as Matthew reports that *suddenly there was a violent earthquake*. This was the second strong tremor in the last three days, certainly a wake-up call for many in Jerusalem and even us today! It is during this earthquake that *an angel of ADONAI came down from heaven, rolled away the stone and sat on it*. The other Gospel writers refer to two angels, but this is not a problem. As is so often the case, it simply reflects the reality that different eyewitnesses notice different details.

This manifestation could not be a mere mortal, as *his appearance was like lightning and his clothes were white as snow*. Once again, the writer seems to be at a loss for words to describe something incomprehensible—the *Shekhinah* Glory of God (cf. Ezekiel 1; Matthew 17; etc.). With the moving of the stone over the burial cave and the supernatural angelic appearance, it is little wonder that fear struck the witnesses. We should not forget that professional Roman soldiers were guarding the tomb to ensure that there would be no trouble from the Messianic disciples. It says a lot about the intensity of the situation that even these hardened soldiers were *so terrified that they trembled and became like dead men*. In fact, Matthew makes use of a play on words by using the root word for earthquake to describe the trembling of the soldiers (cf. Matthew 27:51)!

The angel could also see the terror of the two Miryams and tried to convince them to *not be afraid*. The angel acknowledged their original purpose for coming to the tomb as *looking for* Yeshua *who was executed on the stake*. They had come to bring spices or a memorial for their rabbi, but they were not ready for the angel's announcement: "He is not here, because he has been raised—just as he said!" The use of the passive verb underscores the important truth that Yeshua did not raise himself as the Messiah, but it was the Father—The God of Abraham, Isaac, and Jacob—who performed the dramatic miracle. The Resurrection is, in that sense, God's confirmation that Yeshua is indeed his son, the *Mashiach* for Israel and all the nations.

The general belief in the resurrection of all people at the end time has long been a central doctrine in Judaism. Many scriptures testify of its promise (cf. Job 19:25-27; Isaiah 26:19; Daniel 12:1-2), as do several Talmudic references. There has even been some debate among the rabbis about the possible resurrection of the Messiah himself. The classic passage of Isaiah 53 ("he will see his offspring") was traditionally interpreted by the early rabbis as referring to *Mashiach* (cf. Tractate Sanhedrin 98a). In another fascinating passage, the rabbis state that the first Messiah (*Mashiach ben Yosef*) will be killed in the last battle, but he will be resurrected by the second Messiah (*Mashiach ben David*) (cf. Tractate Sukkah 52a).

A later commentary explains it this way: "When Messiah ben Yosef is killed, his body will remain cast out in the streets for forty days, but no unclean thing will touch him until Messiah ben David comes and brings him back to life, as commanded by the Lord. And this is the beginning of the signs which he will perform, and this is the resurrection of the dead which will come to pass" (*Hai Gaon, Responsum* as quoted in Patai, *The Messiah Texts*, p. 169). Many modern Jews might be surprised by these interpretations, as since the Middle Ages (starting with Rashi), many of these passages were reapplied not to the Messiah but to the sufferings of the Jewish people in general. But the historical teaching of the resurrection of the Messiah was in some manner clearly part of the debate in Jewish theology. In this light, the closing chapter of Matthew's account takes on special interest as he highlights the details of the bodily resurrection of Yeshua of Nazareth.

In the midst of their shock, the two Miryams are exhorted by the angel to "come and look at the place where he lay." The tomb had been opened and the stone moved not just for Yeshua's sake but so the witnesses could enter the tomb to see for themselves. The women are told to verify the empty tomb and to *go quickly and tell the talmidim*. It is remarkable that the first witnesses to the resurrection of Yeshua were women. Although Jewish women had many civil rights and protections within their biblical culture, it was a commonly held doctrine that a woman was not an acceptable witness in many legal proceedings. This was deduced from the *Torah* passage that speaks specifically of "men" who have a legal controversy. Therefore, it was concluded that witnesses must be men, not women or minors (cf. Tractate Yoma 43b speaking to Deuteronomy 19:17). This was not so much a judgment against women but a recognition that they had only certain responsibilities, whereas men had the greatest responsibilities in ancient society. Most of this was directly related to the practical belief that women were exempt from the positive commandments, as they were often time-sensitive and therefore difficult for a busy homemaker to fulfill (cf. Tractate Kiddushin 1.7).

One reason that the gender of the witnesses is so striking is that a person seeking to write the strongest and most convincing account of such an important event would probably not relish inclusion of this detail. If, for example, the account was fabricated, Jewish elders or Yeshiva rabbis would almost certainly have been reported as the first witnesses! On the other hand, it confirms to us that the gospel writers were not concerned about developing a biased account but rather simply recording the actual facts as they transpired. The fine details of this report thus contribute to its veracity. The angel exhorts the women to go testify to the disciples that Yeshua *has been raised from the dead*. They are also to relay the message that the risen *Mashiach* is *going to the Galil,* where they *will see him* with their own eyes.

Frightened yet filled with joy, the two Miryams quickly depart to search for their Messianic brothers. They must have still had a bit of apprehension in their own spirits, however. They had seen the empty tomb and experienced the dramatic events of that early morning, but they had not actually seen the risen Yeshua for themselves. That was about to change, as *suddenly* Yeshua *met them and said, "Shalom!"* His resurrection was now confirmed, and they literally *took hold of his feet* and *fell down in front of him.* In the flurry of emotion, Yeshua feels the need to assure them with the words "don't be afraid!" Again the simple yet powerful reality of the situation is portrayed, as the women are described as fearful. In other religious accounts, the writer might be tempted to paint the witnesses as heroic and strong, but Matthew's account is very believable as we consider the entire situation. Yeshua reiterates the words of the angel that they are to *tell* his *brothers to go to the Galil* and *they will see him* there. The women continue their journey, now invigorated by their own eyewitness encounter with the risen Yeshua.

While there was great joy and anticipation among the women, the scenario was quite different for some of the religious and political authorities. Some of the Roman *guards went into the city and reported to the head cohanim everything that had happened.* They also had been eyewitnesses to the same events of that early morning of *Yom Rishon*/the first day of the week—the earthquake, the angelic appearances, and the empty tomb. Yet they were the very ones who had been commissioned to guard the tomb in order to thwart any potential problems.

Matthew is careful to point out that only *some* of the guards were seeking to meet with the authorities. Perhaps some of the military eyewitnesses followed a more natural conclusion and became believers in the Messiah for themselves.

The remaining Roman guards *met with the elders* and came up with a coordinated response to the problem of the empty tomb. It was decided that the guards would be paid *a sizable sum of money* with the condition that they report an adapted account of the events. They were to *tell people* that the *talmidim came during the night and stole the body* while they were *sleeping*. How ironic that the very event that the guards were to prevent now becomes the story that they are to tell!

Of course, there are several difficulties with this false account. How did the soldiers know what actually happened if they were sleeping? What would their supervisors say if the soldiers were guilty of such a dereliction of duty? The leaders anticipate some of these problems, as they note they will keep the guards out of trouble if the governor hears of the situation. Perhaps they would be able to accomplish that, since Pilate probably had larger concerns in his kingdom and had delegated the guard duty to the supervision of the Jewish authorities. Whatever the reason, we are told that *the soldiers took the money and did as they were told.* In Matthew's account (some thirty years after the event), *this story spread* as the main explanation for the empty tomb.

Other possible explanations for the empty tomb have also been put forth. Some skeptics have proposed what has been called the "Wrong Tomb" theory. This explanation asserts that the women (and later the men) accidentally went to the wrong tomb, which happened to be empty. Although possible, this is highly unlikely, as it would require us to believe that the women forgot, within a matter of hours, where their beloved rabbi was buried. Furthermore, if this was somehow the case, those opposed to Yeshua could have stopped any false rumors of resurrection by simply going to the correct tomb and producing the body. However, the dead body of Yeshua was never found by either his friends or enemies.

Another popular explanation for the empty tomb is what is called the "Swoon" theory. This account attests that Yeshua did not actually die on the execution-stake but merely fainted from exhaustion and loss of blood. Everyone thought he was dead (even the Roman professionals) when, in fact, he was about to revive himself in the cool of the tomb. Lest we think these are merely ancient stories, it should be noted that popular author Hugh Schonfield published his version of this account, entitled "The Passover Plot," in the 1960s. But the Swoon theory has too many problems to be seriously considered. Could Yeshua really survive and revive himself after the horrific experience of Roman crucifixion? Also, who would have moved the heavy stone—the disciples or Yeshua himself? And how could it have been moved in the presence of the Roman guards?

Ultimately, none of these explanations for the empty tomb hold up under detailed examination. Add to this the dramatic transformation of the *talmidim* in the days to follow. If they had conspired to steal the body, how can one account for their dramatic spiritual change? They went from being a fearful and doubtful group to a dynamic community that would soon turn the ancient world upside down. Would they have suffered or even died for what they knew was a hoax? The most logical explanation for the empty tomb in light of all these details is that the disciples actually saw the risen Yeshua! Perhaps the greatest apologetic argument for the Resurrection of Yeshua is the changed lives of his closest followers and the impact they had on first-century Israel. More than 2000 years later, we are still talking about it, and many lives testify of an encounter with the living Yeshua as King Messiah.

The Commission for His Followers 28:16-20

The last segment of Matthew's account culminates with a personal appearance of Yeshua and his commission to his followers. The writer properly notes that it was the *eleven talmidim* who *went to the Galil where* Yeshua *had told them to go*. This number reflects the inner circle of Yeshua minus Y'hudah, who had tragically met his own death. It seems fitting that the Messianic group heads back to the Galil, where the earliest ministry of Yeshua had commenced. When they saw Yeshua, the group *prostrated themselves before him*, although we are told that *some hesitated*. The former group acted on their new conviction that Yeshua is the risen *Mashiach* and, as such, is worthy of their worship (as the term denotes). All the way to the end of his account, Matthew honestly records some of the lingering doubts among the disciples. We know from other accounts about the skepticism of *T'oma*/Thomas (*Yochanan*/John 20:24-29), as well as the disciples by Emmaus who did not recognize Yeshua at first (Luke 24:16). With his numerous Resurrection appearances, it would not be long before all of the disciples were strong believers and were joined by a large growing number of new Messianic Jews (I Cor. 15:6).

The final words of Yeshua to his *talmidim* must be of the utmost importance. First, he assures them that *all authority in heaven and on earth has been given* to him as the risen *Mashiach*. Perhaps he needed to restate this truth after the events of his humiliating death. Nonetheless, Yeshua fulfilled his exact calling as *Mashiach ben Yosef* to suffer for the sins of Israel and the entire world. Yet it is because of the resurrection power that his authority is confirmed.

As Yeshua conquered the greatest enemy of mankind, he proved that he had received the blessing of the Father and the resultant authority over all. The next phrase is closely connected to this idea, as he commands the disciples to *therefore go*. It is in a participle form, clearly stating that the *talmidim* have a new mandate. It could be translated as "having gone," which gives it a sense of command and also an expectation that they are already on their way! What are they to do while they are going? The imperative form is reflected in the next verb "make *talmidim*/disciples." The main focus of Yeshua's commission is for the *talmidim* to go and make new *talmidim*. This is consistent with the principle in rabbinic literature "to raise many disciples" (Pirke Avot 1:1). How much more so for the disciples of the Messiah!

The things that the disciples have seen and experienced are meant to be passed on to those around them. It is called "Good News" because the Kingdom of God is now very close to those who seek it. Sins may be forgiven through the finished work of Yeshua, and we are offered a close relationship with the God of Israel as we place our trust in Yeshua as our King Messiah. So good is this news that Yeshua elsewhere calls it "abundant life," as we walk in a new awareness of God's blessings through Messiah (*Yochanan*/John 10:10). Good news like this is meant to be shared!

Most naturally, these disciples would start sharing these blessings with their own Jewish brothers first. In a sense, the good news is always directed to the Jewish people first, as we were the ones who have the first covenants promising the Messiah. If he has come, then it is only fitting that the Jewish community should be the first to hear! Not surprisingly, we find emphasis in Scripture on sharing this new covenant "to the Jew first" (Romans 1:16) and "starting in Jerusalem" (Acts 1:8).

Yeshua's Great Commission extends beyond the Jewish people, however, as the disciples are commanded to make other disciples *from all nations* as well. Even with the focus on Israel, it should not surprise anyone that this good news is for all peoples. This was actually part of the earlier covenants between God and Israel, in which Abraham was predicted to be a blessing to the Gentiles (Genesis 12:3) and Isaiah reminds his generation of their calling to be a light to the Nations (Isaiah 49:6).

The Hebrew word *goyim* in this context would also be inclusive of the Jewish people, so it is understood that this Great Commission is for all peoples, Jew and Gentile alike. Simply put, the Messiah has now come and all peoples should be invited to participate in the abundant life he offers! It is unfortunate that sometimes the world (even our people) misunderstands the zeal of Messianic believers to share our faith in Yeshua. This is not meant to be merely a "conversion campaign" to bring people over to our side. Given the original intent of Yeshua, it is clear that we are to share with others simply because we have been blessed in our walk with the risen Yeshua. Today's believers should be careful not to come across as angry religious people trying to convince others. It is more like a beggar telling another beggar where to find some bread!

The next phrase in Yeshua's command gives us more details about how to make new *talmidim*. The disciples are told that new followers should be identified by *immersing them*. The followers would have naturally thought of ritual immersion (*t'vilah*) in water as a sign of the new adherents. Immersion in a kosher *mikveh* (pool) has long been a common practice in Judaism to symbolize various spiritual truths. In biblical times, the *mikveh* was a place of ritual cleansing after a healing (Leviticus 15) or to prepare for the holy days (Leviticus 16). Likewise, a woman was to go to the *mikveh* after her monthly cleansing (*nidah*), as is still practiced today by observant Jewish women.

Most informative in these words of Yeshua is the fact that immersion was a common requirement for non-Jews who wanted to convert to Judaism in the first century. At that time, a Gentile was told to bring a Temple sacrifice, be circumcised, and to take a ritual *mikveh* as a symbol of his sincere desire to follow the God of Israel (Tractate Yevamot 47a). It is not immersion itself that cleanses, as seen by the fact that it is always after a cleansing that a person takes a *mikveh*. In fact, one must thoroughly wash himself or herself before entering the waters of the *mikveh*.

All of this is informative as we consider the command of Yeshua. The disciples are not merely to immerse others so they are ritually cleansed, but they are to administer immersion upon those who have already been cleansed by their faith in Yeshua. Simply put, an understanding of *mikveh* confirms that baptism itself does not bring salvation but is a sign that a person has saving faith in Yeshua. This understanding of *mikveh* might have prevented a lot of division and denominational splits in Christian history. Since *mikveh* was very well known to Yeshua's disciples, the next phrase is an important qualifier as to the type of immersion to be used.

In first-century Judaism, there were numerous types of immersions, as stated above. Yet, Messiah is not talking about any of the rabbinic or *Torah* immersions commonly known at that time. That is why this immersion is to be into *the reality of the Father, the Son and the Ruach HaKodesh*. It is a *mikveh* not in the name of Moses or for preparation of *Shabbat* but in the reality (the Name) of the triune God. It is assumed in the New Covenant that Jews would already know about Father God as well as the *Ruach* of God. What is distinctive about this immersion is that it is in the Name of Yeshua as the Messiah. For those who embrace Yeshua as their Messiah and intend to live their life in submission to him, this immersion is a symbol of that commitment. Although Jews should have a biblical understanding of the concept of God (*Elohim*) and the Spirit (*Ruach*), there is no doubt that controversy surrounds the concept of a triune revelation of God.

For modern Jews, much of the aversion to such theology is actually rooted in the perception that such a belief would amount to idolatry or conversion to a different religion. We are told multiple times that God is a single entity and there is no other aspect to his self-revelation, as it is written, "There is no other God besides me, a just God and a Savior; there is none beside me" (Isaiah 45:21). This perspective is affirmed time and again throughout rabbinic theology and the *Siddur*/prayer book, as reflected in such prayers as the Yigdal, "*Eyn lo d'mut ha-guf v'eyno guf...*/He has no semblance of body, nor any body, nothing compares to his holiness." Messianic Judaism heartily affirms this idea that God is unique.

While we understand some of these statements in rabbinic Judaism (especially when seen as a response to historic Christianity), we take exception when they appear to fail to address some detailed statements in Holy Scripture. Although the term "God" is often understood as referring to a distinct oneness, there are some compelling questions as to what that actually means in biblical Hebrew. For example, the word most often used for "God" is *Elohim,* which is in the plural form. This could be interpreted as many gods, but when the singular God of Israel is referred to, it is used with a singular verb (Genesis 1:1). Clearly one God is meant, but there seems to be some mystery to that oneness.

How interesting that the very next verse speaks of the *Ruach Elohim* as part of the creation process, implying that this, too, is a manifestation of God (Genesis 1:2). Add to this the intriguing verse 3 of Genesis, where God's first words are an exhortation to "let there be light." This is all good until one realizes (as the rabbis have pointed out) that there are no light sources until Day 4 of Creation! Where is the light coming from? Messiah is the light from God, as Yeshua himself claimed (*Yochanan*/John 8:12). So, the first three verses of the *Torah* speak of God's revelation in three different manifestations.

Another piece of evidence is found in the most central declaration of Scripture and Judaism: *"Sh'ma Yisra'el!* ADONAI *Eloheynu* ADONAI *Echad*/Hear O Israel! The LORD our God, the LORD is One" (Deuteronomy 6:4). Clearly God is reminding us that the God of Israel is unique and there is no other god. However, the Hebrew word *echad* is not so simply translated. It can mean "one," but it is often used in the *Torah* to describe a unity of various parts. It is the word used to describe the composition of a day; evening and morning are called *"yom echad*/one day" (Genesis 1:5). The word is also used to describe the bond between husband and wife within marriage, *"basar echad*/one flesh" (Genesis 2:24). In both cases, two different entities are united together; they remain distinct and yet are unified. This has implications for our understanding of God, as he himself uses the same word to describe his nature.

There are also many puzzling verses that use plural pronouns to describe the work of God. One such verse is "let us make man in our image" (Genesis 1:26). The rabbis have long speculated what this verse might entail, suggesting everything from God speaking to angels or simply using poetic Hebrew. That it is not entirely understandable is reflected in the ancient *midrash*:

> "Rabbi Shmuel bar Nachman in the name of Rabbi Yonaton said, that at the time when Moses wrote the *Torah*, writing a portion of it daily, when he came to this verse which says, 'And Elohim said, let us make man in our image after our likeness,' Moses said, 'Master of the universe, why do you give herewith an excuse to the sectarians [*minim*, the early Messianic Jews]? God answered Moses, 'You write and whoever wants to err, let him err'" (Genesis Rabba 1:26).

Such passages show us that when dealing with the nature of God, we would be wise to let the Scriptures speak to us and to study with a spirit of humility. It is a deep subject, and there is much more evidence to consider in the *Tanakh*. It is not a surprise that some of the mystical literature comes amazingly close to presenting a more open view of the mystery of God's nature.

> "Come and see the mystery of the word *YHVH*: there are three steps, each existing by itself: nevertheless they are One, and so united that one cannot be separated from the other. The Ancient Holy One is revealed with three heads, which are united into one" (Zohar, Vol. III, p. 288, Vol. II, p. 43).

These are intriguing and deep concepts with which theologians have grappled over the centuries. Later Christian theologians attempted to explain these ideas within some church councils (e.g., Nicea in 325 AD) and from a Greek context. While Messianic Jews affirm the concept of the tri-unity of the one God, we may not necessarily agree with the Greek words and explanation. It is most unfortunate that there was not one Jewish Messianic theologian invited to participate in the Council of Nicea. Undoubtedly, some of the Hebrew background would have made a great contribution to this doctrinal discussion. Even though it is good and proper to ask some deeper questions about the nature of God, we should emphasize that Yeshua himself called the *Sh'ma* the greatest commandment (cf. Mark 12:28-34). One thing is for sure: Whatever the New Testament teaches about the pluralistic aspect of the one God, it must be consistent with the full revelation of the *Tanakh* (cf. Matthew 5:17).

Some conclusions from a Messianic Jewish perspective lead us to view God as One and yet as a mysterious plurality within that unity. This is reflected in the words of the Great Commission of Yeshua, as the disciples are to go "in the Name" (reality) of *the Father, the Son, and the Ruach HaKodesh*. It must be pointed out that even with the mention of the three realities of God, Yeshua uses the singular word "name" in describing all three. This is consistent with the mystery of the one God revealed in a plurality of manifestations.

If this is in fact the correct interpretation of the *Torah*, then this would be the perfect way to describe the triunity within the oneness of Elohim. New *talmidim* are to receive a special mikveh "in the Name" (singular) of the threefold revelation of God (plural). No doubt this sounded very different to many first-century Jews, as it does to many modern Jews. But the bottom line is this: If this revelation is consistent with the *Tanakh,* then we should embrace it. If it is incorrect according to the standards of the *Tanakh* (not just rabbinical interpretations), then we should reject it. It is ultimately a mystery, but the more one studies this issue, the more amazingly consistent it appears.

The final words of Yeshua's commission include an important exhortation. As the *talmidim* (and us) are to go and make other disciples, they are also to be *teaching them to obey everything* that Yeshua commanded. Once again the original language uses a participle form to show that "teaching" is a requisite part of the main verb "make disciples." The content of Yeshua's teaching would, of course, include all of the distinctive and unique insights that came from his ministry. Since he himself put great emphasis on the *Torah* and the Prophets (Matthew 5:17-18), Messianic Jews must also teach the entire Scripture as an essential part of Yeshua's commission.

Though we do not look at the *Torah* through the authority of Orthodox or more modern tradition, we similarly value the *Torah* as comprised of teaching directly from God. Messianic Judaism looks at this *Torah* through the lens of Yeshua and in light of the Messiah's ministry in our midst. It is this fulfilled and beloved *Torah*/Instruction that his *talmidim* are to teach and obey as followers of King Messiah. Although some followers of Yeshua seem to question the validity of *Torah* today, for Messianic Jews and non-Jews affiliated with our movement, the *Torah* becomes even more amazing. *Mashiach* has come and has taught us the deep spiritual riches of the *Torah*, so we appreciate it even more!

This final Great Commission could have sounded rather overwhelming to those early Jewish believers (as it does to us!). But the final words recorded by Matthew are a source of great comfort and hope. Yeshua promises, "I will be with you always, yes, even until the end of the age." There is seemingly no way that this Great Commission can be accomplished, even through the best efforts of Yeshua's followers.

Our strength and resources are limited. We many times seem like such a small remnant in contrast to the massive unbelieving world around us. But Yeshua reminds his disciples that they are not limited to their own resources! He is the resurrected King Messiah, and will be present with his people from here on out. After the next 40 days, Yeshua will ascend to the right hand of God the Father (Acts 1), but even that event should not discourage his *talmidim*. Shortly thereafter, on the day of *Shavuot*, the *Ruach* would be poured out on the faithful remnant (Acts 2). This empowering would provide the necessary presence of Messiah in the lives of the believers in order to fulfill their mandate.

History records the amazing events that transpired for the early Messianic Jews and later the Gentile believers. What started as a band of 12 common Jewish men was transformed into a dynamic movement that literally turned the ancient world upside down. God is also doing some amazing things in our own day. Over the last 40 years, the world has seen the rebirth of a modern Messianic Jewish synagogue movement, and the Good News of Yeshua is reaching virtually every people group worldwide.

Yeshua's commission applies just as much to all of us who are his modern *talmidim*. It appears that we are living in the days when the last chapter of Jewish history and world history is about to be written. It seems the best is yet to come! We can be assured of that because he will be with us always. May we serve God with gladness as we anticipate the soon return of Yeshua—King Messiah!

GLOSSARY

Adonai Echad	The Lord is One (Deut. 6:4)
afikoman	the broken middle matzah of the Passover Seder
aliyah	going up, especially to Jerusalem
Amidah	18 benedictions (plus one added after 70 CE)
ashrey	happy are those; opening phrase of many Psalms and prayers
asur	rabbinic term for forbidden actions
avot/toledot	Fathers. 39 Father commandments; many descendants
b'rakhah	blessing
b'ris	covenant (Ashkenazi pronunciation)
b'rit	covenant (Sephardic pronunciation)
b'rit milah	covenant of circumcision, often referred to as just *b'ris* or *b'rit*
bar	son (Aramaic)
Bar/Bat Mitzvah	Son/Daughter of the Commandment

barukh habah b'shem Adonai	blessed is he who comes in the name of the Lord
bat-kol	lit. "daughter voice" but used to describe a voice coming from the heavens
ben	son (Hebrew)
beit	house
Beit-Din	house of judgment; local rabbinic court
Beit-Ha'Mikdash	The Holy Temple
Beit-Hillel/Shammai	House of Hillel/Shammai; opposing first-century rabbis
bimah	pulpit, platform
birkat ha'mazon	blessing after a meal
b'nai Yisra'el	sons of Israel
challah	Sabbath bread
chametz	leaven
chevra kaddisha	burial society
Cohanim	Priests, the sons of Aaron
Cohen hagadol	The High Priest
davvening	Yiddish for praying
Eretz-Yisra'el	The Land of Israel
erusin	betrothal; engagement
Gemara	commentary on the *Mishnah*
get	divorce decree
Gei-Hinnom	Hell
goyim	non-Jews, Gentiles
Haftarah	section read from the Prophets

haggadah	Passover booklet of liturgy and readings used during seder
halakhah	rabbinic interpretive law
hallel	praise Psalms 113-118
HaShem	The Name; substitute for the name of God *(YHVH)*
huppah	wedding canopy
Josephus	first century Jewish historian
kal v'chomer	light to heavy; how much more
kàshrut	dietary laws
Kefa	Peter
kehilah	congregation
ketubah	marriage contract
kiddush	sanctification, often a cup of wine to "set apart" an event
kippah (kippot)	Hebrew for skullcap(s)
klal	rabbinic general principle
kosher	fit for consumption, clean (primarily used to describe food, but can be applied to situations that are "fit," or "clean," like "kosher behavior")
kosher l'Pesach	kosher for Passover
Levi'im	sons of the tribe of Levi
lulav	palm branch of *Sukkot*/Feast of Tabernacles
maror	the bitter herb eaten at Passover; usually ground horseradish
mashal	parable

Mashiach	Hebrew for Messiah
Mashiach ben David	Son of David, refers to King Messiah
Mashiach ben Yosef	Son of Joseph, refers to the Suffering Messiah
matzah	the unleavened bread used for Passover (and other times)
m'zuzah	doorpost, but used to describe a small box containing two handwritten biblical passages (Deut 6:4-9 and Deut. 11:13-21) on parchment; the box attached to the doors of homes
midrash	rabbinical commentary on the *Torah*
mikveh	special pool constructed for ritual water immersion
minchah	afternoon Temple sacrifice
Mishnah	the Oral Law written down about 200 AD based on the *Torah* (the Written Law)
mitzvah (mitzvot)	commandment(s), good deed(s)
mutar	rabbinic term for permitted actions
natilat yadaim	washing the hands
niddah	removed, separated (the period when a woman is forbidden to have sexual contact with her husband)
nisuin	marriage
olam haba	the age to come
olam hazeh	this age
ol ha-Torah	the yoke (responsibility and blessing) of the *Torah*

oneg	joyful celebration, often refers to a meal after Shabbat morning services.
oy!	woe (but untranslatable!)
P'rushim	Pharisees
Pesach	Passover
Rashi	acronym for Rabbi Shlomo Yitzaki (1040-1105 AD), a famous and influential rabbi
Rambam	acronym for Rabbi Moshe ben Maimon, also known as Maimonides (1135-1204 AD) a famous and influential rabbi
Rosh Hashanah	Jewish New Year, head of the year
Ruach HaKodesh	Holy Spirit
Sanhedrin	Israel's religious supreme court until 70 AD
seder	order (Passover meal)
Sh'khinah	Glory of God
sh'khitah	ritual slaughtering procedure
Sh'ma	refers to Deuteronomy 6:4-6; Hear (oh Israel)
Sh'ol	the place of the dead
Shabbat	Sabbath
shadkhan	marriage broker, matchmaker
shakharit	daily morning prayer services
shaliach (sh'lichim)	representative(s), apostle(s)
shalom	peace, health, contentment
Shavuot	Pentecost, Feast of Weeks
shel rosh	head *t'fillin*, designated for the head
shel yad	hand *t'fillin*, designated for the hand

sheva b'rakhot	seven blessings at a Jewish wedding
shiddukhin	arrangements preliminary to betrothal
Shim'on	Simon
shofar	ram's horn (other animals' horns are sometimes used)
shokhet	kosher butcher
siddur (siddurim)	prayer book(s)
simcha	joyous occasion
s'mikhah	laying on of hands or ordination
sukkah	booth for Feast of Tabernacles
Sukkot	Feast of Tabernacles
t'fillah	prayer
t'fillin	phylacteries, leather boxes strapped to the forehead and hand used for prayer
t'shuvah	repentance
t'vilah	to totally immerse
tallit	prayer shawl
tallit katan	small prayer shawl worn under shirt
talmid (talmidim)	disciple(s) or student(s)
Talmud	codified body of rabbinic thought; *Mishnah* plus *Gemara*. Completed in 6th century.
Tanakh	acronym for The Hebrew Scriptures: <u>T</u>orah (Law), <u>N</u>eviim (Prophets), <u>K</u>etuvim (Writings)
Targum	translation into another language
tashlikh	ceremony of repentance that takes place at a body of water on Rosh Hashanah

Torah	Law or Instruction; five books of Moses
Tractate	a book of the *Talmud*
treif	non-kosher
Tz'dukim	Sadducees
tzedakah	righteousness, charity
tzitzit, tzitziyot	fringe(s) worn on a garment
yarmulke	Yiddish for head covering
Yerushalayim	Jerusalem
Yeshua	Jesus, salvation
Yeshua HaMashiach	Jesus the Messiah
yetzer ha-tov (ha-ra)	the good (or evil) inclination of mankind
YHVH	(Yud-Heh-Vav-Heh) the Hebrew letters for the ineffable Name of God
Yom Kippur	Day of Atonement

BIBLIOGRAPHY

Abbott-Smith, G. *A Manual Greek Lexicon of the New Testament.* Edinburgh: T & T Clark, 1973.

Birnbaum, Philip. *A Book of Jewish Concepts.* New York: Hebrew Publishing Company, 1975.

_____, ed. *Maimonides Code of Law and Ethics: Mishneh Torah.* New York: Hebrew Publishing Company, 1974.

Bivin, David. *Understanding the Difficult Words of Jesus.* Shippensburg: Destiny Image, 1994.

Boteach, Shmuel. *The Wolf Shall Lie with the Lamb - The Messiah in Chassidic Thought.* Northvale, New Jersey: Jason Aronson, 1993.

Boyarin, Daniel. *Border Lines—The Partition of Judaeo-Christianity.* Philadelphia: University of Pennsylvania Press, 2004.

Brown, Michael. *Answering Jewish Objections to Jesus (5 Volumes).* Grand Rapids: Baker Books, 2003.

Buxbaum, Yitzhak. *Jewish Spiritual Practices.* Northvale, New Jersey: Jason Aronson Inc., 1994.

Carroll, James. *Constantine's Sword—The Church and The Jews*. New York: Houghton Mifflin Company, 2001.

Cohen, Abraham. *Everyman's Talmud*. New York: Schocken Books, 1975.

_____. *The Twelve Prophets*. New York: Soncino Press, 1985.

Cohen, Shaye. *The Beginnings of Jewishness*. Berkeley: University of California Press, 2000.

Cohn, Haim. *The Trial and Death of Jesus*. New York: Ktav Publishing House, 1977.

Cohn-Sherbok, Dan, ed. *Voices of Messianic Judaism*. Baltimore: Messianic Jewish Publications, 2001.

Danby, Herbert. *The Mishna*. New York: Oxford University Press, 1991.

Daube, David. *Collected Works of David Daube*, vol. 2. Berkeley: The Robbins Collection, 1992.

_____. *The New Testament and Rabbinic Judaism*. Peabody, Massachusetts: Hendrickson Publishers, 1956.

Davies, W. D. *Paul and Rabbinic Judaism*. Philadelphia: Fortress Press, 1980.

Edersheim, Alfred. *The Life and Times of Jesus the Messiah*. Grand Rapids: Eerdmans Publishing, 1984.

Encyclopedia Judaica. Jerusalem: Keter Publishing House, 1972.

Epstein, I. (ed.). *The Soncino Talmud (CD software)*. Brooklyn: Soncino Press, 1995.

Eisenman, Robert and Wise, Michael. *The Dead Sea Scrolls Uncovered.* New York: Barnes & Noble, 1992.

Falk, Harvey. *Jesus the Pharisee.* New York: Paulist Press, 1985.

Feinberg, Jeffrey. *Walk! Genesis through Deuteronomy.* Baltimore: Lederer Messianic Publications, 1999.

Fischer, John. *The Gospels in Their Jewish Context (*MP3/DVD *series).* Clarksville: Messianic Jewish Publishers, 2011.

_____. *Siddur for Messianic Jews.* Palm Harbor, Florida: Menorah Ministries, 1988.

Flusser, David. *The Sage from Galilee.* Grand Rapids: Eerdmans Publishing, 2007.

Friedman, David. *They Loved The Torah.* Clarksville: Messianic Jewish Publishers, 2001.

Fruchtenbaum, Arnold. "The Life of Messiah from a Jewish Perspective" (DVD series). San Antonio: Ariel Ministries, 2010.

Glaser, Mitch and Zhava. *The Fall Feasts of Israel.* Chicago: Moody Press, 1999.

Grudem, Wayne. *Systematic Theology.* Grand Rapids: Zondervan, 1994.

Hilton, Rabbi Michael and Father Gorian Marshall. *The Gospels and Rabbinic Judaism.* Hoboken: Ktav Publishing House, 1988.

Jeremias, Joachim. *Jerusalem in the Time of Jesus.* Philadelphia: Fortress Press, 1988.

Juster, Daniel. *Jewish Roots.* Pacific Palisades: Davar, 1986.

Kaiser, Walter; Bock, Darrell; Enns, Peter. *Three Views on the New Testament Use of the Old Testament*. Grand Rapids: Zondervan, 2008.

Kasdan, Barney. *God's Appointed Times*. Baltimore: Lederer Messianic Publications, 1993.

_____. *God's Appointed Customs*. Baltimore: Lederer Messianic Publications, 1996.

Keener, Craig. *Matthew—IVP Commentary*. Downers Grove: InterVarsity Press, 1997.

Kinzer, Mark. *Post-Missionary Messianic Judaism*. Grand Rapids: Brazos Press, 2005.

Klausner, Joseph. *Jesus of Nazareth*. New York: Menorah Publishing Company, 1979.

Klein, Isaac. *A Guide to Jewish Religious Practice*. New York: The Jewish Theological Seminary of America, 1979.

Lachs, Samuel Tobias. *A Rabbinic Commentary on The New Testament*. Hoboken: Ktav Publishing House, 1987.

Levine, Amy-Jill. *The Misunderstood Jew: The Church and the Scandal of the Jewish Jesus*. San Francisco: HarperCollins, 2006.

Martin, Ernest. *Secrets of Golgotha*. Portland: ASK Publishers, 1996.

Morris, Leon. *The Gospel According to Matthew*. Grand Rapids: Eerdmans, 1999.

Neusner, Jacob. *A Rabbi Talks with Jesus*. New York: Doubleday, 1994.

Patai, Raphael. *The Messiah Texts*. New York: Avon Books, 1979.

Pentecost, J. Dwight. *The Words and Works of Jesus Christ*. Grand Rapids: Zondervan, 1981.

Prager, Dennis and Telushkin, Joseph. *Why The Jews?* New York: Simon & Schuster, 2003.

Resnik, Russell. *Creation to Completion: A Guide to Life's Journey from the Five Books of Moses*. Clarksville: Messianic Jewish Publishers, 2006.

Rienecker, Fritz and Rogers, Cleon. *Linguistic Key to the Greek New Testament*. Grand Rapids: Zondervan, 1982.

Safrai, Shmuel. "The Value of Rabbinical Literature as an Historical Source" (article). Jerusalem: JerusalemPerspective.com, 2009.

Sanders, E. P. *Judaism—Practice and Belief 63 BCE-66 CE*. London: SCM Press, 1992.

_____. *Jesus and Judaism*. Philadelphia: Fortress Press, 1985.

Scherman, Nosson. *The Rabbinical Council of America Edition of The Artscroll Siddur*. Brooklyn: Mesorah Publications, 1990.

_____. *Tanach: The Torah, Prophets and Writings*. Brooklyn: Mesorah Publications, 1996.

Sigel, Phillip. *The Halakhah of Jesus of Nazareth According to the Gospel of Matthew*. Atlanta: Society of Biblical Literature, 2007.

Soulen, R. Kendall. *The God of Israel and Christian Theology*. Minneapolis: Fortress Press, 1996.

Spangler, Ann and Tverberg, Lois. *Sitting at the Feet of Rabbi Jesus: How the Jewishness of Jesus can transform your faith*. Grand Rapids: Zondervan, 2009.

Stern, David. *Complete Jewish Bible*. Clarksville: Jewish New Testament Publications, 1998.

_____. *Jewish New Testament Commentary*. Clarksville, Maryland: Jewish New Testament Publications, 1992.

_____. *Messianic Judaism—A Modern Movement with an Ancient Past*. Clarksville, Maryland: : Messianic Jewish Publications, 2009.

Thiede, Carsten Peter. *The Dead Sea Scrolls and the Jewish Origins of Christianity*. New York: Palgrave, 2001.

Tree of Life Bible, The New Covenant. Shippensburg, PA: Destiny Image Publishers, 2011.

Vermes, Geza. *Jesus in His Jewish Context*. Minneapolis: Fortress Press, 2003.

Wagner, Jordan. *The Synagogue Survival Kit*. Northvale, New Jersey: Jason Aronson Inc, 1997.

Whiston, William. *Josephus' Complete Works*. Grand Rapids: Kregel Publications, 1960.

Young, Brad H. *Meet The Rabbis: Rabbinic Thought and the Teachings of Jesus*. Peabody, Massachusetts: Hendrickson Publishers, 2007.

_____. *The Parables: Jewish Tradition and Christian Interpretation*. Peabody, Massachusetts: Hendrickson Publishers, 1998.

OTHER RELATED RESOURCES

Available at Messianic Jewish Resources Int'l. • www.messianicjewish.net
1-800-410-7367
(Prices subject to change.)

Complete Jewish Bible: *A New English Version*
—Dr. David H. Stern

Presenting the Word of God as a unified Jewish book, the *Complete Jewish Bible* is a new version for Jews and non-Jews alike. It connects Jews with the Jewishness of the Messiah, and non-Jews with their Jewish roots. Names and key terms are returned to their original Hebrew and presented in easy-to-understand transliterations, enabling the reader to say them the way Yeshua (Jesus) did! 1697 pages.

Hardback	JB12	$34.99
Paperback	JB13	$29.99
Leather Cover	JB15	$59.99
Large Print (12 Pt font)	JB16	$49.99

Also available in French and Portuguese.

Jewish New Testament
—Dr. David H. Stern

The New Testament is a Jewish book, written by Jews, initially for Jews. Its central figure was a Jew. His followers were all Jews; yet no other version really communicates its original, essential Jewishness. Uses neutral terms and Hebrew names. Highlights Jewish references and corrects mistranslations. Freshly translated into English from Greek, this is a must read to learn about first-century faith. 436 pages

Hardback	JB02	$19.99
Paperback	JB01	$14.99
Spanish	JB17	$24.99

Also available in French, German, Polish, Portuguese and Russian.

Jewish New Testament on Audio CD or MP3

All the richness of the *Jewish New Testament* beautifully narrated in English by professional narrator/singer, Jonathan Settel. Thrilling to hear, you will enjoy listening to the Hebrew names, expressions and locations as spoken by Messiah.

20 CDs	JC01	$49.99
MP3	JC02	$49.99

Jewish New Testament Commentary
—Dr. David H. Stern

This companion to the *Jewish New Testament* enhances Bible study. Passages and expressions are explained in their original cultural context. 15 years of research. 960 pages.

Hardback	JB06	$34.99
Paperback	JB10	$29.99

Jewish New Testament & Commentary on CD-ROM

Do word searches, studies and more! And, because this is part of the popular LOGOS Bible program, you will have the "engine" to access one of the top Bible research systems. As an option, you'll be able to obtain and cross reference the Mishnah, Josephus, Bible dictionaries, and much more! Windows 3.1+ only.

JCD02	$39.99

Good News According To Matthew
—Dr. Henry Einspruch

English translation with quotations from the Tanakh (Old Testament) capitalized and printed in Hebrew. Helpful notations are included. Lovely black and white illustrations throughout the book. 86 pages.

	LB03	$4.99
Also available in Yiddish.	LB02	$ 4.99

Messianic Judaism *A Modern Movement With an Ancient Past*
—David H. Stern

An updated discussion of the history, ideology, theology and program for Messianic Judaism. A challenge to both Jews and non-Jews who honor Yeshua to catch the vision of Messianic Judaism. 312 pages

LB62	$17.99

Restoring the Jewishness of the Gospel
A Message for Christians
—David H. Stern

Introduces Christians to the Jewish roots of their faith, challenges some conventional ideas, and raises some neglected questions: How are both the Jews and "the Church" God's people? Is the Law of Moses in force today? Filled with insight! Endorsed by Dr. Darrell L. Bock. 110 pages

English	LB70	$9.99
Spanish	JB14	$9.99

Yeshua *A Guide to the Real Jesus and the Original Church*
—Dr. Ron Moseley

Opens up the history of the Jewish roots of the Christian faith. Illuminates the Jewish background of Yeshua and the Church and never flinches from showing "Jesus was a Jew, who was born, lived, and died, within first century Judaism." Explains idioms in the New Testament. Endorsed by Dr. Brad Young and Dr. Marvin Wilson. 213 pages.

LB29	$12.99

Gateways to Torah *Joining the Ancient Conversation on the Weekly Portion*
—Rabbi Russell Resnik

From before the days of Messiah until today, Jewish people have read from and discussed a prescribed portion of the Pentateuch each week. Now, a Messianic Jewish Rabbi, Russell Resnik, brings another perspective on the Torah, that of a Messianic Jew. 246 pages.

LB42	$15.99

Creation to Completion *A Guide to Life's Journey from the Five Books of Moses*
—Rabbi Russell Resnik

Endorsed by Coach Bill McCartney, Founder of Promise Keepers & Road to Jerusalem: "Paul urged Timothy to study the Scriptures (2 Tim. 3:16), advising him to apply its teachings to all aspects of his life. Since there was no New Testament then, this rabbi/apostle was convinced that his disciple would profit from studying the Torah, the Five Books of Moses, and the Old Testament. Now, Rabbi Resnik has written a warm devotional commentary that will help you understand and apply the Law of Moses to your life in a practical way." 256 pages

LB61	$14.99

Walk Genesis! Walk Exodus! Walk Leviticus! Walk Numbers! Walk Deuteronomy!
Messianic Jewish Devotional Commentaries
—Jeffrey Enoch Feinberg, Ph.D.

Using the weekly synagogue readings, Dr. Jeffrey Feinberg has put together some very valuable material in his "Walk" series. Each section includes a short Hebrew lesson (for the non-Hebrew speaker), key concepts, an excellent overview of the portion, and some practical applications. Can be used as a daily devotional as well as a Bible study tool.

Walk Genesis!	238 pages	**LB34**	$12.99
Walk Exodus!	224 pages	**LB40**	$12.99
Walk Leviticus!	208 pages	**LB45**	$12.99
Walk Numbers!	211 pages	**LB48**	$12.99
Walk Deuteronomy!	231 pages	**LB51**	$12.99
SPECIAL! Five-book Walk!	5 Book Set **Save $10**	**LK28**	$54.99

The Gospels in their Jewish Context
—John Fischer, Th.D, Ph.D.
An examination of the Jewish background and nature of the Gospels in their contemporary political, cultural and historical settings, emphasizing each gospel's special literary presentation of Yeshua, and highlighting the cultural and religious contexts necessary for understanding each of the gospels. 32 hours of audio/video instruction on MP3-DVD and pdf of syllabus.

LCD01 $49.99

The Epistles from a Jewish Perspective
—John Fischer, Th.D, Ph.D.
An examination of the relationship of Rabbi Shaul (the Apostle Paul) and the Apostles to their Jewish contemporaries and environment; surveys their Jewish practices, teaching, controversy with the religious leaders, and many critical passages, with emphasis on the Jewish nature, content, and background of these letters. 32 hours of audio/video instruction on MP3-DVD and pdf of syllabus.

LCD02 $49.99

They Loved the Torah *What Yeshua's First Followers Really Thought About the Law*
—Dr. David Friedman
Although many Jews believe that Paul taught against the Law, this book disproves that notion. An excellent case for his premise that all the first followers of the Messiah were not only Torah-observant, but also desired to spread their love for God's entire Word to the gentiles to whom they preached. 144 pages. Endorsed by Dr. David Stern, Ariel Berkowitz, Rabbi Dr. Stuart Dauermann & Dr. John Fischer.

LB47 $9.99

The Distortion *2000 Years of Misrepresenting the Relationship Between Jesus the Messiah and the Jewish People*
—Dr. John Fischer & Dr. Patrice Fischer
Did the Jews kill Jesus? Did they really reject him? With the rise of global anti–Semitism, it is important to understand what the Gospels teach about the relationship between Jewish people and their Messiah. 2000 years of distortion have made this difficult. Learn how the distortion began and continues to this day and what you can do to change it. 126 pages. Endorsed by Dr. Ruth Fleischer, Rabbi Russell Resnik, Dr. Daniel C. Juster, Dr. Michael Rydelnik.

LB54 $11.99

Matthew Presents Yeshua, King Messiah *A Messianic Commentary*
—Rabbi Barney Kasdan
Few commentators are able to truly present Yeshua in his Jewish context. Most don't understand his background, his family, even his religion, and consequently really don't understand who he truly is. This commentator is well versed with first-century Jewish practices and thought, as well as the historical and cultural setting of the day, and the 'traditions of the Elders' that Yeshua so often spoke about. Get to know Yeshua, the King, through the writing of another rabbi, Barney Kasdan. 448 pages

LB76 $29.99

God's Appointed Times *A Practical Guide to Understanding and Celebrating the Biblical Holidays* – **New Edition.**
—Rabbi Barney Kasdan

The Biblical Holy Days teach us about the nature of God and his plan for mankind, and can be a source of God's blessing for all believers–Jews and Gentiles–today. Includes historical background, traditional Jewish observance, New Testament relevance, and prophetic significance, plus music, crafts and holiday recipes. 145 pages.

English	**LB63**	$12.99
Spanish	**LB59**	$12.99

God's Appointed Customs *A Messianic Jewish Guide to the Biblical Lifecycle and Lifestyle*
— Rabbi Barney Kasdan

Explains how biblical customs are often the missing key to unlocking the depths of Scripture. Discusses circumcision, the Jewish wedding, and many more customs mentioned in the New Testament. Companion to *God's Appointed Times*. 170 pages.

English	**LB26**	$12.99
Spanish	**LB60**	$12.99

Celebrations of the Bible *A Messianic Children's Curriculum*

Did you know that each Old Testament feast or festival finds its fulfillment in the New? They enrich the lives of people who experience and enjoy them. Our popular curriculum for children is in a brand new, user-friendly format. The lay-flat at binding allows you to easily reproduce handouts and worksheets. Celebrations of the Bible has been used by congregations, Sunday schools, ministries, homeschoolers, and individuals to teach children about the biblical festivals. Each of these holidays are presented for Preschool (2-K), Primary (Grades 1-3), Junior (Grades 4-6), and Children's Worship/Special Services. 208 pages.

LB55	$24.99

Passover: *The Key That Unlocks the Book of Revelation*
—Daniel C. Juster, Th.D.

Is there any more enigmatic book of the Bible than Revelation? Controversy concerning its meaning has surrounded it back to the first century. Today, the arguments continue. Yet, Dan Juster has given us the key that unlocks the entire book—the events and circumstances of the Passover/Exodus.

By interpreting Revelation through the lens of Exodus, Dan Juster provides a unified overview that helps us read Revelation as it was always meant to be read, as a drama of spiritual conflict, deliverance, and above all, worship. He also shows how this final drama, fulfilled in Messiah, resonates with the Torah and all of God's Word. — Russ Resnik, Executive Director • Union of Messianic Jewish Congregations. 144 Pages.

LB74	$10.99

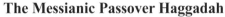

The Messianic Passover Haggadah
Revised and Updated
—Rabbi Barry Rubin and Steffi Rubin.

Guides you through the traditional Passover seder dinner, step-by-step. Not only does this observance remind us of our rescue from Egyptian bondage, but, we remember Messiah's last supper, a Passover seder. The theme of redemption is seen throughout the evening. What's so unique about our Haggadah is the focus on Yeshua (Jesus) the Messiah and his teaching, especially on his last night in the upper room. 36 pages.

| English | LB57 | $4.99 |
| Spanish | LBSP01 | $4.99 |

The Messianic Passover Seder Preparation Guide
Includes recipes, blessings and songs. 19 pages.

| English | LB10 | $2.99 |
| Spanish | LBSP02 | $2.99 |

The Sabbath *Entering God's Rest*
—Barry Rubin & Steffi Rubin

Even if you've never celebrated Shabbat before, this book will guide you into the rest God has for all who would enter in—Jews and non-Jews. Contains prayers, music, recipes; in short, everything you need to enjoy the Sabbath, even how to observe havdalah, the closing ceremony of the Sabbath. Also discusses the Saturday or Sunday controversy. 48 pages.
LB32 $6.99

Havdalah *The Ceremony that Completes the Sabbath*
—Dr. Neal & Jamie Lash

The Sabbath ends with this short, yet equally sweet ceremony called havdalah (separation). This ceremony reminds us to be a light and a sweet fragrance in this world of darkness as we carry the peace, rest, joy and love of the Sabbath into the work week. 28 pages.
LB69 $4.99

Dedicate and Celebrate!
A Messianic Jewish Guide to Hanukkah
—Barry Rubin & Family

Hanukkah means "dedication" — a theme of significance for Jews and Christians. Discussing its historical background, its modern-day customs, deep meaning for all of God's people, this little book covers all the how-tos! Recipes, music, and prayers for lighting the menorah, all included! 32 pages.
LB36 $4.99

The Conversation
An Intimate Journal of the Emmaus Encounter
—Judy Salisbury

"Then beginning with Moses and with all the prophets, He explained to them the things concerning Himself in all the Scriptures." Luke 24:27
If you've ever wondered what that conversation must have been like, this captivating book takes you there.
"The Conversation brings to life that famous encounter between the two disciples and our Lord Jesus on the road to Emmaus. While it is based in part on an imaginative reconstruction, it is filled with the throbbing pulse of the excitement of the sensational impact that our Lord's resurrection should have on all of our lives." ~ Dr. Walter Kaiser President Emeritus Gordon-Conwell Theological Seminary. Hardcover 120 pages.

LB73 $14.99

Growing to Maturity
A Messianic Jewish Discipleship Guide
—Daniel C. Juster, Th.D.

This discipleship series presents first steps of understanding and spiritual practice, tailored for the Jewish believer. It's purpose is to aid the believer in living according to Yeshua's will as a disciple, one who has learned the example of his teacher. The course is structured according to recent advances in individualized educational instruction. Discipleship is serious business and the material is geared for serious study and reflection. Each chapter is divided into short sections followed by study questions. 256 pages.

LB75 $19.99

Growing to Maturity Primer: *A Messianic Jewish Discipleship Workbook*
—Daniel C. Juster, Th.D.

A basic book of material in question and answer form. Usable by everyone. 60 pages.

TB16 $7.99

Proverbial Wisdom & Common Sense
—Derek Leman

A Messianic Jewish Approach to Today's Issues from the Proverbs Unique in style and scope, this commentary on the book of Proverbs, written in devotional style, is divided into chapters suitable for daily reading. A virtual encyclopedia of practical advice on family, sex, finances, gossip, honesty, love, humility, and discipline. Endorsed by Dr. John Walton, Dr. Jeffrey Feinberg and Rabbi Barney Kasdan. 248 pages.

LB35 $14.99

That They May Be One A Brief Review of Church Restoration Movements and Their Connection to the Jewish People
—Daniel Juster, Th.D

Something prophetic and momentous is happening. The Church is finally fully grasping its relationship to Israel and the Jewish people. Author describes the restoration movements in Church history and how they connected to Israel and the Jewish people. Each one contributed in some way—some more, some less—toward the ultimate unity between Jews and Gentiles. Predicted in the Old Testament and fulfilled in the New, Juster believes this plan of God finds its full expression in Messianic Judaism. He may be right. See what you think as you read *That They May Be One*. 100 pages.

LB71	$9.99

The Greatest Commandment
How the Sh'ma Leads to More Love in Your Life
—Irene Lipson

"What is the greatest commandment?" Yeshua was asked. His reply—"Hear, O Israel, the Lord our God, the Lord is one, and you are to love Adonai your God with all your heart, with all your soul, with all your understanding, and all your strength." A superb book explaining each word so the meaning can be fully grasped and lived. Endorsed by Elliot Klayman, Susan Perlman, & Robert Stearns. 175 pages.

LB65	$12.99

Blessing the King of the Universe
Transforming Your Life Through the Practice of Biblical Praise
—Irene Lipson

Insights into the ancient biblical practice of blessing God are offered clearly and practically. With examples from Scripture and Jewish tradition, this book teaches the biblical formula used by men and women of the Bible, including the Messiah; points to new ways and reasons to praise the Lord; and explains more about the Jewish roots of the faith. Endorsed by Rabbi Barney Kasdan, Dr. Mitch Glaser, & Rabbi Dr. Dan Cohn-Sherbok. 144 pages.

LB53	$11.99

You Bring the Bagels, I'll Bring the Gospel
Sharing the Messiah with Your Jewish Neighbor
Revised Edition—Now with Study Questions
—Rabbi Barry Rubin

This "how-to-witness-to-Jewish-people" book is an orderly presentation of everything you need to share the Messiah with a Jewish friend. Includes Messianic prophecies, Jewish objections to believing, sensitivities in your witness, words to avoid. A "must read" for all who care about the Jewish people. Good for individual or group study. Used in Bible schools. Endorsed by Harold A. Sevener, Dr. Walter C. Kaiser, Dr. Erwin J. Kolb and Dr. Arthur F. Glasser. 253 pages.

English	**LB13**	$12.99
Te Tengo Buenas Noticias	**OBSP02**	$14.99

Making Eye Contact With God
A Weekly Devotional for Women
—Terri Gillespie

What kind of eyes do you have? Are they downcast and sad? Are they full of God's joy and passion? See yourself through the eyes of God. Using real life anecdotes, combined with scripture, the author reveals God's heart for women everywhere, as she softly speaks of the ways in which women see God. Endorsed by prominent authors: Dr. Angela Hunt, Wanda Dyson and Kathryn Mackel. 247 pages, hardcover.

LB68 $19.99

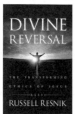

Divine Reversal
The Transforming Ethics of Jesus
—Rabbi Russell Resnik

In the Old Testament, God often reversed the plans of man. Yeshua's ethics continue this theme. Following his path transforms one's life from within, revealing the source of true happiness, forgiveness, reconciliation, fidelity and love. From the introduction, "As a Jewish teacher, Jesus doesn't separate matters of theology from practice. His teaching is consistently practical, ethical, and applicable to real life, even two thousand years after it was originally given." Endorsed by Jonathan Bernis, Dr. Daniel C. Juster, Dr. Jeffrey L. Seif, and Dr Darrell Bock. 206 pages

LB72 $12.99

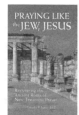

Praying Like the Jew, Jesus
Recovering the Ancient Roots of New Testament Prayer
—Dr. Timothy P. Jones

This eye-opening book reveals the Jewish background of many of Yeshua's prayers. Historical vignettes "transport" you to the times of Yeshua so you can grasp the full meaning of Messiah's prayers. Unique devotional thoughts and meditations, presented in down-to-earth language, provide inspiration for a more meaningful prayer life and help you draw closer to God. Endorsed by Mark Galli, James W. Goll, Rev. Robert Stearns, James F. Strange, and Dr. John Fischer. 144 pages.

LB56 $9.99

Growing Your Olive Tree Marriage *A Guide for Couples from Two Traditions*
—David J. Rudolph

One partner is Jewish; the other is Christian. Do they celebrate Hanukkah, Christmas or both? Do they worship in a church or a synagogue? How will the children be raised? This is the first book from a biblical perspective that addresses the concerns of intermarried couples, offering a godly solution. Includes highlights of interviews with intermarried couples. Endorsed by Walter C. Kaiser, Jr., Rabbi Dan Cohn-Sherbok, Jonathan Settel, Dr. Mitchell Glaser & Natalie Sirota. 224 pages.

LB50 $12.99

In Search of the Silver Lining *Where is God in the Midst of Life's Storms?*
—Jerry Gramckow

When faced with suffering, what are your choices? Storms have always raged. And people have either perished in their wake or risen above the tempests, shaping history by their responses...new storms are on the horizon. How will we deal with them? How will we shape history or those who follow us? The answer lies in how we view God in the midst of the storms. Endorsed by Joseph C. Aldrich, Ray Beeson, Dr. Daniel Juster. 176 pages.

LB39 $10.99

The Voice of the Lord *Messianic Jewish Daily Devotional*
—Edited by David J. Rudolph

Brings insight into the Jewish Scriptures—both Old and New Testaments. Twenty-two prominent Messianic contributors provide practical ways to apply biblical truth. Start your day with this unique resource. Explanatory notes. Perfect companion to the Complete Jewish Bible (see page 2). Endorsed by Edith Schaeffer, Dr. Arthur F. Glaser, Dr. Michael L. Brown, Mitch Glaser and Moishe Rosen. 416 pages.

LB31 $19.99

Kingdom Relationships *God's Laws for the Community of Faith*
—Dr. Ron Moseley

Focuses on the teaching of Torah—the Five Books of Moses—tapping into truths that greatly help modern-day members of the community of faith. 64 pages.

LB37 $8.99

His Names Are Wonderful
Getting to Know God Through His Hebrew Names
—Elizabeth L. Vander Meulen and Barbara D. Malda

In Hebrew thought, names did more than identify people; they revealed their nature. God's identity is expressed not in one name, but in many. This book will help readers know God better as they uncover the truths in his Hebrew names. 160 pages.

LB58 $9.99

Train Up A Child *Successful Parenting For The Next Generation*
—Dr. Daniel L. Switzer

The author, former principal of Ets Chaiyim Messianic Jewish Day School, and father of four, combines solid biblical teaching with Jewish sources on child raising, focusing on the biblical holy days, giving fresh insight into fulfilling the role of parent. 188 pages. Endorsed by Dr. David J. Rudolph, Paul Lieberman, and Dr. David H. Stern.

LB64 $12.99

Fire on the Mountain - *Past Renewals, Present Revivals and the Coming Return of Israel*
—Dr. Louis Goldberg

The term "revival" is often used to describe a person or congregation turning to God. Is this something that "just happens," or can it be brought about? Dr. Louis Goldberg, author and former professor of Hebrew and Jewish Studies at Moody Bible Institute, examines real revivals that took place in Bible times and applies them to today. 268 pages.

LB38 $15.99

Voices of Messianic Judaism *Confronting Critical Issues Facing a Maturing Movement*
—General Editor Rabbi Dan Cohn-Sherbok

Many of the best minds of the Messianic Jewish movement contributed their thoughts to this collection of 29 substantive articles. Challenging questions are debated: The involvement of Gentiles in Messianic Judaism? How should outreach be accomplished? Liturgy or not? Intermarriage? 256 pages.

LB46 $15.99

The Enduring Paradox *Exploratory Essays in Messianic Judaism*
—General Editor Dr. John Fischer

Yeshua and his Jewish followers began a new movement—Messianic Judaism—2,000 years ago. In the 20th century, it was reborn. Now, at the beginning of the 21st century, it is maturing. Twelve essays from top contributors to the theology of this vital movement of God, including: Dr. Walter C. Kaiser, Dr. David H. Stern, and Dr. John Fischer. 196 pages.

LB43 $13.99

The World To Come *A Portal to Heaven on Earth*
—Derek Leman

An insightful book, exposing fallacies and false teachings surrounding this extremely important subject... paints a hopeful picture of the future and dispels many non-biblical notions. Intriguing chapters: Magic and Desire, The Vision of the Prophets, Hints of Heaven, Horrors of Hell, The Drama of the Coming Ages. Offers a fresh, but old, perspective on the world to come, as it interacts with the prophets of Israel and the Bible. 110 pages.

LB67   .$9.99

Hebrews Through a Hebrew's Eyes
—Dr. Stuart Sacks

Written to first-century Messianic Jews, this epistle, understood through Jewish eyes, edifies and encourages all. 119 pages. Endorsed by Dr. R.C. Sproul and James M. Boice.

LB23 $10.99

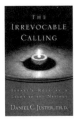

The Irrevocable Calling *Israel's Role As A Light To The Nations*
—Daniel C. Juster, Th.D.

Referring to the chosen-ness of the Jewish people, Paul, the Apostle, wrote "For God's free gifts and his calling are irrevocable" (Rom. 11:29). This messenger to the Gentiles understood the unique calling of his people, Israel. So does Dr. Daniel Juster, President of Tikkun Ministries Int'l. In *The Irrevocable Calling*, he expands Paul's words, showing how Israel was uniquely chosen to bless the world and how these blessings can be enjoyed today. Endorsed by Dr. Jack Hayford, Mike Bickle and Don Finto. 64 pages.

| LB66 | $8.99 |

Are There Two Ways of Atonement?
—Dr. Louis Goldberg

Here Dr. Louis Goldberg, long-time professor of Jewish Studies at Moody Bible Institute, exposes the dangerous doctrine of Two-Covenant Theology. 32 pages.

| LB12 | $ 4.99 |

Awakening *Articles and Stories About Jews and Yeshua*
—Arranged by Anna Portnov

Articles, testimonies, and stories about Jewish people and their relationship with God, Israel, and the Messiah. Includes the effective tract, "The Most Famous Jew of All." One of our best anthologies for witnessing to Jewish people. Let this book witness for you! Russian version also available. 110 pages.

| English | LB15 | $ 6.99 |
| Russian | LB14 | $ 6.99 |

The Unpromised Land *The Struggle of Messianic Jews Gary and Shirley Beresford*
—Linda Alexander

They felt God calling them to live in Israel, the Promised Land. Wanting nothing more than to live quietly and grow old together in the country of refuge for all Jewish people, little did they suspect what events would follow to try their faith. The fight to make *aliyah*, to claim their rightful inheritance in the Promised Land, became a battle waged not only for themselves, but also for Messianic Jews all over the world that wish to return to the Jewish homeland. Here is the true saga of the Beresford's journey to the land of their forefathers. 216 pages.

| LB19 | $ 9.99 |

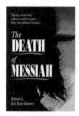

Death of Messiah *Twenty fascinating articles that address a subject of grief, hope, and ultimate triumph.*
—Edited by Kai Kjaer-Hansen

This compilation, written by well-known Jewish believers, addresses the issue of Messiah and offers proof that Yeshua—the true Messiah—not only died, but also was resurrected! 160 pages.

LB20 $ 8.99

Beloved Dissident *(A Novel)*
—Laurel West

A gripping story of human relationships, passionate love, faith, and spiritual testing. Set in the world of high finance, intrigue, and international terrorism, the lives of David, Jonathan, and Leah intermingle on many levels--especially their relationships with one another and with God. As the two men tangle with each other in a rising whirlwind of excitement and danger, each hopes to win the fight for Leah's love. One of these rivals will move Leah to a level of commitment and love she has never imagined--or dared to dream. Whom will she choose? 256 pages.

LB33 $ 9.99

Sudden Terror
—Dr. David Friedman

Exposes the hidden agenda of militant Islam. The author, a former member of the Israel Defense Forces, provides eye-opening information needed in today's dangerous world.

Dr. David Friedman recounts his experiences confronting terrorism; analyzes the biblical roots of the conflict between Israel and Islam; provides an overview of early Islam; demonstrates how the United States and Israel are bound together by a common enemy; and shows how to cope with terrorism and conquer fear. The culmination of many years of research and personal experiences. This expose will prepare you for what's to come! 160 pages.

LB49 $ 9.99

It is Good! *Growing Up in a Messianic Family*
—Steffi Rubin

Growing up in a Messianic Jewish family. Meet Tovah! Tovah (Hebrew for "Good") is growing up in a Messianic Jewish home, learning the meaning of God's special days. Ideal for young children, it teaches the biblical holidays and celebrates faith in Yeshua. 32 pages to read & color.

LB11 $ 4.99

These books, by the founders of our organization, were some of the first books of their kind, ever. They were instrumental in bringing many Jewish people to faith in Yeshua and helped launch Messianic Jewish Publishers and the Messianic Jewish movement.

A Way In The Wilderness *Essays in Messianic Jewish Thought*
—M.G. Einspruch

Did the Jews kill Jesus? Is the New Testament anti-Semitic? Immortality in Jewish thought. What is a Jew? These are just a few of the topics addressed. Written by well-known Jewish believers in the Messiah--Victor Buksbazen, Daniel Fuchs, Henry Einspruch, and more. Thousands of copies of this book have been shared with seekers around the world. Includes a chapter on Messianic prophecy. A classic and valuable resource! "Excellent. One cannot improve upon it." *--the late Messianic Jewish scholar, Rachmiel Frydland* 112 pages.

LB04	$ 7.99

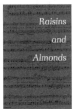

Raisins And Almonds
—edited by Henry & Marie Einspruch

Poetry, testimonies, music, photographs, illustrations, brief essays and points to ponder. Edited by Henry and Marie Einspruch, this little book has been shared with thousands around the globe! Now it's your turn to pass it on to your Jewish friends. 87 pages.

LB05	$ 5.99

The Ox, The Ass, The Oyster
—edited by Henry & Marie Einspruch

A collection of articles and stories originally presented over the radio in Yiddish (now in English). This book is presented in the hope that it will challenge the reader to compare the mundane, materialistic things of everyday life, with the world of truth, justice, love, judgment, and forgiveness. 100 pages.

LB06	$ 5.99

Would I, Would You?
—edited by Henry & Marie Einspruch

Here are the stories of 14 Jewish people who became believers in Yeshua, including an Orthodox rabbi! Includes the 53rd chapter of Isaiah in Hebrew and Yiddish. Another little gem that has been distributed to thousands around the world. 95 pages.

LB07	$ 5.99

The Man With The Book

The life and testimony of Henry Einspruch, translator of the Yiddish New Testament and founder of The Lederer Foundation, the parent company of Messianic Jewish Publishers and Resources. 20 pages.

LB08	$ 2.99

------ :: ------ NOTES ------ :: ------

------ :: ------ NOTES ------ :: ------

------ :: ------ NOTES ------ :: ------

------ :: ------ NOTES ------ :: ------

ABOUT THE AUTHOR

Barney Kasdan is rabbi of Kehilat Ariel, a thriving Messianic synagogue located in San Diego, CA. He holds degrees from Biola University (B.A.) and Talbot School of Theology (M.Div.). He also completed a year of post-graduate study at American Jewish University (formerly University of Judaism) in Los Angeles. Rabbi Kasdan is ordained through the Union of Messianic Jewish Congregations (UMJC) and has served on numerous committees including as its President (1998-2002). He has written numerous articles regarding Messianic Judaism and is author of the popular books *God's Appointed Times* and *God's Appointed Customs* (Messianic Jewish Publishers).

Among his various duties, he also serves as a Chaplain for the San Diego Police Department. He and his wife Liz reside in San Diego and have four grown children.